Motivation, Ability and Confidence Building in People

To Jan, with love . . .

. . . Mac

Motivation, Ability and Confidence Building in People

Adrian Mackay

AMSTERDAM • BOSTON • HEIDELBERG • LONDON • NEW YORK • OXFORD
PARIS • SAN DIEGO • SAN FRANCISCO • SINGAPORE • SYDNEY • TOKYO

Butterworth-Heinemann is an imprint of Elsevier

Butterworth-Heinemann is an imprint of Elsevier
Linacre House, Jordan Hill, Oxford OX2 8DP
30 Corporate Drive, Suite 400, Burlington, MA 01803, USA

First edition 2007

British Library Cataloguing in Publication Data
A catalogue record for this book is available from the British Library

Library of Congress Cataloguing in Publication Data
A catalogue record for this book is available from the Library of Congress

ISBN–13: 978-0-7506-6500-1
ISBN–10: 0-7506-6500-9

For information on all Butterworth-Heinemann publications
visit our web site at http://books.elsevier.com

Printed and bound in Great Britain

07 08 09 10 11   10 9 8 7 6 5 4 3 2 1

Contents

Preface   xiii
About the author   xv

PART 1 INTRODUCTION   1

Chapter 1   A Short History of Management   3

Learning Outcomes   3
Peter Drucker Did it First!   3
So Why Bother Studying Management Theories?   5
One Hundred Years in the Making   5
Human Relations Management   9
Leadership, Motivation and the Organisation   10
The MAC Factors   14
Summary   15
Questions   15
References   15
Further Reading   16

PART 2   MOTIVATION BUILDING   17

Chapter 2   A Definition of Motivation   19

Learning Outcomes   19
How Much Do You Know About Motivation?   19
Towards a Definition   20
Human Capital Management   23
Empowerment and Motivation   24
The Motivation Questionnaire   25
Summary   26
Questions   27
Reference   27
Further Reading   27

Chapter 3   Are They Motivated?   28

Learning Outcomes   28
What Does and Does Not Motivate People?   28
A Happy Work Ethic   32
How to Find Out What Motivates   33

Summary   34
Questions   34
References   35
Further Reading   35

Chapter 4   Approaches to Motivation   **36**

Learning Outcomes   36
Frederick Taylor   37
Henri Fayol   38
Frank and Lillian Gilbreth   39
Henry Gantt   39
Mary Parker Follett   40
Elton Mayo   41
Douglas McGregor   41
Abraham Maslow   42
Kurt Lewin   43
Frederick Herzberg   45
Robert Tannenbaum and Warren Schmidt   47
Rensis Likert   48
Robert Blake and Jane Mouton   49
Peter Drucker   50
John Adair   51
W. Edwards Deming   53
Robert House   54
Richard Hackman and Greg Oldham   55
Rosabeth Moss Kanter   57
Chris Argyris   58
Robert McNamara   59
Charles Handy   59
Tom Peters and Robert H. Waterman Jr   60
Victor Vroom   62
Clayton P. Alderfer   64
Hersey and Blanchard's Situational Leadership   65
Summary   66
Questions   66
References   67
Further Reading   67

Chapter 5   Motivating Individuals   **68**

Learning Outcomes   68
Energy at Work   69
Workspace   71
Trust   72
Disgruntled Employees   74
Turning Theory into Practice to Enable People's Motivation to Shine 76

Summary   78
Questions   78
Reference   79
Further Reading   79

Chapter 6   Motivating Teams   **80**

Learning Outcomes   80
What Motivates a Team?   81
Team Leadership   85
On the Need for Conversation   86
The Place of Teams   88
Meredith Belbin and Team Roles   89
Meetings Management   92
Summary   99
Questions   100
References   100
Further Reading   101

Chapter 7   Effort, Performance and Reward   **102**

Learning Outcomes   102
The Relationship Between Effort, Performance and Rewards   103
Effort and Performance   105
Expectation and Motivation   109
Performance   111
Rewards   117
Summary   123
Questions   123
References   124
Further Reading   124

Chapter 8   Selling the Vision   **125**

Learning Outcomes   125
The 'Centre for Leadership Studies – Europe' Model   126
Psychological Contract   132
A Passion for Business   133
Summary   134
Questions   135
References   135
Further Reading   135

Chapter 9   Mackay's Motivation Development Model   **136**

Learning Outcomes   136
Background to the Motivation Development Model   137
Task Motivation Control Orientation   138

Relationship Orientation 142
Adapting to the MDM 146
Evaluating a Scenario 150
Summary 152
Questions 152
Further Reading 152

PART 3   ABILITY BUILDING 153

Chapter 10   The Learning Organisation 155

Learning Outcomes 155
On the Need for Learning 156
Learning from Failure 157
The Learning Organisation 159
Organisational Learning 164
Investors in People 167
The EFQM Model and Learning 168
Learning Management Systems 168
Summary 169
Questions 170
References 170
Further Reading 171

Chapter 11   Lifelong Learning and CPD 172

Learning Outcomes 172
Introduction to Learning 173
The Meaning of Adult Education 182
Lifelong Learning 183
Continuing Professional Development (CPD) 185
Summary 186
Questions 186
References 187
Further Reading 187

Chapter 12   Individual Learning Styles 188

Learning Outcomes 188
A Process for Personal Change 189
Awareness of Competence 191
Johari Window 193
Kolb Learning Styles 195
Jarvis Experiential Learning Model 198
Howard Gardner's Multiple Intelligence 199
VAK: Visual–Auditory–Kinaesthetic Learning Styles Model 204
Bloom's Taxonomy of Learning Domains 205
Donald Kirkpatrick's Training Evaluation Model 207

Summary   208
Questions   209
References   209
Further Reading   210

Chapter 13   Management Style and Ability Development   211

Learning Outcomes   211
Early Theories   212
People vs. Production   216
Authority vs. Freedom   217
Supportive vs. Directive Behaviour   218
Effectiveness Orientation   220
Transformational Leadership Style Inventory   222
Summary   225
Questions   225
References   225
Further Reading   226

Chapter 14   Mackay's Ability Development Model   227

Learning Outcomes   227
Background to the Ability Development Model   228
Task Ability Control Orientation   229
Relationship Orientation   232
Adapting to the ADM   237
Evaluating a Scenario   239
Summary   242
Questions   242
Further Reading   243

PART 4   CONFIDENCE BUILDING   245

Chapter 15   Self-esteem   247

Learning Outcomes   247
What is Self-esteem?   248
Why is it Important?   249
Evaluating Self-esteem   250
The Cause of Low Self-esteem   250
How to Deal with Bullying in the Workplace   252
Transactional Analysis or the 'OK Corral'   254
Improving your Self-esteem   258
Improving Others' Self-esteem   259
Emotional Intelligence   260
Summary   264
Questions   264
References   265
Further Reading   265

Chapter 16 Assertiveness   **266**

Learning Outcomes	266
What is Assertiveness?	267
Thomas–Kilmann Conflict Mode Instrument	268
Aggressive and Submissive Behaviour	269
The Rewards of Assertive Behaviour	270
Assertive Behaviour in Action	271
Assert your Rights at Work	275
Dealing with Difficult People at Work	276
Assertive Customer Complaint Handling	278
Summary	279
Questions	279
Reference	279
Further Reading	279

Chapter 17 Achievement   **280**

Learning Outcomes	280
The Fundamentals of Achievement	281
Optimism and Pessimism	284
Managerial Achievement (Mach One)	285
Theories about the Desire for Achievement	286
Become Motivated to Study	293
Summary	295
Questions	295
References	296
Further Reading	296

Chapter 18 Building Confidence Through Constructive Feedback   **297**

Learning Outcomes	297
Why Build Staff's Confidence?	298
A Manager's Self-confidence	302
Tips for Giving and Receiving Feedback	302
Criticism vs Constructive Feedback	303
Daft Things Managers Should Not Say	306
Summary	308
Questions	308
References	308
Further Reading	309

Chapter 19 Mackay's Confidence Development Model   **310**

Learning Outcomes	310
Background to the Confidence Development Model	311
Task Confidence Control Orientation	313
Relationship Orientation	317

Adapting to the CDM   323
Potential Criticisms of the Model   326
Evaluating a Scenario   327
Summary   329
Questions   329
Further Reading   330

PART 5   LOOKING FORWARD   331

Chapter 20   Times are Changing   **333**

Learning Outcomes   333
Change Defined   334
'Times are a-Changing'   334
Why Do Organisations Have Such a Problem with Change?   337
Dealing with Resistance to Change   340
Managing Organisational Change   342
How to Plan an Effective Change Programme   345
Motivating People Through Change   348
How to Get Others to Participate – A Guide for Change Agents   352
Summary   353
Questions   353
References   353
Further Reading   354

Chapter 21   The Future of Work   **355**

Learning Outcomes   355
Tracking Future Trends   356
The Growth of Legislation   359
Information Technology and Working Practices   361
E-learning   367
Flexible Working   369
Working from Home   372
Working Part-time   377
Interim Working   378
Family Fortunes   379
The Future for Women in Work   382
Work/Life Balance   383
Work with Meaning   387
Summary   390
Questions   390
References   391
Further Reading   391

Index   392

Preface

You have been the inspiration behind this book – so thank you! Well, people just like you: people in jobs, as employers and as employees. Inspiration has come from my former managers and my staff, my clients, and those delegates on the thousands of training courses I have delivered or attended over the past 30 years.

As a tutor on the Chartered Management Institute certificate and diploma courses, through attending classes myself as a delegate at University College Northampton, attending my MBA classes at Hull University Business School and working with the Chartered Management Institute, tutoring at St Gallen Business School in Switzerland, as a sports coach and RFU Referee in rugby, and in delivering management development workshops as far apart as Manhattan and Istanbul, I have noticed an enduring theme when it comes to study, work and play – wherever one looks, it is down to *people* doing these things successfully.

It occurred to me that three factors need to be in place for success to follow – and for people to be fully effective, success requires all three to the same degree.

Obviously, we need people that want to do things; people that want to do the right things and do things right. People who can be bothered to do what is required in the appropriate fashion; bothered to do things better, cheaper, faster – bothered to do what their organisation's stakeholders want. We recognise this as a person's *motivation*. In my studies, courses and reading I discovered a wealth of information and research from others trying to understand this most pressing human emotion. These ideas have been distilled into a pragmatic model of how managers (or those tasked with a leadership role, such as team leaders and supervisors) can apply some of these approaches in practice to manage the process of bringing out the best in other people – that is, motivation building in people.

But no matter how willing an individual might be to undertake a task, no amount of effort will produce the desired outcomes if people don't know what to do. How to do their jobs, how to learn how to do their jobs better and why be bothered to learn in the first place are all key issues that need to be addressed. We recognise this as a person's *ability*. A natural starting point for any tutor is to understand how people learn, but it is also fundamental for any coach, supervisor or manager to know how to instil improved competences in others. 'Sending them on a course', standing them up against a wall and lecturing them to death are not enough to improve someone's ability – such activity might just switch them right off and so become a barrier to their further learning. This text builds on a foundation of how people learn and offers a parallel model to that on motivation building, enabling readers to explore their approach to helping other people learn – that is, ability building in people.

The popular academic and professional texts have addressed these two factors at length. There is over a century of motivational theory to draw upon, where ability development has gone hand in hand. However, there seems to be a shortfall in the literature on how to go about developing someone's self-assurance and belief in themselves. We recognise this as a person's *confidence*. Even if someone has the motivation to undertake a task and has the relevant know-how to do it, they will often be held back through concerns about 'what if': 'What if I make a mistake?', 'What if they get cross?', 'What if I forget something?' As a manager, have you ever had a perfectly competent and motivated person check something with you – yet you know they are just offloading the decision onto you rather than using the confidence of their own conviction? Have you ever wondered why problems seem to occur when you are there, magically getting sorted when you are away? This text addresses the confidence factor as well, providing the reader with a model, again using a parallel framework as for the other two factors, to explore their style in developing the self-esteem and self-reliance of others – that is, confidence building in people.

I have battled with all three from time to time as manager, tutor and parent; as instructor, trainer and coach; as colleague, team member and individual. I needed a practical guide when dealing with people. Not just in their motivation building – after all, if I was motivated, why couldn't I get them motivated? And not just in developing their ability – how could I pick up the skills yet they couldn't pick them up from me? And even if I was feeling anxious internally – how could I appear confident while other people couldn't do the same but allow their nerves to get the better of them?

This is your practical guide to the three factors. To assist the reader in making the text accessible, this text is presented in five sections, each with a companion web page for students, tutors and practitioners to explore the subject further, found at http://books.elsevier.com/management? isbn=0750665009.

First, we take an overview of the subject of managing people and review a short history of management.

The second section on motivation starts with an understanding of what motivation is and explores approaches to evaluating the motivation of people. Students and management practitioners will find a full review of the last hundred or so years of management theory, a useful summary that underpins the practical approaches in later chapters. Both individual and team motivation are discussed before exploring the link between effort, performance and rewards; the importance of 'selling' a picture of the future is also emphasised. The final chapter of this section presents Mackay's Motivation Development Model, illustrated by a series of case examples of someone who is clearly unmotivated to do their job through to a situation where they are going above and beyond their job brief.

The third section addresses ability building. The text does more than look at individual learning styles – it explores the subject from a wider perspective of the learning organisation and lifelong learning. From there, Mackay's Ability Development Model looks at differing approaches to encourage someone who starts on day 1 in a new organisation, learning the ropes, right through to full competency in their tasks. Again, a case study approach is favoured, drawing on everyday situations giving both student and seasoned practitioner clear, easy-to-relate-to situations.

Confidence building forms the fourth section and considers the development of self-esteem, assertiveness and achievement. This section will be of value to the individual reader for themselves as well as for managers – or those tasked with a leadership role, such as team leaders and supervisors – guiding others to build their confidence. Mackay's Confidence Development Model is a particular innovation and follows similar principles as the other two models, simplifying understanding of the ideas for all readers.

Finally, Part 5 rounds off the text with a pragmatic look at managing change and the future of work to place the models in the context of the real world, both for today and tomorrow.

So, I hope that this text does inspire you, the reader, as people like you have inspired me. I hope that you have the *motivation* to explore the text, are able to improve your *ability* to manage people and have the *confidence* to apply the ideas in practice.

Adrian 'Mac' Mackay
Moreton Pinkney

About the author

Adrian 'Mac' Mackay is Managing Partner with Duncan Alexander and Wilmshurst, Training and Development Advisors, and is a Director of DAW Limited, that specialises in providing innovative marketing solutions. Mac's interests are advising professional people on marketing, as well as management skills, leadership and improved performance, and client care. He has recent international experience in Europe and the USA and has worked with many varied organisations, both large and small.

He co-authored *Below-the-Line Promotion* (1992), *Fundamentals of Advertising, second edition* (1999) and *The Fundamentals* and *Practice of Marketing, fourth edition* (2002) with John Wilmshurst; is editor of *The Practice of Advertising, fifth edition* (2004); he co-authored *The Veterinary Receptionist* with John Corsan and is also sole author of *Recruiting, Retaining and Releasing People* (2007) – a companion text to this book.

Mac is an Honours graduate in Physiology and Nutrition from Leeds University (1977), he holds a Diploma from the Chartered Institute of Marketing (1983), a Masters Degree in Strategic Marketing (1994), was elected to the Faculty of the Chartered Institute of Marketing and is a full Member of the Chartered Management Institute (2002); he is a former subject specialist on their accredited programmes. He achieved a Postgraduate Certificate in Management from University College Northampton (2006).

Mac coaches a local junior rugby team and is an East Midlands RFU Society Referee. He is married to Jan; they share five fabulous children and live in Northamptonshire.

Part 1

Introduction

1

A Short History of Management

Managers learn in business school that relationships are either up or down, but the most important relationships today are sideways. If there is one thing that most of the people in management that I know have to learn is how to handle relationships where there is no authority and no orders.

Professor Peter Drucker

Learning Outcomes

By the end of this chapter you will:

- Have had a brief overview of management theory as it has developed over the last century
- Understand the value of theory underpinning your practice
- Discover why so many 'theories' have had a shelf life
- Recognise the importance of motivation in the workplace
- Have had an introduction to some of the key influencers in management thinking.

Peter Drucker Did it First!

The challenge for management writers is finding things to say that Peter Drucker has not already said better. One just has to read a couple of his books for the first time – from the *Concept of the Corporation* (1946) to *Management Challenges for the 21st Century* (1999) – to realise that this is no exaggeration.

'Drucker's primary contribution is not a single idea, but rather an entire body of work that has one gigantic advantage – nearly all if it is essentially right' (Collins, 2004). While others wrote widely on management before Drucker (e.g. Taylor on efficiency or Follett on motivation), it was Drucker who first wove the threads into a coherent picture. In the foreword of *The Practice of Management* (1954), Jim Collins wrote, 'This is the first book to look at management as a whole, the first that attempted to depict management as a distinct function, managing as specific work, and being a manager as a distinct responsibility'. Drucker proposed that limiting access to management jobs to 'people with a special academic degree' would be a mistake – anticipating by half a century both the rise in MBA programmes and the failure of management 'theories'.

Professor Drucker explains, 'Teaching 23-year-olds in an MBA programme strikes me largely as a waste of time. They lack the background of experience. You can teach them skills – accounting and what have you – but you cannot teach them management.' Drucker's view is that management is neither an art nor a science but a practice – in which achievement is measured not by academic awards but by results.

The Practice of Management also had a piece of 'modern wisdom', that management is about innovation. 'Every unit of the business should have clear responsibility and definite goals for innovation,' he wrote – whether 'selling or accounting, quality control or personnel management'. When people today speak of 'business process innovation', they are restating Drucker.

His early work warned of 'the imaginative isolation of the executive' – the tendency for managers to become so absorbed in their work that they become blind to emerging opportunities or threats. He feels that information technology has made matters much worse. 'Executives are totally flooded with inside data to the exclusion of outside data.'

In *Concept of the Corporation*, he described in detail his ideas for 'self-governing plant communities' in which workers would play a central role in setting priorities and formulating policies. He considers his '. . . ideas for the self-governing plant community and for the responsible worker to be both the most important and the most original', he wrote years later in his autobiography, *Adventures of a Bystander*. He feels that the labour movement stifled the self-governing plant community; by representing the workers the unions stopped every direct relationship between management and employees.

However, Drucker feels that the rise of the knowledge workers – a phrase he coined in *The Age of Discontinuity* (1969) – has changed the rules away from the shop-floor. Communities of practice reaching across boundaries are often stronger than bonds within a particular company. As he pointed out in *Managing in Turbulent Times* (1980), successful organisations must learn to think of themselves as orchestras, not armies. Today, he explained, a multinational is a network of alliances for manufacturing, distribution, technology and so on. Sometimes there is stock participation as an indication of commitment but not for control. These companies are held together by strategy and information, not ownership. 'Managers learn in business school that relationships are either up or down, but the most important relationships today are sideways. If there is one thing that most of the people in management that I know have to learn it is how to handle relationships where there is no authority and no orders.'

Hence the need for managers to excel at relationships in which they have little authority and even less control. And that cannot be learnt in the lecture theatre or from a book.

So Why Bother Studying Management Theories?

> *The more extensive a man's knowledge of what has been done, the greater will be his power of knowing what to do.*
>
> Benjamin Disraeli, British Prime Minister

We all have our preferred methods of learning (see Chapter 12) and many of us like to 'try things out' and discover the practical uses of a new 'tool'. We may not much like the idea of sitting back, reflecting on our experiences and trying to put those experiences into a logical framework or theory.

Yet a theory may well help us better understand our experiences and help us better use the knowledge we have gained. Theory and practice support each other: theoretical knowledge can often give us a good base for developing our practical skills.

So, take time to reflect. Consider and relate the theories outlined in this book to your own practical experience. Experiment and see if the theory makes sense to you and helps your understanding of the subject. If, having done all of that, the theory does not help you, then identify the reasons why and put that theory aside. A theory is only useful if it helps you better understand and use your own knowledge.

A theory that all management theories have a life cycle was published in America in 1993 in a magazine called *Planning Review*. It is believed that the theory originated in the Massachusetts Institute of Technology in Boston. It is outlined in Figure 1.1. The cause of the failure frequently lies in the stage of Overextension: organisations looking for the quick-fix flavour-of-the-month. As the originators imply: announce the new system; arrange some training courses; and then sit back and wait for the magic to work. If only business management were so simple!

Whenever we consider a theory, especially one that has been criticised or derided, we need to reflect on how much of the criticism is due to flaws in the original theory and how much is due to the theory being misapplied in practice.

One Hundred Years in the Making

Managers' beliefs about how to get the best out of people at work have changed as the 20th century has progressed. This section briefly outlines those changing beliefs and refers to a few of the many researchers who have influenced management thinking.

The approach in the opening years of the last century was very much in line with the views of Frederick Taylor – the father of scientific management – and other work study practitioners such as Gantt. They believed that jobs could be standardised and workers could

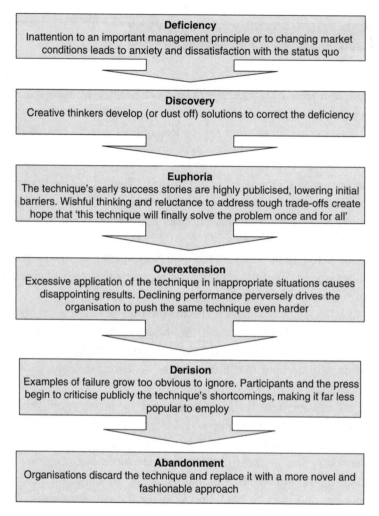

Figure 1.1 All management theories have a life cycle.

produce more if they had the right rest breaks to reduce fatigue, the right tools for the job and the right monetary reward in terms of a piecework bonus. Such concepts are sometimes referred to as Rational–Economic models.

Given the situation of increasing industrial production and a largely unskilled and un-educated immigrant workforce in the USA, the scientific management approach did bring benefits. However, it took no account of workers as individual human beings.

With her concern for creative experience, democracy and for developing local community organisations, Mary Parker Follett is an often forgotten, but still deeply instructive, thinker for educators on motivation at the beginning of the 20th century.

By the late 1920s, Elton Mayo (usually acknowledged as the founder of Human Relations Management) was conducting research at the Hawthorne Works of Western Electric Co.

in Chicago. The aim of his research was to find the relationship between the lighting of the work area and the productivity of a work group, where they found that a key factor in productivity improvement was the social relationships of the work group. This will be explored further in a later section.

Starting in the 1950s there was a growth in what was called behavioural science: attempts to define and explain the behaviour of individuals and groups. The concepts that were developed are sometimes referred to as self-actualising models.

In the mid-1950s, Frederick Herzberg produced what is often known as his Hygiene/Motivator theory. He defined certain factors linked to the job environment that cause dissatisfaction with a job: the Hygiene factors. These encompass things such as style of supervision, physical working conditions and pay. They must be right to avoid dissatisfaction, but increasing them above the appropriate level will not increase motivation.

The factors he refers to as Motivators, that encourage people to put extra effort into a job, are the ones inherent in the job itself: a sense of achievement, advancement, recognition and so on.

Another key researcher, Abraham Maslow, categorised people's needs into five primary classifications arranged in a hierarchy. Each level must be satisfied to some extent before the next becomes dominant. The basic needs are:

- Physiological: basic physical and biological needs
- Safety: physical and psychological security
- Social: love, affection and social relationships
- Esteem: self-respect, independence and prestige
- Self-realisation: self-fulfilment, accomplishment and personal identity.

It is these needs that act as internal motivators – both within and outside work.

Douglas McGregor showed how a leader's assumptions about other people dictate that leader's approach. He defined a set of assumptions called Theory X which stated that the average human being dislikes work and needs to be directed, coerced and controlled. Such assumptions result in an autocratic leadership style – which, in turn, results in the behaviour predicted by the Theory X assumptions! His alternative set of assumptions, which he labelled Theory Y, are about people being imaginative, responsible and able to exercise self-control. These assumptions lead to a more participative leadership style – and thus the behaviour predicted by the assumptions.

The Tannenbaum and Schmidt Continuum links in with McGregor's Theory X and Y and shows how a leader's style of decision-making can be authoritarian (Theory X) or may give subordinates a significant amount of freedom in making a decision (Theory Y).

The 1960s also saw a focus on the effects of different leadership styles. Rensis Likert and Blake and Mouton, with their Managerial Grid, all highlighted the need for leaders to balance their concern for people with their concern for productivity. Likert's research particularly highlighted the increased productivity that can result from an employee-centred approach rather than a more productivity-centred one.

As the 1970s gave way to the 1980s, there developed a realisation that the way people were managed was intricately linked with the structure and the culture of the organisation in which they worked. John Adair looked at the task, the team and individuals as three interlinked areas for leaders to address.

Deming's work on Total Quality Management (not his own phrase for it) highlighted the importance of managers understanding their people because they could only achieve results through their teams. He stressed that leadership was about helping people to do a better job and involved training those people in the new skills needed to keep up with change. He also emphasised the need for trust, two-way communication, the breaking down of barriers between departments, and allowing pride of workmanship.

Around this time, also, Peters and Waterman published their book *In Search of Excellence*. They identified eight common yardsticks of the successful company, one of which was 'Productivity Through People'. Among the ideas this yardstick encompassed was:

- Treating people like adults
- Expecting ideas and suggestions as a routine
- No ivory towers
- Reinforcement of good work with quick praise and immediate small, visible rewards
- Constant harping on the 'people' theme in conversation
- 'Less is more' – less corporate management means more individual management
- Obsessive sharing of information to beat NETMA (nobody ever tells me anything!)
- Small units so people know each other.

Other writers and researchers, such as Charles Handy and Rosabeth Moss Kanter, have all highlighted the forthcoming changes in organisation structure and the consequential effects on the way we manage people within – and outside – the organisation.

In such a brief summary of around 100 years' research into such a complex subject, I have inevitably:

- Lost many of the subtleties of the original research
- Omitted details of many other worthy researchers who have contributed to our fund of knowledge about how we can obtain people's true commitment to their jobs.

The purpose of this summary is to try to illustrate that today's people management principles are an extension of those that have been developing throughout the 20th century. Concepts such as smaller organisational units and 'fad phrases' such as 'empowerment' and 'self-managed teams' are evolutionary rather than revolutionary; they have been influenced by social, technological, economic and legal changes. The aim of this text is to pull together the thinking of the various theorists and practitioners to provide the reader with a pragmatic approach to motivation, ability and confidence building of those people around them upon which organisational success depends.

Human Relations Management

The concept of Human Relations Management, as distinct from Scientific Management, developed in the mid-1920s. The movement is closely linked with Elton Mayo and with the Hawthorne Experiments – so named because they took place in the Hawthorne Works of Western Electric in Chicago (Mayo, 1949).

The concept is also referred to as Social Relationships because it highlighted the importance of groups at work.

The first experiment, begun in 1924, was to establish the most cost-effective level of lighting for various assembly works. After several controlled experiments, the researchers concluded that the increases in productivity had no predictable link to lighting levels but must be due to some other factor.

In 1927, Mayo started a two-year series of experiments with a group of girls assembling relays. The experiments focused particularly on the effects of the length of the working week, the use of rest pauses and the provision of group incentive pay. Once again, no direct link was found between these factors and the increased productivity. Instead, it was concluded that the determining factors were:

- A more friendly and attentive supervisory style.
- The girls having more control over the way they carried out their tasks.
- The girls becoming a cohesive social group rather than isolated individuals.
- The high morale that developed through such factors and also because the girls felt 'special' – they had been singled out to take part in an important experiment. This last factor has become known as the Hawthorne Effect, the idea that people perform better when they receive special attention, such as at the time of a change.

A final experiment was carried out with a group of men working in the bank-wiring room. This experiment was to discover as much as possible about the influence of group pressure on an individual worker to restrict output – despite the existence of group incentive pay.

The experiment established that individuals had to conform to a number of group norms if they were to be accepted as a member of the group:

- You should not turn out too much work. If you do, you are a 'rate-buster'.
- You should not turn out too little work. If you do, you are a 'chiseller'.

- You should not tell a supervisor anything that will get a fellow worker into trouble. If you do, you are a 'squealer'.
- You should not attempt to maintain social distance or 'act officious'. If you are an inspector, for example, you should not behave like one.

Mayo shared some of Taylor's scientific management beliefs in the use of a methodical approach to increasing productivity and in the importance of the supervisor. However, whereas Taylor focused on the individual worker, Mayo concluded that group membership helped productivity more than social isolation.

Some years later, two American sociologists (D. C. Miller and W. H. Form) summarised the findings from the Hawthorne Experiments:

- Work is a group activity.
- The social world of the adult is primarily patterned about work activity.
- The need for recognition, security and sense of belonging is more important in determining workers' morale and productivity than the physical conditions under which they work.
- A complaint is not necessarily an objective recital of facts; it is commonly a symptom manifesting disturbance of an individual's status position.
- The worker is a person whose attitudes and effectiveness are conditioned by social demands from both inside and outside the workplace.
- Informal groups within the workplace exercise strong social controls over the work habits and attitudes of the individual worker.
- The change from an established to an adaptive society tends continually to disrupt the social organisation of a workplace and industry generally.
- Group collaboration does not occur by accident; it must be planned for and developed. If group collaboration is achieved, the work relations within a workplace may reach a cohesion which resists the disrupting effects of adaptive society.

Leadership, Motivation and the Organisation

In considering the subjects of leadership and motivation, we cannot ignore the effect of the organisation itself.

As leaders, the environment in which we operate will always condition our behaviour. We will be constrained by, for example: the culture of the organisation; our own leader's expectations; the type of work undertaken; and the particular circumstances surrounding an event. We will also be influenced by the skills of the staff we lead.

In the last 25 years or so there has been an increasing amount of research into the relationship between an organisation, the behaviour of its leaders and the ways in which these affect the commitment of employees to their work.

The work of Frederick Taylor on Scientific Management and of Elton Mayo in his Hawthorne Experiments both showed how the culture of an organisation affects leadership and motivation. Changes in organisation structure will, therefore, have an effect on motivation and on expectations of what is required of a leader. Conversely, if we seek greater commitment from individual employees we need to provide the right organisation structure and culture to encourage such commitment.

This section gives a very brief, and selective, outline of some of the key research findings. They are arranged in rough chronological order.

Eric Trist (1950)

He researched the effects of increasing mechanisation in British coal mining and, as a result, developed the concept of the 'open social–technical system'. An organisation must consider not just the physical effects of technological change but also the psychological and social effects. These effects must be considered as one interdependent whole to create an effective working environment.

The system also needs to be open to the influence of the environment in which the organisation operates so that it is responsive to change. Nothing lasts forever.

W. Edwards Deming and J. M. Juran (1950s)

Both these industrial engineers are closely linked with the concepts of Total Quality Management (TQM). However, both recognised that for TQM to be successful, the culture of the organisation needed to lead to the right kind of leadership behaviour.

Deming's 14 Points for Management is a list that integrates principles both of organisation and of people management.

In Juran's view, quality is indissolubly linked with human relations and teamwork.

Chris Argyris (1957)

He suggested that the structure and management beliefs of an organisation often inhibited the individual in developing from the behaviour of an infant to that of a mature adult.

In 1970, along with Donald Schön, he examined the paradoxical pressures on individuals in an organisation that wanted both to be stable and to react dynamically to change.

Victor Vroom (1964)

The fundamentals of expectancy theory include three basic elements:

- *Expectancy* – refers to an individual's perception that their efforts will result in performance, such as higher productivity or reduced waste.
- *Instrumentality* – refers to a person's perception that the performance will result in certain positive or negative outcomes, such as promotion, increased wages, greater fatigue or loneliness.
- *Valence* – refers to the value the person attaches to various outcomes that result. One may assign a negative valence to fatigue but a positive valance to more wages.

In his model, Vroom popularised his theory that:

$$\text{Motivation} = \text{Valence (Instrumentality)} \times \text{Expectancy}.$$

Edgar H. Schein (1978)

He analysed motivation and the way it is affected by an organisation's culture. In particular, he emphasised the psychological contract that exists between the employee and the organisation based on their mutual expectations.

He also linked the psychological contract to the concept of the career anchor: the factors that encourage individuals to remain in the organisation.

Tom Peters and Robert H. Waterman (1982)

They identified eight characteristics shared by 43 successful organisations in *Fortune*'s top 500 companies. Their basis for success was that these organisations had consistently beaten their competitors over a 20-year period on six financial yardsticks and on their record of product innovation.

Their eight characteristics for success are:

- A bias for action – getting on with it
- Close to the customer – learning from the people they serve
- Autonomy and entrepreneurship – fostering innovation and nurturing 'champions'
- Productivity through people – treating the rank and file as a source of quality
- Hands-on, value-driven – management showing its commitment
- Stick to the knitting – stay with the business you know
- Simple form, lean staff – some of the best companies have a minimum of headquarters staff
- Simultaneous loose–tight properties – autonomy in shop-floor activities plus centralised values.

In their research, Peters and Waterman analysed the organisations using the 7S Model they developed at McKinsey:

- Structure
- Strategy
- Systems
- Style of management
- Skills (the corporate strengths)
- Staff
- Shared values.

Rosabeth Moss Kanter (1983)

This US sociologist, consultant and author has studied the ways in which traditional bureaucratic organisations inhibit the use of individual talents and lock people into predetermined roles, and has identified ways in which such talents can be released.

Her work has focused particularly on managing the creative potential of staff as an organisation changes. She also perceived that organisations would need to have flatter hierarchies, decentralised authority, autonomous work groups and other such empowering strategies.

Going alongside such changes she also, in 1989, considered how the globally competitive cooperation would develop. Among her proposed new strategies were: smaller, centralised head offices; contracting out of company services; the creation of strategic affiances; and portable employability. This last strategy, with its implications for the lifetime career ladder in a company, has major implications for the way we obtain commitment from employees.

Charles Handy (1989)

This Irish writer on business and organisations has concentrated particularly on the implications of the changing organisation for work and society.

His earliest work, in the 1970s, explored the culture of organisations. He is particularly known for classifying organisations according to the characteristics of four Greek Gods: Zeus, Apollo, Athena and Dionysus.

His more recent books have concentrated on the shift away from lifetime employment in a single company; different and more radical forms of organisation structure; and the challenge for managers in managing the knowledge workers of the future.

Peter Martin and John Nicholls (1990)

They developed a conceptual model of ways to create commitment, based on research in 14 UK companies who regarded the establishment of such commitment as a high priority. The core of their model is three pillars, which must be built if commitment is to be achieved:

- *A sense of belonging to the organisation* – this is created by making sure the workforce is informed, involved and sharing in success
- *A sense of excitement in the job* – this comes from an appeal to the higher-level needs of pride, trust and accountability for results
- *Confidence in management leadership* – this stems from management paying attention to authority, dedication and competence.

Peter Wickens (1994)

Based on his experience as a senior executive in car manufacturers, such as Ford and Nissan, he has developed the concept of the ascendant organisation. This concept recognises that, for an organisation to achieve long-term, sustainable success there must be the right balance between the commitment of the people and control of the processes. The 'behavioural scientists' concentrated their attention on people's commitment, while the 'scientific management' school of thought concentrated almost exclusively on the control of the process. Wickens's principle is that both are needed for success.

Wickens also identifies the key characteristics which a leader will need to have to be successful in an ascendant organisation: personal attributes – such as empathy, determination and integrity; strategic perspective – such as being able to create a strategic vision and relate goals and action to that strategic vision; ability and willingness to communicate appropriately with others; and a commitment to achievement of high standards.

This sample of current ideas on organisational structure and culture shows some common trends:

- A changing society, with differing expectations of what working life is likely to provide, changing customer expectations of the way organisations should behave
- Organisations having to change to meet not only these changing social expectations, but also in response to changing economics in a global marketplace
- Changes in the style of leadership needed to gain employee commitment in a dynamic organisation that can respond rapidly to the demands of its market.

The various theories will be explored in more detail in Chapter 2, with particular emphasis on practical application in the real world.

The MAC Factors

This text in the following chapters aims to draw on the fine works of previous authors and build three practical models for today's manager – it is only if an individual is *Motivated* to do a job, has the *Ability* to undertake the task and possesses sufficient *Confidence* that success will follow. It is every manager's responsibility to address these three factors in equal measure – it is on their shoulders that the future prosperity of their organisation, the individuals in it and the community at large rests so squarely.

Summary

In this chapter you have:

- Briefly reviewed management theory as it developed over the last century
- Understood the value of theory to underpin your practice
- Discovered why so many 'theories' have had a shelf life – and how to avoid similar traps
- Recognised the importance of motivation in the workplace
- Reviewed some of the key influencers in management thinking.

Questions

1. What are *your* main reasons for studying management theory – what do you hope to gain?
2. Review any 'theories' or 'fads' that your organisation, or one that you have studied, has implemented in the past. What stage are they at – or identify why the approach failed.
3. Who do you consider to be the most influential management writer in the last 100 years; substantiate your answer with reasons.
4. Consider the 'McKinsey 7S Model' in the context of your organisation, or one that you have studied, and comment briefly on each of the seven areas. Are the approaches in each area of the organisation aligned? Support your reasons with examples. If there are any misalignments, what would you recommend to make improvements?

References

Collins, J. (2004) In *The Daily Drucker: 366 Days of Insight and Motivation for Getting the Right Things Done*, Butterworth-Heinemann.

Drucker, P. (1954) *The Practice of Management*, Butterworth-Heinemann.

Mayo, E. (1949) *The Social Problems of An Industrial Civilisation*, Routledge, Kegan & Paul.

Vroom, V. H. (1964) *Work and Motivation*, Wiley, New York.

Further Reading

Drucker, P. (2003) *The Essential Drucker: The Best of Sixty Years of Peter Drucker's Essential Writings on Management*, Harper Collins.

Organizational Behavior: Foundations, Theories & Analysis (2002) Oxford University Press, USA.

Walton, M., Foreword by Deming, W. E. (1992) *The Deming Management Method*, Mercury Business Books.

Part 2

Motivation Building

2

A Definition of Motivation

People are the only source of competitive advantage left to us today.

Michael Porter

Learning Outcomes

This chapter, and the companion web pages, have been written as a general guide for managers and cover key elements of the National Occupational Standards for Management and Leadership (*Working with People – Units 19 and 21–23*); the chapter also covers some of the requirements of the Chartered Management Institute's Diploma in Management compulsory and optional modules as far as 'people' resources are concerned, and some of the demands of the CIPD Professional Development Scheme – particularly the *People Management and Development* module. It also serves as an introduction to this text's section on motivation.

By the end of this chapter you will:

- Understand what motivation is – and what it is not
- Uncover some possibly hitherto misunderstood facets about motivation
- Understand the importance of managing human capital professionally
- Recognise the role of 'empowerment' when managing people.

How Much Do You Know About Motivation?

Motivation has been a much discussed topic in management and supervisory circles for years and yet it remains a complex, elusive concept. No matter what rung of the management ladder you are on, the aspect of motivation you are probably most concerned with is how to apply motivational theory to the job. Figure 2.1 is a list of statements that deal with both motivational theory and practice. Read each statement and decide whether it is true or false.

Check your answers with the comments at the end of the chapter.

		True	False
1	You can motivate your workers	☐	☐
2	To keep people challenged, a manager should assign more work than they can handle	☐	☐
3	Motivation lies outside the job	☐	☐
4	Some workers are unmotivated	☐	☐
5	Food motivates a rat to run a maze	☐	☐
6	There's only one level of motivation – full blast	☐	☐
7	Keeping employees guessing on their progress keeps them motivated	☐	☐
8	Publicity about organisation and employee achievements enhances motivation	☐	☐
9	Allowing employees to participate in making decisions has a good effect on their work	☐	☐
10	Most people want to do a good job	☐	☐

Figure 2.1   Motivation theory and practice – true or false?

Towards a Definition

*Motivate – v. **1** Supply a motive to; be the motive of. **2** Cause (a person) to act in a particular way. **3** Stimulate the interest (of a person in an activity).*

The Oxford Dictionary of Current English

This definition is a good example of the problems associated with the concept of motivation. In essence, there seem to be two conflicting views of motivation.

In one way, the definition indicates that motivation is where someone (perhaps a team leader) causes someone else (a team member) to act in a certain way. In another way, it appears that motivation is something that someone uses as a motive for doing things.

This apparent conflict reflects an ongoing debate by researchers into motivation. Traditional views of leadership and motivation reflected a 'passive' view of motivation. In effect, people required strong leaders to motivate them towards certain goals. If someone says they are demotivated and we offer them a bag of cash or threaten to sack them, and then they get on with the task in hand, what has happened? This approach to motivation implies that the leader had to motivate his or her team member through various rewards and/or punishments. However, as we shall see in Chapter 4, there are many more 'active' models of motivation.

Motivation is typified as an individual phenomenon where every person is unique and all the major theories of motivation allow for this uniqueness to be demonstrated in one way or another. Chapter 4 explores the myriad of theories around motivation in more depth, but a short introductory review is included here.

The job of a manager in the workplace is to get things done through others. To do this, most people think that the manager should be able to 'motivate' employees. However, motivation practice and theories are difficult subjects, touching on several disciplines. In spite of enormous research, basic and applied, the subject of motivation is not clearly understood and more often than not poorly practised. To understand motivation one must understand human nature itself – and herein lies the problem.

Motivation is described, usually, as intentional. That is, motivation is assumed to be under the worker's control, and behaviours that are influenced by motivation, such as effort expended, are seen as choices of action. (Chapter 7 looks at the relationship between effort, performance and reward.) One can look at motivation as a deficiency, a need that must be fulfilled. Hunger is a motivation – it is an internal force, food *per se* is not – it is the satisfaction and is external. Once it is 'internal' and we have had sufficient and are satiated, more food is not a motivation, in fact it might be the opposite!

Motivation is multifaceted. The two factors of greatest importance are:

1. What gets people activated (arousal)
2. The force of an individual to engage in desired behaviour (direction or choice of behaviour).

The purpose of motivational theories is to predict behaviour. Motivation is not the behaviour itself and it is not performance. Motivation concerns action, and the internal and external forces that influence a person's choice of action. In terms of the forces that can influence an individual to take an action, the generic choices of a manager might include:

- Positive reinforcement
- Effective discipline and punishment
- Treating people fairly
- Satisfying employee needs
- Setting work-related goals
- Restructuring jobs
- Basing rewards on job performance.

Clearly these are basic strategies, although the 'mix' in the final recipe will vary from place to place. Essentially, there is a gap between the individual's actual state and some desired state, and managers try to reduce the gap. Motivation can be viewed as a means of reducing and manipulating this gap; it is influencing others in a specific way towards goals specifically stated by the motivator, conforming within organisational constraints.

One can categorise three main models of motivation, roughly in order of their historical appearance. These are:

- *The rational–economic model* – this view of motivation is linked to the classical view of management, which suggests that people are primarily motivated by their own financial and material rewards.

- *The social model* – this view of motivation was influenced by the human relations school. Experiments (such as the Hawthorne Experiment – see Chapter 1) suggested that people at work were motivated by recognition, sense of belonging and social interaction.
- *The self-actualising model* – this model owes a great deal to the behavioural science school. The self-actualising model holds that human beings have an inherent need to fulfil their potential. However, a person's potential is a very individual thing determined by her or his personality. Behavioural scientists developed various models which help managers to understand the psychological make-up of individuals.

One of the issues that must be linked to 'potential' is its relative nature; humans are pack animals and attainment is seen by individuals as relative – relative to what we did before (our personal best), any siblings, our neighbours, colleagues or even an industry benchmark. While envy is frowned upon by both religion and philosophy, we habitually compare ourselves to others. But how do these comparisons influence our behaviour and feelings?

Envy can have two effects: the envious man thinks that if a neighbour breaks a leg, he will appear to be able to walk better himself; but it is also possible to be spurred on by the achievements of others – so-called 'admiring envy'.

If we are motivated by the desire to match or surpass the achievements or possessions of others, might envy be necessary for the successful working of the market economy? So, is admiring envy necessary for an effective and productive organisation? People at work often want what the people above them have – a better job (however defined), more money, a more luxurious office, a personal assistant – and this forms a large part of what motivates people to do a good job.

But again, it is relative. One's position on the ladder is as important as the absolute height of the ladder. In a study of satisfaction with pay levels of 16 000 workers in a range of organisations, workers at Warwick University found that a person's position in the pay ranking was a significant predictor of how happy people were with their salary – even after allowing for absolute pay levels and distance from the average pay level.

Flatter organisations and open-plan offices mean that many of the visible trappings of achievement relative to others have gone. We have new feathers to show off our plumage: the lightness of a laptop, the smallness of a phone, whether one turns left when boarding a plane. However, these are often inadequate; people are becoming territorial and in need of space again at work – their own space. We are status-seeking creatures and the office has become an important space for signalling our position, for parading our feathers.

We are motivated to achieve something that is important to us, particularly if we admire those that have it or recognise that possessing it puts us ahead of those that don't. However, once we have something it ceases to motivate – that need is satisfied. We might be motivated to hold on to it, of course, if we feel threatened that we might lose something we value.

Human Capital Management

Today, the phrase 'a good man manager' should be restated, politically correctly, as 'a good people manager'. However, how does this concept relate to that of human capital management and the motivation of that 'capital'?

Management itself involves a combination of both technical knowledge and personal traits. Technical knowledge can come in the form of an understanding of the theories of motivation, for example, and traits from understanding the characteristics or behaviours of a good manager. For much of the 20th century, Taylorist[1] driven 'scientific management' gave the impression that it was primarily (if not solely) technical factors that mattered. Today, increasingly, this mechanistic approach is being softened by a greater emphasis on people/values-driven issues. Daniel Goleman (1995) made a strong case for emotional intelligence as a key differentiator in success of managers that could 'tune in' to the emotional side of themselves and others. The behavioural approach focuses on people (rather than techniques) and argues that it is people that make things happen; it argues that change is not a technical issue, but that it is critically dependent on how progress is defined and perceived.

When we think of progress it implies a change for the 'better' and any definition of 'better' is essentially a reflection of the values of those involved. It is these values issues that critically influence the level of individual commitment. Competence without commitment is not a sound basis for either effective decision-making or operating performance.

In the end, management is not about mere manipulation – people quickly see through this and hence the high levels of cynicism in many organisations. It is about helping people really to believe in what they are doing (pure McGregor Theory Y?[2]).

Here management focuses on being committed to the interests (and hence motivations) and development of employees, which can only be done if staff believe in what they are doing, want to do it and recognise that management is there to help them become more effective in doing it. A good people manager believes in the value of people, and treats them fairly and with respect, hence that vital element of trust is established and grown. But how often does this happen in practice? Management, of course, involves a combination of what you do and the way that it is done.

It could be argued that a people/values-driven approach is reflected in the phrase 'human capital management'. However, while it might well reflect much of its spirit, the phrase is frequently identified with the more formalised, technical and manipulative, even cold and

---

[1] Frederick Winslow Taylor's (1856–1915) ideas led to the concept of dividing work between those who did it (workmen) and those who supervised and planned it (managers).

[2] Professor Douglas McGregor (1906–1964) of the Massachusetts Institute of Technology felt that the basic beliefs managers have influence the way organisations are run. Theory X and Theory Y featured in his book *The Human Side of Enterprise*. Theory Y managers believe in the integration of individual and organisational goals.

calculating, agendas and the words themselves (using the words 'capital' and 'management' so closely together) can easily be interpreted as reflecting that concern.

This human capital management approach is now about to be extended into 'human capital accounting', which some argue is an even more potentially 'dehumanising' development. Few would consider this development (and phrase) an ideal solution, especially when one hears a chief executive wax lyrically about people being the company's best assets only for the individuals to discover they are 'virtual' and are, if not entirely, ignored in company accounts, which is much more insulting to the workforce at all levels.

Talking about people as 'assets' may not be ideal but surely it is better than not mentioning them explicitly at all?

There are probably better phrases than 'human resources' (or 'human remains' as one group of embittered employees viewed themselves) or 'human capital' and many would not hesitate to welcome it. There is little wrong with the use of the phrase 'people assets' in itself. Problems only arise when the underlying organisational culture is interpreted as essentially exploitative. It is this general lack of trust in so many organisations today that, inevitably, makes many organisational changes extremely difficult.

Overall, the concept of 'human capital management' (and its extension into 'human capital accounting') is, by no means, inherently incompatible with the phrase 'a good people manager', but the rhetoric gets in the way of focusing on the essence of the real meaning that we are trying to convey, which is that people and values are the key to both effective management and organisational performance.

As long as that is (and is seen to be) the driving motive behind what we do and the way we do it, semantic arguments over language, rightly, become irrelevant. Unfortunately, as that is so rarely the case, language becomes both the message and the messenger and, perhaps, too often there is much more behind the two different phrases than is generally recognised. As Lord Brown of Madingley (CEO of BP) said, *'Technologies can be bought; what we need is the talent to implement them.'* And that requires people that want to do it.

Empowerment and Motivation

Is empowerment motivation? Henry Ford pointed out that with workers you get a free brain with every pair of hands. Managers have long been aware that they were not getting their staff to perform to their potential. So how do they raise staff performance? The mantra became 'empower' them to perform. Trust them to take decisions was the philosophy behind self-managed teams. Give people the authority and the resources they need, then get out of the way – even let them define their direction within a broad canvas. In practice, too many managers found it hard to let go.

The idea originated from W. Edwards Deming, who was brought in to reinvigorate Japanese industry after the Second World War and became empowerment's modern advocate. By linking the Japanese instinct for consensus with the industrial concept of teamwork, he suggested that the way to continuous improvement came through empowerment. In the 1980s, alarmed at the success of Japanese rivals, Western industrialists launched Total Quality Management (TQM). Quality circles, consisting of empowered staff, would deliver the performance. Sadly, the pervading attitude of command and control could not accept the freedom. As a consequence, the results generated by TQM and the endless paper-work required to achieve compliance with quality benchmarks proved counter-productive. Motivation waned.

Sadly, again practice did not live up to the promise. All too often when staff were 'empowered', little power was actually given to them. If power was actually given, it was quickly taken back again.

In order to find and keep the best talent, there are five key questions that you need to answer clearly for every employee:

- Where are we going?
- What are we doing to get there?
- What do you want me to do?
- What will you do to help me do it?
- What is in it for me when I do?

Repeat answering these five questions frequently and every time there is a change, large or small. Invite dialogue with your people to find out if you are reaching your aim of having them work 'on purpose'. Does their current work feel purposeful and – no less importantly – does yours?

The Motivation Questionnaire

Answers to the questionnaire in Figure 2.1:

1. False. You don't motivate your workers; motivation is an internal force. In fact, motivation is the need to fulfil a deficiency. Once a person's need is satisfied, that person is no longer motivated. You supply the satisfaction, not the motivation itself.
2. False. Assigning more work than people can handle doesn't keep them challenged. The catchword here is 'more'. You should assign more *challenging* work or give employ-ees more *responsibility* to stretch their capabilities – job enrichment rather than job enlargement.
3. True. Motivation doesn't lie in the job; it lies inside a person and can be satisfied anywhere. Many people find their jobs, or at least some aspects of their jobs, satisfying. As supervisor or manager, you can provide different kinds of job satisfaction for your employees – for example: recognition; advancement; responsibility; reward.

25

4. False. Everyone is motivated. There are apparent differences in amounts of motivation because of the way people satisfy their needs. For example, a file clerk who turns down the opportunity to become a secretary may seem unmotivated to some people. However, if that person's needs are satisfied by being an excellent file clerk, that person is motivated.

5. False. Food doesn't motivate the rat – hunger does. Hunger is one of the basic, physiological needs and food satisfies that need.

6. False. Full blast is not the only level of motivation. No one is motivated equally towards all tasks. For example, even the most enthusiastic file clerk will get more satisfaction from one aspect of the filing job than from another.

7. False. Keeping employees guessing on their progress doesn't keep them motivated. In fact, it has been shown that interest and performance are improved when employees have goals to work towards and feedback on how they are progressing towards those goals. Employees' performance and interest deteriorate when they are no longer informed.

8. True. Publicity about organisation and employee achievements enhances motivation by fulfilling an employee's need for esteem and respect. The employee's image of the organisation, which is affected by publicity, influences that employee's motivation to work toward the organisation's goals.

9. True. The more you can involve an employee in decisions that affect his or her job, the more motivated that employee will become in working towards established goals. The highest level of participation is letting the employee actually make the decision. But it has also been shown that workers are positively motivated if they are allowed to make recommendations to those who will make the decision, or at least learn from the decision-maker the alternatives being considered.

10. True. Most people want to do a good job as they see it. Discrepancies in performance occur when their idea of a job well done differs from your idea of what constitutes a good job. As a manager or supervisor, your responsibility is to communicate to them your standards or, in other words, what a 'very good job' is as you see it.

Summary

In this chapter you have:

- Reviewed a definition of motivation
- Evaluated your understanding of motivation, recognising there are three basic 'theories' about the subject:
  - The rational–economic model
  - The social model
  - The self-actualising model

- Recognised the importance of managing human capital professionally
- Explored the role of 'empowerment' when managing people, and linked that to understanding and communicating the strategy of the organisation.

Questions

1. Consider your current situation. What would motivate you to work or study harder? How does this differ from your colleagues? Discuss the differences.
2. If you did not need to work for the financial rewards, what part of your job or your study would you still enjoy doing. What rewards does it bring?
3. What it is about the place where you work or study that demotivates you? What can you do about these influences?
4. While probably sharing a dislike of 'management speak' with the author, what must you as a manager do really to live up to the concept of 'empowering' your staff?

Reference

Goleman, D. (1995) *Emotional Intelligence*, Bantam Books, New York.

Further Reading

In addition to Goleman's book listed above:

Harvard Business School (2005) *Motivating People for Improved Performance* Harvard Business School Press.

3

Are They Motivated?

The floggings will continue until morale improves.

Anon

This chapter, and its companion web pages, have been written as a general guide for managers and cover key elements of the National Occupational Standards for Management and Leadership (*Working with People – Units 19 and 21–23*); the chapter also covers some of the requirements of the Chartered Management Institute's Diploma in Management compulsory and optional modules as far as 'people' resources are concerned, and some of the demands of the CIPD Professional Development Scheme – particularly the *People Management and Development* module. Its main thrust is to review best practice in running a staff audit.

By the end of this chapter you will:

- Recognise that motivation is often about changing behaviours
- Be able to consider a range of incentives available to managers that are attractive to staff
- Explore five key strategies to exert influence on people
- Understand best practice when planning and implementing a staff appraisal system.

What Does and Does Not Motivate People?

Management literature is full of actual case histories of what does and does not motivate people. Outlined here is a tentative initial broad selection of the various practices that have been tried in order to draw lessons for the future.

The traditional Victorian style of strict discipline and punishment not only failed to deliver the goods, it also left a mood of discontent and resentment amongst the working class.

Punishment appears to have produced negative rather than positive results and increased the hostility between 'them' (the management) and 'us' (the workers). In contrast to this, the 'carrot' approach, involving approval, praise and recognition of effort, has markedly improved the work atmosphere, produced the 'goods' and given the workers enormous satisfaction.

In January 2006, the British Psychological Society Conference in Bournemouth heard of research into disciplinary methods by Liverpool John Moores University that constant praise is the best way to make children behave (*The Daily Telegraph*, 2006). The report claimed that teachers that increase the amount of praise for good behaviour and reduce criticism directed at unruly pupils notice a 'dramatic' improvement in discipline. When teachers were persuaded to raise the amount of praise from 54 to 85 per cent and reduce 'telling-offs' from 46 to 15 per cent, the result was 6 per cent of pupils disrupting or failing to work compared with nearly a quarter before the change. So, 'catch someone doing something right' seems to be the motivation mantra.

People often say that the manager's main task is to motivate his or her team. What they really mean is managers need to provide the things that get people activated and influence individuals to engage in the desired behaviour. Managers need to do this both individually and collectively, so that staff can deliver the 'goods' and also derive satisfaction from it.

This may appear somewhat contradictory, but it seems to work. The main tools in the manager's kitbag for producing the desired change in behaviours (i.e. motivating the team) are:

- Approval, praise and recognition
- Trust, respect and high expectations
- Loyalty, given that it may be received
- Improvement in the competencies of individuals to undertake a task
- Building confidence and self-esteem
- Removing organisational barriers that stand in the way of individual and group performance (smooth business processes, systems, methods and resources)
- Job enrichment
- Good communications
- Financial incentives.

While everyone will have their preferences, the list is arranged in some order of importance for many – it is interesting to note that cash is way down the ladder of motivators for many people. This will be explored in more detail in Chapter 5.

It may be that organisations want productive and responsible workers, even happy ones, but the ultimate aspiration seems to be for free workers – and for work that liberates, rather than limits, the individual. There is a growing demand from employees for 'job autonomy', which means having a greater say over how, where and when their job is done, with, perhaps above all, an expanded opportunity for learning.

As far back as 1848, John Stuart Mill wrote in *Principles of Political Economy*:

After the means of sustenance are assured, the next in the personal wants of human beings is liberty; and (unlike the physical wants, which as civilisation advances become more moderate and more amenable to control) it increases instead of diminishing in intensity as the intelligence and the moral faculties are more developed.

Mill's central argument was that freedom is a vital dimension of our humanity, one that becomes more important in societies where basic needs are universally met, and was a century and a half ahead of its time.

Today, as a society we have many opportunities for freedom of expression, choice of lifestyle, education opportunities and individual consumption patterns. However, on the work front, things are not so free. More service sector jobs and an increase in the proportion of skilled jobs have increased the opportunities for individual discretion; moreover, non-manual work gives more freedom than life on the factory floor. Job satisfaction and lower stress levels are found to be closely related to the degree of control workers have over their time and their jobs. Behind pay, people leaving the public sector ranked 'the lack of freedom to do the job the way I want' as their reason for leaving to join the private sector.

However, for too many people, the choices about how their job is done are being made way above their heads. While some people sacrifice their time for the sake only of the resulting salary, for many it is not only just a way to pay the bills but an opportunity to associate with others in a joint endeavour, to define ourselves and develop new skills. But winning freedom at work is no easy task.

While demands for freedom have an indirect but nonetheless real impact on organisational performance, the labour market is not so sensitive; employers respond to workers' needs only when workers raise the cost of indifference. In other words, it is only when workers 'vote with their feet' and walk away from jobs that cramp their individuality will the labour market respond (Reeves, 2005). However, most organisations find it hard to create work that is truly liberating, yet it is what many individuals look for when they make their job choices. There is a significant difference between conscripts and volunteers and, indeed, in how they are managed.

Compulsion vs persuasion

Persuasion is far more powerful than compulsion – even for conscripts, just as the pen is mightier than the sword! Managers have a much better chance of success with all employees if they use persuasion rather than compulsion. The former builds morale, initiative and motivation, whilst the latter quite effectively kills such qualities. The three basic components in persuasion are:

- Suggest
- Play on the person's sentiments
- Appeal to logic.

Once convinced, the person is sufficiently motivated as to deliver the 'goods'. The manager will have achieved the goal quietly, gently and with the minimum of effort. It is, in effect, an effortless achievement.

Looking at the options in more detail, when one considers the alternatives, there is a range of influencing strategies that can be used to change others' behaviours, each with differing effects. Each of five influencing strategies and their possible effects are explored below.

Push

The person or persons being influenced feels a force pressurising (or pushing) them to change behaviour. This can be effective in achieving rapid behaviour changes where attitude shifts or long-lasting effects are not really important. However, it can have unpredictable or negative after-effects, particularly on whether someone will be motivated to maintain the required change in behaviour to get the work done.

Examples of 'push' behaviour would include:

- *Coercion* – 'I really think you should because every one else is and you don't want to be left out, do you?'
- *Threats* – 'If you don't, you'll be in big trouble when the boss finds out . . . '
- *Blocking* – 'I can't agree to that, you'll have to go elsewhere . . . '.

Pull

This involves the provision of positive forces to pull the person or persons along with you, but it relies on your status and/or personality. It produces short-term rather than long-term results; moreover, behaviour rather than attitude change is likely to accrue.

Examples of 'pull' behaviour would include:

- *Rewards* – 'OK, once you have done that, I can offer you . . . '
- *Recognition* – 'That will be a good departmental achievement to put onto the company intranet'
- *Charisma* – 'Oh go on, do it just for me . . . please!'

Persuade

This is particularly useful when all parties have equal power and there is a need for long-term working relationships to be maintained. The effects can be short-term and long-term, changing attitudes that affect behaviour.

Examples of 'persuasive' behaviour would include:

- *Logic* – 'Just look at the cost/benefit analysis and you'll see that...'
- *Propaganda* – 'Did you read that independent report that said that...?'
- *Self-discovery* – 'Why don't you have a go and let me know what works?'

Preventative

This can be used to delay or prevent an issue being considered, actioned or decided. It is most useful when the other party has more power (like the boss), but can backfire by irritating the other person and creating adverse impressions.

Examples of 'preventative' behaviour would include:

- *Delay* – 'I can't do that until I have finished the course...'
- *Avoidance* – 'I do not feel confident in tackling that...'
- *Ignoring* – not doing what was asked or changing the subject.

Preparatory

These behaviours are concerned with creating the right atmosphere or climate for other actions. They tend to be long-term in their implementation and effect, but need careful planning and are not to be viewed as the overnight panacea. They are particularly effective when used in conjunction with other strategies.

Examples of 'preparatory' behaviour would include:

- *Butter 'em up* – 'This is one area where you will excel; it is right up your street...'
- *Timing* – 'Leave this until after the holidays when we have staff back off leave...'
- *Image* – 'This will be good for you to bring up at your appraisal...'.

While we can exert the most appropriate influencing strategy, combination or sequence of the above approaches to achieve an end goal, how can we ensure that the workers are contented?

A Happy Work Ethic

The days of working 18-hour days for an insatiable employer, rarely seeing one's family, never going out with one's spouse/partner, spending limited free time drinking to excess so that one ends up burned out and mentally exhausted by such a lifestyle is on the way out.

With a diminishing labour pool, expanding demands from employees, and new legislation from both the UK government and Brussels, the concept of life/work balance is becoming more acceptable.

The traditional 'slave driver' employer is now recognising that a happier, more fulfilled workforce delivers better productivity then an exhausted, demoralised one. It is no longer fashionable to be exhausted. Wider flexibility and innovation in employment practices – including options like working part-time, job sharing, unpaid leave and career breaks, where employees can buy an additional seven weeks' holiday – are being adopted by employers for two reasons. Not only to build retention but also due to the fact that, beyond pay and career development, people want flexibility from their employer; they want to feel valued and supported.

As a further initiative, many organisations are exploring the benefits of mentoring to help people find new ways to develop and advance themselves. Mentoring need not be just a problem-solving exchange, but also a way to access different tasks in the organisation, shared issues and common circumstances from which both parties may learn new strategies. Mentoring will be explored in more detail in later chapters.

How to Find Out What Motivates

A survey conducted among the Chartered Management Institute's membership (*Management Today*, 2004) reveals that 82 per cent of them still rely on the annual appraisal for information about their people and their attainments, despite that fact they also make it clear that they feel that the annual appraisal tells them little of value and is too often considered a waste of time for all concerned. There is often a big difference between what people in boardrooms think is going on and what the people who actually do the day-to-day work on the value chain think is going on.

In most organisations, there are just a few, often quite simple changes in how people are managed that might make a huge difference to bottom-line results. Sadly, so many managers do not have the information they need to tell them what they are – and only a tiny proportion of managers have even identified the questions they need answers to. Although many organisations claim that 'our people are our greatest asset', managers often take few active steps to engage them in the business, to achieve better outcomes from their labours or to ensure that they are making the best possible use of their peoples' talents.

Employees are a tremendous source of information on how to improve the organisation, but 'running a survey' is not such a straightforward procedure. Rather than simply a 'temperature-taking' process, employee surveys should be used to identify areas of needed improvement that have a high impact on organisational performance. They can be used to uncover staff feelings and attitudes to their employer, whether they are particularly motivated and what motivates them.

While a traditional 'opinion' survey can be helpful, a more strategic approach to surveys can provide organisations and leaders with:

- Measurement of the effectiveness of critical business processes
- Valuable information for managers to help them guide the organisation
- A focus for change on issues that can provide the organisation with significant competitive advantage
- Ideas to help achieve a better client focus
- Feedback on behaviours that support critical business practices.

To review how best to undertake a professional staff survey, see the online companion web pages.

Summary

In this chapter you have:

- Seen that motivation is often about changing behaviours
- Identified a range of incentives available that are attractive to staff
- Explored five key strategies to exert influence on people – push, pull, persuade, preventative, preparatory
- Reviewed best practice when planning and implementing a staff appraisal system.

Questions

1. Other than the ideas given in the text, what more modest things might a manager offer as an incentive for people in your organisation?
2. Imaging that you, as the production manager, were asked to get a group of people on an assembly line to work to a different shift pattern to improve productivity, what strategy would you use to exert influence? Justify your reasoning – and if that was not successful, what alternative might you consider?
3. Imagine that your senior management team wishes to introduce a staff evaluation in your firm and you have been asked to contract an external consultancy to run it for you. What criteria would you use to assess the appropriateness of the firm you employ?
4. How would you break the news to your department that a staff evaluation scheme is going to be introduced? Write some notes covering what you would need to say.

References

The Daily Telegraph (2006) 6 January, p. 7.
Management Today (2004) December, p. 10.
Reeves, R. (2005) *Management Today*, February, p. 25.

Further Reading

Aten, J. 'Making Association-audits Staff-friendly'. An article from: *Association Management* as HTML file from www.amazon.com (search 'staff audits').

4

Approaches to Motivation

Too many people let others stand in their way and don't go back for one more try.

Rosabeth Moss Kanter

Learning Outcomes

This chapter, and its companion web pages, have been written as a summary of fundamental management thinking over the last century and cover key elements of the National Occupational Standards for Management and Leadership (*Working with People – Units 19 and 21–23*); the chapter also covers some of the requirements of the Chartered Management Institute's Diploma in Management compulsory and optional modules as far as 'people' resources are concerned, and some of the demands of the CIPD Professional Development Scheme – particularly the *People Management and Development* module.

Over the years, much has been written and researched into the theories of motivation. While we introduced some in Chapter 1, this chapter looks at other individuals' thoughts and concepts. It is by no means intended as a definitive summary, but is intended as a more thorough review of the subject for both the student of management and the practitioner – and lays the foundation for new approaches to Motivation, Ability and Confidence building in People.

By the end of this chapter you will:

- Have a clear idea of the key management theories over the last 100 years
- Be able to compare and contrast the various theories
- Have an understanding to underpin your management practice in the workplace
- Have an understanding of the basis of Mackay's Motivation, Ability and Confidence Development Models introduced in later chapters of this text.

Frederick W. Taylor

The man generally recognised as being the 'father of scientific management' was
F. W. Taylor. He was an industrial engineer working in the USA around the end of the 19th
century. His aim was to replace individual judgement or opinion with scientific research and
knowledge. He perceived that the resulting increase in working efficiency would improve
the status of labour and society in general (Taylor, 1947).

Taylor believed in the 'economic man' theory of the economist Adam Smith: that individuals are interested in, and directed by, their own economic well-being. Unlike Smith,
however, he believed that managers also had an important role to play in determining how
work should be done, assigning qualified workers and motivating the workers.

Taylor conducted a number of experiments to illustrate how his principles could be used
to improve production methods.

The Yard Crew

In the Midvale steelworks, he observed how workers used the same shovel to move ash, iron
ore or coal. This meant that the weights they lifted depended on the density of the material.
By using time study, he found that most material was moved in a given period if the weight
carried was around 21.5 pounds – just less than 10 kg. He then provided the workers with
shovels of different size and shape for the different materials so that they would always
carry around 21.5 pounds. The result was increased output per worker.

The Pig-iron Handlers

In the same steelworks he came to the conclusion that the workers were working too hard
and for too long, making the wrong movements and resting too frequently. By offering one
of the workers a bonus to work as Taylor directed, he demonstrated an increase of nearly
300 per cent in the amount of pig-iron handled. The worker who took part in the experiment
also earned nearly 60 per cent more pay.

The Ball-bearing Inspectors

Taylor's time studies in a bicycle wheel factory indicated that the girls who inspected the
ball-bearings were working at a leisurely pace. He improved productivity by moving the
girls further apart, so that the girls could not talk with each other, reduced overall working
hours, gave several rest periods and paid on a differential piece rate.

There are four key features in the methods devised by Taylor:

- All decision-making, control and coordination lies with management – the managers think, the workforce does.
- There is a rigidly defined system for carrying out each task, for which workers are trained. This system will take into account the best tools and physical conditions, as well as defining rest periods.
- Workers are motivated through higher pay, directly linked to output.
- Workers are only selected, and retrained, if they can regularly achieve the required output. For example, Taylor specified 'husky men' to be pig-iron handlers.

Taylor's methods certainly showed benefits when used with a US workforce composed of poorly educated immigrants who often had a poor command of English. The organisation's productivity improved, as did the pay of individual workers. However, the systems he devised were cold, rational ones that treated the workers as automatons, taking no account of human feelings and behaviour. It was also seen that the organisation gained more than the workers and that there were fewer jobs available as a result of Taylor's productivity improvements.

Henri Fayol

A French engineer, his key work was *Administration Industrielle et Generale* (1916). He belongs to the Classical school of management theory, and was writing and exploring administration and work about the same time as F. W. Taylor in the USA.

While both have a task focus, their approaches are quite different. Fayol was particularly interested in authority and its implementation, while Taylor concentrated on work organisation (e.g. efficiency). In many ways, their views illustrate some of the differences between the USA and Europe. He advocated a consistent set of principles that all organisations need to run properly.

His five functions still form the basis of much of modern management thought and action:

- Plan (and look ahead)
- Organise
- Command
- Coordinate
- Control (feedback and inspect).

He also identified 14 principles that he saw as common to all organisations:

- Specialisation/division of labour
- Authority with responsibility

- Discipline
- Unity of command
- Unity of direction
- Subordination of individual interests
- Remuneration
- Centralisation
- Chain/line of authority
- Order
- Equity
- Lifetime jobs (for good workers)
- Initiative
- *Esprit de corps.*

Frank and Lillian Gilbreth

Frank and Lillian Gilbreth, who particularly specialised in the work-study technique of micro-motion study, invented and refined such a system, roughly between 1908 and 1924. Gilbreth also gave his name to a unit of measure used in such studies, the 'Therbligs'. These comprise a system for analysing the motions involved in performing a task. The identification of individual motions, as well as moments of delay in the process, was designed to identify unnecessary or inefficient motions and to utilise or eliminate even split seconds of wasted time.

In their writings from about 1915 to 1920, the Gilbreths begin to talk about 15–16 'motion cycles', but rarely named them all and did not allude to any comprehensive system. Indeed, it was not until the late summer of 1924, shortly after Frank's death, that the entire Therblig System was presented in two articles (Gilbreth and Gilbreth, 1924). While Motion Study and Therbligs have been reviewed and used by other authors, Mogensen (1979) and Barnes (1980) developed the most important improvements on the Gilbreths' original work.

To find out more about Therbligs and to see them in chart form, go online to the companion web pages.

Henry Gantt

Henry Gantt is the third well-known pioneer of scientific management and worked with Taylor in the USA. He is to be remembered for his humanising influence on management, emphasising the conditions that have favourable psychological effects on the worker. He is particularly remembered as the person who developed bonus plans and control charts that were particularly good at visualising work, as a result of which he gave his name to the now frequently used bar chart, which is used for scheduling multiple overlapping tasks over a time period. These charts were particularly innovative as they scheduled work against time rather than quantity, volume or weight.

Henry Gantt also focused on motivational schemes, emphasising the greater effectiveness of rewards for good work (rather than penalties for poor work). He developed a pay incentive system with a guaranteed minimum wage and bonus systems for people on fixed wages. Also, Gantt focused on the importance of the qualities of leadership and management skills in building effective industrial organisations.

Mary Parker Follett

Mary Parker Follett occupies a very significant place in the development of thinking and practice around adult and informal education, as well as in management development. Her contribution can be seen in three particular arenas:

- Involvement in, and advocacy of, community centres in the first two quarters of the 20th century did a great deal to establish them as an important social and educational form.
- Her theorising around the notions of community, experience and the group, and how these related to the individual and to the political domain, broke new ground – and was considered 'far ahead of her time' (Konopka, 1958). It provided a key element in the development of the theorising and practice of group work and community development and organisation. For example, her argument that democracy could only work if individuals organised themselves into neighbourhood groups, and people's needs, desires and aspirations were attended to, was fundamental to the sorts of thinking that emerged.
- She was able to help key figures like Henry Croly and Eduard Lindeman not only to develop their thinking, but also to access important sources of financial help.

In 1925, she presented an influential paper, '*The Psychological Foundations of Business Administration*' to executives at the annual conference of the Bureau of Personnel Administration in New York. She argued that the ideas she had been developing with regard to communities could equally be applied to organisations; we have seen a similar shift in recent years around the notion of social capital. She argued that organisations, like communities, could be approached as local social systems involving networks of groups. In this way she was able to advocate the fostering of a 'self-governing principle' that would facilitate 'the growth of individuals and of the groups to which they belonged'. By directly interacting with one another to achieve their common goals, the members of a group 'fulfilled themselves through the process of the group's development'.

Today, Mary Parker Follett is remembered for her pioneering work on management – although her contribution was soon forgotten after her death in 1933 (especially in the USA). In terms of current debates around management her perspective is hardly revolutionary, but then its radicalism and 'soft' orientation stood well outside the mainstream.

Elton Mayo

The Hawthorne Experiments were conducted from 1927 to 1932 at the Western Electric Hawthorne Works in Chicago, where Harvard Business School professor Elton Mayo examined productivity and working conditions. The studies grew out of early experiments at the plant into the effect of light on productivity (Chapter 1). Since the amount of light did not influence productivity on the relay assembly line, they began to enquire what did. While investigating the effect that fatigue and monotony had on productivity – by aiming to influence output by altering variables such as rest breaks, working hours, temperature and productivity – he stumbled on a principle of human motivation that would revolutionise theory and practice of management.

By segregating six workers for the study under a supervisor that was more a friendly observer than strict disciplinarian, he noted that they became a team and it had given itself totally and spontaneously to cooperation in the experiment. Thus, they felt themselves to be participating freely in the activity happy in the knowledge that they were working without coercion from above or limitation from below. They felt that they were working under less pressure than before. Medical check-ups revealed that they had no signs of cumulative fatigue and absence from work declined by 8 per cent.

It was also noted that each worker had flexibility in how they assembled the components of the relay, sometimes varying the method to alleviate boredom, and the more intelligent the individual, the greater the variety. This finding is similar to research findings into the fact that achievement had a motivating effect. It was recognised that the experimental group had considerable freedom of movement and were not 'bossed' by anyone; under these conditions the group developed an increased sense of responsibility and instead of discipline from managers being imposed, it came from within the group itself.

Douglas McGregor

Sigmund Freud suggested that people are lazy; they hate work to the extent that they avoid it; they have no ambition, take no initiative and avoid taking any responsibility; all they want is security, and to get them to do any work, they must be rewarded, coerced, intimidated and punished. This formed the basis of the so-called 'stick-and-carrot' approach to management. If this theory was valid – later called *Theory X* – managers would have constantly to monitor their staff, whom they cannot trust and who will refuse to cooperate. Sadly, in such an oppressive atmosphere, for both staff and manager, there was no room for achievement and little creative work.

On the other hand, Douglas McGregor believed that people want to learn and that work is their natural activity to the extent that they develop self-discipline and self-development – so-called *Theory Y*. Their reward is not so much in cash payments but in the freedom to do difficult and challenging work by themselves. The manager's job is to integrate the human wish for self-development into the organisation's need for maximum productive efficiency in achieving its goals. Therefore, the basic objectives of both are met and with imagination and integrity, and the enormous potential of the human capital can be realised.

The theory of management roles emanating from these two contrasting approaches has intuitive appeal, yet the theories only describe a limited aspect of leadership and management behaviour. Because the research on which they were based included limited empirical support, generalisations on how to motivate people are problematic.

Abraham Maslow

Abraham Maslow was an American psychologist who, during the 1940s, developed the concept of a hierarchy of human needs. His ideas influenced other behavioural scientists in the 1950s and 1960s, including Frederick Herzberg, Douglas McGregor and Rensis Likert.

Maslow (1954) defined five levels of human need in an ascending order of priority. A lower level must be substantially satisfied before we consider a higher-level need. But a need that has been satisfied no longer controls our behaviour; it no longer motivates. Over the years, various labels have been attached to the five levels of need. In Maslow's original terms, they are in ascending order:

- *Physiological.* These are the physical needs that are fundamental to survival, such as air, food, water, sleep, sex, excretion, physical activity and no extremes of temperature. Unless these are met we will not even begin to think about higher-level needs. Very often we attend to these needs almost without thinking about them – until something goes wrong. For example, we breathe with comparatively little conscious thought until we choke on a piece of food – then all our attention is turned to the problem of obtaining air. There is a hierarchy in physiology too. Throwing a loaf of bread to a hungry, drowning man will not be helpful; while it is not particularly buoyant his hunger needs are being ignored in favour of the need to breathe!
- *Safety.* Once our physical needs are met we will turn our attention to ensuring our bodily and mental safety and the continued supply of our basic physiological needs. We will seek security: survival, the avoidance of pain, and comfort.
- *Love.* This is also often referred to as *social* or *belonging needs*. Feeling secure, we will look to fill our need to belong: to be with other people with whom we share similar ideas and values, and in whose company we feel relaxed and at ease; to find love – as opposed to sex – and affection.
- *Esteem.* Social needs met, we will turn our attention to meeting our need to feel that we are important and respected by others. We may seek formal status, recognition of our specific abilities or almost any combination of these – in addition to self-respect.

- *Self-actualisation.* This is the top level and is also referred to as *self-fulfilment* or *self-realisation needs.* When all other levels have been satisfied we turn our attention to this need – which takes many different forms in different people. For example, it may be a need to paint creatively, compose music, serve others or do something that has never been done before in that way. We may not even require others to know about it so that it doesn't come into the reckoning. It is the drive to 'be what one must'.

Managers need to consider each level and relate them to the workplace – find some ideas online on the companion web pages.

According to Maslow, if we aim to have a motivated individual by giving satisfaction through meeting his or her needs, we need to identify the individual's needs and then arrange things so that we can satisfy those needs while getting the work done.

In identifying individual needs, we need to remember that:

- The bottom levels of need are more capable of being satisfied, the higher levels less so. If we satisfy a goal in the higher levels of need we are much more likely just to set ourselves a new and more difficult goal to reach. Thus, it is the higher-level needs which tend to encourage us to greatest long-term effort, because the need is less likely to be ever fully satisfied.
- The theory is about meeting a person's needs overall, not just at work, and we cannot do a proper analysis without knowing the individual's circumstances outside work. It may be that an individual is happy working alone because their belonging needs are more than satisfied by social interests outside work.
- We are all individuals, fortunately, whereas theories are generalisations. For a particular person the needs may operate in a different sequence, and some may even be absent. Maslow, for example, found some people for whom self-esteem seemed more important than love.
- Individuals will have different ideas on what constitutes 'satisfaction' at a particular level. One person's cod and chips is another's caviar.
- The importance of particular needs may vary during our lifetime and, if a lower, previously satisfied level is threatened, we will turn our attention back to that threatened level. In times of high levels of unemployment we may remain in an uninteresting job solely to meet our physiological and safety needs, since it may be difficult to find a more fulfilling occupation.

Kurt Lewin (1890–1948)

One of the most interesting pieces of work in which Lewin was involved concerned the exploration of different styles or types of leadership on group structure and member behaviour. This work involved collaboration with Ronald Lippitt, among others (Lewin et al., 1939;

also written up in Lewin, 1948). They looked to three classic group leadership models – 'democratic', 'autocratic' and '*laissez-faire*' – and concluded that there was more originality, group-mindedness and friendliness in democratic groups. In contrast, there was more aggression, hostility, finding scapegoats and discontent in '*laissez-faire*' and 'autocratic' groups (Reid, 1981). Lewin concluded that the difference in behaviour in autocratic, democratic and *laissez-faire* situations is not, on the whole, a result of individual differences. Reflecting on the group experiments conducted with children he had the following to say:

> *There have been few experiences for me as impressive as seeing the expression in children's faces change during the first day of autocracy. The friendly, open and cooperative group, full of life, became within a short half-hour a rather apathetic looking gathering without initiative. The change from autocracy to democracy seemed to take somewhat more time than from democracy to autocracy. Autocracy is imposed upon the individual. Democracy he has to learn.*
>
> (Lewin, 1948)

The impact of variations in style on motivation will be explored in Chapter 9.

Another key area of interest for Lewin was *field theory*. For him, behaviour of individuals was determined by the totality of an individual's situation. In Lewin's field theory, a 'field' is defined as '*the totality of coexisting facts which are conceived of as mutually interdependent*'. Individuals were seen to behave differently according to the way in which tensions between perceptions of the self and of the environment were worked through. The whole psychological field, or 'life space', within which people acted had to be viewed in order to understand behaviour. Within this, individuals and groups could be seen in topological terms (using map-like representations). Individuals participate in a series of life spaces (such as the family, work, school and church) and these are constructed under the influence of various force vectors.

Lewin is also remembered for his three-step model for change in organisational development: unfreeze–change–refreeze. The central concept is that the organisation needs to be shaken out of its current rigid values and modes of operation first, and then changed, before being set running in a new mode with new values. Many a consultant created the tension to break the old ways of working by the change agent charging high fees! However, most people would argue today that refreezing is not a good idea as change is constant.

More of a psychologist than a management advisor, Lewin is renowned for his work with the US government during the Second World War. His work on social dynamics later made him instrumental in the creation of the T-Group movement ('T' for team).

Further details on the T-Group movement can be found online on the companion web pages.

Frederick Herzberg

Frederick Herzberg is an American psychologist who has conducted research on human motivation at work and its effects on the individual's job satisfaction and mental health. His work, in many ways, complements Maslow's theory of The Hierarchy of Needs (Herzberg, 1956).

Herzberg interviewed 200 accountants and engineers in Pittsburgh to find out what made them satisfied and dissatisfied in their jobs. The replies showed that, in general, the experiences they regarded as satisfying were not just the opposite of those that gave rise to dissatisfaction. For example, an individual may have disliked the job because of poor working conditions or indecisive management, but very rarely would that individual say that the job was liked because of good conditions and decisive management.

On the one hand, he suggested that there are *dissatisfiers* that affect how dissatisfied a person feels. Obviously, these play little part in motivating people. The dissatisfiers tend to be tangible. For example:

- Pay
- Company policy
- Level of supervision
- Working conditions
- Relationships.

On the other hand, there are the *satisfiers* that are necessary for people to feel motivated. Satisfiers are feelings or perceptions and fall into five broad categories:

- The work itself
- Achievement
- Recognition
- Responsibility
- Advancement (i.e. promotion).

If there is a scale from dissatisfied through neutral to satisfied, varying the dissatisfiers can alter a person's position on the scale that runs from dissatisfied to neutral, while varying the satisfiers can alter a person's position on the scale that runs from neutral to satisfied (see Figure 4.1).

Putting right the problems that cause dissatisfaction will bring people up to a neutral position of being neither satisfied nor dissatisfied. Adding yet more of the same (for example, making working conditions even better) will not make people positively satisfied: that needs something else.

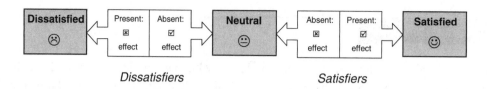

Dissatisfiers   Satisfiers

Figure 4.1 Adaptation of Herzberg's two-factor theory of motivation showing how the presence or absence of dissatisfiers and satisfiers have their causal effects.

Table 4.1 Herzberg's two sets of factors affecting motivation

Hygiene factors – job context	Motivators – job content
Technical and managerial competence of leadership	The work itself, especially interesting and challenging work
Organisation's policies and administration	Achievement from the task
Working conditions	Having responsibility
Interpersonal relations (can also be a motivator)	Prospects for advancement and development in the job
Pay	Recognition by the organisation or outsiders
Status and security	

Herzberg concluded that there are two sets of factors influencing motivation (see Table 4.1). These are largely independent of each other and affect behaviour in different ways.

Some factors will cause dissatisfaction if they are not right for the people in the organisation; Herzberg calls these 'hygiene factors'. Just as refuse collection, sanitation and so on reduce the chances of disease while not making people positively healthy, so putting right the causes of dissatisfaction will not positively motivate people – it just stops them from being demotivated.

A second set of factors accounts for positive feelings of satisfaction. These are the motivators. (Equivalents in health are presumably things like physical fitness and a proper diet.)

So what are these two sets of factors?

- *Hygiene factors* are about job *context* – when people felt dissatisfied at work they were concerned about the environment (in the broadest sense) in which they were working
- *Motivators* are about job *content* – when people felt satisfaction at work this had to do with the jobs they were doing.

Herzberg says that the hygiene factors describe the job environment – so how does one treat people on their jobs? Treat them so they have a minimum of dissatisfaction.

The motivators must be built into the job itself – so how does one use people in their jobs? Utilise their abilities so they get achievement, recognition for achievement, interest, responsibility, and they can grow and advance in their work.

It is key to note that when one speaks of achievement, that must not be a false sense of achievement. Building the motivators into jobs – what Herzberg calls job enrichment – is not a gimmick or a psychological trap to make employees feel important when in reality they are not. Job enrichment is a hard, serious, rewarding business and if it cannot be approached honestly it had best not be tried at all.

Critics of Herzberg's research can be found online on the companion web pages.

Robert Tannenbaum and Warren Schmidt

Robert Tannenbaum and Warren Schmidt devised a simple continuum model (see Figure 4.2), which shows the relationship between the level of freedom that a manager chooses to give to a team and the level of authority used by the manager. As the team's freedom is increased, so the manager's authority decreases. This is a positive way for both teams and managers to develop.

While the model concerns delegated freedom to a group, the principle of being able to apply different levels of delegated freedom can be applied to individuals. For managers, one of the key responsibilities is to develop the team. The model suggests that a manager should delegate and ask a team to make its own decisions to varying degrees according to their abilities. There is a rising scale of levels of delegated freedom that can be used when working with a team. Over time, a manager should aim to take the team from one end to the other, up the scale, at which point the manager should also aim to have developed one or a number of potential successors from within the team to take over. Since this process can take a year or two, or even longer, managers need to be patient, explain what they are doing, and be aware constantly of how the team is responding and developing. This theme will be developed further in Chapter 14.

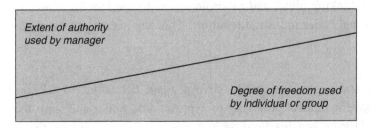

Figure 4.2 Adaptation of the Tannenbaum and Schmidt continuum.

Rensis Likert

According to Rensis Likert (1961), the best managers in business and government give an insight into how a much more effective system of management should operate.

He described low-efficiency departments as having supervisors who, being job centred, keep workers busy through a prescribed work cycle at a satisfactory time rate. The job is reduced to component parts, with trained people to do them and constant pressure to achieve output using all the resources available.

However, he noted that high-efficiency departments have supervisors who, being people centred, focus on the human aspects and build effective work groups pursuing high achievement goals. The supervisors attempt to know employees as individuals. They give general rather than detailed supervision, with overall targets rather than prescribing methods. They accept maximum participation in decision-making and see employees as capable of joining in the decision-making processes.

Likert suggested four systems of management (by ideal types):

1. *Exploitive authoritative.* Management uses fear and threats; communication is top down with most decisions taken at the top; superiors and subordinates are distant. This was seen as an extension of McGregor's Theory X.

2. *Benevolent authoritative.* Management uses rewards; information flowing upward is restricted to what management wants to hear and while policy decisions come from the top some prescribed decisions may be delegated to lower levels. Superiors expect subservience lower down.

3. *Consultative.* Management offers rewards and occasional punishments; big decisions come from the top while there is some wider decision-making involvement in details lower down. Communication is downward while critical upward communication is cautious.

4. *Participative group management.* Management encourages group participation and involvement in setting high performance goals with some economic rewards. Communication flows in all directions and is open and frank with decision-making through group processes. Each group is linked to others by persons who are members of more than one group called 'linking pins', and subordinates and superiors are close. The result is high productivity and better industrial relations. This was seen as an extension of McGregor's Theory Y.

A manager and supervisor should always adapt behaviour to take account of actual employees, adapting general principles to expectations, values and skills they have. According to Likert (1967), organisations should generate the conditions that encourage every manager to deal sensitively with them.

While it is possible to have job-centred, tough management that can achieve high productivity through systems of control, there will still be unfavourable 'them and us' attitudes amongst employees towards work and management, with a higher labour turnover and greater labour and management conflict.

Social scientists help obtain objective measurements in organisations of such variables as:

- Members' loyalty to the organisation
- How individuals' goals interact with the organisation's goals
- Motivation
- Trust and confidence between different hierarchical levels
- Communication and whether each manager or supervisor is correctly informed of the expectations, obstacles, problems, reactions and failures of employees
- How each manager or supervisor provides assistance to employees based on understood expectations.

This is the interaction–influence system (between employees and organisation), and evaluates why it is improving or deteriorating and what is required to improve matters. Objective information and the authority of facts have to come from the social scientist's tools, so that an enhanced human behaviour-based law of the situation (originally Mary Parker Follett) is revealed for the purposes of action.

An organisation should have an integrative unity where what happens matters to the individual and matters to the organisation equally and are as one. This is system 4.

Robert Blake and Jane Mouton

In 1964, Dr Robert Blake and Dr Jane Mouton developed a model that conceptualises management styles and relations they termed the Leadership Model Grid Theory. They were two of the leading pioneers of leadership consulting and transformational change in organisations. Steeped in behavioural science, grid learning has been successfully adapted to corporate, governmental and academic bodies to effect dynamic and lasting change.

Their grid uses two axes: 'Concern for people' is plotted using the vertical axis and 'Concern for task' is along the horizontal axis. They both have a range of 1 to 9. The notion that just two dimensions can describe managerial behaviour has the attraction of simplicity. Figure 4.3 illustrates the grid. Questionnaires are used to evaluate an individual manager's style, and the results can be plotted and visualised on the grid.

The various management styles are described by reference to the coordinates on this grid. High concern for people and low concern for production is known as 1,9 – 'country club management'. Its opposite is 9,1 – 'authoritarian management' – obedience being the order of the day with a high concern for the task or productivity and a low concern for people.

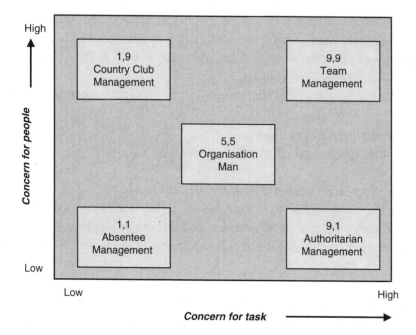

Figure 4.3 An adaptation of Blake's Leadership Model Grid Theory.

Some of these phrases have entered the rhetoric of management, where some had 'trial by 9,1'. Despite recent attempts to reinterpret what Blake and Mouton offered, they did suggest that 9,9 team management was the ideal style of management.

Peter Drucker

Amongst the many management initiatives devised by Drucker, Management by Objectives (MBO) is one of the simplest yet so often poorly applied. MBO relies on the defining of objectives for each employee, and then comparing and directing their performance against the objectives that have been set. It aims to increase organisational performance by aligning goals and subordinate objectives throughout the organisation. Ideally, employees get strong input to identifying their objectives, time scales for completion and so forth. MBO includes ongoing tracking and feedback in the process to reach objectives.

MBO was first outlined in his book *The Practice of Management* in 1954. According to Drucker, managers should avoid the activity trap, getting so involved in their day-to-day activities that they forget their main purpose or objective. One of the concepts of MBO was that instead of just a few top managers, all managers of a firm should participate in the strategic planning process, in order to improve implementation of the plan.

Another concept of MBO was that managers should implement a range of performance systems, designed to help the organisation stay on the right track. Clearly, MBO can be seen as a predecessor of Value-Based Management.

The principles of MBO are:

- Cascading of organisational goals and objectives
- Specific objectives for each member
- Participative decision-making
- Explicit time period
- Performance evaluation and feedback.

MBO also introduced the SMART method for checking the validity of the objectives, which should be 'SMART':

- Specific
- Measurable
- Achievable
- Realistic[1]
- Time-related.

Goal setting is discussed in more detail in Chapter 6 of Mackay (2007).

In the 1990s Drucker put the significance of this organisational management method into perspective when he said, 'It is just another tool. It is not the great cure for management inefficiency... MBO works if you know the objectives; 90 per cent of the time you don't.'

John Adair

British-born John Adair developed his Action-Centred Leadership Model while lecturing at Sandhurst Royal Military Academy and as assistant director and head of the leadership department at The Industrial Society. As this was during the 1960s and 1970s, in terms of management theories, Adair's work is relatively recent.

His work certainly encompasses and endorses much of the previous thinking on human needs and motivation by Maslow, Herzberg and Fayol, and his theory adds an elegant and simple additional organisational dimension to these earlier works. Very importantly, Adair was probably the first to demonstrate that leadership is a trainable, transferable skill, rather than it being an exclusively innate ability.

---

[1] Some would argue that a 'Realistic' objective is achievable and thus the R should be 'Results-orientated' building to a bigger picture, or 'Resourced' to check that the objective can be achieved with appropriate resources.

He helped change the perception of management to encompass leadership, to include associated abilities of decision-making, communication and time management. As well as developing the Action-Centred Leadership Model, he has written over 25 books on management and leadership.

Adair is now a management consultant and also has his own publishing company in Surrey, England. He also maintains links with the University of Surrey, where he was the first UK chair of leadership studies, 1979–83.

Adair suggests that leadership is different to management. All leaders are not necessarily great managers, but the best leaders will possess good management skills. One skill-set does not automatically imply the other will be present.

Adair's explanation used the original word meanings to emphasise this: leadership is an ancient ability about deciding direction, from an Anglo-Saxon word meaning the road or path ahead, knowing the next step and then taking others with you to it. Managing is a later concept, from the Latin '*manus*', meaning hand, and more associated with handling a system or machine of some kind. The original concept of managing began in the 19th century, when engineers and accountants started to become entrepreneurs.

Adair further suggests that there are valuable elements of management not necessarily found in leadership – for example, administration and managing resources. Likewise, leadership contains elements not necessarily found in management – for example, inspiring others through the leader's own enthusiasm and commitment.

The Action-Centred Leadership Model is Adair's best known work, in which the three elements – achieving the task, developing the team and developing individuals – are mutually dependent, as well as being separately essential to the overall leadership role (see Figure 4.4).

Moreover, Adair set out these core functions of leadership and says they are vital to the Action-Centred Leadership Model:

- Planning – seeking information, defining tasks, setting aims
- Initiating – briefing, task allocation, setting standards

Figure 4.4 Adaptation of John Adair's Leadership Model.

- Controlling – maintaining standards, ensuring progress, ongoing decision-making
- Supporting – individuals' contributions, encouraging, team spirit, reconciling, building morale
- Informing – clarifying tasks and plans, updating, receiving feedback, interpreting
- Evaluating – feasibility of ideas, performance, enabling self-assessment.

Therefore, the Action-Centred Leadership Model does not stand alone; it must be part of an integrated approach to managing and leading, and should also include a strong emphasis on applying these principles through training.

Adair's eight rules in motivating people are:

- Be motivated yourself
- Select people who are highly motivated
- Treat each person as an individual
- Set realistic and challenging targets
- Remember that progress motivates
- Create a motivating environment
- Provide fair rewards
- Give recognition.

W. Edwards Deming

Deming was an electrical engineer and statistician who is regarded as the founding father of quality management. He worked at the Western Electric Hawthorne plant in Chicago (around the time of Elton Mayo's famous experiments there) and was involved in statistical process control. In 1950, he started work in Japan and is credited with helping the Japanese overcome their original reputation for shoddy quality.

Deming's philosophy was to regard the customer as the most important part of the production line and to aim to have customers who were more than satisfied: customers who would give repeat business and encourage others to become customers.

He also highlighted the importance of managers understanding their people because they could only achieve results through their teams. He stressed that leadership was about helping people to do a better job, and involved training those people in the new skills needed to keep up with change. He also emphasised the need for trust, two-way communication, the breaking down of barriers between departments, and allowing pride of workmanship.

As part of his philosophy he developed and refined, over 20 years or more, his 14 Points for management. Quoted in Deming's own words, these are:

1. Create constancy of purpose for continual improvement of products and service.
2. Adopt the new philosophy created in Japan.
3. Cease dependence on mass inspection: build quality into the product in the first place.
4. End lowest-tender contracts; instead, require meaningful measures of quality along with price.
5. Improve constantly and forever every process for planning, production and service.
6. Institute modern methods of training on the job for all, including management.
7. Adopt and institute leadership aimed at helping people to do a better job.
8. Drive out fear, encourage effective two-way communication.
9. Break down barriers between departments and staff areas.
10. Eliminate exhortations for the workforce – they only create adversarial relationships.
11. Eliminate quotas and numerical targets. Substitute aid and helpful leadership.
12. Remove barriers to pride of workmanship, including annual appraisals and Management by Objectives.
13. Encourage education and self-improvement for everyone.
14. Define top management's permanent commitment to ever-improving quality and productivity, and their obligation to implement all these principles.

Deming's name is often linked with that of Joseph M. Juran, another pioneer in quality management. Juran also worked at the Hawthorne plant in the 1920s – as an industrial engineer. He, too, promoted the importance of quality in the 1950s and worked in Japan from 1953.

Juran's approach is biased towards the human aspects of quality management and he has criticised Deming for being too biased toward statistical quality control. Juran foresees the corporation of the future having a business plan that incorporates quality targets in the same way that sales and financial targets are currently incorporated. He also sees empowerment and teamwork as keys to achieving quality. In his view, quality is indissolubly linked with human relations and teamwork.

Robert House

In 1971 Robert House put forward the Path–Goal Theory that says that a manager can affect the performance, satisfaction and motivation of a group by:

- Offering rewards for achieving performance goals
- Clarifying paths towards these goals
- Removing obstacles to performance.

However, whether the manager can do so effectively would depend on situational factors. Thus, according to House, there are four different types of leadership styles depending on the situation:

1. *Directive leadership* – where the leader gives specific guidance of performance to subordinates.
2. *Supportive leadership* – where the leader is friendly and shows concern for subordinates.
3. *Participative leadership* – where the leader consults with subordinates and considers their suggestions.
4. *Achievement-orientated leadership* – where the leader sets high goals and expects subordinates to have high-level performance.

The situational factors of the Path–Goal Theory are:

Subordinate's personality

- Locus of control – a participative leader is suitable for subordinates with internal locus of control; a directive leader is suitable for subordinates with external locus of control
- Self-perceived ability – those that perceive that they have a high ability do not like directive leadership.

Characteristics of the environment

- When working on a task that has a high structure, directive leadership is redundant and less effective
- When a highly formal authority system is in place, directive leadership can again reduce workers' satisfaction
- When subordinates are in a team environment that offers great social support, the supportive leadership style becomes less necessary.

Richard Hackman and Greg Oldham

Hackman and Oldham (1980) originally proposed their Job Characteristics Theory as a three-stage model, in which a set of core job characteristics impact a number of critical psychological states, which in turn influence a set of effective and motivational outcomes (see Figure 4.5). Most subsequent research has omitted the critical psychological states, focusing instead on the direct impact of the core job characteristics on the outcomes (i.e. a two-stage model). Results from Behson et al. (see http://www.chrms.org/library/critic/critic1a.htm)

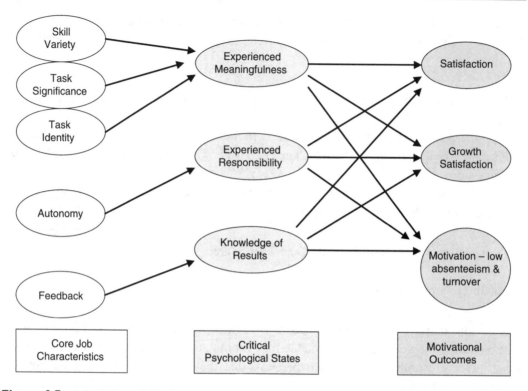

Figure 4.5 Adaptation of Hackman and Oldham's Job Characteristics Model.

suggest that, while the two-stage model demonstrates adequate fit to the data, information on the critical psychological states is important for both theoretical and practical reasons.

Interestingly, the researchers found that 'autonomy' is the core job characteristic that has the strongest link to motivational outcomes. Allowing an individual personal control over how they achieve the defined outcomes of their task is a key to successful change in employee attitudes, behaviours and value orientation. Moreover, this classical theory has many facets to consider, not least the implications of the 'critical psychological states' that have impact in workplace change initiatives, including Just-In-Time (JIT), Total Quality Management (TQM) and Management By Objectives (MBO).

In practice, the following approaches implement concepts from the Job Characteristics Model:

- Combine tasks – affects skill variety, task identity and task significance
- Group tasks into natural work units – affects task significance and task identity
- Give workers contact with customers – affects skill variety, autonomy and feedback
- Vertically load jobs – affects autonomy
- Open feedback channels – affects feedback.

Rosabeth Moss Kanter

Rosabeth Moss Kanter is a Harvard Business School professor, bestselling author and ex-editor of the *Harvard Business Review*. She came to prominence with *The Change Masters* (1988) – accurately dubbed a thinking person's manager *In Search of Excellence*. Primarily a sociologist, she retains a strong interest in utopian communities – this is most recently expressed in her co-authorship of *Common Interest, Common Good: Creating Value Through Business and Social Sector Partnerships* (1999). Her most recent book *E-volve!* (2001) provides Kanter's determinedly humanistic view on what it takes to succeed and thrive in the new economy featuring companies such as e-Bay and CNBC.com.

She suggests that the most important things a leader can bring to a changing organisation are passion, conviction and confidence in others. Too often executives announce a plan, launch a task force and then simply hope that people find the answers – instead of offering a dream, stretching their horizons and encouraging people to do the same. That is why she says, 'Leaders go first'. However, given that passion, conviction and confidence, she suggests that leaders can use several techniques to take charge of change rather than simply react to it. In nearly 20 years working with leaders, she found the following classic skills to be equally useful to CEOs, senior executives or middle managers who want to move an idea forward (from an interview with Rosabeth Moss Kanter; go to www.business.com/directory/management/management_theory/):

- *Tuning in to the environment.* Leaders have to listen both inside and outside the organisation and need to create the opportunities to interact with *people* to find out what is going on. Look not just at how the pieces of one's business model fit together but for what doesn't fit. For instance, she suggests, pay special attention to customer complaints, which are often the best source of information about an operational weakness or unmet need. Also, search out broader signs of change – a competitor doing something differently or a customer using your product or service in unexpected ways.
- *Challenging the prevailing organisational wisdom.* Leaders need to develop what she calls 'kaleidoscope thinking' – a way of constructing patterns from the fragments of data available and then manipulating them to form different patterns. They must question their assumptions about how pieces of the organisation, the marketplace or the community fit together.
- *Communicating a compelling aspiration.* One cannot sell change, or anything else, without genuine conviction, because there are so many sources of resistance to overcome: 'We've never done it before; we tried it before and it didn't work.' 'Things are OK now, so why should we change?' Especially when pursuing a true innovation as opposed to responding to a crisis, managers have to make a compelling case. Leaders talk about communicating

a vision as an instrument of change, but she prefers the notion of communicating an aspiration. 'It's not just a picture of what could be, it is an appeal to our better selves, a call to become something more. It reminds us that the future does not just descend like a stage set; we construct the future from our own history, desires and decisions.'

- *Building coalitions.* Change leaders need the involvement of people who have the resources, the knowledge and the political clout to make things happen. Work with the opinion shapers, the experts in the field, the values leaders.

- *Transferring ownership to a working team.* Once a coalition is in place, managers can enlist others in implementation. Remaining involved, the leader's job is to support the team, provide coaching and resources, and patrol the boundaries within which the team can freely operate. But rather than simply ask others to execute a fully-formed change agenda, develop a broad outline, informed by your environmental scan and lots of good questions, from which people can conduct a series of small experiments. Thus, confer team ownership, but allow people to explore new possibilities in ways that do not compromise the company or the budget.

- *Learning to persevere.* Rosabeth Moss Kanter's personal law of management, if not of life, is that everything can look like a failure in the middle. One of the mistakes leaders make in change processes is to launch them and leave them. There are many ways a change initiative can get derailed, but stop it too soon and, by definition, it will be a failure; stay with it through its initial hurdles and good things may happen.

- *Making everyone a hero.* Remembering to recognise, reward and celebrate accomplishments is a critical leadership skill – and it is probably the most underutilised motivational tool in organisations. There is no limit to how much recognition managers can provide, and it is often free. Recognition brings the change cycle to its logical conclusion, but it also motivates people to attempt change again. So many people get involved in and contribute to changing the way an organisation does things that it is important to share the credit. Change is an ongoing issue, and managers cannot afford to lose the talents, skills or energies of those who can help make it happen.

Chris Argyris

He suggested that organisations need to be redesigned for a fuller utilisation of their most important asset, the workers, in particular their psychological energy. The pyramidal structure will be relegated to the background and decisions will be taken by small groups rather than by a single boss. Satisfaction in work will be valued over material rewards. Work should be restructured in order to enable individuals to develop to the fullest extent. At the same time, work will become more meaningful and challenging through self-motivation.

Argyris also undertook some fundamental work on individual learning that will be explored further in Chapter 12.

Robert McNamara

Upon his discharge from the air force, McNamara joined the Ford Motor Company; he was elected a director of the company in 1957 and became company president in 1960. At the request of President-elect John F. Kennedy, McNamara agreed to serve as Secretary of Defence of the United States, a position he held from 1961 until 1968. He became president of the World Bank Group of Institutions in April 1968, retiring in 1981.

When he came into the Kennedy administration from Ford, he was perceived as a manager of large organisations par excellence. In 1967 he suggested that management is the gate through which social, economic and political change, indeed change in every direction, is diffused though society. In an interview in April 1996 with Harry Kreisler, he was asked to explain a comment made in 1962, *'Running the Department of Defence is not different from running Ford Motor Company, or the Catholic Church, for that matter. Once you get to a certain scale, it's all the same.'*

Robert McNamara explained that that was a simplification. He drew the parallel between running the Defence Department, which at times carries a responsibility for putting the youth of his country at the risk of death, and requires many of the same skills, attitudes, philosophical values and approaches as does managing Ford or the Catholic Church.

For him, the key ingredient was first to have an objective, and he felt that Pope John had an objective for the Catholic Church. He had an objective for the Ford Motor Company and had an objective for the US government, then headed by John F. Kennedy.

McNamara said that if you don't have an objective, you can't expend your power to achieve the objective. The President's job is to help lead the country, not as a dictator but as a persuader. To lead a democracy, you need a concept of values and objectives, and you need then to put your concepts at risk in the forum of public debate, and have them debated and hopefully move the people to support them and move the society to them. Kennedy thought that way too.

Charles Handy

Ireland-born writer and broadcaster Charles Handy has had an interesting influence on organisational thinking and popularised a typology of cultures and organisations. His four cultures are very easy for people to understand, and groups readily identify with them and begin to explore their culture through the models he uses. Handy also uses four Greek gods to illustrate his basic approaches and the organisational cultures that result:

- *Power culture.* This is like a web with a ruling spider. Those in the web are dependent on a central power source, where rays of power and influence spread out from a central figure or group. In a *Zeus* organisation, power derives from the top person, and a personal relationship with that individual matters more than any formal title or position. Examples would include small entrepreneurial companies and political groups.

- *Role culture*. This is often referred to as a bureaucracy, controlled by procedures, role descriptions and authority definitions. Coordination is at the top. Job position is central, where individuals value predictability and consistency so that many may find it harder to adjust to change. An *Apollo* culture creates a highly structured, stable company – a bureaucracy – with precise job descriptions, usually with a single product.
- *Task culture*. This is very much a small team approach – such as the network organisation – where small organisations are cooperating together to deliver a project. The emphasis is on results and getting things done. Individuals are empowered with discretion and control over their work so that the organisation is flexible and adaptable. The *Athena* culture emphasises talent and youth, with continuous team problem-solving. One example would be consultancies.
- *Person culture*. Here the individual is the central point. If there is a structure it exists only to serve the individuals within it. The culture only exists for the people concerned; it has no superordinate objective. Such organisations tend to have strong values about how they will work. These values are very difficult for the organisation to manage. A *Dionysus* 'existential' organisation exists so that individuals can achieve their purposes – e.g. university, a medical practice, other professional groupings.

Each culture stems from different assumptions about the basis of power and influence, what motivates people, how people think and learn, and how change should occur.

Tom Peters and Robert H. Waterman Jr

In Search of Excellence was published in 1982, and remains one of the biggest selling and widely read business books ever. Peters and Waterman found eight common themes which they argued were responsible for the success of the chosen corporations, which have become pointers for managers ever since.

Peters and Waterman were both consultants on the margins of McKinsey, based in the San Francisco office. In 1977 McKinsey director Ron Daniel launched two projects; the first and major one, the Business Strategy project, was allocated to top consultants at McKinsey's New York corporate HQ and was given star billing. Nothing came of it. The second 'weak sister' project (as Peters called it) concerned Organisation – structure and people. The Organisation project was seen as less important, and was allocated to Peters and Waterman at San Francisco. Peters travelled the world on an infinite budget, with licence to talk to as many interesting business people he could find about teams and organisations in business. He had no particular aim or theory in mind. In 1979 McKinsey's Munich office requested Peters to present his findings to Siemens, which provided the spur for Peters to create a 700-slide, two-day presentation. Word of the meeting reached the US and Peters was invited to present also to PepsiCo, but unlike the hyper-organised Siemens, the PepsiCo management required a tighter format than 700 slides, so Peters produced the following eight themes:

1. A bias for action, active decision-making – 'getting on with it'.
2. Close to the customer – learning from the people served by the business.
3. Autonomy and entrepreneurship – fostering innovation and nurturing 'champions'.
4. Productivity through people – treating rank and file employees as a source of quality.
5. Hands-on, value-driven – management philosophy that guides everyday practice, management showing its commitment.
6. Stick to the knitting – stay with the business that you know.
7. Simple form, lean staff – some of the best companies have minimal HQ staff.
8. Simultaneous loose–tight properties – autonomy in shop-floor activities plus centralised values.

The platform for Peters and Waterman, onto which the *In Search of Excellence* research and theorising was built, was the McKinsey 7S Model, with the following elements:

1. Structure
2. Strategy
3. Systems
4. Style of management
5. Skills – corporate strengths
6. Staff
7. Shared values.

This model is represented in Figure 4.6.

Peters and Waterman examined 43 of *Fortune* 500's top performing companies. They started with a list of 62 of the best-performing McKinsey clients and then applied performance measures to weed out what they thought to be the weaker companies. General Electric was one of the casualties which failed to make the cut. Peters says that one of his personal drivers in carrying out his research was to prove that certain established methods – particularly heavily systemised philosophies and practices – were wrong, notably those used by Xerox, and advocated by Peter Drucker and Robert McNamara. Peters says that he wanted – with a passion – to prove how crucial people are to business success, and to release business from the 'tyranny of the bean counters'.

As Peters explained in 2001:

> *Start with Taylorism, add a layer of Druckerism and a dose of McNamaraism, and by the late 1970s you had the great American corporation that was being run by bean counters...*

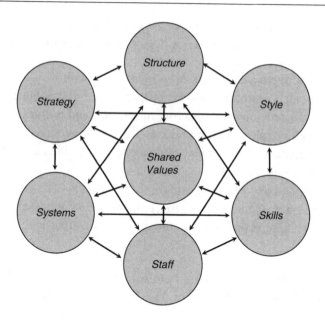

Figure 4.6 Adaptation of the McKinsey 7S Model.

Contrast this with what Peters says became the essential message of *In Search of Excellence*, simply:

- People
- Customers
- Action.

Peters says that *In Search of Excellence* turned these 'soft' factors into hard ones, when previously the only 'hard factors' were considered to be the 'numbers'.

Peters also said in 2001 that other than certain wrong companies highlighted – Atari and Wang, for instance – *In Search of Excellence* 'absolutely nailed the eight points of the compass for business at that time' (1982), but that its central flaw was in suggesting that these points would apply forever, when they most certainly have not.

Peters said finally in his 2001 interview that were he to write *In Search of Excellence* today, he would not tamper with any of the eight themes, but he would add to them: capabilities concerning ideas, liberation and speed.

Victor Vroom

Vroom's 'Expectancy Theory' is an extension of the 'contingency' approach (Vroom, 1965; Vroom and Deci, 1978). Here, the leadership style should be tailored to the particular situation and to the particular group. In some cases, it is suggested, it is better for the manager of the group to decide and in others the group arrives at a consensus. Moreover, it was seen to be important to reward the individual with what he or she perceives as important, rather than what the manager perceives.

In this way, it was suggested that behaviour results from conscious choices among alternatives whose purpose is to maximise pleasure and minimise pain. Together with Edward Lawler and Lyman Porter, Vroom suggests that the relationship between people's behaviour at work and their goals was not as simple as first imagined by other researchers. Vroom realised that an employee's performance is based on individual factors such as personality, skills, knowledge, experience and abilities.

The Expectancy Theory states that individuals have different sets of goals and can be motivated if they believe that:

- There is a positive correlation between efforts and performance
- Favourable performance will result in a desirable reward
- The reward will satisfy an important need
- The desire to satisfy the need is strong enough to make the effort worthwhile.

Vroom's Expectancy Theory is based upon the following three beliefs:

- *Valance* – the emotional orientations people hold with respect to outcomes (rewards). Managers must understand the depth of the want of an employee for intrinsic (satisfaction) or extrinsic (money, promotion, time off, benefits) rewards.
- *Expectancy* – employees have different expectations and levels of confidence about what they are capable of doing. Mangers need to uncover what resources, training or supervision employees need.
- *Instrumentality* – the perception of employees whether they will actually get what they desire even if it has been promised by a manager. Here, management must ensure that promises of rewards are fulfilled and that employees are aware of that.

Vroom suggests that an employee's beliefs about Expectancy, Instrumentality and Valance interact psychologically to create a motivational force such that the employee acts in ways that bring pleasure and avoid pain. He suggested that this force can be calculated using the following formula:

$$Motivation = Valance \times Expectancy\ (Instrumentality)$$

This formula can be used to indicate and predict such factors as job satisfaction, one's occupational choice, the likelihood of staying in the job and the effort that one might expend at work.

Clayton P. Alderfer

Existence, Relatedness, Growth – or ERG Theory (Alderfer, 1969) – is a model devised in reaction to Maslow's Hierarchy of Needs. Alderfer defined three categories of human needs that are said to influence a worker's behaviour: existence, relatedness and growth. These are explained thus:

- *Existence needs* – physiological and safety needs (such as hunger, thirst and sex) which are related to Maslow's first two levels.
- *Relatedness needs* – social and external esteem (involvement with family, friends, co-workers and employers) which are related to Maslow's third and fourth levels.
- *Growth needs* – internal self-esteem and self-actualisation (desires to be creative, productive and to complete meaningful tasks) which are related to Maslow's fourth and fifth levels.

While Maslow contended that access to the higher levels required satisfaction in the lower-level needs, according to Alderfer the three ERG areas are not stepped in any way (see Figure 4.7).

ERG Theory recognises that the order of importance of the three categories may vary for each individual and recommends that managers must recognise that an employee has multiple needs to satisfy simultaneously. According to ERG Theory, just by focusing on one need at a time, managers will be unable to effectively motivate individuals.

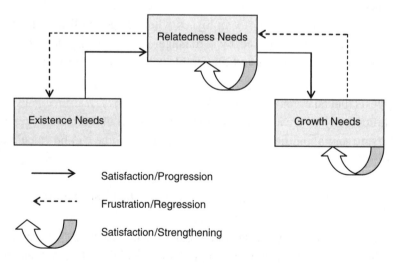

Figure 4.7 Adaptation of ERG Theory, after Alderfer.

Moreover, ERG Theory acknowledges that if a higher-level need remains unfulfilled, the person may regress to lower-level needs that appear easier to satisfy. This is known as the frustration–regression principle; it has an impact on workplace motivation. For example, if growth opportunities are not available to employees, they may regress to relatedness needs and socialise more with co-workers. If managers recognise these conditions early, steps can be taken to satisfy the frustrated needs until the subordinate is able to pursue growth again.

Hersey and Blanchard's Situational Leadership

The basic assumptions around this model is that leaders should adapt their style to follower 'maturity', based on how ready and willing the follower is to perform required tasks (that is, their competence and motivation; see Figure 4.8).

There are four leadership styles that match the four combinations of high/low readiness and willingness. The four styles suggest that leaders should put greater or less focus on the task (task orientation) in question and/or the relationship (relationship orientation) between the leader and the follower. Chapter 13 provides more detail of the basic styles and applicability.

Kenneth Blanchard (of the *One Minute Manager* fame) has written a short and very readable book on the approach. It is simple and easy to understand, which makes it particularly attractive for practising managers who do not want to get into heavier material. It also is accepted in wider spheres and often appears in college courses.

It is limited, however, and is based on assumptions that can be challenged, for example the assumption that at the 'telling' level, the relationship is of lower importance. It is the

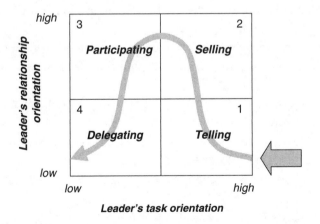

Figure 4.8 Adaptation of Hersey and Blanchard's Situational Leadership Model.

aim of this book to explore the further application of the model as it affects motivation, ability and confidence.

The simplicity, applicability and adaptability of this model is such that it will be a cornerstone to the Motivation, Ability and Confidence building development models explored later in this text.

Summary

In this chapter you have:

- Reviewed the key management theories over the last 100 years
- Seen that there is a key element in them all – the *people* that actually do the work!
- Developed an understanding to underpin your management practice in the workplace
- Have an understanding of the basis of Mackay's Motivation, Ability and Confidence development models introduced in later chapters of this text.

Questions

1. Among a group of colleagues or fellow students, list those things that make you unhappy at work and those things that 'motivate' you. Compare and contrast your findings with Herzberg.
2. Maslow's Hierarchy of Needs has been popular for over half a century. Why do you think that is? Look at each of the five levels and define what it is that 'motivates' you in your place of work or study, and make suggestions on how things could be improved for you at each level.
3. Consider a manager that you know. Where are they on an autocratic–democratic continuum? What evidence do you have to support your answer and how effective do you feel they are?
4. Consider the Hersey/Blanchard Situational Leadership Model. What is the most appropriate style to use for:
   - A committed and talented worker?
   - A new recruit on their first day?
   - Someone that used to do a good job reliably but has missed some key detail in their work?
   - An enthusiastic worker who has made some progress but does not know their entire job?

References

Alderfer, C. P. (1969) 'An Empirical Test of a New Theory of Human Need', *Psychological Review*.

Barnes, R. (1980) *Motion and Time Study*, 7th Edition, John Wiley, New York.

Blake, R. R. and Mouton, J. S. (1964) *The Managerial Grid*, Gulf, Houston.

Gilbreth, F. and Gilbreth, L. (1924) *Management and Administration*, August, pp. 151–154; September, pp. 295–297.

Hackman, J. R. and Oldham, G. R. (1980) *Work Redesign*, Addison-Wesley, Reading, MA.

Herzberg, F. (1956) *Work and The Nature of Man*, World Publishing.

Konopka, G. (1958) *Eduard C. Lindeman and Social Work Philosophy*, University of Minnesota Press, Minneapolis.

Lewin, K., Lippitt, R. and White, R. (1939) Patterns of Aggressive Behaviour in Experimentally Created Social Climates', *Journal of Social Psychology*, Vol. 10, pp. 271–299.

Lewin, K. (1948) *Resolving Social Conflicts: Selected papers on group dynamics* (G. W. Lewin, ed.), Harper & Row, New York.

Likert, R. (1961) *New Patterns of Management*, McGraw-Hill.

Likert, R. (1967) *The Human Organization: Its Management and Value*, McGraw-Hill.

Mackay, A. R. (2007) *Recruiting, Retaining and Releasing People*, Butterworth-Heinemann.

Maslow, A. H. (1954) *Motivation and Personality*, Harper & Row, New York.

Mogensen, A. (1979) *Common Sense Applied to Motion and Time Study*, John Wiley, New York.

Moss Kanter, R. (1988) *The Change Masters: Corporate Entrepreneurs At Work*, Unwin Paperbacks, London.

Reid, K. E. (1981) *From Character Building to Social Treatment: The history of the use of groups in social work*, Greenwood Press, Westpoint, CT.

Taylor F. W. (1947) *Scientific Management*, Harper & Row.

Vroom, V. H. (1965) *Motivation in Management*, American Foundation for Management Research, New York.

Vroom, V. H. and Deci, E. I. (1978) *Management and Motivation*, Penguin, Middlesex, UK.

Further Reading

In addition to the texts used as references, the following is a useful resource:

Harvard Business School (2005) *Motivating People for Improved Performance* Harvard Business School Press.

5

Motivating Individuals

...we've introduced e-mail-free Fridays to encourage our staff to pick up the phone or walk across the office and talk to one another.
    David Radcliffe, CEO of Hogg Robinson, writing in *Management Today*, January 2005, p. 6

Learning Outcomes

This chapter, and its companion web pages, have been written to provide a practical agenda for busy managers aiming to provide the right environment for individuals' motivation to come through. The chapter has been written to cover some further elements of the National Occupational Standards for Management and Leadership (*Working with People – Units 19 and 21–23*). It covers some of the requirements of the Chartered Management Institute's Diploma in Management compulsory and optional modules as far as 'people' resources are concerned, and some of the demands of the CIPD Professional Development Scheme – particularly the *People Management and Development* module.

By the end of this chapter you will:

- Recognise the place of an individual's 'energy' as a key resource
- Discover the value of people actually 'talking' to each other rather than e-mailing a person next to them!
- Have met a five-point agenda to re-energise ourselves
- Recognise the most sought-after facilities favoured by staff
- Know the value of trust in the workplace and strategies to build and maintain it
- Be able to turn theory into practice to enable motivation to come through.

Energy at Work

The Business Energy Survey 2004 was undertaken by the Chartered Management Institute in partnership with Adecco (see http://www.managers.org.uk/researchreports). The survey found that too many UK businesses are still failing to understand the wants and needs of their employees and workplace energy is dangerously low in some organisations. Around one-third (35 per cent) of respondents admit to having no energy on weekday evenings and 24 per cent use the weekend solely to recover from work.

In terms of workloads and working hours, the survey found that:

- One in five managers work 14 hours more a week than their normal working hours
- Almost half (43 per cent) feel they are overloaded with work
- Forty per cent of managers admit to missing family commitments because of work
- A quarter think that their organisation has an 'authoritarian' culture, with 28 per cent feeling exploited, and 30 per cent believe their organisation responds to change in an ad hoc, haphazard way
- Sixty-one per cent class 'sense of purpose' as the biggest motivating factor, whereas only 12 per cent see 'pay' as the main driving force
- One-third of managers want flexible working initiatives like compressed working weeks, but less than 5 per cent believe that this will happen.

This survey shows that energy levels among UK managers are dangerously low, while employees are not afraid to work at this level provided their ideas are heard and they can be made to feel valued, empowered and are allowed to work more flexibly.

> *What is a man without energy? Nothing, nothing at all.*
>
> Mark Twain

If the 1980s were about the quest for money and the 1990s the quest for time, the 2000s have become the energy decade. According to the Henley Centre, business people now regard energy as more important than money, information and space, and only just behind time; one in four think that within five years energy will be their most important resource.

Current debates about information fatigue, time squeeze, work/life balance or productivity are really about energy – and our need for more of it. Energy is a priceless business asset – across organisations as well as in individuals. Jack Welch (former CEO at GE – General Electric) suggested that successful managers need high personal energy and, equally, are able to energise others. Senior managers inject energy into the right part of the organisation at the right time. New recruits are expected to bring new energy into the workplace.

For organisations, employee energy is a critical ingredient for success, yet meetings, presenteeism and increasing bureaucracy are significant drains. Progressive firms think about time and space, creativity and communication, but also measure and invest in energy – as this is the factor that affects all the others. Some firms are clearly taking this aspect seriously.

The e-mail-free Fridays at Hogg Robinson are an attempt to encourage staff to pick up the telephone or walk across the office to talk to one another. The aim is to help them to realise the benefits of the spoken word and avoid the negative sinking feeling as they open their inboxes and are faced with hundreds of electronic messages vying for their attention. One Scottish bank has a defined protocol to manage their internal e-mails (see Box 5.1).

Hogg Robinson is keen to motivate their workforce in other ways too, and has devised schemes that both reward employees and recognise commitment to the organisation. All staff are invited to share power-boating days on the Solent, or enjoy the facilities of the corporate boxes at Twickenham and Ascot. They also run an employee recognition award scheme called 'Thanks'. While they have regular awards for nominated employees, they also have an annual awards event – Employee of the Year – where the winner receives a round-the-world trip.

Box 5.1: E-mail protocols at 'NAG'

E-mail guidelines
The European Leadership Team has committed to the following guidelines to help ensure effective and relevant communication and to free up time to focus on our customers and growing our businesses.

Effective communication
- First preference: talk face-to-face
- Second preference: pick up the phone
- Third preference: send an e-mail.

Prioritising e-mails
- To help us manage and reduce the flow of e-mails, we commit to follow a protocol that every e-mail should be marked in the 'Subject' section as follows:
  - *If you require a decision*: please add 'Decision' after the subject – e-mails to be reviewed as first priority
  - *For input/getting my views*: please mark as 'Response required' – e-mails to be dealt with within 48 hours
  - *For information*: please mark either 'For information or FYI' – e-mails for information and do not expect a response.
- E-mails that do not comply with this protocol should be returned to sender with no action taken.

As a client-focused company, Hogg Robinson recognises the need to exceed client expectations and achieve business objectives. They also acknowledge the benefits of an included and motivated workforce – paraphrasing Henry Ford, with every employee you get a free brain that is a huge energy source when harnessed. Hogg Robinson has a lower staff turnover than the industry average and they aim to reduce it still further. David Radcliffe, CEO of Hogg Robinson, writing in *Management Today* (January 2005), said, 'We're committed to evolving our work/life balance options to match our ever-changing personal requirements, listening to our staff and responding to their needs.'

If an individual has lost energy some detective work is often required. Try to identify when things started to go wrong:

- Maybe some 'satisfiers' are missing
- Maybe new 'dissatisfiers' are occurring
- Perhaps good positive feedback from their manager is missing
- If a role does not stretch the jobholder, remuneration and status are poor substitutes
- Greater responsibility/influence/autonomy often re-energise
- Poor organisation performance can be taken personally by senior people, producing a downward spiral of self-doubt and self-criticism.

The good thing about the source of demotivation deriving from recognised shortcomings in our working lives is that we can choose to do something about them either within the current organisation or by moving to a more appropriate job. When energy levels decline as a result of changes in our personal lives, easy solutions are harder to come by. While individuals differ in their approach to problems, clearly the death of a family member, the birth of a child, long-term sickness, the beginning or end of a significant personal relationship can all cause us to re-evaluate work and its importance in our lives. As personal priorities shift, one may need to accept that work may no longer be a driving force in our lives and we may change our work to reflect revised priorities more closely.

You will find five simple approaches to try to start to re-energise yourself online on the companion web pages.

In Clive Woodward's story of England's rise to 2003 Rugby World Cup glory, *Winning!*, after a training session with the Royal Marines he identified certain members of the then elite rugby squad who had low energy – they were the ones that held the squad back. There were no 'energy sappers' in the squad that lifted the World Cup in Australia.

Workspace

As reported in *Management Today* (2003), most workers are ashamed or disappointed about their workplaces and yearn for better working accommodation. Moreover, they are ready,

Table 5.1 Staff facilities really wanted compared to actually provided

	Really wanted (%)	Actually provided (%)
Relaxation/thinking space	56	20
Gym	53	14
Restaurant	41	31
Child care/elderly care	27	6
Shower	27	39
Cultural activity	12	7
Concierge service	9	3

willing and able to make sacrifices to get it. Nearly one-half of those surveyed would forgo one week annual leave, some would take a £1000 a year pay cut, while others would swap medical insurance for a better workplace. Surprisingly, 45 per cent might change employers for a better working environment even if the role, salary and benefits were no better.

It is clear that the working environment is becoming central in recruitment, retention and motivation of the best people. While it is recognised that a well-designed workspace makes a valuable contribution to the achievement of business objectives, it would seem that few are getting it right. Most managers would agree that a better work environment can reduce stress, improve morale, reflect corporate culture, reinforce brand identity, help retain staff and improve productivity; nearly one-third of those surveyed would actually be ashamed to bring clients or contacts into their own workplace.

Thus, there seems to be a gap between understanding theory and implementation in practice. With the boom in DIY, so many property makeover shows on television and celebrity interior decorators, we are all much more aware of our physical environment than before. Sadly, the aspiration of staff is not being turned into corporate reality and discontentment is spreading.

What most managers want are workplaces that are better designed for their needs – with additional leisure and social facilities that traditional 'Gradgrind' Dickensian approaches have failed to deliver. Nearly three-quarters of managers surveyed believe that having such amenities would contribute to higher levels of satisfaction in the workplace (see Table 5.1).

Trust

As such a rare commodity, being trusted gives any manager significant advantages over those who are not. Being trusted matters so much today – not just in politics but for business organisations too. It underpins many business issues from customer loyalty, sales, health and safety, as well as leadership and affecting job satisfaction and career prospects.

We know from Enron scandals and elsewhere that formal rules don't suffice: values, integrity and the spirit of agreement are as important to success as the letter of the law. Moreover, trust drives profitability. While new customers are attracted to brands and organisations they trust, existing customers remain loyal, employees increase productivity and stay. They are also more motivated and efficient if they can give and receive trust. Trust matters if you are trying to motivate anyone, sell to a customer, share ideas, generate new opportunities, take risks and innovate, prevent or solve a problem – the list goes on.

While improved business performance alone is worth building trust for – the consequence of its absence is more damaging than just having a neutral situation. When trust is undermined there is a high price to pay. To gain and retain trust, managers should:

- Create an atmosphere and expectation of trust by speaking about it and being an example of it.
- Take immediate responsibility for trust in their work area:
  - Look out of the window to give credit to others when things go well
  - Look in the mirror to apportion responsibility when things go wrong.
- Trust others and reinforce trust in others rather than rely on power, control and an overload of rules.
- Be clear and honest about their intent, without hidden agendas; seek to be understood, rather than confuse.
- Be open, honest and sincere.
- Have the organisation's and the employees' interests to heart, building a legacy for a collective spirit rather than pursuing a personal agenda.
- Be consistent. Rather than being inflexible or insensitive to different situations, a trusted manager will always treat people fairly; uphold standards of behaviour and performance, no matter what. Their values and principles are obvious, which leads to predictable responses.
- Confront people without being confrontational, especially when tackling performance issues.
- Wear their passion on their sleeve, showing clearly what they care about. People will follow a manager who is committed to a project, company or brand. Passion and self-motivation are infectious.
- Speak from the heart – not just the head. Trusted managers admit if they don't know or if they are wrong.
- Have integrity – are honest, keep confidences and promises, respecting others.

■ Use their power positively and productively, enabling them to do the right thing rather than support an ego. Better informed decision-making, less time wastage and earlier problem detection and resolution are the by-products.

High-trust firms spend more time and energy on customers than internal politics and benefit from motivated confident employees. However, it is no 'quick fix', to be used as required, but a genuine belief system (see Chapter 6). Managers do not trust their people for their own gain but because it is the right thing to do and in the end all stakeholders benefit.

Disgruntled Employees

Beware. The Internet empowers – and not always positively. It has become the favourite tool of corporate infighters and the disaffected employee. Howard Raines resigned in 2003 as editor of the *New York Times* after a period in which he tried to ride roughshod over rivals. In a previous era he might have succeeded and been able to retire the disgruntled old-timers and ride out the period of discontent. Had he succeeded in energising the right parts of the organisation at the right time, he would have won the rewards that America usually bestows on successful leaders. Unfortunately, disgruntled employees were able to leak to competitors their dissatisfaction. Raines had to resign not so much because he had lost the trust of his staff, but since it was so obvious that he had lost that confidence. Leaders like Raines could no longer maintain authority through fear and fire disaffected employees.

From this we learn that it is becoming harder to manage change, particularly in highly competitive business environments like publishing newspapers in New York. Managers have to accept that, by and large, most employees at whatever level are disaffected. They are paid too little for what they feel they give to the firm; they are promoted too slowly, passed over and humiliated.

Box 5.2

On a railway journey into Marylebone in May 2006, the author – and the rest of the carriage – overheard one young female manager explain to her mobile phone caller how she had been selected for a project but someone else was given the project control. All he had asked of her was to manage data entry: a seemingly mountainous job of extreme tedium. She felt overworked and sought refuge in cocktails on a midweek girls' night out and had been 'completely wasted'! She needed to speak with her boss about her pay freeze but had not found the right moment with him. She also mentioned that she had been trying to recruit a new technician. When they had taken references from a possible candidate they discovered that they had lied on their CV – and their reference had reported 142 days sick leave in two years and would not employ them again. The applicant had only mentioned four weeks off with a sprained ankle. Apparently, they were likely to offer them the job anyway, as they could not recruit technicians to their location. A recipe for disaster.

Few have realised their dreams, they blame everyone around them and everyone above them in particular.

Managers have come to believe that they are able to control their multi-centred organisations through e-mail and telephones. However, modern communications – from the growth of e-mails, 'weblogs' and web bulletin boards in particular – have also given destructive power to bitter employees. Managers may have been able to hire and fire, but today's employee has the Internet: more people today have the opportunity to 'publish and be damned' in a publishing revolution with a greater influence on common people than Caxton's first printing press.

Many companies are discovering that an Internet-enabled workforce thrust under the media spotlight is not a pleasant sight. Moreover, shareholders and analysts will soon become aware of employee discontent as the public exposure of staff grumbles becomes the norm. In the meantime, do not become the manager that puts change initiatives ahead of employee comfort.

Managers that want to make good people feel better should consider the following 10 ideas:

- Manage by example – let your people see you as a model of peak performance.
- Set clear goals with clear measures – work with individuals to get goals agreed and show them how to measure their own performance.
- Work with all team members as individuals – explain how to raise one's game from good to excellent.
- Take time to acknowledge – rather than move straight onto the next goal, show your appreciation of achievements to date.
- Show commitment to each and every person – develop a clear understanding of each person's motivators and help them achieve their own personal desires.
- Use the appropriate 'carrot' – reward for performance rather than purely just for competency. This will help people give their best.
- Balance skill and challenge – too many challenges can lead to anxiety, surplus skill leads to boredom.
- Be there for support – keep in contact as required to help people stay on track. Listen to people and help develop their problem-solving skills rather than provide the solution every time.

- Reduce identified distractions – what gets in the way of your people doing a great job?
- Reflect in real time – keep current with activities rather than run post-mortems. This will help raise awareness in your people and ensure that their experiences are valued.

Turning Theory into Practice to Enable People's Motivation to Shine

Turning to the straightforward theories of motivation we explored in Chapter 4, there is much that a manager can do practically to help keep staff focused on the objectives of their job role and stop other issues getting in the way. We take a pragmatic look at the situation in the workplace.

Physical needs

Here managers need to pay attention to the working environment and take appropriate and timely action to put things right when necessary. For instance, if someone complains that their office is draughty because of an ill-fitting door, or their computer screen has reflections from the skylight, or the food in the canteen is diabolical, don't ignore these complaints. Investigate the situation and try to solve the problem. Remember, if someone is cold because they're sitting in a draught, squinting because they can't read their screen or hungry because the food is inedible, satisfying their physical needs will be their number one priority. Your project, budget, report, schedule, presentation or whatever will come a very poor second on their list.

Security needs

People need to feel a sense of security about the future and a measure of confidence about their continued employment. Although one cannot promise job security if that is not likely to be the case, managers can:

- Let people know what you expect of them and how they are doing – note Drucker's 'MBO' in Chapter 4.
- Keep people informed about changes by being open and honest with information, and sharing this equally so that everyone knows where they stand – note trust in the section above.
- Be fair and impartial and treat everyone equally – no grudges, no favourites.
- Avoid using the threat of loss of employment (through downsizing, for example) as a 'stick' to encourage people to work harder. This is a 'Theory X' manager's tactic and it doesn't work. Instead of motivating people, fear acts as a demotivator and ultimately results in physical, mental and emotional stress.

Social needs and recognition motivator

Because people need to feel accepted by society in general, and their friends, family and work colleagues in particular, managers can make a real contribution to meeting this need by:

- Creating an overall team atmosphere of approval. This involves personally avoiding gossip, back-biting and rumour-mongering, and demonstrating to your people that these activities have no place on the team – see Chapter 6.
- Celebrating individual and team success. Giving credit where credit is due. Acknowledging the long hard slog, as well as special efforts – remember to 'look out of the window' when credit is due.
- Treating people as individuals and recognising (and showing that you recognise) that everyone has a life outside of work – work/life balance.
- Including everyone 'in', regardless of how you might personally feel about an individual – again, teamworking and ownership are key.
- Providing resources and delegating tasks with fairness and objectivity.

Self-esteem and interest motivator

People do best in jobs where they are challenged and stretched. Job satisfaction and the ability to feel good about their work are key motivators.

Managers can help by:

- Allocating tasks to people that will use their skills to their utmost ability.
- Providing development opportunities so that people can expand their knowledge, skills and abilities.
- Making sure people have sufficient time and resources to produce high-quality work – should the 'R' in 'SMART' be 'Resourced'?
- Listening to people and taking them seriously.
- Carrying out regular performance reviews and appraisals.
- Providing constructive feedback – see Chapter 18.
- Noticing and acknowledging individual effort.
- Offering genuine encouragement and praise when it is appropriate.
- Appreciating that for some people status symbols and job titles are important for their sense of self-esteem and self-worth.

Self-actualisation and advancement motivator

This is often the hardest state to achieve and feel fully satisfied, as theory suggests that all other areas must be satisfied for this motivator to be realised. However, while some people can find a happy state through their own endeavours, managers can make a valuable contribution to the situation for individuals, including:

- When people are ready, provide really challenging opportunities so that they can demonstrate their full capabilities and fulfil their true potential.
- Give people more responsibility than they expect (but keeping within the guidelines of what you know is possible and manageable for them).
- Allow people to influence decisions.
- Enable people to take a real sense of ownership ('This is my idea, so I'm going to make it work').
- Allow people the freedom to use their initiative and bring their own intellect and creativity to the job.
- Set up a 'self-fulfilling prophecy' by showing people that you believe in them and that they are capable of achieving great things.

Summary

In this chapter you have:

- Seen how an individual's 'energy' is a key resource
- Identified e-mail protocols used in one organisation to improve dialogue between people
- Seen a five-point agenda to re-energise ourselves – eat well, exercise, identify energisers, avoid de-energisers, reflect on what you admire
- Seen that somewhere to 'think' is the most sought-after facility favoured by staff
- Reviewed strategies to build and maintain trust in the workplace
- Explored an agenda of ideas to put into practice to enable motivation to come through in the workplace.

Questions

1. Who, in your workgroup, 'energises' people? Justify your decision with examples of what they do in practice – and how can these behaviours be encouraged in others?
2. In your workgroup devise workable protocols for your e-mail communications to increase the interpersonal dialogue in the organisation, reduce the time wasted managing e-mails and yet maintain the productivity of people.
3. What facilities in your place of work do your people want to improve their attitude to the organisation? How will you find out?
4. Consider the practical ideas identified earlier in the chapter. Write your own agenda of things that you might do to improve matters at each level.

Reference

Management Today (2003) June, p. 53.

Further Reading

Raynor, C. and Adam-Smith, D. (eds) (2005) *Managing and Leading People*, Chartered Institute of Personnel and Development.
Woodward, C. (2004) *Winning!*, Hodder & Stoughton.

6

Motivating Teams

I made it a habit... to give a quick debrief after every game. Instead of being harsh with the boys for not giving enough, or some such nonsense, I would try and focus on what they had done right, keep it brief, and set the stage for improving for the next game.

Sir Clive Woodward on team management early in his career when with Henley RFC

Learning Outcomes

Teams of people come together both formally and informally to achieve particular aims – this chapter, and its companion web pages, address the key facets of the management of teams and how to run their meetings more effectively. The chapter has been written to cover key elements of the National Occupational Standards for Management and Leadership (*Working with People – Units 19 and 21–23*) and it covers some of the requirements of the Chartered Management Institute's Diploma in Management compulsory *Unit C44 – Effective Communication and Information Management* and the 'maintain an effective project management environment' section of the optional *Unit O45 – Principles of Project Management*. It is also of value to those studying the optional *Unit O42 – Developing Personnel and Personnel Performance*. This chapter will also be of value to those studying the CIPD Professional Development Scheme – particularly the *People Management and Development* module.

By the end of this chapter you will:

- Recognise some of the dynamics of teamworking that fulfils fundamental motivators of people, building on the theories outlined in earlier chapters
- Look at the practical example of motivating a team of technical people
- Understand the key place of conversations in teamworking
- Review the seminal work of Belbin on team roles
- Recognise the phases that team development goes through
- Explore a more effective approach to team meetings through identifying problems and what to do about them.

What Motivates a Team?

When someone asks, 'How do you motivate teams?' one wonders if there are some deeper, hidden questions that need to be addressed:

- 'How did the team get demotivated in the first place?'
- 'Was the team initially motivated and then somehow lost it?'
- 'Who has to motivate whom anyway?'
- 'Can you motivate a team in any case?'
- 'What is motivation anyway?'

So, in answering the question of techniques for motivating a team, we have to ask some other more fundamental questions regarding the whole issue of motivation.

We saw in Chapter 4 that in the 1950s and 1960s researchers such as Abraham Maslow, Eric Trist, Fred Herzberg, Vroom and Deci (1978) and many others proposed an 'active' model of motivation. Maslow's work in particular redefined motivational theory. He argued that all people were driven or motivated by a hierarchical set of needs. The basic need is the need for survival – food, water and shelter. Once this need is satisfied, the need for security of the survival needs becomes more significant or motivating. The security need is then overtaken by the need for social contact and a sense of belonging. Once a person is in a position of belonging to a social group, the emergent need is to be given esteem by that group or, in other words, to be seen as a valued member of the group. After esteem, the need for self-esteem emerges as a strong motivator and finally the most powerful need for self-actualisation emerges. Maslow's model clearly places motivation as something within a person rather than something provided by another person and team dynamics as pivotal.

Herzberg's work was more focused in organisations and, working with many people within organisations, he concluded that there were two sets of motivational factors. The demotivators or dissatisfiers were a set of organisational factors which 'turned people off'. Factors such as company benefits or culture, job security, physical working conditions, salary (or perceived inequity of salary compared to others) and interpersonal or team relations generally led to lower levels of motivation. However, if these factors were perceived to be adequate they did not cause higher levels of motivation. In effect, the absence of demotivators simply meant that people did 'a fair day's work'. To obtain higher levels of motivation, Herzberg argued that satisfiers or motivators such as advancement, the nature of the work tasks, responsibility, recognition, opportunity for growth, a sense of achievement and autonomy were crucial in high-performance motivation.

While there have since been many variations and extensions to Maslow's and Herzberg's work, their fundamental validity is unchallenged, as we'll see later. Most contemporary

Physical working conditions		
Salary	Physiological/survival	
Company benefits	Security	*Extrinsic Needs*
Job security	Social	
Interpersonal/team relations		
Opportunities for growth		
Work/task nature	Self-Esteem	
Responsibility		*Intrinsic Needs*
Recognition	Self-Actualisation	
Achievement		
Autonomy		

Figure 6.1 Relationship between motivation theories.

motivation theory agrees that there are intrinsic and extrinsic motivation factors which align with Maslow's and Herzberg's initial work (see Figure 6.1).

For most people, extrinsic needs require an external environment, for example a job or income, to be satisfied. A job or career will satisfy survival, security, social and esteem needs; however, as shown by Herzberg, a poor working environment would leave these 'lower' needs unsatisfied. The intrinsic or 'higher' needs are internally governed by each person and factors such as autonomy, growth, responsibility and so on are the major determinants of high motivation.

The relationship between extrinsic and intrinsic motivation resolves the conflict in the definition of motivation we used in Chapter 2. A leader can motivate his or her people by addressing factors such as working conditions, physical environment, team interpersonal relations and basic rewards. However, the more powerful or high-performance motivation needs are within each person and are controlled by each individual team member, not the leader.

As a result, to impact the high-performance intrinsic motivation, a project manager or team leader must address the external factors such as autonomy, opportunity for growth and so on.

Developing on the Herzberg and Maslow work, Richard Hackman and Greg Oldham (1980) analysed the intrinsic motivation impact of job and job tasks. As shown in Figure 4.5, they developed the Job Characteristics Model, which proposed that each job contains a number of core job dimensions and if these core job dimensions are improved then the person undertaking the job develops an internal belief in the meaningfulness of the job, responsibility for and understanding of the relationship between their effort and the results. These internal states lead to improved personal and work outcomes, such as high intrinsic motivation, high-quality work and so on.

In effect, Hackman and Oldham provide a structured model for improving intrinsic motivation. Their model has been validated in many organisations in their experience of group working with computer and other project teams (Cougar and Zwacki, 1980; Thomsett, 1990).

Using the work of Maslow, Herzberg, Hackman and Oldham, it is possible to propose a simple and powerful approach to motivating creative project teams. This approach builds on the participative approaches to project management developed over the past few years.

In 1996, *Inc* magazine conducted a survey of US workers regarding critical factors bearing on employees' satisfaction and job performance. The results showed striking similarity to the studies of Herzberg, Hackman and Oldham of the 1970s and 1980s.

What turned on US workers in 1996 were:

- An opportunity to do what they do best every day
- A supervisor or a colleague who cares about them
- Their opinions are listened to and taken into account
- The job offered opportunities for growth and learning
- The mission of the employer makes the employees feel that their jobs are important
- They have the materials and equipment to do their job right.

It is the author's experience that most technically qualified people (including lawyers and other professional service people) have their extrinsic needs met by their jobs and that the key to motivating these people is in the intrinsic needs arena. When looking at project work of technical people – such as computer technicians – the project manager/team leader cannot, in effect, directly motivate such a team member but, by focusing on the nature of project work, the project tasks and the broader organisational environment of projects, the project manager can create a more motivating environment for their teams.

To put it simply:

Changing the job for a person changes motivation levels for that person.

The challenge for IT project management

In many organisations, there is a cultural and attitudinal gap between computer and other technical service or creative teams and the broader organisation. As discussed by Thomsett (1993), there have emerged significant differences in organisational culture and business focus of the computer and business areas.

This gap has often meant that many business people perceive that their IT teams are non-responsive, inward-looking, technology-obsessed 'geeks', and that the best way to deal with IT is to leave them isolated in their 'technology pit' and for the business people to develop their own Business Case and requirements for the project and to throw these documents into the 'pit of technologists'. In many organisations, the business experts are responsible for the development of the project's scope, objectives, benefits analysis, costs and so on. The IT teams are simply seen as hands-off service providers.

In many organisations, this gap between the technical service providers and their business clients is further widened through the use of business analysts who are placed between the IT team and the business people, and account managers who are often the managerial interface between IT and business. The existence of this gap has major impacts on the motivation of IT teams. Thomsett has proposed that there are three levels of intrinsic motivation that apply for computer and other creative teams. Each level of motivation is stronger and more significant than the lower level.

Level 1 motivation – technical excellence

This level of motivation is the most common in IT teams. Since the IT teams are remote from their business clients and other stakeholders, they are forced to sub-optimise their intrinsic motivation to the areas of skill variety, autonomy and feedback (see Hackman and Oldham's model, Chapter 4).

In effect, the computer expert simply undertakes the project based on system specifications with a maximum of technical excellence (high feedback) and with the use of as many new techniques and technology as possible (skill variety and autonomy). The feedback is generally from peers and is based on the technical elegance and innovation of the solution.

Level 2 motivation – client partnership

This level of motivation builds on Level 1 motivation. The project team member is 'out of the pit' and is working in partnership with the business client and other stakeholders. At this level, the team is able to see the 'big picture', and the task significance and task identity become more important. Skill variety, feedback and autonomy are also enhanced as the team needs to learn and understand the business issues associated with the project.

At this level of motivation, the team member will often choose different, less technical solutions (than those that would be chosen in Level 1) that are based on the business view rather than the pure technical view.

Level 3 motivation – adding value

This level of motivation is the highest and builds on Level 2 motivation. The project team member is working in partnership with the business client and stakeholders, and they are all focused on the 'added value' of the project. At this level, the task significance and task identity are optimised, as well as skill variety, feedback and autonomy.

At this level of motivation, the team members are totally aware of and focused on the life-cycle impact and cost-benefit of the product or system they are developing. The economic and organisational impact of the project have been developed by all team members during the initial project planning sessions and all team members (not just the project manager and project leaders) are committed to a successful project and subsequent life-cycle issues.

This concept of high-performance motivation is not only consistent with the theoretical work of Herzberg, Hackman and Oldham, but has been validated in a number of practical situations.

Members of project teams that are 'out of the pit' and working in full partnership with their business clients towards the realisation of project benefits consistently report that they enjoy working in this manner and that they experience higher levels of motivation.

How to motivate IT teams?

The case of IT teams can be found online on the companion web pages.

Team Leadership

One does not have to be a pseudo or crypto socio-biologist to recognise three fundamental characteristics of the human species:

- *We are social animals.* We live in groups where we need/like/prefer the company of others; we like inclusion and fear exclusion. We punish with ostracism, solitary confinement and abolition to 'Coventry'.[1]
- *We need to get along with others.* This is learnt from an early age, yet those adults who somehow did not pick up the fundamentals have to go to remedial social skills training or emotional intelligence facilitation classes. Social skills are about perception, charm and flexibility – they are about reading others, what they signal visually and vocally, amusing them and being aware about how one is coming across. The second fundamental skill after knowing how to get along is to know how to get ahead of others. In every social group there is a status hierarchy.
- *We have a belief system.* All social groups have one, almost a 'religion' of sorts, and it fulfils various functions to give meaning to the vagaries of life. The more successful an ideology or religion, the more it speaks to the deep and fundamental yearnings of human beings. People need a positive identity, a good story of their past, a sense of purpose and so on. People die for their beliefs: a sad fact noted from the earliest of times to the present-day suicide bombers. People will endure great hardship and deprivation for a belief system.

Therefore, to lead a team you have to demonstrate that you have, can and will get along with (all) others that you need to deal with at work; get ahead of the rest of your peers, competitors and the press; and be able to communicate a coherent ideology relevant to the company, the product or service you are offering, and the employees.

---

[1] Being 'sent to Coventry' is a term to indicate that a person is being ignored.

Remember, as Einstein warned:

> *The major problem in communication is the illusion that it has occurred.*

On the Need for Conversation

So, if we need to be able to get along with others and inspire them with some sense of purpose and direction, we had better be able to have a conversation with them. For professional service providers, it is a startling marketing fact that 'people buy people'. *People* have business problems and *people* look for *people* to solve them. In this technological age the people who succeed will be the people who can *talk* to other people. The need to meet, mingle, make contacts and conversation is even more important in the 21st century's Internet working world. Managers likewise have to be able to hold a conversation.

In the new millennium, we will all be technically adept, but those who succeed will be the people who can talk to other people. With social skills on the decline, those that have them will shine in any situation.

'Talk' – conversation – is how we relate, explain, persuade, sell, converse, amuse, learn, motivate and connect. No matter what walk of life we pursue, we need to be able to break the ice, approach strangers, and start, build and maintain conversations. We cannot build strategic partnerships, business and social relationships and business-to-business models unless we communicate in conversations.

Conversations are maintenance for relationships and relationships between people are a company's greatest asset. If people are not working together then they are essentially a group of gifted individuals. Thus, the ability to hold good-quality conversations with each other – and with the outside world – is becoming a core organisational and individual skill.

However, conversation is not just communication – it is intrinsically creative. It takes one idea, adds another and mixes it with a third. Communication is about swapping data, while real conversation catches fire. It involves more than just sending or receiving information. Creativity and organisational improvements come from conversations between people rather than the activity of isolated geniuses. Conversations also do not stick to agendas like meetings tend to; they roam freely across a range of issues from the personal to the corporate, including given work projects. However, in the corporate jungle it seems that jargon and the appearance of expertise is paramount. Who really knows what a paradigm is, let alone how to shift it? The language of business life so often aims to kill conversations rather than promote them: hence the popularity of Bullshit Bingo used to pass the time in 'lose-the-will-to-live' meetings (see Figure 6.2). We will explore how to make team meetings more motivational in a later section.

Fed up with the same old meetings? – here is something to change all that:				
Bullshit Bingo How to play – simply tick off five words or phrases as they occur and shout BINGO, it is that easy!				
REVISIT	GAME PLAN	BANDWIDTH	HARDBALL	OUT OF THE LOOP
SYNERGY	TAKE THAT OFFLINE	STRATEGIC FIT	PARADIGM SHIFT	UNDER THE BLOTTER
BALL PARK	PROACTIVE, NOT REACTIVE	WIN-WIN SITUATION	THINK OUTSIDE THE BOX	FAST TRACK
SEE WHO SALUTES THIS ONE	QUID PRO QUO	SLIPPERY SLOPE	TICKS IN BOXES	MINDSET
KNOCK-ON EFFECT	THE BOTTOM LINE	PULL OUT ALL THE STOPS	LESSONS LEARNT	TOUCH BASE
GO THE EXTRA MILE	PUT THIS ONE TO BED	THE BIG PICTURE	MOVE THE GOALPOSTS	MOVERS AND SHAKERS
RESULTS-DRIVEN	EMPOWER EMPLOYEES	NO BLAME	STRETCH THE ENVELOPE	WAKE UP AND SMELL THE COFFEE

Figure 6.2 The Bullshit Bingo game card.

Organisations need to increase physical, financial and human capital – but social capital sets the human dimension in operation and builds synergy in the workplace, getting the skills and attributes of people motivated towards a common goal: improved performance. In all walks of life, social capital is generated and accumulated through conversations.

When working with 'One Account', senior managers realised that 'if they only knew what they know – they could double their profits'. This alluded to the fact that they had complex knowledge management systems about their clients, but only by sharing the knowledge could they realise that potential. Their best knowledge management systems were strong networks sustained by conversations and while their IT systems might help, they could also hinder if not constructed and managed correctly. The best IT systems help put people in touch with each other, rather than trying to take the place of people being in touch.

Managers are beginning to realise that conversations are a defence against stress and other mental health problems – people with good social relationships are much less likely to be stressed or anxious. In a staff satisfaction survey undertaken at a south coast financial services firm, we discovered that the change from a large central staff canteen to a series of 'kitchenettes' on each of eight floors stifled interdepartmental collaboration and communication. While they had e-mail, proper interaction was absent. They were advised to have a coffee in the company of their colleagues rather than their e-mails? Try it yourself!

The Place of Teams

Teams are not the same as other groups; they need to be planned, built and maintained. A number of people who happen to work together in the same place may not operate as a team and may not need to. A team has a distinct characteristic – it is a group working together to achieve a common purpose and may be composed of people drawn from different functions, departments or disciplines. Increasingly, teams are groups that are set up for a specific project, are empowered to steer and develop the work they do, and are responsible for their achievements.

Successful team building can:

- Coordinate individuals' efforts as they tackle complex tasks
- Make the most of the personal expertise and knowledge of everyone involved, which might otherwise remain untapped
- Raise and sustain motivation and confidence as individual team members feel supported and involved
- Encourage members to spark ideas off each other, to solve problems and find appropriate ways forward
- Help break down communication barriers and avoid unhealthy competition, rivalry and point-scoring
- Raise the level of individual and collective empowerment
- Support approaches such as TQM, Just-in-Time management, customer care programmes and Investors in People
- Bring about commitment to and ownership of the task in hand.

However, teams may not be the answer in every situation. There are circumstances where teams may be unsuitable – for example, they may not fit in some organisational cultures where there are rigid reporting structures or fixed work procedures. A team approach can be the wrong approach, especially:

- Where one person has all the knowledge, expertise and resources to do the job on their own
- When there is no real common purpose and a group is wrongly called a team.

Meredith Belbin and Team Roles

There can be inordinate amounts of pressure within teams because one flaw of decisions made by teams or committees is that the majority inevitably persuade the minority – even if they are wrong! However, it is recognised that teams fulfil a social need. People feel comfortable in groups with others who think like them. It's why we join clubs! In practice, groups, through effective leadership, develop 'norms' or codes of acceptable behaviour where newcomers will be expected to conform.

The Cambridge psychologist, Meredith Belbin, identified eight different roles that people play when working in a team situation. The term 'team role' describes the way in which an individual will operate and function within a team and encompasses the way he or she relates to and communicates with others in the team and contributes to the team.

The eight team roles are as follows:

- *Monitor evaluator.* A good judge, analytical, thorough, cautious and unemotional, seeing all options but may lack enthusiasm, tact or diplomacy.
- *Teamworker.* Sociable, averts friction, loyal and diplomatic, able to support others but can be indecisive, particularly when they have to choose whether to put people or the task first.
- *Implementer.* Reliable and efficient, well organised and a sensible, self-disciplined person; while able to put concrete plans of action together, they can be inflexible and resistant to change.
- *Completer.* Painstaking, gets it right and often an anxious person never assuming that it will be 'alright on the night'; very conscientious and will take care of the details, but they do have high expectations of themselves and everyone else on the team and will not tolerate a slapdash approach from others.
- *Plant.* An ideas person, creative, solves tricky problems and can be unorthodox; while contributing original thought they can live 'in the clouds' and not attend to the detail or communicate particularly well.
- *Resource investigator.* Extrovert, develops contacts and is a 'people person', positive, optimistic and has diplomacy, giving energy to the team, but can lack stamina, losing heart quickly if the rest of the team do not lend support and moving on to something else.
- *Coordinator.* Mature, confident, clarifies goals, calm and controlled, they can be skilled communicators, strong and steady; they can unify a team, keeping focused on the outcomes, yet they can lack ideas and sparkle.

- *Shaper*. Dynamic, gets around problems, pushy and impulsive with 'thick skin'; they can shape a team's efforts in a practical course of action but can be insensitive to other's feelings and needs, so are likely to provoke and upset others.

One other type of person has been identified who has a particularly important role to play in many teams:

- *Specialist*. Focused, dedicated individuals with rare skills that bring to the team particular knowledge or expertise, they are often introverted and can be more concerned with the technicalities of the solution than pragmatism or the impact on the human dimension.

In an ideal world, when building effective teams, one would have eight (or nine) people, each of whom would be comfortable operating in one of each of the eight (or nine) Belbin team roles. Such a perfect mix is very rare and one is much more likely to have highly unsatisfactory combinations. So, Belbin's attributes of 'winning teams' are more likely to focus on:

- *The attributes of the team leader* – their ability to manage conflict between team players yet still achieve the desired outputs or goals
- *A spread of mental abilities and personal attributes* – appropriate to the team objectives and tasks to be undertaken
- *Team roles matching individual attributes of members* – where people are asked to make a contribution according to their personal characteristics rather than 'square pegs in round holes'.

Determinants of team effectiveness

The effectiveness of an individual, as discussed in Chapter 5, is no different when considering the work of teams – their sole purpose is to be effective and achieve more as a team than the sum of the individuals working on their own could muster.[2] The effectiveness of the team is determined by a number of key factors:

- *Size of group*. Some cynics would suggest that the success of a team is inversely proportional to the size of the group: the bigger the group the longer it takes to reach consensus. However, as we have seen, the optimal size of a group would appear to be from five to eight people. The reason for this may be that as pack animals living in 'families' this is the optimal size of a social unit. When the group size extends beyond 10 people, two groups soon form and so on.

---

[2] For more on effectiveness in defining job descriptions, running appraisals and setting goals, see Mackay (2007).

- *Skills/attributes of members*. If the requirements of the task are beyond the capabilities of the group, no amount of effort on their part, without some developmental input, is likely to produce the outcomes required.
- *The task in hand*. Similarly, the task needs to interest and inspire the team, so the outputs need to be worth the effort or 'desired' before the team expend energy.
- *Resource/support available*. This is crucial to keep the team on track. While assets like cash and technology might be available, do they get support from other individuals outside the team in order to fulfil their tasks – particularly, do they have the time to do the necessary work?
- *External recognition*. Along with support is recognition. Cross-functional teams need to know that their efforts involved with the team will be appreciated when it comes to appraisal with their line manager.
- *Leadership style*. The most appropriate style of leadership must be in place to get the best out of the team. The style will depend on each individual's motivation, ability and confidence. As we explore below, a team will evolve through a series of developmental stages, each requiring a particular leadership style.
- *Group interaction patterns*. With a variety of team member roles identified above, the group dynamics are crucial to team success. The ability of each individual to communicate through 'conversations' comes into play.
- *Motivation and rewards*. As we explore in Chapter 7, the rewards for success must match the needs, wants and desires of the team collectively, yet there may also be individual agendas that should be taken into account to ensure team effectiveness.
- *Stages of group development*. These are explored in more detail in the following section.

Stages of group development

There are five stages of team/group development, each requiring a particular style of management. Different teams develop at different rates and go into the stages to different degrees. The stages are not empirical but serve as a useful analysis of group developmental dynamics.

The five stages of group development are:

1. *Forming*. This is the initial stage, where the group forms for the first time. Members and leader will be apprehensive about the whole project, their role, the tasks ahead and the performance expected of them. Thus, the team leader must be well prepared and take control, yet still allow opportunities for the group to shape the way they work; this builds ownership among the members. Note that forming could take weeks or even months.
2. *Storming*. This is a phase involving conflict, although not all groups experience 'storming'. At this stage, individual agendas emerge and conflict with roles individuals are

expected to play within the team. Typical behaviour may include sarcasm, hostility towards individuals, jokes at individual's expense and negative comments. Leaders must not enter into the conflict but should enlist support and listen to individuals.

3. *Norming*. At this stage, the team begins to work together and a sense of cohesiveness appears. Here, group 'norms' become established as a team identity emerges and members begin to show that they want to belong to it. It is important that the team leader builds on this stage, nurturing the conditions.

4. *Performing*. This stage is only reached by passing through at least two of the previous stages. Now the team becomes fully operational and productive. Once the team is 'on the right track' and progressing well, leadership becomes less of an issue. Without having a flexible style, some leaders find it hard to withdraw. However, there is a new role for the leader – that of being a 'resource' for the team.

5. *Mourning*. Not often taken into account, but it occurs when the group disbands as the work is completed. Individuals may go on to form new groups and people may feel a sense of loss for the old ways. This is particularly noticeable after redundancy, redeployment, relocation or retirement. In this situation, individual performance, confidence and feelings of self-worth suffer – and the leader may be left with nothing to lead!

Meetings Management

Managers spend a great deal of time in meetings, often ineffectively and usually with a growing sense of frustration. Why are so many ineffective, and how can we make them more effective?

Most communication is non-verbal, reported to be somewhere between 55 and 75 per cent – depending on your source! We are an evolved species and are designed for face-to-face communications; it is the only form of interaction that is instinctive – all others are learned. However, that does not mean that every interaction has to be in person. While former Asda chairman Archie Norman held his meetings standing up to speed things along, and never for more than half an hour at a time, there are other options to consider before actually holding a meeting.

From e-mail, video and teleconferencing, instant messaging to 'collaboration tools', there are a number of alternatives to more flipcharts and chocolate digestives!

E-mail is a powerful tool for keeping in touch but as a meeting substitute it is flawed. Words alone may cause problems because our latent insecurities can be triggered by other people; words can easily be taken 'the wrong way'. Send in haste and repent at your leisure. With the ever-increasing use of e-mail (and its teenage cousin the mobile phone text) a new phenomenon has spawned: the e-mail bully. These are people who tend to avoid 'real' encounters and use indirect communications to browbeat others into doing what they want – particularly colleagues that copy in the 'boss' to add extra authority. These people are generally cowards, yet it is easier to lose your temper with a depersonalised e-mail than with the real person. Personal issues and professional problems at work are better solved face to face, yet many people might not open up to a manager until their confidence improves (see Chapter 18). Serial internal e-mailers would do better to stop and think about how their e-mail 'missive' will be received and what it says about them before they press 'Send'. Would the recipients be pleasantly surprised if they picked up the phone or actually gave them a visit?

Of all the man-made voice communication tools, the telephone is the oldest and the one that we are most familiar with. Talking on the phone is second nature and most 10-year-olds can master it. (However, some teenagers temporarily lose the capacity to converse with adults when they answer a phone!) Even technophobes can pick up a receiver and dial a number, while 'call-divert' and 'hold' may baffle them. When it comes to getting together with distant colleagues, teleconferencing is becoming increasingly popular.

According to BT, it is a multibillion global market and growing rapidly – they estimate that there are over 20 000 conference calls a day in the UK alone. They are an effective way for teams of people to keep in touch, limit waffle and are quicker than face-to-face meetings. Out of politeness, we tend to give visitors 30 minutes of our time, even if we could achieve the same result in five minutes on the phone. Teleconferences are immediate when sorting the unexpected problem; add in web-based collaboration software, that allows people to look at and work on shared documents through their PC or laptop, and teleconferencing is beginning to look like a sharper tool in the meetings toolbox.

However, teleconferencing is not so good for people that never meet; hence the potentially most powerful meeting substitute of all – videoconferencing. Combining speech and vision (and with more sophisticated systems) presentation and document-sharing capability, it is the next best thing to being there. This is particularly popular in the USA, where east and west coast offices of firms have regular progress meetings by videoconference. However, training is important and there is still a place for face-to-face events – by videoconference there is little eye-to-eye contact, the focus of body language.

Good meetings mean more effectiveness

It is popular to grumble about meetings; indeed, this pastime can become a dangerous obsession so that, in some organisations, the climate is such that managers find it very difficult to conduct effective meetings. Jokes and 'laws' about meetings proliferate and the well-known VideoArts *Meetings – Bloody Meetings*, although admirable, may have unwittingly contributed to the myth that meetings are a nuisance. Perhaps the typical management attitude to meetings is best summed up by a story relayed by a financial manager. He recounted the final act of a long and difficult meeting when, after more than two hours, little had been achieved and the only decision that they were about to make was a time for the next meeting so that they could continue their fruitless endeavours. After much diary searching the chairman thought he had found a consensus and announced 'How about next Wednesday?' To which one of those present replied with a groan, 'Oh no, not Wednesday – that ruins two weekends!'

So what is the message? It is that senior management should encourage and cultivate a 'good meetings climate', because in doing so they will improve:

- *Communication.* A business organisation is, by definition, two or more people engaged in commercial pursuit. Organisations cannot cohere or achieve goals without communicating and effective meetings play an essential part in this process.
- *Policy formulation and planning.* These activities require ideas, discussion and debate on key issues and on alternatives. They benefit from the collective wisdom of the management team and carefully considered proposals and options. This process can only take place in meetings.
- *Decision-making.* Some decisions have to be made in formal meetings (or endorsed by them) because of constitutional or statutory requirements – for example, Cabinet, council and boardroom decisions. But there are many circumstances in which the quality or durability of a decision will be enhanced if it is subjected to careful (and urgent!) consideration in a meeting at which those responsible for implementation or affected are present.

Better communication, better planning and improved decision-making will have a positive effect on the bottom line, and this is a justification for giving thought and energy to improving meetings.

Do we need a meeting?

If so many managers express the view that they spend too much time in meetings, perhaps they should not be there in the first place. It is undoubtedly the case that some meetings should never have been called, so it is worth exercising the discipline of asking 'Do we need a meeting?' before setting one up. Box 6.1 is a useful checklist that can be used to determine whether there is a need for a meeting.

Box 6.1: Checklist – do we need a meeting?

Do the rules require a meeting?
So many formal meetings are required by statute or constitution, and they have to be called and held in accordance with the rules. Although they often seem tedious and pointless, such meetings are consistent with open, democratic administration and provide some reassurance to those with an interest in the organisation concerned.

Is there a need to communicate?

How often do you hear the complaint 'Nobody tells us anything'? When a business is proposing change there may be a strong case for holding briefing meetings in order that a positive attitude can be encouraged. The great advantage of a meeting over a written briefing is the two-way nature of the communication. So, if you want to avoid rumour and distortion, you want to change attitudes or you want to take people with you, consider the case for a meeting or series of meetings.

Is there a need for team building?

Well-conducted meetings can do much to build a good team. Leaders of the best sports teams, and winning generals, have recognised the benefits of the 'here's how we win' meeting and the same thing can work in business.

Do I need advice and guidance before making a decision?

It doesn't follow that if the answer is yes, a meeting is required, since a few phone calls or a one-to-one discussion may achieve the desired result. However, collective advice reviewed and weighed in a meeting will often lead to a better decision. It has to be recognised, though, that some managers who are poor decision-makers use meetings as a device for delaying or compromising when they would have been better taking speedy action.

Have we got a problem or crisis that can be better dealt with by a group solution?

Not quite the same as the last point, because in this instance there is a crisis and a need for urgent action, but there are many circumstances in which a 'war cabinet' approach is needed – for example, an unexpected takeover bid, a lightning strike, a serious accident. The crisis may involve several departments or call for a range of specialist views or skills; the sooner they are all brought together in a meeting the better.

A positive answer to one of the questions in the checklist suggests that a meeting is needed – but just by calling a meeting you don't communicate better, build teams, make good decisions or solve problems. Many meetings, which undoubtedly should have been held, fail. Let us now consider why this happens.

Why do meetings fail?

Meetings can be broadly classified into formal and informal. The formal category embraces all those meetings that are required by some written constitution, Articles of Association or Statute. The conduct of formal meetings is usually governed by rules or custom and the membership controlled by election or some form of qualification.

By far the more frequent and managerially important meeting is the informal type, which may be a regular or ad hoc problem-solving type of meeting. Whatever the type, the chances are that they fail from time to time or, in some cases, all the time! But why?

People problems

Since a meeting is a social group it is not surprising that they reflect the weaknesses and idiosyncrasies of their members. For example:

- An incompetent Chair
- An idle committee secretary
- Interpersonal conflict between members or departmental rivalries (the 'point-scoring' syndrome)
- An anti-meeting culture (the 'this is going to be a waste of time' syndrome)
- Mistrust or envy by those outside the meeting (the 'what are they up to' syndrome)
- Ill-conceived membership – for example, vertical or diagonal slice when a peer group is demanded.

Planning problems

The varied and awkward nature of human beings does not mean that meetings are always going to be difficult and ineffective provided someone gives some thought to the structure and content. More typically, what happens is that there is:

- Insufficient notice of a meeting or silly timing
- No understanding of the aim – 'why are we here?'
- No agenda or a badly structured agenda
- Poor paperwork – 'these figures don't add up!'
- A feeling that 'we've discussed all this before'.

Progress

It is a common complaint that, after a meeting, even a productive meeting, nothing happens. For example, there is no:

- Record or minute circulated
- Action or follow-up on decisions taken
- Continuity between meetings
- Upward reporting.

It follows, therefore, that to achieve better meetings something has to be done to change managers' attitudes towards meetings, and this can be achieved with attention to the three Ps: people, planning and progress.

Solutions to problems with meetings

People

It is worth giving attention to three 'people' factors: attitude, selection and training.

1. *Attitude.* Much damage is done because managers lack a positive approach to meetings. To encourage a positive view:
   - Avoid the word 'committee'. Bureaucracy and inactivity are too closely associated with the word committee, so where possible stop using it. Consider alternatives, using active descriptions such as working party, task force and action group, or using descriptions that emphasise efficiency or excellence, like quality circle, profit improvement group, etc.
   - Emphasise importance and urgency. Senior managers have a key role to play in emphasising the importance of the work done in meetings and by encouraging their own staff to take a positive attitude by, for example, arriving at meetings on time, by preparing for meetings and by constructive contribution.

2. *Selection.* We rightly take time and care to recruit managers, but rather less concern is shown when assembling a group to perform some managerial task. It seems that the 'least busy' or 'muggings' turn' principle is often applied. When forming a meeting group such matters as intellectual ability, experience, seniority, need for confidentiality, representational and personality factors all need to be considered. The group will have an aim similar to a manager's job description and there is therefore a case for preparing a 'group specification'. Obviously, in some circumstances, the group task pre-selects the group, but there will be many occasions when members of a working party or task force should be carefully selected.

   If care in picking members is important, the choice of Chair is often critical to the effectiveness of a meeting. There are occasions when seniority or status leaves no room for consideration, but when there is a choice, personality and skills such as listening, managing time, prioritising, summing up, fairness, firmness, impartiality, etc. must be taken into account.

3. *Training.* Once the importance of meetings is recognised, the need for simple but effective training follows. There are short courses on effective meetings, training films and videos, and useful booklets. Any training aimed at improving the effectiveness of meetings will also help change the attitude to them. Don't overlook the special training needs of the Chair and of the secretary (preparing agendas, taking notes, writing action reports).

Planning

Once management attitudes are positive, the climate is right for effective meetings but this won't happen unless the Chair and the secretary give some thought to what they want to achieve and how they intend to set about it – in other words, planning. Specifically, they will need to:

- Time meetings to be cost-effective and acceptable to the members. Try holding them last thing in the afternoon – they are less likely to run over time, unlike ones held mid-morning!
- Fix the location to be convenient and free of interruption and distraction.
- Clarify their terms of reference or aim.
- Plan and prepare an agenda. Define each item with an objective or outcome to focus the mind of attendees. Some informal meetings may not need a written agenda as long as everyone knows why they are there and what is to be covered.
- Consider the need for supporting papers, which should be well written, up-to-date and accurate.
- Consider the need for prior consultation and discussion on difficult issues in order to prepare the ground and save valuable time at the meeting.

In crises, meetings have to be called at short notice and little preparation is possible. In these circumstances, the Chair's role becomes even more significant, as does the post-meeting progress, of which more below.

Progress

If one had to nominate one single factor that has contributed to the 'bad press' that meetings enjoy it would not be easy, but post-meeting inactivity would be high on my list. Nothing will have a greater potential for convincing managers that they are wasting their time if they can see no cause and effect relationship between the outcome of the meeting and subsequent action or if they are continually covering old ground. If something positive happens they will soon begin to change their attitudes to meetings. What needs to be done?

- *Circulate a record of the meeting.* Call them minutes if you like, but if you are free of procedural requirements, it might be better to describe them as an 'Action and Information Report'. (One firm used to call theirs 'Hot AIR'; while that might undermine the attitude to meetings, the action points did get read!) In any event it is a good thing to have an 'action column' in the record, with agreed completion times, so that the names of those responsible for carrying out the agreed decisions can be noted. This puts the action manager on the spot and goes some way towards avoiding the 'I didn't realise I was supposed to do anything' reaction.
- *Take managerial action.* This means taking an interest in what happens post-meeting – asking for a progress report and generally encouraging and prodding to ensure that matters are progressed.
- *Report post-meeting progress.* Let those at the meeting and others know what has happened. This may encourage others and it will enhance the status of meetings.

Checklists of seven ways to better meetings

Given that the priority is to produce a better meetings climate by encouraging a positive attitude, there is much that the individual manager can do to improve his own performance in meetings, be they the Chair or just a member. As a reminder and as a guide to better practice, two checklists (Box 6.2) are provided, one for the Chair and one for the member. Use these lists as a reminder. A bit more thought and some effort could do much to improve the effectiveness of your meetings.

Box 6.2: Checklists for better meetings

For the Chair
1. Know your committee (terms, rules, members)
2. Prepare (compile agenda, plan meeting)
3. Consult before the meeting (i.e. prepare the ground)
4. Be firm but fair
5. Convey sense of urgency/importance
6. Listen
7. Seek consensus/agree the action.

For the member
1. Prepare/know your facts; consult subordinates before the meeting
2. Don't be late
3. Accept the Chair
4. Be constructive
5. Don't lose your cool
6. Question if in doubt
7. Fight your corner – but don't waste time.

Summary

In this chapter you have:

- Seen that the dynamics of teamworking fulfil a fundamental motivator of people – a sense of belonging
- Looked at a practical example of how to motivate a team of technical people
- Recognised the key place of conversations in teamworking

- Looked at the nine Belbin team roles – *Monitor evaluator, Teamworker, Implementer, Completer, Plant, Resource investigator, Coordinator, Shaper* and *Specialist*
- Recognised the five phases of team development – *forming, storming, norming, performing* and *mourning*
- Reviewed an effective approach to team meetings, dealing with three common causes of problems – people, planning and progress.

Questions

1. Think of someone in your organisation who has impressed you with his or her high level of motivation; list three or four factors that have convinced you of this person's high level of motivation. Think of someone who has struck you as having a low level of motivation; list three or four factors that convinced you of this person's low level of motivation. What conclusions do you draw from your two lists for managers of such people?
2. List four factors that have, at some stage in your working life, caused you to work harder and more enthusiastically, and four that have discouraged you and made you work less energetically and less willingly. What conclusions do you draw from your two lists for managers?
3. Imagine that you are pulling together a group at work to manage a short-term project. What would you want the 'ground rules' to be for the way that you worked together? For example, attend meetings on time, let everyone make a contribution, etc.
4. Consider a team or workgroup of which you are familiar. What stage of group development are they now? Give reasons for your answer. How could the team be better managed through the phases?

References

Cougar, J. D. and Zwacki, R. A. (1980) *Managing and Motivating Computer Personnel*, Addison-Wesley, New York.

Inc (1996) Vol. 16, No. 7, June.

Mackay, A. R. (2007) *Recruiting, Retaining and Releasing People*, Butterworth-Heinemann.

Thomsett, R. (1990) *Building Effective Project Teams*, American Programmer, Summer.

Thomsett, R. (1993) *Third Wave Project Management*, Prentice-Hall, Englewood Cliffs, NJ.

Vroom, V. H. and Deci, E. I. (1978) *Management and Motivation*, Penguin, Middlesex, UK.

Further Reading

Fisher, K. (2000) *Leading Self-Directed Work Teams: A Guide to Developing New Team Leadership Skills*, McGraw-Hill Education.

Gordon, J. (2002) *Organisational Behaviour – A Diagnostic Approach*, 7th Edition, Prentice-Hall, Englewood Cliffs, NJ.

Streibel, B. J. (2002) *The Manager's Guide to Effective Meetings*, McGraw-Hill Education.

7

Effort, Performance and Reward

Genius is 99 per cent perspiration and 1 per cent inspiration.

Albert Einstein

Learning Outcomes

It is expected that if someone puts in effort, they will perform in a particular way, which will produce a given outcome that in turn will produce a level of satisfaction – this chapter, and its companion web pages, address the key facets of the management of performance and explores rewards in the context of motivation. The chapter has been written to cover key elements of the National Occupational Standards for Management and Leadership (*Working with People – Units 19, 21, 22, 26 and 27*), and it covers many of the requirements of the Chartered Management Institute's Diploma in Management, compulsory *Unit C45 – Managing Performance* and the 'improve personnel effectiveness' of the optional *Unit O42 – Developing Personnel and Personnel Performance*. This chapter will also be of value to those studying the CIPD Professional Development Scheme – particularly the *Leadership and Management* and *People Management and Development* modules.

By the end of this chapter you will:

- Understand the relationship between effort, performance and reward
- Recognise the importance of feedback to good performance
- Explore the subject of job enrichment
- Understand how to develop another's role in the organisation
- Uncover a range of rewards in the workplace from the 'everyday' to the more comprehensive benefits package.

The Relationship Between Effort, Performance and Rewards

The relationship illustrated in Figure 7.1 shows a cycle suggesting that if someone puts in the effort, they will perform in a particular way, which will produce a given outcome that in turn will produce a level of satisfaction. If that is sufficient, the effort will be repeated. As we shall see, it is the *links* that are important and it is here that managers can have a significant impact on an individual's motivation.

The effort–performance link

There will be little motivation if this link is weak. For the link to be strong, people must believe that their efforts have a good chance of producing the desired performance. Managers need to be able to communicate what performance is required in terms that people can understand.

Four main factors affect this link:

- *Ability.* If people are poorly selected or poorly trained for the task, they will not have the ability to do the job. Allocate tasks appropriately to those best suited to do them or ensure that there is sufficient support for them to learn the skills.
- *Clarity of objectives.* People must know exactly what is expected of them and know themselves whether the job is being done to the required standard. Focus on the 'outputs' of the job and the tangible elements of what is required.
- *Communication.* Do not assume that they know what is required – don't ask if they understand, ask if you have explained things appropriately.
- *Resources.* Make sure that they have the materials, equipment, information and time to do the job – time is often forgotten.

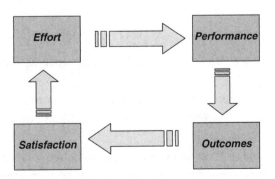

Figure 7.1 The relationship between four factors that affect motivation.

The performance–outcomes link

Once the performance standard has been reached, the outcomes can be desirable or undesirable.

There are two essential types of outcomes:

1. *Intrinsic*. Those that result directly from the performance and are not given by someone:
   - Self-respect
   - Sense of achievement
   - Learning something
   - Feeling of having done something worthwhile
   - Feeling of having contributed something useful
   - Fatigue, largely a negative outcome on its own.

   These outcomes are more closely linked to performance as someone else does not give them. They are generated by the performance itself and are very important to create a strong performance–outcomes link.

   Good job design or job enrichment is important here.

2. *Extrinsic*. Those that are awarded by someone else and can be both positive as well as negative:

   Positive outcomes
   - Salary and bonuses
   - Other benefits, e.g. private health care
   - Praise
   - Time off, e.g. more holiday time
   - Promotion
   - Status.

   Negative outcomes
   - Loss of pay
   - Loss of status
   - Social punishments.

   These outcomes are less closely related to performance as they depend on someone else to 'give' them.

   For this link to be strong, the person must believe that if their performance is good, a desired outcome – that they want – is likely to follow. Trust is a key ingredient.

   Managers may not be able to influence some outcomes (e.g. pay, promotion or time off), but they can give praise and recognition for good performance. They can also design jobs well.

Outcomes–job satisfaction link

For this link to be strong, the outcome must be of value. Do not assume that any given outcome is of value to all staff. Remember that people have different needs and motivations; an outcome must be of value to the individual.

Feedback

Feedback is essential to motivate people to perform well. If they are never told how they are doing they may not really know and will soon become demotivated. Feedback must be rapid – both positive to praise good performance and constructive to correct poor performance.

Invent occasions to give feedback if necessary, e.g. an informal chat with an individual. Praise in front of the individual's peers, corrective behind closed doors. Praise the individual, criticise the act.

Team meetings can be held regularly to give feedback to a group. Feedback to a group in praise of good performance can generate good team sprit.

So, in summary of this section, identify and limit *their* dissatisfiers, look for job enrichment in *their* terms and ensure that the rewards are there for better performance – they work better than sanctions for poor performance. See Chapter 18 for a guide to giving and receiving feedback, and *Recruiting, Retaining and Releasing People*, by the same author (Mackay, 2006), for a guide on how to appraise work done.

Effort and Performance

When in pursuit of improved performance, we know that there is no simple link between effort and performance. So often we may feel that the more effort we apply, the better the results will be. There is lots of 'parental guidance' on the subject: 'the more you put in, the more you'll get out', '. . . all it needs is a bit of elbow grease',[1] '. . . just try a bit harder (with your studies)'. If we don't apply any effort into a task, we are unlikely to reap rewards. However, what is the link between effort and performance, and how can managers influence the causal link?

Herzberg (1956) suggested that there are two separate sets of factors that influence the way a person feels about his or her job – his Two-Factor Theory of Job Satisfaction (see also Chapter 4).

The effects of the satisfiers tend to be longer lasting than the effect of the dissatisfiers. Experience suggests that dissatisfaction can be avoided by improving the 'work environment', i.e. the benefits and working conditions. However, no amount of improvement in them will motivate a person to work more effectively and achieve better outcomes.

---

[1] 'Elbow grease' refers to the effort required when polishing or sandpapering.

Job enrichment is seen as a way to improve jobs to increase satisfaction, and hence motivation, and it relates to the Two-Factor Theory of Job Satisfaction. Note, however, it is a supplement to paying people fairly and providing them with decent working conditions – not a substitute. It is about treating people well and giving them responsibility and recognition. It does not involve redesigning a business completely. An individual manager at any level, e.g. a first-level supervisor, can influence them.

Table 7.1 illustrates four principles of job enrichment and the related motivator that can influence job performance.

A complete unit of work

When Henry Ford was looking at his workers on an automotive production line, it was recognised that people were more productive when they took responsibility for the assembly of whole units in production of a vehicle, rather than part of an assembly. However effective Gilbreth was in devising a 'Therblig' of activity (see Chapter 4), if the person was only involved with part of the whole picture and did not have opportunity to see the final outcome, their motivation – or 'sense of purpose' – was compromised.

So, rather than have someone compile, say, a small mailing shot (too small to subcontract to a mailing house) and just stuff envelopes, get them to monitor responses too. They might also be involved in updating the database from those responses. There may be a case for asking them to present a modest report on their findings from the mailing – number of replies, enquiries, orders, etc.

Table 7.1 The four principles of job enrichment and the related motivator that can influence job performance

Principle	Motivator
Give a person a complete unit of work	Achievement Recognition Responsibility
Give extra authority	Achievement Recognition Responsibility
Introduce new and more difficult tasks	Achievement Recognition Responsibility
Give people specific or specialised tasks so that they become 'experts'	Achievement Recognition Responsibility Advancement

This approach affects three key motivators:

- *Achievement.* The whole job being done is complete in itself and people can see that they have achieved something; it is finite and has parameters.
- *Recognition.* This is where individuals can gain a full sense of self-worth as their staff, peers and more senior colleagues can see that they have completed and been responsible for clear outcomes of a definitive piece of work.
- *Responsibility.* The jobholder feels an internal sense of responsibility for all facets of the work and there is less chance of a '*that wasn't my fault*' attitude developing.

When someone is given a whole piece of work there is a better chance of an '*if it is going to be, it is down to me*' attitude developing. Provided that people have the ability and confidence in place too, the appropriate behaviours tend to follow.

Extra authority

Managers often think that when they ask someone to undertake a task on their behalf they are delegating to them the 'responsibility' to achieve a particular outcome. However, as a manager, the responsibility stays with the manager. The manager can delegate the authority to achieve a particular outcome through enabling the follower to make decisions appropriate to achieving a particular goal. And people like to have control over the 'how' a job is to be done and to have 'ownership' of the goal reached – Maslow's self-actualisation. Giving people extra authority can achieve this.

An account director in a Home Counties advertising agency was looking after accounts totalling several millions; he could not, however, have authority to order his own stationery items – they had to be approved by one of the managing directors. He was told he could not have his own hole-punch as his secretary must do all his filing: not the most pragmatic way of dealing with things when the account director was working late preparing something for the following day.

While a very elementary example, it does show how frustrating it can be not to allow people to have simple authority over how they do their work. But authority can be broader and more substantial than ordering one's own stationery. If people are being managed by objectives, provided that they agree that the objectives are SMART (see Chapter 4), being given authority within appropriate parameters to achieve those outcomes is a positive influence on behaviour.

This approach affects three key motivators:

- *Achievement.* That the individual is being trusted works both ways, from manager to staff member and the other way too. People get that sense of achievement as, previous to having the authority granted, there were more restrictions over how the work may be done as well as what is to be done.

- *Recognition*. As with a complete unit of work, individuals can gain a sense of self-worth as their staff, peers and more senior colleagues can see that they have been given responsibility to exercise that authority over aspects of their work.
- *Responsibility*. While responsibility for the overall outcomes rests with the manager, people will take a sense of pride in exercising their authority sensibly as they would fear that authority being taken away if they abused it.

Introduce new or more difficult tasks

People rise to a challenge. Sadly, most employees do not feel particularly challenged in their work. They may find *doing* their work a challenge because so many demotivators are in place, but that is not the same as having work that stretches their abilities. There is growing evidence that more and more people are doing work that, in skill terms, are simply beneath them. As people's expectations of what they want from life – and work – rise, they discover that being able to do their job with their eyes closed is a mixed blessing.

There is increasing evidence that managers and professionals, in particular, are suffering work-related stress; one in 10 people work more than 60 hours a week and almost half blame their workload. A combination of the speed at which one has to work and the number of tight deadlines faced creates an 'index of work'; almost half of managers in the UK think their job requires them 'to work very hard', up from less than a third in 1992 (*Management Today*, 2003a). This is a sign not of work being too hard, but too shallow.

People find problem-solving motivating; just look at the popularity of game shows, crosswords, 'sudoku' and even pub quizzes. The fewer opportunities for accomplishment a job contains, the more likely people are to fill the void with working fast for long hours to persuade themselves and others that their work has a purpose.

However, taking on new or more difficult tasks and solving how to do them, while intrinsically rewarding, also builds a feeling of self-worth – just as there is a feeling of uselessness when things don't go so well. This is only possible if people have the *ability* to do the task and the *confidence* that, if they should err, someone will back them up and sort it out for them without the fear of direct recriminations. Once these two areas are addressed, then *motivation* will tend to follow.

Handled carefully, this approach affects three key motivators:

- *Achievement*. Being able to do something new holds its own rewards, particularly working out how to do it oneself.
- *Recognition*. That colleagues recognise the new abilities adds to self-esteem; that person has new skills and becomes more valuable for the team as a whole.

■ *Responsibility*. Being able to do something challenging is only really satisfying if the person is able to undertake activities that use those newly found skills. Only if someone has the skills to do a task to a particular level of competence will they have the confidence and the full motivation to do the work to the appropriate standard.

Specific or specialised tasks

Building on from being given new and more challenging tasks, people find training motivating; it can show a person that the organisation is making an investment in them, and some managers use further training as a reward for loyalty and an individual's contribution. A person's skills are something they take with them into their future, whoever they work for. Naturally, 'being sent on a course' to 'sort someone out' is no substitute for poor management!

Remember, too, that people appreciate having the opportunity to offer something special to the work group or organisation. Maybe it is something outside the usual work activity, like being the first-aider or fire warden, or perhaps the person becomes the 'reception champion' with responsibility to make recommendations on improvements and organise its redecoration.

This approach affects four key motivators:

■ *Achievement*. Again, being able to do something new holds its own rewards.
■ *Recognition*. As with new or more difficult tasks, colleagues recognising the new abilities adds to self-esteem; that person has new skills and becomes more valuable for the team as a whole.
■ *Responsibility*. With the new skills, the jobholder may be expected to take on new responsibilities and, provided that person is able to undertake those activities that use those newly found skills, motivation follows.
■ *Advancement*. The satisfaction that comes from completing a more complex jigsaw, managing to programme a new – and advanced – mobile phone or master a complex piece of work carries with it individual satisfactions, each to their own level of advancement. With advancement more responsibilities often mean a regrading or higher job evaluation. While more money is often recognised as a reward for advancement, many people doing a 'technical' job or in one of the professions – like law or accountancy, for example – would rank advancement as being more rewarding than the salary increase alone.

Expectation and Motivation

In the late 1960s, several writers worked on what became known as the expectancy theory of motivation: the amount of effort put in by an individual will depend on what result the individual expects from that effort (see Victor Vroom, Chapter 4). Consider two alternative views of a situation:

Leader: 'If Lynn makes a good job of that project, she'll be well placed for promotion and moving on to more interesting work.'

Lynn: 'If I make too good a job of this project, I'll probably get lumbered forever with jobs of this type.'

Whether Lynn does a good job will depend on what she herself believes will be the likely consequences, not what the leader thinks. She may be mistaken or she may be right, but there is no doubt that motivation depends on the individual's perceptions rather than on some objective reality. So, even if you have correctly identified that a person is striving to meet a particular need and that his or her doing what you want will help meet that need, motivation will not take place unless that person sees the same connection.

When deciding whether to put in a special effort, the individual is asking three questions, perhaps subconsciously.

1. Will the effort achieve results?
   'If I try harder to complete this on time will I actually meet the deadline or will it be a waste of effort?'
2. Will the results be rewarded?
   'If I meet the deadline, will I get more interesting work, or praise from the boss, or be held in high esteem by the rest of the group – or will nothing happen?'
3. Will the reward be worth the effort?
   'Is more interesting work, or a word of praise from the boss, really worth staying late for? Does the reward help satisfy my needs?'

Only if the answer is 'yes' to all three questions will the extra effort be made. Motivation depends on the individual's speculation about what is likely to happen, even though some of these perceptions may be mistaken. This is very easily forgotten. (It can work both ways, of course. An individual may put in a tremendous effort in the belief that it will lead to promotion, when in fact there will be no opportunities for promotion for anyone.)

The practical lesson here is not that we are powerless to motivate people. Rather, we need to pay attention to how they see things, talking to them to find out what their perceptions are and – if we know they are mistaken – giving information to help change these views.

Discussing the above three questions will often do more to motivate staff than reorganising work and creating new opportunities. It is also within all managers' power to do.

The concept of expectancy can be extended to consider what expectations people have of their work. Huw Benyon (1973), a sociologist, wrote about what it was like to work in the Ford car factory. A quote from one worker, appearing on the back cover, gives a good example of expectations about work:

> *It's strange this place. It's got no really good points. It's just convenient. It's got no interest. You couldn't take the job home. There's nothing to take. You just forget it. I don't want promotion at all; I've not got that approach to the job. I'm like a lot of people here. They're all working here but they're just really hanging around, waiting for something to turn up . . . It's different for them in the office. They're part of Fords. We're not, we're numbers.*

With such expectations, an employee is unlikely to be motivated to put in much effort.

In an early study by J. H. Goldthorpe and others (1968), they investigated the views of workers in three leading firms in Luton. They found that, although most of the people interviewed had jobs which gave them little direct job satisfaction, they had no thoughts of leaving and had high opinions of their firms. The level of pay and job security were the two predominant reasons given for staying in the job.

The authors concluded that workers have different orientations to work based on the rewards they expect from their working life. They gave examples of three types of orientation and their related expectation:

1. *Instrumental orientation.* Work is not a central life interest to this individual, who works primarily for the economic rewards expected. This is the orientation of many who work on assembly lines or in call centres.
2. *Bureaucratic orientation.* Work is seen as service to the organisation with the expectation of steadily increasing income, social status and lifetime security. This is the orientation of many who entered traditional banking, insurance or civil service jobs.
3. *Solidaristic orientation.* Work is seen as a group activity and economic rewards may be sacrificed in favour of expected group loyalty. This orientation was seen during the Hawthorne Experiments and is often found in, for example, the police or fire services.

The authors stressed that these three orientations are not necessarily mutually exclusive and that they are not the only possibilities.

Performance

Research by the Centre for Research into Business Activity (CeRiBA) suggested that the most productive firms have significantly higher proportions of skilled workers (*Management Today*, 2003b); the top 10 per cent of firms measured by productivity hire workers with, on average, two years more education compared with the bottom tenth. On further investigation it was realised that the difference in skills levels accounted for less than 10 per cent of the productivity gap between firms at the top and those at the bottom. Investment, capital availability and technology employed seemed to carry more weight. Why did higher skill levels correlate with higher productivity, yet higher skill levels did not account for much of that higher performance?

Proving that X is correlated with Y is not the same as saying that X is the *cause* of Y. In this instance, it seems that highly productive firms, having become more successful, are able to attract and pay workers with higher skills. Only by looking over time at the performance of firms, and the skills of their staff, could this be proved or disproved.

There are two sides to performance: being effective (doing the right things) and being efficient (doing things right). Improved performance needs to consider both facets.

Improving effectiveness

As discussed in Mackay (2007), the first step in helping someone become more effective is to think in detail about their job in output terms. Peter Drucker (1954) coined the term 'management by objectives', where one focuses on the output or objectives of a job (see Chapter 1). These 'outputs' are generally referred to as effectiveness areas. The problem is, however, that too many jobs are described in terms of inputs, not outputs: in terms of input areas and not in terms of *effectiveness* areas.

Remember, all effectiveness areas should meet four tests:

- Output
- Measurability
- Importance
- Authority.

Refer to Mackay (2007) to review how to evaluate someone's effectiveness.

Tests for effectiveness areas

So, thinking about your own job, how will you measure your effectiveness in output terms? Are you now making some of the mistakes that have been indicated here? Why not try the exercise of listing what you think your outputs are – they may turn out to be activities in some part – and asking '*Why?*' until you realise you cannot control the variance? This kind of activity is quite definitely done best on a team basis, as other people can contribute ideas and tend to be somewhat more objective. See also the section on apparent effectiveness.

Improving efficiency – why bother?

When we talk about improving efficiency, we are talking about improving the way in which we do something. Within today's organisations, this means identifying ways of reducing the number of errors that occur, reducing waste in processes and increasing our ability to get things right first time.

When we talk about improving efficiency in the context of our organisation we will come to link this with the identification of improvement opportunities and with the way in which we organise ourselves to address these opportunities and the use of 'improvement initiatives'.

Essentially, the elements that we will need to discuss when improving efficiency are, how do we:

- Identify and prioritise problems or opportunities?
- Organise them within the organisation?
- Manage their solution?

Developing a Role Effectiveness Model (REM)

It is important to look at the role of each individual task someone might do in the fulfilment of the department or organisation's overall purpose. Such an analysis reveals just what might get in the way of each individual doing their best job each and every time – i.e. how to be *effective* in that role. To do this, we need to look at the process where we are trying to add value; here we take a defined input, process it and produce an output for our internal – or external – customer.

In order for an individual to do that piece of work, there are four key criteria that must be satisfied. If they are not, the process fails and a chain of events will be set in motion. Unchecked, these lead to failure in the hands of that most critical of assessors – the ultimate customers we serve.

The development of a Role Effectiveness Model for each of an individual's key activities is a fundamental part of achieving significant improvements in the firm (see Figure 7.2). It starts with a clear definition of a process that is a clear piece of work for the person in question. The input and output requirements are agreed, so that it is clear what the process is

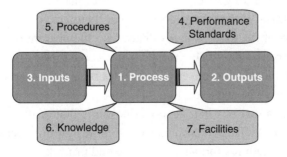

Figure 7.2 The sequence for development of a Role Effectiveness Model.

113

trying to do in terms of the customer/supplier chain running across the organisation. There are four other needs that will prevent the process going wrong that also need to be defined so that the process can meet the output requirements. Let us look at each component in more detail:

1. *The process.* This is the key piece of work that an individual has to fulfil in order to meet their overall purpose. Each task should be taken in turn, starting with the highest priority, and be defined clearly. If the task can be subdivided into a substantial piece of work, then it may be more appropriate to look at two separate REMs for that task.

   Once the process is defined, it will be essential to define its scope, i.e. when does it begin and end? This exercise may go some way to evaluate whether the task should be subdivided.

   Does the individual understand it fully? This is one area that needs to be agreed for any task to be undertaken successfully.

2. *The output.* This is a key part of any job. Unless the outputs are clear, then the process cannot hope to deliver what is required. It must be clear not only who the customers are but also that *all* their requirements are known *and* agreed. Once this is done and understood, then it is easier to meet their needs rather than leave it to assumption.

   One of the most difficult areas is the agreement of what performance measures are to be used to evaluate the output. The measurement may be in terms of timeliness, cost implication or accuracy. In order for the evaluation to be rational and not emotional, ideally some form of numerate evaluation must be sought at the outset and agreed by both parties.

3. *The input.* Only when the output has been agreed can the input that must be sought to meet those outputs be established. As with the outputs, the inputs will need to be defined and the supplier – or suppliers – agree to all the requirements. Again, these requirements will have a numerical basis to them, along with other conformance criteria.

   Once the outputs of a process have been agreed, and the inputs defined, then the overall process from inputs through the process to the outputs can be studied to ensure that the process is operating effectively. To ensure that the process successfully meets those output needs, and that nothing goes wrong, there are four further areas that can be investigated as part of the process study. These are the prevention needs.

4. *Quality performance standard.* Has the person receiving our output reached agreement on the standard required? Moreover, does the person following the process know the standard that they have to achieve?

5. *Procedures.* One area that so often gets overlooked is that of the procedures that need to be followed for the task. This is particularly true in marketing environments, where there are often no clear procedures for, say, designing and printing brochures. Nonetheless, if a given output is required, and more than one person may be working on the task in a given

period, then to have a clear guide of what logos, type-styles and approval procedures one has to follow will help prevent errors.

Continual improvement and a changing environment (internal and external) will necessitate that these procedures, once written, are consistently reviewed. Changes for change's sake and being out of date are equally damaging to the department and the organisation. In both cases, the delivery to the output requirements must be a fundamental guide to the procedures.

6. *Knowledge*. Again, an area so often overlooked, particularly in some departments where junior staff are left to 'learn on the job'. An individual may need specific training – albeit informally – in order to carry out a specific task.

One must remember that skill and experience both play an important role in the application of knowledge.

7. *Facilities*. While one might look to ensure that they have the right equipment for the task, it will be important to ensure that other resources are also available for the task – particularly time.

Prevention requirements shortfall

If there is going to be a limitation on any of the final four key areas at any juncture, this will have an impact on the output of the process. Managers will be able to address the shortfall before it affects the output.

However, any shortfall may require a change to the output and a revision agreed with the customer. This is far more preferable to letting them receive something less than they expected.

Performance appraisal and performance management

Most organisations are being pressured for improved performance and managers are being asked to get more from fewer resources. At the same time, employees in many organisations are asking for better and more direct feedback on their performance. The performance of an organisation depends directly on the performance of its key people. Most progressive organisations therefore have, or are implementing, a system of performance appraisal – most regularly a goals-orientated system, as described below.

Improved performances will not just happen, they must be managed!

Helping senior managers and their subordinates to focus on priorities within their jobs is the first step to managing performance. A performance appraisal system allows an individual manager to achieve clarity with his/her member of staff about their precise job and the goals they should be achieving within it.

Those organisations that aspire towards a high-performance culture are strong on:

- Clarity about objectives and goals
- Continuous assessment of performance and feedback
- Recognition for performance.

This is a basic part of the managerial function of all line managers. Optimum performance is best achieved by the above three steps. The aim is to have a goals-orientated approach. It is usually a motivating experience for employees to see clearly achievable goals in front of them and to be recognised by management when they achieve these goals. Therefore, we need to develop key objectives for individuals.

The overall objective of a performance appraisal system may differ from one organisation to another. Specific objectives will depend on the needs of the organisation at a particular time, but try not to have too many. In general, any system of appraisal or review is likely to include the following objectives:

- *Improvement of individual performance*. Management should not be afraid to state clearly that improving individual performance comes first. Departmental and organisational performance should improve as a consequence.
- *Personal development of the employee*. Employees must be able to see some benefit to themselves from a performance appraisal system. Adopting the personal development of the employee as a key objective will demonstrate this, in which case management must ensure delivery of this development.
- *Deeper understanding of the job*. Very often managers and subordinates, always under pressure from lack of time, do not fully understand the key elements of one another's jobs. A successfully operated performance appraisal system, along the lines described in these notes, greatly facilitates this understanding:
  - It institutes direct dialogue on a regular basis
  - The focus is on the job itself
  - It considers the performance of the individual within the job.

Four facets of appraisal systems that can be considered as 'best practice' would include:

- *Focus is on the real needs of the group, firm or organisation*. A key element within a performance appraisal system that is goals orientated is that it focuses on the needs of the firm and not on esoteric values unrelated to pressures within the business. This clearly benefits line managers, when firm-wide and/or departmental goals can be adapted to form part of an individual's goals.
- *Improved communications*. In a busy, over-pressured working environment, managers frequently fail to allow time to communicate adequately with their staff. A goals-orientated

system facilitates communication about the really important issues concerning achievement in a particular job. Typically, the quality of this communication is better and deeper than normal day-to-day discussions.

■ *Management commitment.* None of the benefits described will be fully realised unless senior management takes a very active interest in the process of performance appraisal and its management. Their commitment to this is vital.

■ *Commitment is a set of behaviours.* Thus, all managers must be seen to do things differently after the introduction of such a system. You only know an individual is committed to a new process if you see them clearly behaving in a manner consistent with the new process.

Building confidence through a 'goals-orientated appraisal system' is explored further in Mackay (2007).

Pay and performance

Employees want to feel that their good work is appreciated and appropriately compensated. However, most employees say that they do not believe that there is a clear relationship between their pay and their job performance (Duncan Alexander & Wilmshurst, 2006).

Although arithmetically impossible, most employees believe that their performance is above average. Each, therefore, believes that he or she should be paid above average. Similarly, most employees feel that they are not adequately paid compared to those performing similar work in other organisations. They therefore also believe that their pay is below the level of their job performance.

Employees often perceive that there are poor performers in their organisation who are earning as much if not more than they earn. They thus conclude, 'If that lazy so-and-so is still here, they must be underpaying me for my good work'.

Supervisors often do not have the know-how, measures or courage to differentiate between poor, average and above-average performers. They take the simple way out and give everyone the same pay increases each year.

Many employee surveys consistently show that employees say that tying pay to performance is very important to them; this is found to be particularly true in unionised organisations, where the union has negotiated contracts that require their employer to tie pay increases to years of service rather than performance.

So, what can management do? Explore the online companion web pages for some ideas.

Rewards

Psychologists have focused more attention on the power of consequences – rewards, punishment and removing something unpleasant – to change behaviour than any other method.

Some behaviour modifiers use only this method; others do not use it at all. However, it is not known exactly how reinforcement works; alternative suggestions have been put forward. So, do rewards:

- Strengthen the habit (response tendencies in a specific situation)?
- Merely give us information, letting us know which responses result in the pay-offs we want?
- Act primarily as pay-offs for performing a certain action, thus motivating us?

This has been a controversy for decades; perhaps the answer lies somewhere between all three.

Surprisingly, rewards will sometimes reduce the frequency of the preceding behaviour, i.e. have the effects of punishment. In some circumstances, extrinsic rewards are harmful, e.g. rewards (like 'pay') may turn a fun activity into 'work', lower the motivation to do the 'work' and reduce the amount of innovativeness or thinking done about the 'work' at hand, thus making behaviour more automated and stereotyped (see Box 7.1).

Threatening and pressuring students to do better is harmful, but giving praise, offering to help and giving encouragement is helpful. Repeatedly rewarding the student for completing easy tasks results in the student feeling less able and being less motivated. Even rewarding excellence with honour rolls and status may be detrimental if students restrict their interests or avoid hard courses to keep their extrinsic rewards high. There are no simple rules to the use of rewards.

To complicate matters further the effectiveness of a reinforcer (reward), of course, depends on the individual. Listening to loud music is a great reward for some people; it's punishment for others. Accumulating a lot of money is critical for some and rather meaningless for others. Likewise, failure affects people differently. For the success orientated, a failure experience increases the drive to succeed and to try again to accomplish the task. If personality-wise a person focuses primarily on avoiding failure, a failure is

---

Box 7.1: Rewards limiting performance

Alex (15) and Duncan (18) are often quite happy to help their Dad around the house with various DIY projects, coming and going as they please, doing as much or as little as they want, yet often working with their Dad way into late evening. When pay-per-hour was offered, they accepted but then felt *obliged* to do the work and so it became a chore, limiting their involvement to a few hours preferring TV to DIY.

So, material rewards may not be best placed where there are intrinsic motivations in doing work.

too punishing and they may lose interest in the task; they won't try it again (see Chapter 10, on learning from failure). Hence, one has to find the most meaningful reinforcer.

In the workplace, how do you keep your employees motivated, enthusiastic and eager to succeed when we are surrounded by fiscal despondency and you haven't got the budget to pay them as much as you'd like? You need to keep the best people to achieve good organisational performance in easier times. Let us explore some options for providing rewards at work? A checklist, not all of which is within the scope of all managers to apply, is suggested in Box 7.2.

Rewards for attendance

It seems that working at the UK Department for Work and Pensions had got to such a sorry state that, in October 2005, the DWP Minister Lord Hunt announced that the government had decided to offer cash bonuses and cheap holidays (via travel vouchers) in an effort to reward

---

Box 7.2: Some options for non-cash rewards

- Direct praise
- Peer recognition
- Outings, representing company
- Certificate or plaque
- Nice lunch or dinner out
- Special awards dinner/banquet
- Personal call or visit from CEO
- Tickets to sporting events, concerts
- Social function
- Letter of recognition – especially from most senior person
- Sport or outdoor activity
- Verbal praise
- Additional training
- Passing on customer compliments
- Press release
- Additional responsibilities
- Time off
- Car parking space
- New or updated tools to do job better
- Taking other responsibilities off hands.

---

civil servants for turning up to work rather than pulling a 'sickie'. At the Department, the 134 820 staff took, on average, 12.6 days sick a year at a cost of £100 million to the taxpayer (*The Daily Telegraph*, 2005). This number of days off (often Fridays or Mondays) exceeds the average for the public sector, estimated by the Chartered Institute of Personnel and Development at 10.3 days a year, and is far worse than the private sector average of 6.8 days – and the number of days taken sick is probably lower still amongst the self-employed!

The August before, Royal Mail offered staff who didn't take sick leave for six months the chance to win one of 37 Ford Focus cars. More than 90 000 staff received a £150 holiday voucher and attendance rose by 11 per cent. Prior to the scheme, approximately 10 000 of Royal Mail's 170 000 staff called in sick every day.

The CBI, representing businesses, says around 15 per cent of all absences are false sickness claims.

Fat cats

At the 2005 UK Enterprise Summit, business leaders joined the Chancellor Gordon Brown with the aim of making Britain more enterprising. The conference concluded with the assertion that the current British culture did not properly appreciate the contribution business makes. This deterred people from seeking a career in commerce, whether that is in large, established organisations or through starting businesses of their own.

Traditionally, being in 'trade' was considered to be 'common'; educated people headed to the professions rather than commerce. Today, management traineeships with the country's major companies are sought after in the same way as training contracts with the major law firms. However, while British attitudes have warmed towards business, they differ markedly from that seen in America. Is the UK media to blame?

There have been many column inches berating the salaries of some executives and some of the criticism seems to owe as much to jealousy as trying to see fair play for shareholders. Business people berated for their bonuses might wonder why an uncouth teenager with some fancy footwork earning four times the national yearly average wage each week can be greeted with such praise while it is taken for granted that a CEO will deliver the profits whatever the opposition.

In America, there is little objection to financial rewards that are far higher than those in the UK, as often some of that money goes to good causes, business people endowing their old colleges and sharing some of their rewards with various charitable endeavours; moreover, they create wealth and opportunity for their employees too. This wins some of the public plaudits the UK counterparts appear to seek. While British business people give relatively generously, they tend not to boast about it. And the media doesn't always focus on the wider social benefits.

Writing in *Management Today* in 2004, Patience Wheatcroft (Business and City Editor of *The Times*) suggested that business leaders should change tack:

> *Perhaps they should change their approach and broadcast the fact that their success, as well as that of their company, is to the country's benefit. That might even persuade the tabloids to lionise leaders rather than pillory them as fat cats.*

At the end of October 2005, retailing entrepreneur Philip Green received a £1.2 billion dividend from Arcadia, the Top Shop, Dorothy Perkins and Evans group he bought for £850m three years ago. Many tabloids reported that it is the biggest dividend paid to a UK individual and takes the total that his Monaco-based family has taken out of their BHS and Arcadia retailing empire to £1.6 billion. However, others reported a comment from Mr Green, who defended the size of the dividend (Rankine, 2005): '*If this was one of the venture capitalists they'd be taking twice this number,*' he said. '*In any business we've bought, we haven't sold and leased back all the assets, we've kept them all. We haven't ratcheted the business off the roof.*'

Flexible benefits packages

Benefits have traditionally been based on holiday, pension and private medical insurance to recognise age and reward seniority rather than desirability or choice. However, managers now realise that the benefits people want depend on their individual circumstances.

The 'gold standard' private sector benefits package would be along the lines of that shown in Box 7.3.

Box 7.3: The 'gold standard' private sector benefits package

Headline salary: £25 000
Benefits:
Bonus (15%) – £3750
Employer's pension contribution (10%) – £2500
Life assurance (4 × salary) – £100
Income protection – £350
Medical insurance of the family – £1000
Car – £7500
Total value of package: £40 200

Lloyds TSB Group has been running a 'state-of-the-art' flexible benefits package since January 2003. The scheme, branded 'Flavours', is based on allocating 4 per cent on top of their monthly salary to spend, as they wish, on a range of benefits offered by the company. They can add up to 50 per cent of their actual salary to that allowance or opt to take the cash and no benefits. Around a half of staff have signed up to the programme, choosing benefits in three key areas:

- Health – full medical insurance, dental care and cash plans
- Leisure – holiday, retail and childcare vouchers, tax-free home PC purchase and a learning account
- Future life planning – pension, accident, critical illness and life assurance cover.

As the benefits are 'purchased' out of salary, there are double savings on tax and National Insurance. The most popular has been holiday trading – staff are allowed to buy or sell up to five days' holiday a year.

The company also offers a share ownership scheme, including a save-as-you-earn plan that, after five years, can be used to buy shares priced as they were at the start of the programme – given the depressed market of late, these options are starting to look like a good long-term benefit.

While long-term benefits encourage people to stay, it is also a good incentive in recruitment. However, the company is beginning to think beyond money as the major means of motivating people. While the 1980s might have been about money and the size of the last bonus, in the mid-2000s 'time' is the new money and quality-of-life issues have come to the fore. A 2003 survey by American Express (*Management Today*, 2003c) found that nearly a fifth of people who received a cash bonus could not remember what they spent their money on and only 9 per cent used it for the intended purpose of treating themselves to something memorable.

When it comes to sales rewards, IBM's eServer team blended 'old' (retail gifts) with 'new' (24/7 updates and information via the Web) and achieved a 250 per cent increase in trade participants and a 42 per cent increase in sales (Fisher, 2005). They were hyperlinked to other IBM sites for back-up and it became a main gateway for communication. It appears that instant gratification via the Web reinforces desired and desirable behaviour in a way that more conventional slow incentives rarely match.

While 60 years have lapsed since Abraham Maslow proposed his Hierarchy of Needs, his theory remains watertight. Once we have enough to clothe, feed and shelter our families, money is a low-level motivator for most people. This is replaced by the desire for recognition, status and ultimately the need to express ourselves through our work – Maslow recognised that few get this far.

Thus, job satisfaction, enjoyment and feeling part of a social group at work become some of the most effective benefits a business can offer – and they are cheaper than private medical cover. Things like career breaks and the opportunity to undertake voluntary work – to put something back – give the opportunity for company and staff to have a psychological contract to be proud of. Good management and a feeling of being involved and recognised are some of the best benefits that a company can give. The cost is in management time and they have a disproportionately positive effect on people's attitude to their employers.

Summary

In this chapter you have:

- Explored the relationship between effort, performance and reward, noting that four key facets should be addressed to improve performance – achievement, recognition, responsibility and advancement
- Recognised the importance of feedback to good performance
- Explored the subject of job enrichment and noted four key areas:
    - Give a person a complete unit of work
    - Give extra authority
    - Introduce new and more difficult tasks
    - Give people specific or specialised tasks so that they become 'experts'
- Looked at the Role Effectiveness Model, noting four areas that affect the output of a job:
    - Quality performance standards
    - Procedures
    - Knowledge
    - Facilities
- Uncovered a range of rewards in the workplace from the 'everyday' to the more comprehensive benefits package.

Questions

1. Choose a job of which you are familiar (this could be your own job, or the job of a colleague or subordinate). Analyse the job in terms of the five core characteristics, identifying areas in which it could be improved:
    - Skill variety
    - Task identity
    - Task significance
    - Autonomy
    - Feedback.

2. Develop a Role Effectiveness Model for your job. What are the potential shortfalls in achieving the desired outputs? How might you address these?
3. Thinking about the people in your organisation, how can their jobs be enriched by:
   - Giving a person a complete unit of work
   - Giving extra authority
   - Introducing new and more difficult tasks
   - Giving people specific or specialised tasks so that they become 'experts'.

References

Benyon, H. (1973) *Working For Ford*, Penguin.

The Daily Telegraph (2005) 20 October, Business Pages 1.

Drucker, P. (1954) *The Practice of Management*, Butterworth-Heinemann.

Duncan Alexander & Wilmshurst (2006) Data on file from staff audits.

Fisher, J. G. (2005) *How to Run Successful Incentive Schemes*, Kogan Page.

Goldthorpe, J. H. et al. (1968) *The Affluent Worker: Industrial Attitudes and Behaviour*, Cambridge University Press.

Herzberg, F. (1956) *Work and The Nature of Man*, World Publishing.

Mackay, A. R. (2007) *Recruiting, Retaining and Releasing People*, Butterworth-Heinemann.

Management Today (2003a) May, p. 37.

Management Today (2003b) July, p. 31.

Management Today (2003c) June, p. 75.

Rankine, K. (2005) From www.telegraph.co.uk (filed: 21 October).

Wheatcroft, P. (2004) *Management Today*, March, p. 27.

Further Reading

Baron, A. and Armstrong, M. (2004) *Managing Performance*, Chartered Institute of Personnel and Development.

Mackay, A. R. (2007) *Recruiting, Retaining and Releasing People*, Butterworth-Heinemann.

Rumnler, G. A. and Brache, A. P. (1995) *Improving Performance: How to Manage the White Space on the Organization Chart*, Jossey-Bass Wiley.

8

Selling the Vision

If you don't know where you are going, any road will take you . . .
Advice Tweedle-Dum and Tweedle-Dee gave to Alice in *Through the Looking Glass* by
Lewis Carroll

Learning Outcomes

With today's rapidly changing influences on organisations, why should anyone follow another if they have little idea of where they are going? This chapter, and its companion web pages, look at how to sell the vision of the future for the organisation, attract people to a values-driven business, harnessing the passion in individuals for doing meaningful work in the context of motivating them. The chapter has been written to cover particular elements of the National Occupational Standards for Management and Leadership (*Providing Direction – Units 6, 8, 9 and 11*) and it covers many of the requirements of the Chartered Management Institute's Diploma in Management compulsory *Unit C43 – Planning to meet Customer Requirements* (in respect of stakeholders) and also to 'meet stakeholder requirements' of the optional *Unit O44 – Managing Marketing Activities*. This chapter will also be of value to those studying the CIPD Professional Development Scheme – particularly the *Leadership and Management* and *People Management and Development* modules.

By the end of this chapter you will:

- Understand your role and responsibilities in relation to the mission, aims and objectives of your organisation
- Know the importance of setting a clear vision for your organisation
- Explore measurements of your business from the value of the workforce to the balanced scorecard
- Know how to enact the manager's role in managing the culture of the organisation
- Understand what is meant by 'psychological contract' and explore a model to define it
- Review approaches to developing a values-driven strategy for the business.

The 'Centre for Leadership Studies – Europe' Model

CLS-Europe developed a model to assist managers in defining the necessary facets of the 'complete leader'. It can be considered a 'steering wheel' that managers need to hold to drive the organisation forward. This is shown in Figure 8.1 and has three main 'spokes'.

Vision

Some wise sage said, '*If you don't know where you are going, you are sure to get there*' but, unless we aspire to the Tweedle School of Management, organisations need better steerage.

From the 'Business Energy Survey 2005' it was found that managers were motivated in their work and want to be challenged. The respondents said that a sense of purpose from work (64 per cent) and a sense of achieving their goals (53 per cent) were the main factors driving them – and this was the case across all managerial levels. (As we saw in Chapter 7, managers did not cite performance-related rewards/incentives as something that motivated them at work – only 11 per cent total.)

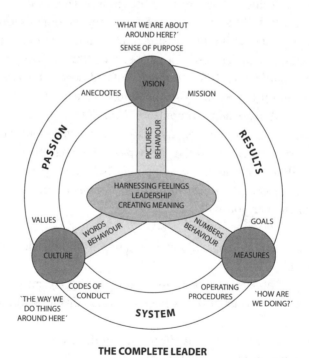

Figure 8.1 The Centre for Leadership Studies 'Complete Leader' Model.

In order to evaluate your own organisation, try answering some fundamental questions:

- How clear are you of the overriding purpose driving your organisation, department or section? It is essential that leaders of various parts of the organisation create a 'picture' of their part and can translate that into something that their team can relate to; this is closely linked to the 'passion' driving the business, of which more later.
- How clear is this overriding purpose to your colleagues? The author was involved in one successful law firm in the Thames Valley where the junior lawyers were of the opinion that the purpose of their firm was to provide 'big 4 × 4s in the car park and second homes in Tuscany' – for the Partners, that is! Not a word about any other stakeholder – least of all junior fee earners!
- How far through the organisation is the overriding purpose shared? For everyone in an organisation to 'pull in the same direction', the overall purpose must be congruent for all.
- Is the mission expressed clearly? We are not speaking about the meaningless rhetoric of a glitzy 'mission statement' stuck on the wall of reception but the true sense of purpose that captures the hearts and minds of all stakeholders towards a meaningful picture of a better future.

It doesn't matter whether you are the CEO or heading up the administration team, the picture created needs to be understood by each level of person involved. Each person needs to feel that they 'fit', that they have a role, that they have a future, that they make a difference. From the 'Business Energy Survey' again: nearly one-half (45 per cent) of all managers claim that the values of their organisation motivate them to a great extent but that there is a distinct difference according to level. Sixty-six per cent of directors, who are more likely to be articulating the organisation's values, claim to be greatly motivated by them, compared to only 28 per cent of junior managers.

Managers largely concur with the need to be customer driven, professional and quality focused – values that are seen to be present in many organisations. However, there is a serious misalignment in terms of how managers' personal values correlate with organisational values. Managers are also keenly seeking environments that are innovative, committed to staff, proactive, trusting and open, yet these values are present in less than 10 per cent of organisations.

- Are the key goals specified? Do they reinforce the overall 'vision'? Individuals may need to have a pathway or steps along the way defined for them so that they can see a way forward. And these steps need to lead to that defined picture of the future.

This latter point leads us to consider the measures that need to be in place to work out whether we are getting there.

Measures

The measures of success of each of the stakeholders in an organisation differ but they, nonetheless, are relevant to them. While CEOs might speak of return on investment or capital employed, what of the administration team? What are their measures of success?

It is a sad truth that 'what gets measured gets done'. So, measuring the wrong things is not effective.[1] So, again, some fundamental questions to consider:

- Do the measures taken to assess performance reflect the overall purpose, vision and key goals? All too often there is not a clear link between a person's key tasks and the 'sense of purpose' of the organisation, and not often referred to at appraisal.
- How widely do you share that information? The author meets many professional people whose performance is only measured as 'billable hours', yet they have no idea how well their organisation – often a partnership – is performing.
- Do you measure how well people live up to the values? How they enact the 'way we work around here'? It was only when the author's business became involved in one charity with a 30-year history that individuals were evaluated by the people they served as whether they were performing in appropriate ways that made a difference.
- How widely is that information shared? A series of workshops were run across the country to feed back that information to all individuals in the charity to assist in the improvement process.
- Is there any other information (e.g. client/staff satisfaction) which you need to collect to give the full picture?

As much as 80 per cent of a company's worth is tied to the value of the workforce (Grossman, 2005), yet recent research by the Chartered Management Institute (CMI) found that, although 90 per cent of managers record various metrics, only 20 per cent thought their measures were effective or even useful.

Measuring the value of the workforce

The value of the workforce is potentially the greatest differentiating source of strategic advantage, the biggest component of most future investment and the organisation's greatest potential asset. It needs to be measured for three key reasons:

- To demonstrate the value of the workforce in achieving strategic business success
- To manage the workforce and other related investments

---

[1] For more on 'effectiveness', see Mackay (2006).

- Corporate governance and information provision following recommendations from the Department of Trade and Industry for the Operating and Financial Review (OFR) sections of annual reports, effective from April 2005 (Accounting for People: http://www. account-ngforpeople.gov.uk/; OFR: http://www.dti.gov.uk/cld/financialreview.htm).

See the companion web pages for suggested key principles for measuring workforce value.

The balanced scorecard

Broad objectives need to be refined into definite goals with specific measures of attainment if they are going to provide clear incentives for performance. In the past, these measures have been too focused on financial results. Today, management needs a broader perspective that incorporates the interests of the various stakeholders and requirements for achieving long-term competitiveness.

For most businesses, the diverse objectives can be incorporated into four perspectives:

- *Financial perspective* – meeting the objectives of shareholders
- *Customer perspective* – meeting customer needs in highly competitive markets
- *Operational perspective* – achieving the key levers that drive performance excellence
- *Internal perspective* – meeting the expectations and building up the capabilities of employees whose skills determine the company's future.

The specific goals will depend upon the nature of the organisation: its industry, manufacturing configuration, service parameters, offering best value, type of customers and the market dynamics. The balanced scorecard has the advantage of not overloading managers with information but giving them the multiple perspectives essential for the strategic development of the organisation.

See the companion web pages for some suggested measures that managers might employ to evaluate their organisation's performance against the four key perspectives.

Culture

In the late 1980s, Gulam Noon set up the family business, Noon Products, supplying a range of ethnic frozen foods to Birds Eye. It was bought out by WT Foods Group plc in 2002 and subsequently a management buy-out was concluded with the help of venture capitalists. Writing in *Management Today*, Sir Noon (2004) suggested three vital ingredients to his firm's success:

- Being in the right market at the right time
- Having the right approach – a shared passion and belief in the products
- Creating an environment of trust and mutual respect among employees.

It is that 'culture' which was most instrumental to their success. Developing a working partnership allowed creativity and innovation to flourish and morale to soar.

Confucius told his disciple Tzukung that three things were needed for government: weapons, food and trust. He added that if the ruler was not able to hold on to all three, he should give up weapons first and food next. Trust, he said, should be guarded to the end, because without trust, nothing is attainable.

Hence, managers need to be consistent in their behaviour and act with integrity to create a culture of trust and respect. Every employee must be given a sense of belonging and a sense that he or she has a vital part to play in achieving the organisation's aims and objectives. So, consider the following questions:

- How clear are you of the 'way things are done' in your organisation?
- What words or phrases would you use to describe this culture?
- How common is this understanding among your key colleagues?
- How far through the organisation is this shared?
- Are the core values explained and understood?
- Are codes of conduct written to explain how people are expected to live up to the values?

Achieving success with 'selling the vision' requires managers to pay attention, not just to the things they do, but to the way in which they do them. One of the inevitable barriers to the pursuit of organisational improvement in the minds of many employees can be the 'lack of management commitment' to that goal. What this usually means is that managers are seen behaving in the same old way, paying lip-service to the vision and not appearing to make an effort to change their style to that consistent with a progressive organisation.

It is not sufficient for managers to feel committed to a goal, they must show it by:

- Making deeds match words
- Ensuring that they enact the manager's role
- Managing the improvement process
- Recognising where responsibility for organisational improvement lies.

Matching deeds with words

It is easy for managers to talk about the importance of the organisation's vision, but their people will evaluate their commitment through what they do.

Managers must:

- Ensure that every action is values driven and builds towards the ultimate goal
- Be consistent in their decision-making and explain why decisions are made
- Know who owns specific problems and has the responsibility and authority to do something about it – and deal with those problems through them!

- Insist on things being right first time and there being no room for second best
- Encourage their people similarly to insist on quality in everything that they do and everything that is done for them
- Constantly reinforce the importance of understanding and meeting all stakeholders' needs as appropriate.

Enacting the manager's role

The activities that a manager involves him or herself in will tell you much about the way in which that person sees the role of the manager.

The visionary executive will:

- Manage the missions and values of the company or their division
- Meet regularly with people at all levels, not relying on formal meeting structures
- Be receptive and enthusiastic about new ideas
- Talk about future goals and long-term outlook
- Pay attention to strengths rather than weaknesses
- Be visible and accessible
- Listen.

At the same time, the visionary executive can still:

- Be decisive
- Be strong
- Be thorough
- Be bottom line focused
- Expect results.

Managing the improvement process

Achieving a vision or goal may require a change in the operating style and all people, not just managers, must take responsibility for helping this change by asking questions like:

- Are we reacting to problems or preventing them?
- Are we working against targets or for continuous improvement?
- Are our decisions made for the sake of expediency or for the sake of quality?
- Are we tackling sporadic problems as they occur or looking for root causes of chronic problems?
- When we hold meetings and discussions, do we look for contention or consensus?
- Do we manage discrete organisational functions or do we manage processes?
- Do we make snapshot measurements or do we measure and manage trends?

In this way, the organisation culture will be one looking to move to a more preventive operating style managing for long-term improvement, not just short-term success.

Recognising where responsibility for organisational improvement lies

Everyone has responsibility for their contribution to the overall vision or goal, but people cannot be held solely responsible for the quality of their work. Around 80 per cent of problems are not caused by people but by failures in systems – particularly information and communication systems, absence of tools or training, inadequate procedures or documentation, or unclear requirements.

To do a job properly people need to:

- Know what to do (requirements)
- Know how to do it (training)
- Have the means to do it (skills, tools)
- Measure performance (how are they doing)
- Take corrective action (ability to respond)
- Have confidence (management support).

It is every manager's responsibility to ensure that their people have all the requirements they need to do their job effectively. Only then can they be truly considered to be responsible for the quality of their output, building towards the organisation's vision, and only then can they be truly held accountable if things go wrong!

Psychological Contract

First used in the early 1960s, the term 'psychological contract' became popular during the economic downturn of the early 1990s, and is defined as '. . . the perceptions of the two parties, employee and employer, of what their mutual obligations are towards each other' (Guest and Conway, 2002). They may be inferred from current or past actions, as well as from statements made by the employer (e.g. during the recruitment or in performance appraisals), thus allowing the obligations to be both informal and imprecise – some seen as 'promises' and others as 'expectations'. In any event, they are believed by the employee to be part of the relationship with their employer.

The psychological contract can be distinguished from the legal contract of employment – this may offer only a limited and uncertain representation of the reality of the employment relationship. The employee may have contributed little to its terms beyond accepting them. The nature and content of the legal contract may only emerge clearly if and when it comes to be tested in an employment tribunal.

Conversely, the psychological contract considers the reality of the situation as perceived by both parties, and may have more effect than the formal contract on the organisational

Table 8.1 A model of the psychological contract (adapted from Guest)

Inputs	Content	Outputs
Employee characteristics	Fairness	Employee behaviours
Organisation characteristics	Trust	Performance
HR practices	Delivery	Commitment

culture. The psychological contract effectively tells employees what they are required to do in order to meet their side of the bargain, and what they can expect from their manager and the job they are asked to do. It may not – indeed, in general it will not – be strictly enforceable, though courts may be influenced by a view of the underlying relationship between employer and employee, for example in interpreting the common-law duty to show mutual trust and confidence.

A useful model of the psychological contract is offered by Professor David Guest of Kings College London (see Table 8.1). In outline, the model suggests that:

■ The extent to which employers adopt people management practices will influence the state of the psychological contract
■ The contract is based on employees' sense of fairness and trust, and their belief that the employer is honouring the 'deal' between them
■ Where the psychological contract is positive, increased employee commitment and satisfaction will have a positive impact on business performance.

A Passion for Business

Imagine trying to have a meaningful relationship with someone whose principles are in stark contrast to your own – you are honest, they lie; you keep within the law, they flaunt it; you want integrity, they couldn't care less. How long would you remain friends, let alone build a business together?

Having congruent values of guiding principles has a place in business just as in social relationships. Having clearly defined and articulated values have played a key part in the success of long-standing organisations such as 3M, Hewlett-Packard, General Electric and Procter & Gamble. Such organisations have realised that by approaching values planning in the right way, individual behaviour can be shaped to promote optimum performance, loyalty, creativity and motivation to the benefit of all concerned.

Organisations need to find common ground and translate organisational values into actionable behaviour that individuals can live in their everyday working lives. So many people today are looking to their work to mean something rather than just to provide a pay cheque.

If organisations want to attract, retain and make teams out of talented people, money alone will not do it. Talented people want to be part of something that offers meaning to their work – something that they can believe in, confers meaning to their work, something to get passionate about.

To do this, an organisation needs to know what it is in business for – over and above making money!

But it is no good hiring external consultants to write impressive-sounding mission statements and a set of inspirational value statements to plaster over the office walls and not changing anything. Unlike politicians that talk about family values then are found to have extra-marital affairs, managers need to do more than pay lip-service to the values – they must live up to them too. The alternative is large doses of cynicism for staff to use as a stick to beat management.

Discovering the core values that drive your people, and hence your business, is not hard – run a professional audit (Chapter 3 will give you some ideas on where to start, or go to www.daw.co.uk for more ideas). Note, however, according to the *Harvard Business Review*, 90 per cent of change programmes fail because of inconsistency between leadership and the 'aspirational' values underpinning the new vision. Even the most common themes can become meaningless if there is too great a gap between words and actions. Don't just 'talk the talk', you need to 'walk the walk'!

Of course, 'meaningful work', 'guiding principles' and 'value-led strategy' do not mean anything to most commercial organisations unless they impact on the bottom line. Tom Heuerman, former change manager at the *Star-Tribune* in Minneapolis and now business consultant, suggests that leaders would not bring him in if their current approach was working and their people were not miserable, conflicted and uninspired. He suggests that his clients take a leap of faith and see whether leading by values to build a passion for their business improves the balance sheet and the energy and feel of the place. If it does not work, he suggests they can drop it and go back to the old ways of working – none of the thousands of organisations that have been led through developing a passion for their business have chosen to go back.

We will explore 'work with meaning' further in Chapter 21 at the end of this text.

Summary

In this chapter you have:

- Seen the three equivalent spokes you need on your wheel to drive the business forward – vision, measures and culture
- Explored your role and responsibilities in relation to the mission, aims and objectives of your organisation
- Seen the fundamental importance of setting a clear vision for your organisation

- Explored measurements of your business from the value of the workforce to the balanced scorecard
- Been introduced to the concept of the 'psychological contract'
- Seen how to enact the manager's role in managing the culture of the organisation
- Been introduced to how to develop a values-driven strategy for the business.

Questions

1. Explore the questions raised in the CLS-Europe Complete Leader Model earlier in the chapter. How does your organisation, or one that you are familiar with, fare?
2. List some of the expectations that an employee may have of their employer and that the employer may have of the employee.
3. What might an organisation do when selecting new staff and when the new recruits join the organisation to assist with developing a two-way understanding of the psychological contract?
4. Evaluate the balanced scorecard. How well does your organisation, or one that you are familiar with, match up to having balanced measures of performance?

References

Grossman, R. (2005) 'Blind Investment', *HR Magazine*, Vol. 50, No. 1, January.

Guest, D. E. and Conway, N. (2002) *Pressure at Work and the Psychological Contract*, CIPD, London.

Mackay, A. R. (2007) *Recruiting, Retaining and Releasing People*, Butterworth-Heinemann.

Motivation Matters (2005) The Business Energy Survey, Autumn, Chartered Institute of Management.

Noon, S. (2004) *Management Today*, September, p. 10.

Further Reading

In addition to the referenced works:

Antonakis, J., Canciolo, A. T. and Sternberg, R. J. (2004) *The Nature of Leadership*, Sage Publications.

9

Mackay's Motivation Development Model

As a manager, the important thing is not what happens when you are there but what happens when you are not there.

Kenneth Blanchard, co-author of *The One Minute Manager*

Learning Outcomes

This chapter, along with its companion web pages, pulls together a range of theoretical approaches to motivation management giving a highly practical model for managers. The chapter has been written to cover particular elements of the National Occupational Standards for Management and Leadership (*Providing Direction – Lead People 9*; *Facilitating Change – Foster Innovation 14*; and many sections of *Working with People*) and it covers many of the requirements of the Chartered Management Institute's Diploma in Management compulsory *Unit C41 – Developing your Management Style* (in respect of developing the trust and support of others), some of the *Effective Communications* elements of compulsory *Unit C44*, and *Unit C45 – Managing Performance*. It is also of value to those studying the optional *Unit O42 – Developing Personnel and Personnel Performance*. This chapter will be of value to those studying the CIPD Professional Development Scheme – particularly the *Leadership and Management* and *People Management and Development* modules.

By the end of this chapter you will:

- Have looked at how much a manager might influence a person's motivation
- Be able to consider both the task being done and the person doing the work – and explore the interaction of the two variables
- Have looked at four levels of motivation and what to do at each level

- Have been introduced to a practical model for motivation development
- Begin to uncover a way of evaluating your management style, its flexibility and its effectiveness in bringing to light another person's motivation.

Background to the Motivation Development Model

One can define an organisation as a selection of people coming together, often in a building of some sort, to undertake collaborative activities of some sort, each using varying amounts of technology, managing resources of some sort, often money, to a defined aim, which we hope they share. At the end of the day, it is whether or not the people engaged in the various activities can be bothered to give up their own time to do what is necessary in exchange for something they value, again often money but, as we know, so much more besides. The challenge facing management thinkers over the last hundred years or more is how we can make the people 'more bothered' to give up their time to do more of what the organisation exists to do.

As we have seen, theories of motivation abound; all of them to varying degrees focus on getting *tasks* done through other *people*.

The purpose of this chapter is to provide a background to the situational Motivation Development Model (MDM) developed by the author and marketed through Duncan Alexander & Wilmshurst. It is built on a background of motivational theories that made their main focus on people vs. tasks (such as Likert, Blake and Mouton, and others) overlaid by Maslow, with its inspiration coming from Tannenbaum and Schmidt and the Blanchard–Hersey Situational Leadership Model – each explored in more detail in Chapter 13.

Through experience it has become apparent that no one individual will be motivated by the same thing all the time and that different people doing the same job need different incentives to achieve the same outcome as the next person. It all depends on what their situation is at the time and the effective manager is able to recognise the dynamics of the situation and respond accordingly.

All this variability may leave the practising manager or 'leader' bewildered about how to address a particular set of circumstances. It is not enough to be flexible, one has to flex in the right manner to be effective. Naturally, a starting point will be an understanding of one's current or preferred style when trying to create the right environment in which a staff member or 'follower' might evolve a higher willingness to achieve a given outcome, and whether that style has flexibility and is effective when flexed.

Leaders may evaluate their motivation development style through the use of a questionnaire. It should be realised that, clearly, it is not possible to develop situations that accurately reflect true-life experiences that one might most easily relate to in the workplace, although the author has made an attempt to provide sufficient variety to illustrate the concept of the MDM.

See the companion web pages for more information.

Questionnaires

In the motivation development elements of the online questionnaire, a number of scenarios have been devised where delegates are asked to consider each situation on its merits and, from the 'clues' in the mini case-scenario, decide on what they would do, if anything, as a consequence. A selection of them has been reproduced in this chapter to illustrate key ideas. They relate largely to Western-style enterprises in both the private and public sector, commercial and not-for-profit, to large and more modest concerns alike.

Naturally, four or five lines of text do not represent the full understanding that an individual 'leader' may have of their 'followers'. Therefore, in practice, a person aiming to motivate a group or individual will have a much better understanding of how they might deal with that given situation. However, the questionnaire is designed to provide enough information to guide the individual on choosing the most *effective* approach to motivation development in the given situation.

Alternative responses

Having considered their likely action, respondents to the questionnaires are then asked to choose which of the four alternative actions (a–d) most closely matches their likely approach to motivation of the individual in the situation given. Again, since the world does not easily divide itself into four separate alternatives, respondents are asked to identify with the one approach that *most closely* resembles what they might actually do. (The reader is invited to be aware of their 'theory-in-action' and 'espoused theory' at this point – see Chapter 10.)

In scanning the alternative approaches, respondents must assess the issue that is most likely to fulfil the follower's needs, wants and desires, and therefore motivate them in the given situation. The alternative style responses will be discussed further below.

Task Motivation Control Orientation

Task motivation control orientation behaviour is the extent to which the 'leader' applies degrees of motivational freedom to the 'follower' when undertaking their tasks or, if there is more than one person, the degree to which the leader controls factors such as:

- Setting working parameters
- Defining outcomes
- Building team dynamics
- Establishing self-evaluation
- Allowing self-direction.

When a leader is trying to get work done through a follower, there is a varying amount of attention that must be given to help the individual find their own motivation in undertaking the task. Let us illustrate this with a case study (see Box 9.1).

In this situation, the leader needs to apply more 'task motivation control' because the follower's motivation to do the job to the required standard cannot be left to chance; in this situation, the follower's *task motivation* – for this task – is low. Leaving someone in this situation alone to find their own satisfaction and motivation in their assigned tasks, when they are clearly not inclined to do it, will not work – in fact, it is likely that, left for too long, the person will become a demotivating force on others in the organisation. So, the leader needs to address the follower's *motivation* before they can be expected to perform.

In this case, the leader responsible for the project will need to set the follower some specific and simple tasks[1] to complete, in line with the project specification, and reinforce their place in the department. The leader needs to tell the follower that these tasks, when completed, will be what is expected from their contracted work on the project and will make a positive contribution to, and be appreciated by, the organisation. The work will need to be closely monitored and every achievement along the route should be appropriately reinforced so the follower builds a sense of security that they are delivering what is expected from their contracted work.

Box 9.1: Helping a new recruit get down to work on a new project

Andrew is a graduate physicist and has been recruited to Duncan Alexander & Wilmshurst on a short-term contract working in the IT department on a specific project. He is a very likeable person, is quite capable and gets on well with others in the firm. However, he seems to have a problem getting up in the morning and getting to work on time! When he gets in, he does not seem to be able to get down to the simplest of tasks; his chatting is becoming a disruptive influence on others in the firm.

It appears that there may be a fundamental mismatch between the individual recruited for the task and what might be attractive for him in terms of work content. While the project may be well within Andy's scope, perhaps the project does not inspire him. Nonetheless, he has taken up the work, is being paid to do it and to achieve specific outcomes in the project brief.

Clearly, this is not a situation where the Senior Partner responsible for IT can leave Andrew with much degree of freedom as, left to his own devices, it appears not much will be done on the project and his chatting would become an increasing problem.

---

[1] Ensuring that they are 'SMART' objectives (see Chapter 4).

Concern for the person is relatively low at this stage; if they don't 'shape up' they will have to 'ship out' – although this should not be used as a warning or threat to try to get anyone motivated!

Let us now consider the follower (Andrew) several weeks into his time at the firm, where he has been able to achieve more things than were expected from the IT project (see Box 9.2).

Now, clearly, the follower has not leapt from the situation in Box 9.1 to the situation in Box 9.2 overnight. Much work has had to be done in developing the follower's motivation. However, it is clear that in this second situation, the follower has achieved the requirements of the project and has gone beyond the expected parameters. If the leader applied the same style as before to affect the follower's motivation what would happen?

If the leader were to set some clear parameters for the new initiatives, tell the follower how much others would appreciate them doing the work and explain how valuable they will be to the organisation, their task motivation control would have been too high and heavy-handed – it would most likely have the opposite effect. As the follower's task motivation maturity is high in this situation, they do not need external influences, the leader can relinquish considerable motivational control and not intervene in the task, simply add their own thanks and appreciation when the time is right.

Box 9.2: Motivating a new recruit several weeks into the project

Andrew has been working for Duncan Alexander & Wilmshurst for several weeks on the IT project. While the project required improvement to the reliability of the broadband connectivity, LAN and knowledge management in the firm, all of which are progressing well, ahead of plan and under budget, Andrew has also been able to provide a 'media station' for staff in the refreshment area from one of the outdated workstations that he renovated one evening.

Andrew was aware of a potential issue arising over Internet access and e-mail use by staff at the firm possibly getting in the way of work, and Partners needing to find a balance between flexibility and control over such matters. Through Andrew's innovation, staff can now access the Internet in the refreshment area for broadcast news and use it for social matters – last minute theatre deals and the like – in their break times and not at their workstations interrupting workflow. Staff all agreed themselves that Internet and e-mail at workstations would be for business matters only; the Partners had not directly intervened.

The Partner overhears others in the firm thanking him for the facility and saying how much he has enjoyed putting his ideas into practice.

So, as far as the task motivation orientation of a leader is concerned, there is a need for the leader to be sensitive to the individual's position (task motivation maturity) on the continuum between 'high task motivation orientation' (where the leader needs to identify, control and implement the motivational influences to get the task underway) and 'low task motivation orientation' (where the leader need not get too involved, since the follower is quite capable of finding their own motivation in doing the work unsupervised).

We can see here a scale of motivation control, but this is only one of the factors. Ability and Confidence are also important issues. If Andrew were not able to do the job required of the project, the Partner would need to address this directly and deal with the problem (see Chapter 14 for a similar approach to ability development). Equally, if Andrew was anxious about a part of his job (damaging equipment outside of warranty, losing valuable information) and would not do it because he was not confident of getting it right, then again the Partner would need to address his confidence (see Chapter 19 for a parallel approach). When he is both able and confident the Partner would need to give much less attention to each of these issues.

Clearly, from the leader's point of view, it is in their interests to get the follower from the high task motivation orientation (where they need to guide the follower in their motivation) to the low task motivation orientation end of the continuum (where the follower becomes largely self-motivated) represented in Figure 9.1.

In order to progress a follower along the continuum, the leader needs to use differing styles to assist the person in their task motivation maturity. As we have seen, the leader may need to be aware of a number of models of motivation as they take the follower along the continuum, such as those outlined in Chapter 4. In this model, we propose four different

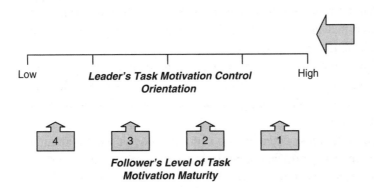

Figure 9.1 The task motivation control orientation continuum. A new recruit, for example, may start towards the right-hand side and the 'leader' would need to take them through four stages to improve their task motivation maturity until the 'follower' is at the left-hand end, where they are fully self-motivated and the leader needs to do less to influence their motivation. Individuals may appear anywhere on the continuum from time to time and indeed can slip back to a lower level of motivation.

approaches to assist the follower with developing their task motivation maturity, of which more later.

So far, our leader, the Partner in the example, has been very 'transactional' in their approach (see Chapter 13). They have not given much attention to the *person* doing the task – the thoughts, feelings and context of the follower – save for recognising that when there is low task motivation maturity (Box 9.1), the person needs clear direction to reinforce their basic *raison d'être* or security at work (because anything less is going to leave too much to chance, which will compromise our follower's progress and indeed have a negative influence on the rest of the organisation). Where there is high task motivation maturity (Box 9.2), the follower would appreciate thanks but otherwise little intervention from the leader (because anything more is going to undermine the follower's confidence that they have done well – i.e. that they can achieve particular outcomes – and probably, in time, their motivation).

Let us turn to the working relationship between the leader and follower.

Relationship Orientation

First, a definition: relationship orientation is the degree to which the 'leader' engages in two-way or multi-way communication, giving 'socio-emotional' support by facilitating inter-actions, active listening and providing feedback to the 'follower'. This means considering the human dimension of the person undertaking the work.

As with task orientation, there is a range of approaches that the leader can take. Their approach will depend on the situation presented by the follower when undertaking the task. The degree to which the leader engages in relationship-orientated approaches will range from lower than average (and that does not mean zero) through to higher than average – the height or degree to which this approach is taken being dependent on the follower's needs and their relationship with the leader.

Again, this orientation can best be illustrated by example (see Box 9.3).

Now, let us consider the situation of our new recruit, Andrew, a couple of days into the job, where he has been able to get going with a few tasks but does not seem to be bothered with others (Box 9.4).

How the leader handles someone who is doing some of what is required of them, perhaps just the minimum to keep their job, but is not willing to do their full duties, perhaps coming up with some excuse or another not to do them, needs careful consideration. The leader needs to consider the follower's motivation maturity.

Simply reinforcing their tasks as part of their job role relies solely on the leader to influence and misses the opportunity to involve others in developing the follower's motivation maturity. The leader needs to address both the task motivation orientation *and* the person doing the task. The leader's style needs to change in order to help the follower improve their motivation further – the follower needs to see their role develop from a personal context into a team function. In other words, the leader and follower need to open a dialogue so that the leader can explain further about the role in such a way that the follower feels they personally are more involved in a group setting.

Box 9.3: Motivation control with a new recruit on the first day into a job

Let us take Andrew, our new recruit. On the first day, when he is exploring the parameters of the project, it is not particularly helpful if the Partner overseeing the project engages in too much open dialogue, asking 'How do you feel we might use IT strategically?' or 'What do you think about our firm and e-commerce . . . ?' It's too soon. As said earlier, Andrew just needs a clear understanding of his role and contribution so he can get on with meeting the requirements of the project.

Followers need leaders to ensure that they have made a positive impact on their role and place in the organisation – that person needs to feel secure as soon as possible and not at a loose end to find their own way. In this situation, the follower is unlikely to respond to too high a relationship orientation – it is too early.

Box 9.4: Motivation control with a new recruit when they are still not doing things they are capable of, and should do, a few days into a job

Let us take Andrew, our new recruit, a couple of days into his new job. The Partner has been monitoring things and finds that the main parts of the project are underway but that there are some other fundamental activities that Andrew doesn't seem to be bothered to do yet is quite capable of doing them. He always seems to find some excuse for not doing them. These shortfalls have annoyed one or two others in the firm who still have to do these things themselves in addition to their usual duties.

The Partner could just tell Andrew, as before, that these tasks are part of the project parameters, he is expected to do them as part of that contract and that he would be appreciated for doing them. Would this high level of motivational control have the desired effect? It might, although since he knows he is doing most other things in the contract, he may not be motivated to do them just because he was told that he should.

So, what of the person, how might he feel about his other duties in the context of the firm?

Here, the Partner can relinquish some of her input into motivation control and bring in peer-group influences.

While Andrew may feel secure in his role, what about his sense of belonging to a peer group that values his contribution? He needs help to develop his own motivation maturity in the role.

The leader can do this by getting others to take an active part in the process of motivation development of the follower. This leader's style now gives an insight into the knock-on effect of the follower's activity as a team function, showing the wider picture of the job, reinforcing the follower's contribution to others. It may be that the follower's work does not have a direct impact on another department; it just means that they do the task, saving someone else time.

The leader is still likely to monitor the situation to ensure that the correct motivational messages come through properly, but may start to guide the follower in becoming aware of it, i.e. more awareness about how other parts of the job contribute to team effort. Naturally, organisational culture plays a part in ensuring other people's contribution to the whole is acknowledged appropriately.

In this way, the follower has discovered something valuable: the fact that others appreciate their contribution to the team effort is fulfilling a sense of belonging, however temporary in the case of the contract worker in our scenario. But there are problems: for the follower to learn about the motivation that can come from being part of a team, they have to have their motivation reinforced by the leader and, particularly, the rest of the team. This requires the manager to relinquish some control of the motivation development to others. This could be a block to both the leader's and follower's progress – the follower might not feel a sense of belonging if their contribution is not appreciated as expected or that, while appreciated, nobody let them know. If this happens, the leader might have to go back to square one and apply more motivation control which, as suggested, might have only a limited and short-term effect.

Let us assume that the team shows their appreciation for his contribution to their efforts, Andrew feels a sense of belonging, so now let us move things forward a few weeks and consider another scenario between him and the Partner (see Box 9.5).

In order to help a follower develop their task motivation maturity, the leader needs to consider their interaction and provide continued 'socio-emotional' support, engaging them in a dialogue about their thought process, inviting them to think about their own feelings and satisfactions from doing a particular piece of work. If the follower comes up with recognising they can build their own sense of worth to the team, they will be able to improve their sense of value without persistent recourse to further input from the team or from the leader. Their feelings of self-motivation would have more impact on them and be longer lasting too.

Once the follower has been able to demonstrate higher levels of task motivation maturity, it is time for the leader to 'let go'. At this stage, the follower is going to need less guidance or feedback – again emphasising that this does not mean they don't get any support – from the leader. Let us finally consider how the Partner might deal with the relationship orientation as far as the work that Andrew did for the refreshment area (see Box 9.6).

So, at the top end of the 'motivation' range, when the follower's task motivation maturity is its highest, followers appreciate being 'left alone' to innovate on their own, being creative without too much involvement from others, save the occasional bit of interest and nod of appreciation. In other words, provided they are aware of others' support and encouragement, they will maintain their task motivation.

Box 9.5: Motivation maturity development with a new recruit when he suddenly appears less motivated a couple of weeks into a job

Andrew, our new recruit, is a couple of weeks into his IT project. He knows that the work he has been doing on the project is of value to others and he has been getting some positive feedback from both the Partner and some of her colleagues in the firm. While still recognising that he is on a short-term contract, he was also invited to play rugby with the Managing Partner last Saturday and was involved with the rest of the staff when they went ten-pin bowling.

While Andrew seemed very willing to attend to the detail of the project and do the less interesting but nonetheless important parts of the work, the Partner in charge has heard that he missed some key information during data entry and some problems have occurred; she ponders what to do.

This time she knows he can recognise the team dynamics and prompts him to think about what it means to him, and during one of their regular project updates asks him, 'So, how's the data input going on the project?' 'Oh, OK' is his non-committal answer. Undeterred she continues, 'OK, so what about the new rates for the tutors in the new year from April 2006?

With this prompt, he recognises that he cannot evade the issue. 'OK, the database is established but the new data just needs to be put in, anyone can do it and, er, I didn't have time.'

With clarity of the specific issue as it might affect others raised, the Partner can then invite Andrew to think about his own feelings if he did the work for the team. 'How do you think you'd feel when you completed the data entry for others and the whole system worked correctly?' 'Well, quite chuffed, I suppose.'

In this scenario, the Partner has not been giving plaudits herself or getting tangible responses from others for Andrew; she has opened him to the opportunity to see self-satisfaction from doing work, knowing the contribution it would make to others, thereby directing him to build his own self-worth from his own actions. While the interaction may take a little longer than taking charge of the task and telling Andrew how much he and his work is valued – he knows that and he has been through that stage already – this approach is likely to have a more lasting effect.

At this stage of Andrew's motivation maturity development, as noted in the quote at the beginning of this chapter, it is not what happens when the Partner is there, it is what happens when she is not.

> **Box 9.6: Self-motivation from a new recruit who identifies a useful business improvement several weeks into the job**
>
> Andrew has been working for Duncan Alexander & Wilmshurst for several weeks now and is completing his main project within time and budget. He looked at the rest area where he and the rest of the staff made coffee and could have their lunch – it was underused. Most people seemed to take their lunch in the company of their e-mails or surf for the latest deals at their desks.
>
> He'd always enjoyed tinkering with computers and had built his own in a varnished wooden box at home – very 1950s. He noticed that a workstation was being replaced so, in his own time, he fitted a faster processor, more RAM and cleared the hard drive. He wired it into the LAN, set up Internet surf protection and a set of his own old small speakers so that it could be used for broadcast radio. He called it the DAW Internet Café – and got people talking together at lunchtime.
>
> As mentioned earlier, The Partner overhears others in the firm thanking him for the facility and saying how much he has enjoyed putting his ideas into practice. He requires little of the Partner in this situation but her thanks would always be appreciated.

Remember, a person's task motivation maturity will be specific for a given area of work; if they attain Level 4 for one task (such as IT developments in our example) the follower is going to be at Level 1 for a new project or a significant job change. For a new project – say, developing a new voice data system – the follower may slip back some way along the task motivation maturity continuum. They may move back in stages or go right back to square one and need the leader's intervention to set some controls again.

Let us put these two dimensions – concern for the task (the person's task motivation maturity) and concern for the person (degree of socio-emotional support and two-way interaction required) into one model (see Figure 9.2), the Motivation Development Model (MDM).

Adapting to the MDM

By taking each level along the task motivation maturity scale, we can identify practical approaches to helping people develop their own motivation that fits with the Motivation Development Model.

Level 1 – *security* of tenure in the workplace

At this level, the 'leader' identifies that they need to take control of the person's most fundamental motivation to ensure that the job gets done. This may be because the 'follower'

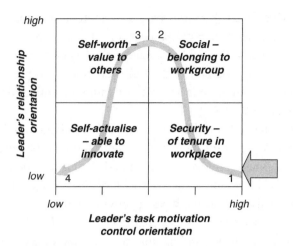

Figure 9.2 Mackay's Motivation Development Model (MDM).

is not at all motivated to do their job, or a large part of their job description's duties, to the required standard. The leader has identified something in the 'task motivation maturity' in the follower that they need to address.

While not threatening a person with disciplinary action as a first choice, it needs to be made clear that this work is expected of them, that others will appreciate their contribution (when it is made) and that the organisation – or their manager as a representative of it – will welcome the task being done to the required standard too. The leader may need to help the follower identify that their task motivation maturity is low – perhaps that their excuses for not doing it are no longer valid – and that they can see the value in doing the task to the required standard.

The leader will also have to monitor progress as the follower will need appropriate feedback to remain motivated – in other words, catch someone doing it right.

At this level, the leader's style is one of establishing the person's *security* at work.

- *Level 1 motivation*. Set controls on the basic level of motivation to get the job started and monitor closely. Give positive feedback where possible.

Level 2 – sense of *belonging* to the workgroup

Here, the 'follower' has demonstrated their motivation to do the task in accordance with their job description and has shown that their motivation is developing. It has to be said that most people start their jobs at least at this level and it is only the most poorly motivated individuals that drop below this level in their task motivation maturity. While most followers will be at or have moved some way along the motivation bar, indicating that the 'leader' needs to be slightly less focused on the basics of motivation, not everyone will by any means be completely motivated in every respect for all tasks.

At this stage, the follower will quickly indicate a need to gain acceptance from their work colleagues. This behaviour on the part of the follower should tell the leader that they would benefit from adopting a different style in order to gain the motivation they need to do the task more completely and effectively.

So, in general terms, the follower is only moderately motivated to do the whole task, but has indicated that they are ready for their further contribution to be recognised more widely. Thus, the leader adopts a more interactive style and develops a team approach of acceptance and mutual support. Therefore, the leader is aware of the context of a person at work and their adapting to a mutually supportive working environment.

Again, the leader will need to identify what controls need to be in place to ensure the feedback is positive and supportive, and monitor to some degree, but the follower may begin to undertake some self-evaluation of their contribution to the team.

At this level, the leader's style is one of developing a *sense of belonging* to the workgroup and relinquishing control of some of the motivating factors.

- *Level 2 motivation.* Explore team dynamics to bring others along and invite others and follower into monitoring positive feedback.

Level 3 – *self-worth* and value to others

When a 'follower' realises that their contribution to the team is appreciated and they are feeling positive about the situation, they will indicate a higher level of motivation maturity and will need somewhat less intervention from the 'leader' but not none at all. This is because, although they are becoming more motivated, the leader still cannot leave them to their own devices because they will not be fully committed and involved. They may not be ready to bring their full potential to the work they do. At this stage, a follower may undertake the majority of their job but still indicate a lack of commitment, attention to detail or some work not being delivered on time.

Now, if the leader is too task motivation orientated and explains why they should as it is part of their job or how much the team/organisation regard their contribution, these approaches will not work in the long run. Next time they give less than they might through a lack of motivation in some area, the follower will need direct support all over again.

Do you want a team of 'dependent energy-sappers' (who keep asking for others to keep them going) or a team of 'energisers' (who are able to feel good about what they are doing – and in turn will make others feel good about what they are doing too)?

At this level, the leader and follower engage in a discussion to explore the follower's feeling of self-worth and their own perspective of value to others. In other words, the leader asks the appropriate questions, such as 'How will you feel about a job well done...?' or 'What do you think others think of someone who gets on with their job...?', or 'What way are you going to make a real difference around here?', etc. The leader can also get the follower to identify how they will recognise how well they are contributing on their own and then they can largely monitor achievement themselves.

It may be that in this situation the follower actually has all the ability in the world to undertake a task but there is some other underlying factor preventing them from getting on with it alone. This is where socio-emotional support is so crucial. Again, telling someone else to give them encouragement as a team member may not be what the individual needs, but a discussion of the issues that can help them find their own self-motivation – especially when no one is looking! At this level, leaders need to be prepared for any ability shortfall and that the follower can actually do the tasks. Equally, there may be something outside of work affecting an individual's motivation or confidence. It may not always be purely motivation that is necessarily lacking at this level.

At this level, the leader's style is one of helping others find their own self-motivation from within.

- *Level 3 motivation.* Help people to establish their own thinking, asking 'What will you feel like when it's done?' and help identify how the follower can reaffirm their own value to others and the organisation.

Level 4 – *self-actualisation* and innovation

Here, the 'follower' is motivated to do the task with little intervention from the 'leader' or anyone else. The leader has confidence in the motivation of the follower and demonstrates through trust and assurances that the individual's innovation and ideas are valued.

Developing trust gives the follower further motivation to continue where they have found their own intrinsic reward in doing the task; they may have the confidence to bring their energy to innovate and discover that the task can be done more efficiently or more effectively than the defined standard.

Finally, they are in no doubt about their own task motivation maturity. Provided no one adversely affects their MAC Factors, all they need from the leader is occasional reinforcement of their personal contribution. Over-supervision or too much 'just checking you are OK' from the leader is not needed, and indeed may damage the relationship and undermine the follower.

At this level, the leader's style is one of allowing self-actualisation in the job – finally letting go for this task.

- *Level 4 motivation.* Reinforce success and ask them for innovative solutions, asking 'Why not?' rather than challenging their ideas.

Evaluating a Scenario

In the following scenario, taken from one of the specific style evaluation questionnaires developed by the author, consider the situation and look for clues as to what level the person is on their task motivation maturity continuum, Levels 1–4. Then look at the four alternative approaches to deal with the problem – what would you do?

You are a manager in a small firm and broke your ankle at an ice-rink with the children. You have been absent from work, missing the first meeting of a cross-functional group you had offered to chair to explore and discuss options available before making recommendations for purchasing an upgrade to the computer system. On your return to work, you found at the second meeting that they are getting on with it; they have developed many good ideas of their own and are near to making a recommendation. You are unsure of your current role and how you should integrate into the team. You would:

a. Let the team carry on as before and you stay on the sidelines.
b. Take over the running of the meeting and make sure it runs to the project brief.
c. Reinforce the good ideas developed thus far and start a discussion on the ideal system requirements.
d. Let them know what a great contribution to the firm they have made to date and take charge of activities.

The clues to this group's task motivation maturity are *'that the group are getting on with it and that they have developed many good ideas of their own'*, suggesting Level 4 and that they are *'near to making a recommendation'* that they are about to complete the task. So, there is nothing to suggest they are compromised – while you had 'offered' to lead it (as Chair) your ideas may have value but there is nothing to suggest that you are the expert and it is a *'cross-functional group'* anyway.

- If you did 'b' and took over confining them to the project brief, you will instantly undermine two good meetings that have moved the goalposts along; you would be lucky not to get your other leg broken!
- If you did 'd' it might reinforce their contribution and value to the firm – but they know that anyway. Their motivation to work as a team is not in question either.
- If you did 'c' you would at least have reinforced their sense of self-worth, having acknowledged that they have come up with some good ideas. However, bringing them back to the project brief may compromise their willingness to innovate and you may find that their ideas generation simply dries up.
- 'a' is the preferred option as it does not undermine your belief that they can bring their ideas to the fore and they will be feeling justly proud of their contribution. Assuming

their ideas are valid, and their recommendations come through into the computer system implemented, they will have great ownership of the outcome. Trusting their task motivation maturity will serve to maintain a relationship of trust between the two parties and they are more likely to innovate in other areas of their work.

In summary, it is important to remember two key parameters of the model, as outlined below.

Task motivation maturity is a two-way process

It is not a one-way street. People do lose their way and slip back along their task motivation maturity continuum; the other factors of Ability and Confidence have an impact on Motivation, as all three 'MAC Factors' are interrelated. Addressing one of the factors can have an influence on the other two. Just because someone can't be bothered to do some small part of their job from time to time, the 'leader' does not have to go right back to square one and control the motivation basics all over again.

Situational effectiveness is clear

Situational effectiveness is easy to comprehend. In the scenario above, the further away we are in our motivation development style from what the 'follower' *needs*, the less our effectiveness. Equally, the closer we are to matching the *current* needs of the follower, given their *immediate* situation (not what they *used* to be like), the more effective we are.

We can evaluate an effectiveness score simply. In the above scenario, which ideally called out for a 'leader' to 'leave them innovating', we could 'score' the responses according to Table 9.1.

Table 9.1 Evaluating the effectiveness of each style – according to the demands of the 'follower' in the scenario in this chapter

Response	Style	Score	Commentary
b	Enforce security	−2	Simply taking over and getting them to stick to the brief will compromise the relationship, so is much less effective
d	Develop belonging	−1	They already work well as a team and they know their contribution is what the firm wants, so nothing is gained
c	Identify self-worth	+1	Reinforcing self-worth is not 'wrong'; it may not compromise the outcomes this time, it is just less effective
a	Leave to innovate	+2	The most effective – it reinforces their ideas now (they'll buy in to the project outcomes) and they'll innovate elsewhere too

For a further evaluation of your situational task motivation maturity style, consult the companion web pages.

Summary

In this chapter you have:

- Explored a way of looking at how much a manager might influence a person's motivation
- Considered both the task being done and the person doing the work – and explored the interaction of the two variables
- Looked at four levels of motivation and what to explore at each level – security, sense of belonging, self-esteem, self-actualisation
- Been introduced to a practical model for motivation development
- Begun to uncover a way of evaluating your management style, its flexibility and its effectiveness.

Questions

1. Thinking of your own situation, what would give you more security in your workplace and what might undermine it?
2. How does your workgroup develop a sense of belonging. How might it do more – other than by running social events outside of work?
3. What particular value do you feel you bring to your workgroup? How might you develop this in others?
4. Given sufficient freedom, what might you like to do on your own initiative to make a significant improvement in the workplace? Make a justified case for your ideas.

Further Reading

Blanchard, K. and Johnson, S. (1983) *The One Minute Manager*, William Collins.
Hersey, P. (1999) *The Situational Leader*, Pfeiffer & Co.
Mackay, A. R. (2007) *Recruiting, Retaining and Releasing People*, Butterworth-Heinemann.

Part 3

Ability Building

10

The Learning Organisation

... the main reason why Britain is the fourth-largest economy today is that it used to be the largest; fourth place represents relative decline.

Stern, 2003, p. 91

Learning Outcomes

With today's rapidly changing influences on organisations, the only sustainable competitive advantage is the ability to learn faster – so how do we develop a learning organisation? This chapter, and its companion web pages, look at how to do just that. The chapter has been written to cover particular elements of the National Occupational Standards for Management and Leadership (*Managing Self and Personal Skills – Unit 3*; *Providing Direction – Unit 11*; *Working with People – Unit 28*; and *Achieving Results – Unit 50*) and it covers some of the requirements of the Chartered Management Institute's Diploma in Management compulsory *Unit C41 – Developing your Management Style* (in respect of developing yourself), some of the compulsory *Unit C45 – Managing Performance* and most of the optional *Unit O42 – Developing Personnel and Personnel Performance*. This chapter will also be of value to those studying the CIPD Professional Development Scheme – particularly the *Leadership and Management* and *People Management and Development* modules as well as people studying any of the CIPD specialist electives in *Learning and Development*.

By the end of this chapter you will:

- See the benefits of developing a learning organisation
- Recognise that the best form of learning is properly managed workplace experience
- Uncover different theories to learning
- Have explored learning in an organisational context
- Had a brief review of Investors in People

- Seen the place of learning in the European Foundation for Quality Management Excellence Model
- Have been introduced to Learning Management Systems.

On the Need for Learning

> *The abandonment by teachers of the traditional methods of teaching reading, known as phonics, precipitated the greatest educational catastrophe of the last 50 years ... (this) represents the greatest educational betrayal of the past 20 years, reducing the life chances of an estimated 4 million children.*
>
> (Clare, 2005)

With a fifth of children leaving primary school not having reached the basic reading standards, there is a problem lying in wait for them and their future employers. And it seems that education standards are slipping throughout the system.

In July 2003, the British government published a new 140-page White Paper, '*21st Century Skills – Realising Our Potential*'. It acknowledged that we now have a workforce in which nearly 8 million people have failed to acquire the equivalent of five decent GCSEs, and where too many still enter the world of work having had a dismal experience of education and training.

Even our graduates, it seems, are not particularly capable. The Forum of Private Businesses conducted a survey of their members in mid-2005. More than half of the 400 firms responding to the survey thought that their graduate employees were 'average to poor' at time-keeping or taking a telephone message. Nearly three-quarters described them as 'very poor, poor or average' at addressing a letter, and more than half thought them 'average' or 'poor' in numeracy and literacy (*The Daily Telegraph*, 2005).

About 21 million of us use information technology in some form at work, but 57 per cent of employers say that their staff are not adequately trained in IT to do their jobs properly (Stern, 2003, p. 93); this mismatch severely undermining UK productivity.

The UK stands 11th out of 15 in the EU for GDP output per head, 18th out of 30 in the OECD (Organisation for Economic Cooperation and Development – see http://www.oecd.org/home/) and has slipped to the fourth largest world economy where once it was at number one. The low-skills culture has been tolerated for so long in the UK that it is hardly surprising that some business leaders have given up hope of seeing any improvement in the situation. Talent is hard to come by and thin on the ground – it seems that poaching other people's staff is the only way of rapidly acquiring the skilled workforce that is needed.

But why train staff who are going to be poached by someone else? Unfortunately, for an OECD nation like the UK, the low-skills, low-cost, low-quality strategy is doomed. China, India and the rest of the developing world are industrialising fast, offering, in some areas, world-class manufacturing and services at a fraction of the cost of the developed world.

Barry Sheerman MP (Labour, Huddersfield) is Chair of the APPGM (All Party Parliamentary Group on Management); he suggests that *'management should be taught as a key component of every child's education and that it should be integrated as an attractive option in further and higher education'*. Equally, he argues, the chance of acquiring management skills cannot be limited to early in the career path – everyone should be offered the appropriate learning opportunity and experiences in the form most useful to them (*Management Today*, 2005).

But the UK corporate sector is spending £10.6 billion on training, where three and a half million employees receive training every month. Firms that are investing in their staff's training do so as they know it will make people more likely to stay and, at a certain point, they require a commitment from the employee in return. Often, a firm paying for an employee's MBA course may require a two-year commitment to remain.

The principal problem is that there is too much training of limited value – a few firms try hard to measure the real value for attending 'soft-skills' training such as leadership, teamworking, coaching, assertiveness or personal effectiveness training. The truth is that many training courses are just perks for managers: nice hotel, use of gym, jacuzzi, fine wines and a good chef.

However, how does one equate learning with training? The best learning is done at work – the best teachers are not trainers, they are talented people doing the job that others are learning to do, with the time and inclination to help others along. These softer skills, in particular, are best taught by example (see 'Social Learning', Chapter 11). If you want to be a great leader, go and work for one.

Rather than abdicating responsibility for learning to outsiders, firms need to build it into everyday life. While it might be easier to write a cheque and send someone off for a few days, it would be better to structure an internal 'course' of learning, which might involve releasing the time of senior staff on a regular basis, building shared learning into reward systems and taking time to find out what the staff already know.

Learning from Failure

Only those who dare to fail greatly can ever achieve greatly.

Robert F. Kennedy

While Homer Simpson's alternative philosophy might be that 'trying is the first step to failure', in the USA failure is more acceptable than in the UK. Once the country of the 'winner', times are a-changing! Failure is now the new success – particularly in the world of celebrities:

- Angus Deayton – sacked from the BBC but earns £20 000 a night as an after-dinner speaker, has landed a part in the film *Making Waves* and the BBC didn't replace him after all.
- Winona Ryder – caught shoplifting at Saks in Fifth Avenue but became the model for Marc Jacobs, the US designer whose clothes she was caught with.
- Jeffrey Archer – did 'time' for perjury, but his *A Prison Diary* netted him £200 000 and his new book *Sons of Fortune* could yield £10 million.
- George Michael – caught doing something 'lewd' in a public lavatory, but went on to make a song about it and is still a pop music chart topper; even being 'slumped in his car' under the influence of class C drugs was no drawback.
- Hugh Grant – caught 'curb-crawling' prostitutes in the US yet has gone on to earn millions for his screen appearances.

Perhaps the 19th century author and publisher Elbert Hubbard was right when he said: *'A failure is a man who has blundered but is not able to capitalise on the experience'.*

In the UK, setbacks such as redundancy – certainly bankruptcy – used to mean career death; now, with our more generous employment practices, they have become a badge of honour. Today, business failure is seen as the price of being on the front edge, having a passion for what you are doing against the odds. In the past, nobody wanted to be branded a failure, but now it shows you are creative – a risk-taker.

However, the US and the UK differed until recently in their approach to bankruptcy. The main purpose of personal bankruptcy in America is to protect the debtor: the process is instantaneous, where the debtor can apply immediately for credit and start again. In the UK, the origins and practice of personal insolvency are different. The American system assumes misfortune, relief and assistance, whereas the English system assumes that inability to pay debts implies at least immorality and recklessness, and probably worse. With a system based on punishment, until the late 1800s bankrupts were sent to debtor's prisons and remained until someone paid off the debt. Today, a bankrupt cannot be a director of a company or manage a business. If they apply for credit, they must announce their bankruptcy – failure to do so may lead to imprisonment.

In the 1990s the source for learning business acumen was focused on management books (like this one!) and MBA courses. However, classrooms and theoretical texts are no longer enough. People want to be inspired and to learn from others' successes – and to learn from their mistakes. Reality business TV (such as *The Apprentice*, *Dragons' Den* and *Risking It All*, even the property development and home make-over programmes) provides a 'warts and all' approach to business activity where the failures are not edited out. Sadly for the participants, they are usually the most entertaining part of the programme.

The programmes do show individuals with an extreme desire to succeed, people with a passion and determination – even if many managers might not want them in their teams. But is this the right reaction? While many may admire an Alan Sugar or Richard Branson – self-made business people who can inspire and entertain – would we know how to manage people like that if they were in our team?

So, here is the challenge for future business leaders: how can individuals with entrepreneurial spirit become integrated into our business organisation?

In a report from Orange (*The Sunday Times*, 2005), it became clear that there was a desire among employees to have the freedom to enjoy and demonstrate their personal values – a trait up to now only associated with the most entrepreneurial individuals or companies. In the future, successful organisations are going to be those that are entrepreneurial enough to encourage development based on the personal beliefs of their employees – and can retain their best staff.

In order to benefit from failure, individuals and organisations have to have the power of reflection and build models of the success and failures – all the emergent literature shows that good leaders milk their experience and admit their own failure. Good leadership rests on the acknowledgement of incompetence; encourage your people to confess their ignorance, because that is where learning and constructive action begins. This notion will be explored further in Model I and Model II learning later in this chapter.

The Learning Organisation

The notion of the 'learning organisation' is closely related to the idea of the 'learning society' and the 'knowledge economy'. The major contributor to this work was Donald Schön, who provided a theoretical framework linking the experience of living in a situation of increasing change with the need for learning. The loss of a stable state means that our society and all of its institutions and organisations are in continuous processes of transformation. There will be no stable states that will endure for a decade – let alone our own lifetimes! Thus, we must learn to understand, guide, influence and manage these transformations, and we need to make the capacity for undertaking them integral to ourselves as individuals as well as to our organisations.

The learning organisation concept was popularised by Peter Senge (1990). He defined learning organisations as 'organisations where people continually expand their capacity to create the results they truly desire, where new and expansive patterns of thinking are nurtured, where collective aspiration is set free, and where people are continually learning to see the whole together'. The basic rationale for such organisations is that in situations of rapid change only those that are flexible, adaptive and productive will excel. For this to

> **Box 10.1: 'If we only knew what we knew, we could double our profits' (quote taken from a management workshop run by the author with 'One Account')**
>
> Some experts in the field of business analysis believe that most organisations already hold or have ready access to 80 per cent of the information required for assessing business development and the competition in the field. The great irony of many large corporations is that by encouraging individual business unit profitability, management often ends up building information barriers. As a consequence of employees wanting their own business unit to succeed, they will often withhold information from another business unit. In such instances, good business practice can work against good intelligence practice – and the organisation can't learn.

happen, he argued, organisations need to 'discover how to tap people's commitment and capacity to learn at all levels'. As Box 10.1 suggests, in many organisations this is not possible.

So, what are the sorts of behaviours and beliefs that are necessary if organisations are to learn and develop? Chris Argyris (1990) has been influential in underpinning our understanding of what guides the learning organisation.

Our starting point is Argyris and Schön's (1974) argument that people have mental maps with regard to how to act in various situations. This involves the way people undertake three important steps: plan, implement and review their actions. Furthermore, they assert that it is these maps that guide people's actions rather than the theories they explicitly use to describe 'why they did what they did' (i.e. *espouse*). The writers went on to say that fewer people are aware of the maps or theories they actually use (Argyris, 1980). One way of understanding this is to say that there is often a split between theory and action. However, Argyris and Schön suggest that two *theories of action* are involved.

Theory-in-use and espoused theory

The distinction made by Argyris between the two contrasting theories of action is between those theories that underpin what we do as practitioners and managers, and those which we use to tell others about our actions. The former can be described as *theories-in-use*. They govern our actual behaviour and tend to be tacit or unspoken structures.

However, when someone is asked how he or she would behave under certain circumstances, the answer usually given is their *espoused theory* of action for that situation. This is the theory of action to which they adhere to, and which, when asked to explain, they communicate to others. (Remember, the theory that actually governs their actions is *theory-in-use*.) The words they use to convey what they do, or what they would like others to think they do, Argyris termed *espoused theory*.

Suppose someone suddenly rushes out of the office unexpectedly; in explaining their actions to a colleague they may come up with some convenient piece of theory. They might explain their sudden departure to others, or even to themselves at some level, by saying that a 'crisis' had arisen with a client. This would be their 'espoused theory'. The 'theory-in-use' (the real reason for leaving) might be quite different. They may have become bored and tired by the paperwork or meeting, been anxious that they might be singled out for some unwelcome task and felt that a quick trip out to an apparently urgent matter would bring welcome relief.

Making this distinction allows us to ask questions about the extent to which the drivers of behaviour fit with espoused theory, and whether inner feelings actually become expressed in actions. In other words, is there congruence between the two? Argyris (1980) made the case that effectiveness results from developing congruence between theory-in-use and espoused theory. A key role of reflection in learning could be to reveal the theory-in-use and to explore the nature of the 'fit'. Much of the business of supervision, where it is focused on the manager's thoughts, feelings and actions, is concerned with the gulf between espoused theory and theory-in-use, or in bringing the latter to the surface. This gulf can be useful; if it gets too wide then there is clearly a difficulty. But provided the two remain connected then the gap creates a method for reflection and for dialogue about management practice.

To help understand theory-in-use we require a model of the processes involved (see Figure 10.1). To this end, Argyris and Schön (1974) initially looked to three elements:

- *Governing variables*. Those controls that people are trying to keep within acceptable limits. Any action is likely to impact upon a number of such variables – thus, any situation can trigger a trade-off among governing variables.
- *Action strategies*. The moves and plans used by people to keep their governing variables or values within the acceptable range.
- *Consequences*. These are what happen as a result of an action. These can be both intended – those actions we believe will result – and unintended. In addition, those consequences can be for the self and/or for others (see also Anderson, 1997).

To give an everyday example, let us consider controlling our winter office temperature with a simple convector heater. Suppose our 'governing variable' was to keep the temperature

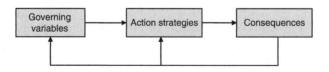

Figure 10.1 Model 'I' of theory-in-use, after Argyris and Schön (1974).

that the office workers agreed on consensus was the most comfortable for work, at $20 \pm 2°C$. Our 'action strategy' will be to set the thermostat to that temperature. The 'consequences' would be the thermostat turning the heating on or off to keep the temperature between the limits.

Where the consequences of a strategy used are what the person wanted, then the theory-in-use is confirmed. This is because there is a match between intention and outcome. However, in more complex situations, particularly when dealing with people, there may be a mismatch between the two and then the consequences may be unintended.

The consequences may also not match, or work against, the person's governing values. Argyris and Schön suggest two responses to this mismatch, and these can be seen in the notion of single- and double-loop learning.

A model for single- and double-loop learning

For Argyris and Schön, learning involves the detection and correction of error. Where something goes wrong, they suggested, the first option for many people is to look for another strategy that will address and work within the governing variables. In other words, given or chosen goals, values, plans and rules are controlling rather than questioned – this is *single-loop learning*.

Taking our office temperature example, suppose that, at midday, the winter sun on the windows was such that the internal temperature rose above 22°; the thermostat on the convector heater would not now be able to function as a temperature control keeping the room temperature within specified limits. So, if the action strategy were revised by readjusting the heating controls, clearly the office would not cool down to within acceptable limits of the governing variable – to keep the office temperature at $20 \pm 2°C$. Hence, in this situation, a different action strategy would need to be employed – installing an air-conditioning unit – to achieve the required consequences.

An alternative response when an error occurs is to question the governing variables themselves, to subject them to critical scrutiny. Argyris and Schön describe this as *double-loop learning*. Such learning may then lead to an alteration in the governing variables and, thus, a shift in the way in which strategies and consequences are framed. This would be the case in a true learning organisation.

Back to our office temperature example; suppose the staff decide to revise their 'ideal' working temperature to be more environmentally friendly to help the organisation reduce its heating bill by 10 per cent – lowering its carbon footprint.[1] The staff then would develop a revised 'governing variable' of winter heating of 18–20°C to include the environmental/cost reduction criteria. This would revise their 'action strategy' by resetting the thermostat.

---

[1] A carbon footprint is the amount of carbon dioxide emitted each year due to the energy we use.

Consequently, if temperatures rose above 20°, in order to keep within their new, revised governing variable they would agree to open the windows rather than use energy to run an air-conditioning unit.

Thus, when the error detected and corrected permits the organisation to carry on its present policies or achieve its present objectives, then that error-and-correction process is *single-loop* learning. Single-loop learning is like our thermostat that learns when it is too hot or too cold and turns the heat on or off. The thermostat can perform this task because it can receive information (the temperature of the room) and take corrective action. *Double-loop* learning occurs when error is detected and corrected in ways that involve the modification of an organisation's underlying norms, policies and objectives.

This process can be represented quite easily by a simple amendment of our initial representation of theory-in-use (see Figure 10.2).

Single-loop learning seems to be present when goals, values, frameworks and, to a significant extent, strategies are taken for granted. The emphasis is on techniques employed and making those techniques more efficient. Any reflection is directed toward making the strategy more effective – a focus on technical issues. It involves following routines and some sort of preset plan – and is both less risky for the individual and the organisation, and offers greater control.

Double-loop learning, in contrast, involves questioning the role of the framing and learning systems that underlie actual goals and strategies. This is more creative and reflective, and involves consideration of the objectives and culture of the organisation. Reflection here is more fundamental: the basic assumptions behind ideas or policies are confronted, hypotheses are publicly tested, and processes are not directly confirmed and are not self-seeking.

How can organisations increase their capacity for double-loop learning? Double-loop learning is necessary if practitioners and organisations are to make informed decisions in rapidly changing and often uncertain environments.

The underlying theory is that the reasoning processes employed by individuals in organisations compromise the exchange of relevant information in ways that make double-loop learning difficult – and all but impossible in situations in which much is at stake. Those people who have created the 'status quo' in their organisation are the least likely to want to allow a change or challenge to it. This creates a dilemma, as these are the very organisational situations in which double-loop learning is most needed.

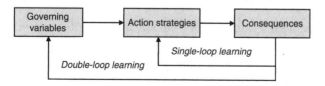

Figure 10.2 Model 'II' of theory-in-use, after Argyris and Schön (1974).

The next step that Argyris and Schön took was to set up two models that describe features of theories-in-use that either inhibit or enhance double-loop learning. The belief is that all people utilise a common theory-in-use in problematic situations. This they describe as Model I – and it can be said to inhibit double-loop learning. Model II is where the governing values associated with theories-in-use enhance double-loop learning.

Model I and Model II

To research deeper into these two models, see online on the companion web pages.

Organisational Learning

Does a 'learner' learn in isolation or is learning organisational? First, a term to help clarify understanding, Organisational Development.

Organisational Development (OD)

Organisational Development is the name given to those activities in the life of an organisation that aim to improve the way that it works – not from a process or technical point of view, but from the point of view of the human system and inter-relationships within the organisation.

In other words, OD is the practical application of the conclusions of the research into how people in the organisation work and how they can work better. Most often, OD is undertaken on a consultancy basis, whereby an external consultant helps the organisation change.

While firms are good at the technical things that they do, they often find it difficult to grapple with the interpersonal matters. The external OD consultant's job is to assist the company in this endeavour. Unfortunately, there is often considerable resistance to their work, since everyone considers themselves an expert in the soft-side of management (despite the evidence that most managers lack skills in this area); outside consultants' work is usually under constant attack – especially because they try to bring about changes that affect people's relationships, status and degrees of openness.

So what is learning?

Theorists have battled with trying to define what learning really is. Four ideas have emerged:

- *Behaviourist* – this movement in psychology looks at the person learning new behaviours in relation to their environment.
- *Cognitive* – considered the mental processes of learning, the act of knowing.

- *Humanist* – concerned with learning for human growth and development; Maslow and others are expressions of this work.
- *Social/situational orientation* – not so much that learners acquire structures or models to understand the world, they participate in frameworks that have structure, so learning involves participation in a community of practice.

So, back to the question, do learners learn in isolation or is learning organisational?

Chris Argyris and Donald Schön (1978) suggest that each person in an organisation constructs his or her own representation or image of the theory-in-use of the whole. The picture is always incomplete – so people are always trying to add pieces to get a view of the whole. It is argued that people need to know their place in the organisation. They suggest that an organisation is like an organism made up of many cells, each of which contains a partial and changing image of itself in relation to the whole; like an organism, the organisation's practice stems from those collective images.

Thus, any organisation is an artefact of the collective individual ways of representing that organisation. To understand organisational learning we must concern ourselves not with static entities called organisations but with the cognitive processes of organising those individuals that make up the organisation. Each person in that organisation is continually trying to know the organisation and to understand themselves in the context of that organisation. To do this, individuals need an external reference – a public representation of their organisation: organisational theory-in-use or a 'map', 'picture' or 'brand image' of their organisation. We saw the importance of this in the 'vision' or 'picture behaviour' of the CLS-Europe Model of the complete leader in Chapter 8.

So, in order to understand organisational learning, we need to join up the individual world of the worker with the world of the whole organisation. By looking at the way that people jointly construct the organisational map (the culture of the organisation), it is possible to define organisational learning – which involves the detection and correction of error – and organisational theory-in-use. For organisational learning to occur, learning ideas, discoveries, inventions, innovations and evaluations that 'correct errors' must be embedded in organisational memory. If it is not captured in the images that individuals have, and the maps they construct with others, then the individual will have learnt but the organisation will not have done so; the way it presents itself to the outside world will not improve.

At the organisational level, single-loop learning occurs when individual members of the organisation respond to changes in the internal or external environment of the organisation by detecting errors that they correct so as to maintain the central features of theory-in-use of the organisation – i.e. maintain the status quo. Double-loop organisational learning is the sort of enquiry that deals with any organisational values that don't 'fit' with the changing world by setting new priorities and norms themselves, together with associated strategies and assumptions.

Thus, Model I organisational learning is characterised by defensiveness, self-fulfilling prophecies, self-fuelling processes and escalating errors. Systems involve a web of feedback loops that make organisational assumptions and behavioural routines self-reinforcing – inhibiting detection and correction of error and giving rise to mistrust, defensiveness and 'I said it wouldn't work' mentalities. In other words, if individuals in an organisation make use of Model I learning, the organisation itself can begin to function in ways that act against its long-term interests – and, therefore, malfunction.

Managers need to create Model II learning at the organisational level. A sequence is suggested on the online companion web pages.

It has often been suggested that 'good' learning can only occur where there is a culture of openness and trust, where 'failures' are seen as an opportunity rather than a problem, and where 'political' behaviour is minimised. However, the very nature of people as individuals or interest groups coming together to form an organisation where the goals and aspirations come about through an ongoing debate determines that bargaining and negotiation are inherently political. So, perhaps it would be wise to incorporate politics into organisational learning, rather than to try to eradicate it.

While we have two models of learning – I and II – which are useful for teaching or sensitising us to consider different and important aspects of organisational life, these models overlook the notion that there may be alternatives between or beyond them. Equally, the suggestion above takes a sequential route through organisational learning; it may be argued that rather than there being a number of phases there could be a number of elements or dimensions working at once.

However, it has given us a way of 'learning our way out' of problems with organisational variables whose strategies and consequences do not meet the demands of the marketplace and as such presents a fair example of straightforward learning theory: that is, learning-in-action. In the classical learning cycle of Kolb (1984), one had to essentially learn by trial and error – whereas one can learn simply by reflecting on the theory-in-action. In other words, it is no longer necessary to go through the entire learning circle in order to develop the theory further. It is sufficient to readjust the theory through double-loop learning.

This is a very significant development and has important implications for educators. In the experiential learning model of Kolb, the educator is in essence a facilitator of a person's learning cycle. To this role can be added that of teacher, coach or mentor, the person who 'helps individuals (managers, professionals, workers) to reflect upon their theories-in-action' (Finger and Asún, 2000).

Sadly, the idea of organisational learning or the learning organisation may have run its course. During the new-economy boom in the late 1990s, learning and knowledge became the new 'hot ideas'. Organisations appointed 'chief knowledge officers' and knowledge management was the in-vogue approach to business; we were all knowledge workers, information was an asset to be managed and it formed the basis of our human capital or value. Unfortunately, managers clung to their old 'Model I' ways: knowledge is power. When managers feared for their jobs in the cycle of economic slow-downs, information stopped flowing up and down the business, making it hard to build a genuine learning organisation – individuals may have learnt but the organisation didn't.

When will they learn?

Investors in People

The Investors in People Standard has long been acknowledged as a business improvement tool, helping organisations of every size, type and location to gain more from their people in support of business goals. It is flexible enough to apply to any organisation and sets a standard for good practice in matching what people can do and are motivated to do with what the organisation needs them to do.

Benefits of being an 'Investor in People' include increased productivity, increased motivation, reduction in staff turnover, and higher customer and client satisfaction. It has been shown that companies recognised as Investors in People consistently outperform non-recognised competitors in terms of productivity and profitability.

A recent study (Databuild, 2004) showed that organisational changes made by companies with the Investors in People Standard ('recognised employers') are twice as profitable as changes made by other companies. Changes made by recognised employers in the three years prior to the study increased profit by 7.16 per cent of sales, or £505 per employee per year, compared to only 3.78 per cent of sales or £197 per employee per year by non-Investor in People organisations.

Developed in 1990 by a partnership of leading businesses and national organisations, the Standard helps organisations to improve performance and realise objectives through the management and development of their people. Since it was developed, the Standard has been reviewed every three years to ensure that it remains relevant, accessible and attractive to all. The most recent review was completed in November 2004.

Investors in People provides a flexible framework, which any organisation can adapt for its own requirements. It mirrors the business planning cycle (plan, do, review), making it clear for organisations to follow and implement in their own planning systems. The framework involves:

- *Plan* – developing strategies to improve the performance of the organisation
- *Do* – taking action to improve the performance of the organisation
- *Review* – evaluating the impact on the performance of the organisation.

The EFQM Model and Learning

The EFQM (European Foundation for Quality Management) is the primary source for organisations throughout Europe that are looking for more than quality, but are also striving to excel in their market and in their business (see http://www.efqm.org). Based in Brussels, the EFQM brings together over 700 member organisations and valued partners situated in every geographical region across the globe.

The EFQM is the creator of the prestigious European Quality Award that recognises the very top companies each year. EFQM is also the guardian of the EFQM Excellence Model, which provides organisations with a guideline on how to achieve and measure their success. EFQM is a not-for-profit membership foundation focused on serving its members' information and networking needs.

They argue that regardless of sector, size, structure or maturity, to be successful, organisations need to establish an appropriate management framework.

The EFQM Excellence Model was introduced at the beginning of 1992 as the framework for assessing organisations for the European Quality Award. Their web page says that it is now the most widely used organisational framework in Europe, and it has become the basis for the majority of national and regional Quality Awards.

The EFQM Excellence Model is a practical tool that can be used in a number of different ways:

- As a tool for self-assessment
- As a way to benchmark with other organisations
- As a guide to identify areas for improvement
- As the basis for a common vocabulary and a way of thinking
- As a structure for the organisation's management system.

More details of the model and a representation can be found online on the companion web pages.

Learning Management Systems

In the future, it is suggested, we will have learning delivered to people in their preferred style and in a timescale relevant to personal needs. A Learning Management System (LMS) offers a different way of using and managing the training function. It offers both learners and organisations control over their future development.

The composition of the LMS may include training administration, registration, scheduling, reporting, skills gap analysis, competency model certification or accreditation testing, compliance auditing and tracking. Working together, they provide a powerful service to the learner. Within organisational guidelines, learners may be able to access their personal training record, view course content, enrol on classroom events, access online discussion groups or information repositories, take online tests and assess their training requirements, plus a host of other functions.

For the organisation an LMS is a point of access to information about an employee's development history and to a course content library and accreditation standard. This enables managers to assess, budget, track and manage employee knowledge. So what does an organisation have to consider before adopting an LMS? A prime concern should be how learning and development are managed currently and where a change could increase the deliverables. Identification of business objectives and ways in which training can help meet these are key. So too is an honest evaluation of an organisation's IT infrastructure and how it will meet the requirement.

The advantages of the LMS to the organisation may include the wealth of information to which they now have access. An LMS also promises that training and HR departments can manage resources in a more efficient and cost-effective way. Administration becomes less cumbersome, and classrooms, tutors, content libraries and access to information are centralised.

But looking at the cost justification of acquisition, how will the organisation measure ROI (return on investment)?

From a learner's perspective, the organisation will be seen to be encouraging self-management of learning by a faster and better identification of training needs. Regular appraisals by the individual and their manager will promote learning and creation of transferable skills and will, in turn, open avenues of career progression. The organisation will benefit by identifying achievers, by honing strengths and addressing areas for improvement.

Training needs analysis will assist just-in-time training to become a reality because the information required to make it happen is immediately available. Cost saving will result because training is targeted on a need-to-know basis rather than blanket coverage.

Of course, the support of senior executives to make the LMS a reality is crucial to its success and communication of its potential benefits to learners needs to be carefully managed. As soon as it is in place, regular monitoring, assessment and appraisal of its use should ensure that both learner and organisation realise its advantages.

All good LMS providers can be found online.

Summary

In this chapter you have:

- Seen the benefits of developing a learning organisation
- Recognised that the best form of learning is properly managed workplace experience
- Uncovered different theories to learning – single- and double-loop learning

- Explored learning in an organisational context
- Had a brief review of Investors in People
- Seen the place of learning in the European Foundation for Quality Management Excellence Model
- Been introduced to Learning Management Systems.

Questions

1. Consider how your organisation views failure. What can be done to ensure that the organisation recognises any shortcomings and allows organisational learning to occur?
2. Review any recent action that you have taken and consider if there was a difference between what you explained to others (espoused theory) and why you really did it (theory-in-use). Can you account for any differences?
3. Consider situations in your workplace and identify any situation where Model II learning took place – the governing variables were changed to achieve better outcomes (see the section on single- and double-loop learning for ideas).
4. What might be (or are) the benefits to your organisation from adopting the Investors in People Standard?

References

Anderson, L. (1997) *Argyris and Schön's Theory on Congruence and Learning* (online). Available at http://www.scu.edu.au/schools/sawd/arr/argyris.html.

Argyris, C. (1980) *Inner Contradictions of Rigorous Research*, Academic Press, New York.

Argyris, C. (1990) *Overcoming Organizational Defenses: Facilitating organizational learning*, Allyn & Bacon, Boston.

Argyris, C. and Schön, D. (1974) *Theory in Practice: Increasing professional effectiveness*, Jossey-Bass, San Francisco.

Argyris, C. and Schön, D. (1978) *Organizational Learning: A theory of action perspective*, Addison-Wesley, Reading, MA.

Clare, J. (2005) *The Daily Telegraph*, 2 December, p. 7.

The Daily Telegraph (2005) 23 August, p. 2.

Databuild (2004) Investors in People Impact Assessment Study; see http://www.investors-inpeople.co.uk.

Finger, M. and Asún, M. (2000) *Adult Education at the Crossroads: Learning our way out*, Zed Books, London.

Kolb, D. A. (1984) *Experiential Learning: Experience as the source of learning and development*, Prentice-Hall, Englewood Cliffs, NJ.

Management Today (2005) November, p. 10.

Senge, P. M. (1990) *The Fifth Discipline: The art and practice of the learning organisation*, Random House, London. A seminal and highly readable book in which Senge sets out the five 'competent technologies' that build and sustain learning organisations. His emphasis on systems thinking as the fifth, and cornerstone, discipline allows him to develop a more holistic appreciation of the organisation (and the lives of people associated with them).

Stern, S. (2003) *Management Today*, November, pp. 91, 93.

The Sunday Times (2005) 30 October, 'Business', p. 6.

Further Reading

Pettit, J. (ed.) et al. (2003) *Development and the Learning Organisation (Development in Practice Readers Series)*, Oxfam.

Lessem, R. (1991) *Total Quality Learning: Building a Learning Organisation (Developmental Management)*, Blackwell.

Mackay, A. R. (2007) *Recruiting, Retaining and Releasing People*, Butterworth-Heinemann.

Sydanmaanlakka, P. (2002) *An Intelligent Organisation: Integrating Performance, Competence and Knowledge Management*, Capstone Publishing.

11

Lifelong Learning and CPD

High-performing leaders are highly conscious of their feelings as they move through life.
From Dotlich, Noel and Walker, *Leadership Passages*, Jossey-Bass, 2005

Learning Outcomes

With people living longer, being expected to be in work longer and moving from one work area to another – quite apart from the rapid rates or change affecting organisations – we have to accept that we need to continue to learn through life. So how do we learn for life? This chapter, and its companion web pages, look at some basic theories of learning. The chapter has been written to cover particular elements of the National Occupational Standards for Management and Leadership (*Managing Self and Personal Skills – Unit 3*; *Providing Direction – Unit 11*; *Working with People – Units 21 and 28*; and *Achieving Results – Unit 50*) and it covers some of the requirements of the Chartered Management Institute's Diploma in Management compulsory *Unit C41 – Developing your Management Style* (in respect of developing yourself), some of the compulsory *Unit C45 – Managing Performance* and most of the optional *Unit O42 – Developing Personnel and Personnel Performance*. This chapter will also be of value to those studying the CIPD Professional Development Scheme – particularly the *Leadership and Management* and *People Management and Development* modules, as well as people studying any of the CIPD specialist electives in *Learning and Development*.

By the end of this chapter you will:

- Explore a selection of learning theories
- Understand the place of lifelong learning
- Explore the subject of adult education
- Recognise that nobody is too old to learn
- See the place of qualifications to support learning
- Understand the role of continual personal development.

Introduction to Learning

The book from which this chapter's opening quote is taken reinforces the fact that life is best understood as a learning journey, and that what comes to us as 'failures' and 'adversity' are all parts of life's rich tapestry. Certainly, humility is a vital part of that landscape, an openness to learn, accompanied by a lack of arrogance. Humility can be viewed as that most elusive quadrant of any individual, distinguishable from mind, body and heart. So, how do we enable that 'openness to learn' to be expressed in ourselves and our people?

We change (i.e. learn) as the result of experience all the time. That doesn't mean that it is easy to change our behaviour, however. If learning to be good were easy, we would all be saints! So, why is self-improvement often difficult? Our ignorance and pessimism about self-control sometimes overwhelms and paralyses us.

Consider how mysterious some behaviour is. Why are some very attractive people shy? Why do some eat and eat until they are fat, unhealthy and damage their self-image? Why do others refuse to eat because they weigh six stones but think they are fat? Why do some drink until they die of liver disease? Why might a person smoke cigarettes until they get throat cancer, lose their windpipe and even then continue to suck the smoke through an air hole in their neck? Why do many put off studying until the last night before an important exam? Why are some of us pessimists and others optimists?

Everyone has a lifetime of experience with learning, especially finding out how to get what we want. We seem to have inherited a brain that is especially adept at learning to cope, but we also learn many self-defeating behaviours. Every person has thousands, probably millions, of learned behaviours or habits. Many are very useful, like brushing teeth, driving a car, talking, etc. Bad habits are probably learned in the same ways as good ones. Replacing bad habits with new, valued ways of behaving probably follows the same learning principles. So, let's understand how to change behaviour by learning more about the process of learning. First, see a case in Box 11.1.

Why was it that Graham found it so difficult to go for his long-term goals, so easily within his reach? Let us first understand the background theories used to explain why we behave as we do. The example will be used to discuss 'attribution theory' in Chapter 17 to underpin why achievement is less then it might have been.

Box 11.1: How procrastination prevented progress and led to disappointment

Graham, the procrastinator
Consider the case of Graham, a second-year sixth-form student, who is a procrastinator. Graham is of average intelligence and wants to be successful as an archaeologist. Yet, he puts off studying, especially physics at A-level in his last year at secondary school.

(Continued)

Box 11.1: Continued

He knows he could learn it but these subjects take time and become boring. He can't just fake his way though a physics exam. Anyway, he says, he can always go to Sixth Form College for a revision year.

Graham has been and still is especially good at sports, particularly rugby, because he is stocky and strong. Also, Graham has many friends, both male and female. It is very hard for him to study when he has so many fun things to do. Lately, he has noticed resenting the teachers who pile on a lot of work. He is doing OK in two subjects but not physics – he needs three good grades to make the University he wants.

Graham is in a reinforcement-rich environment; there are so many enjoyable things to do. Thus, it is hard for studying to compete with all the opportunities to socialise, text his mates, play computer games, party, relax, play sports, listen to music, talk, flirt, have fun, etc. How could studying physics possibly be more enjoyable than all these fun things? This chapter focuses on this kind of dilemma.

(Follow-up at age 38: Graham flunked out of college and didn't make University, got married to a girl in his home town and had three children. His job is secure but uninteresting; it involves operating large earth-moving equipment. He has become a loner and depressed. He and his wife drifted apart. Divorced at 37, he misses his children terribly. He still tends to procrastinate, is late for work, his house is a tip, he doesn't pay his bills on time and makes no plans for the future. He manages to keep his job but isn't likely to be promoted. The dreams of success he had in school seem so far away and futile to him now.)

Learning theories – a background

Learned people have always been interested in learning. Around 2400 years ago, Plato believed that we all had a soul that knew everything. He thought this knowledge was available to us through our 'mind's eye', through introspection and reasoning, not observation. His student, Aristotle, disagreed; he believed we learned through observation and thinking to discover the 'laws of nature'.

Unfortunately, Plato had more influence than Aristotle on Christianity. Thus, the Christian religion set 'man' apart from natural law and since man (not woman) was made in God's image and had 'free will', supposedly man could not be studied scientifically. This opposition to learning by observation lasted for 1500 years. In 1600, philosophers started to speculate about the nature of man again. Some thought there were innate ideas (from Plato), e.g. Descartes and Kant; others believed ideas come from experience, e.g. Hobbes, Locke and Mill, very much like Aristotle and current thinking. For about 300 years, we philosophised about learning. Empirical, careful research on learning only started about 100 years ago. In general, it seems, humans have avoided learning about themselves!

As the Old Testament in the Bible described Adam as being made in God's own image, all the other animals were assumed (even by great philosophers) to be very different from humans; they had no mind, no rational thought, no language, no feelings and no soul; animals were like mechanical machines. However, in 1859, Darwin in *Origin of Species* challenged the separation of animals from humans with his idea of evolution and aroused interest in adaptation to the environment by his idea of survival of the best adapted. Evolution was another way, instead of God's hand, to create humans and all other creatures. A species may come into being and adapt by capitalising on mutant changes and/or by learning how to cope better. People suddenly became interested in psychology, especially in learning to adapt. Learning was also considered another sign of a mind, so psychologists asked, what are the smartest animals? Was learning a mechanical process or a thinking–symbolic–creative, self-controlled process? Is there a continuum from lower animals to humans – do they think like us, as evolution theory suggested, or are they inferior and different organisms?

The 1800s saw some remarkable breakthroughs in understanding learning:

- Hermann Ebbinghaus (1850–1909), a German psychologist, described the laws of learning and forgetting by experimentally studying his own memorisation of thousands of nonsense syllables.
- Ivan Pavlov (1849–1936) was a brilliant, systematic, Russian physiologist who won the 1904 Nobel Prize for his studies of the digestive and nervous systems. For the next 30 years, he carefully explored a kind of learning he called 'conditioned reflex' (classical conditioning), which he believed was the basis of all acquired habits and thoughts.
- At about the same time, a young American studying under William James, Edward Lee Thorndike (1874–1949), established the 'Law of Effect', that states that voluntary (controllable, unlike Pavlov's reflexes) behaviour followed by a satisfying experience tends to be repeated (learned).
- Later, B. F. Skinner (1904–1990) saw 'operant conditioning' as a way of controlling almost all behaviour.

These scientists sought to study experimentally a very simple form of animal learning, which would help explain complex human behaviour. It was a good idea, but it didn't work as well as they had hoped. There have been many other psychologists, following Darwin, interested in learning but these four are founding fathers.

Many researchers have described the ABCs of behaviour (see Figure 11.1), which will be used to explore three basic kinds of learning.

Antecedents are prior conditions, contexts or situations (that may be environmental or internal stimuli) that influence the behaviours of the individual that, in turn, have given consequences. This is a form of 'theory-in-use' as described in Chapter 10.

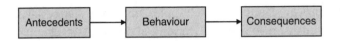

Figure 11.1 The ABCs of behaviour.

Classical conditioning

Learning new associations between the antecedents and subsequent behaviour is classical conditioning. The classic examples of classical conditioning are Pavlov's dogs and Watson's Little Albert. In the 1890s, Pavlov was observing the physiology of the production of saliva by dogs as they were fed when he noticed that saliva was also produced when the person who fed them appeared (without food). This is not surprising – every farm boy for thousands of years has realised, of course, that animals become excited when they hear the sounds that indicate they are about to be fed. But Pavlov carefully observed and measured one small part of the process. He paired a sound, a tone, with feeding his dogs so that the tone occurred several times just before and during the feeding. Soon the dogs salivated to the tone, something like they did to the food. They had learned a new connection: tone with food or tone with saliva response.

Similarly, John B. Watson, an early American psychologist, presented an 11-month-old child, Albert, with a loud frightening bang and a rat at the same time. After six or seven repetitions of the noise and rat together over a period of a week, the child became afraid of the rat, which he hadn't been, something like his fear of the noise. The procedure shows how one might learn to associate a neutral event, called the conditioned stimulus (CS) – the rat – with another event to which one has a strong automatic reaction, called the unconditioned stimulus (UCS) – the scary loud sound.

How can we use this information? What are common, everyday examples of classical conditioning? The ice-cream van and the bakery attract you with jingles and smells previously paired with food. TV advertisers pair their product with beautiful scenes or with attractive, sexy, successful or important people in an effort to get you to like their products more. Studying may be unpleasant for Graham (Box 11.1) because it has been paired with frustration (hating to do it). Much of what we like or dislike is a result of classical conditioning. Let's take drinking beer as an example: on first experience, beer does not usually taste good. However, positive associations of friends together, social acceptance and the feeling of relaxation are all 'conditioned' with the beer, and through repetitions the beer tastes better. So, classical conditioning connects feelings with environmental cues and with behaviours.

Pavlov's experiments dramatically demonstrated the environment's control over behaviour. We are highly responsive to cues in our environment. Some people, for example:

- See dessert and can't avoid eating it
- Act differently with parents than with friends

- Have a place where they can really concentrate and study
- Feel uptight skiving off and get back to work.

In fact, classical conditioning is involved in almost everything we do (even though brushing your teeth isn't the emotional high point of your day, notice how you feel if you don't brush your teeth at the usual time). Thus, changing our environment is one of the most effective self-help methods in learning. Changing our reaction to the environment is another self-help approach based on classical conditioning methods. Indeed, learning to reduce our fears and other unwanted emotions is a major part of gaining control over life.

However, this does not explain all learning behaviour. An adult (or even a five-year-old) probably would not develop fear of a little kitten under the same conditions as Little Albert with the rat; adults know kittens don't make banging noises! The learner is involved in a complex cognitive process of calculating the relationships between stimuli in the environment and behavioural reactions. The person is figuring out what is going on – what causes what or what leads to what (called cognitive maps) – and then acts to get the reinforcer (reward).

Operant conditioning

While Pavlov was studying reflexes, Edward Lee Thorndike observed cats and dogs trying to get out of a cage he had built with a trap door (opened by the animal pulling a string) in order to get food. He concluded that all learning, even in humans, doesn't involve the mind! Learning was, for him, simply the building of a connection between the situation (S) and a response (R), depending on the rewarding or punishing consequences to the animal. His basic conclusion was: rewards strengthen the previous response and punishment weakens the previous response.

In the 1930s, B. F. Skinner built a 'box' in which an animal could get a pellet of food if it learned to press a bar or to peck a light. Thousands of research studies have been done on animals in the Skinner Box. In real life, common examples of operant conditioning would be working for a weekly pay cheque and disciplining a child to change his or her behaviour. The use of rewards and punishment has been known to man for thousands, maybe hundreds of thousands, of years. These response tendencies may be built into the species. Indeed, even animals punish their young for nursing too vigorously or for misbehaving. During the 1960s and 1970s, the use of reinforcement, called behaviour modification, became very popular with psychologists, especially in schools and with the mentally or emotionally handicapped.

The basic idea, straight from Thorndike, is seductively simple: *reward the behaviour you desire in others or in yourself.* There is also a parallel notion: if you don't understand why people do certain things, look for the possible rewards following the behaviour. Then change the reinforcers if you want to change the behaviour. This is also a key method in self-help. Behavioural analysis (understanding the antecedents and consequences) and positive reinforcement are undoubtedly powerful and underused methods, but probably not the solution to all human learning problems. Don't other factors besides reinforcement influence behaviour? What about hoped-for rewards, plans, intentions or powerful emotions?

Nevertheless, the Skinner Box has undoubtedly given us valuable knowledge about different kinds of reinforcement schedules and, as a result, managers know a great deal about getting the most work out of people in highly controlled environments. Advertisers and politicians certainly know how to sell things. But we know a lot less about self-control in more complex situations where people have many alternatives and can make their own decisions and plans.

Operant conditioning involves operating on the environment in very specific ways, namely delivering reinforcers or punishment right after the 'target' behaviour. There are several situations in which behaviour–consequence contingencies might be established:

- You may reward or punish some specific behaviour of someone else, i.e. you are changing his or her environment in hopes of changing his or her behaviour
- Some specific behaviour of yours may be rewarded – or punished – by someone else or by you
- You may engage in some specific behaviour because you expect it to yield some desired change in your environment – i.e. a pay-off.

Furthermore, learning not only involves acquiring a new response, but also learning effectively to use that response in other situations (generalisation) and learning not to use the response in other situations where it won't work (discrimination). Thus, as with classical conditioning, the setting exercises great control over our operant behaviour.

Classical and operant conditioning were not new kinds of learning invented by Pavlov and Thorndike. Conditioning has always existed; no doubt animal trainers, parents, bosses and lovers used rewards, punishment and change of the environment quite effectively 10 000 years ago, much as they do today.

Other examples of operant conditioning are salespersons on a commission and factory workers doing 'piece-work', where the better or faster they work the more they get paid. Likewise, studying for grades, dressing to be attractive, being considerate to make friends, getting angry to get our way, cleaning up our messes for approval or because we enjoy neatness and so forth are behaviours operating on the environment. If they work (yield rewards) the behaviours are strengthened, i.e. become more likely to occur in the future, because they have been reinforced.

There are many other self-modification methods based on operant procedures: self-punishment, negative reinforcement, intrinsic satisfaction, covert (mental) rewards and punishment, extinction (no rewards or punishment after the behaviour).

One more complication is that there are two aspects of self-reinforcement all mixed together. Consider an example: (a) the satisfaction of scoring while practising drop goals in rugby training and (b) having an energy drink as a 'reward' after scoring three in a row.

Do both (a) and (b) actually reinforce *accurate* kicking? Or does (b) only reinforce practising, not accuracy? How do we know? It is suggested that self-rewards and self-praise don't add much reinforcement beyond the satisfaction of doing well. On the other hand, the intrinsic satisfaction of making long drop-kicks isn't exactly *self*-reinforcement (the kicker isn't in total control – they don't make every score and they didn't create the thrill). Good coaches focus on helping people set up the conditions (not reinforcement) that increase their chances of doing what they want to do but haven't been able to do, namely, in my example, make more drop goals. To do this successfully, the coach needs to assess the learning needs of the individual based on their stage or level of competence.

Social/observational learning

In spite of centuries of believing that there is a natural tendency for humans to imitate others, psychologists for most of the 20th century generally assumed that humans didn't learn from observing others. Apparently, this idea came from animals that don't learn very well from observing; animals need to have the experience themselves and be rewarded to learn. However, humans are different. For one thing, most people have a highly developed spoken method of communication that goes with social observation or learning – it is called a language – but we need to listen as well.

We learn from observing models but we don't necessarily copy them. This is called observational learning. In an early study, children watched a film of an adult hitting and kicking a large punch-bag type of doll. Some of the children saw the adult rewarded for the aggressiveness, others saw the adult punished and still others saw no rewards or punishment afterwards. Later, when placed in a similar situation as the adult with the doll, the children were more aggressive themselves if they had seen an adult rewarded for being aggressive. If they had seen the adult punished, they were less aggressive, even though they could imitate the adult perfectly. They had learned behaviour by observing, and learned to monitor and control their behaviour if it might lead to rewards or punishment. Every parent has observed this too.

Although observing an effective model in a film is helpful, seeing a live model works better. Even more effective is watching a live model first and then participating in the activity yourself.

This area of research is called 'Social Learning Theory' because it involves people learning from each other or modelling. Humans can learn what behaviour leads to what outcomes by directly or indirectly (on TV or from books) observing others; they don't have to experience the situation themselves or be rewarded for the new behaviour. In this theory, reinforcement does not strengthen learning, it is simply a pay-off that motivates us to perform the behaviour that leads to the reward.

The observational learner uses his or her head and thinks. He or she must attend to the model, remember what the model did, see the usefulness of the model's behaviour and be able to duplicate the behaviour (after some practice). This kind of learning, along with classical and operant, is also involved in many things we do. We learn how to socialise, to do a job, to intimidate by yelling – all from others. Every one of us can readily see the influence of our parents' model on our habits, preferences, attitudes and patterns of thought. Schools, TV, entertainment stars, religion and other sources provide other models. In complex ways these models help us decide how to behave and what kind of person we want to be – having respected role models in work is important too.

Observational learning involves higher-order thinking, not just thoughtless imitating. The person becomes a controlling factor. We make decisions that direct our lives; our mind is an active 'agent' involved in learning and changing ourselves and our environment.

Many believe that human behaviour is largely self-regulated. We evaluate our own behaviour; the satisfaction felt when we do well is intrinsic reinforcement. It is assumed that self-rewarded behaviour was just as well learned as externally reinforced behaviour – maybe better. The concept of self-efficacy is one's belief about an individual's ability or inability to control their own behaviour, based on personal accomplishments or failures. Clearly, Social Learning Theory involves antecedents (environment), consequences (motivating pay-offs) and complicated cognitive processes.

Also involved in self-control is the concept of 'delay of gratification', which is when we work or wait for a big pay-off instead of taking smaller immediate rewards. Individuals will avoid temptations, including having distracting-but-fun thoughts while waiting, developing a 'plan' for the pay-off and making use of self-instructions. There may be a three-stage model of behavioural self-control in action: self-observation, self-evaluation and self-reinforcement. These theories have evolved to be more and more cognitive.

Many behaviours produce a variety of consequences and it has been suggested that almost all problem behaviours occur when the complex consequences of an action are *both* immediate and delayed, e.g.:

1. Taking immediate pleasures but running into trouble in the long run (smoking, overeating, building loving relationships with two people at the same time, being 'let's-have-a-good-time-orientated' at work).
2. Taking immediate small pleasures but losing out on major satisfactions later on (spending money impulsively as soon as you get it rather than saving your money for major, important purchases later, having a brief affair resulting in losing a good long-term relationship, teasing a person to the point that it becomes a big fight).
3. Avoiding a minor immediate unpleasant situation but risking a major problem (not going to the doctor to have an irregular, dark mole checked; avoiding treatment for an emotional or addiction problem; neglecting to buy condoms or to take the pill).
4. Avoiding a minor immediate unpleasant situation and, thereby, missing out on an important future event (not studying hard enough to get into a University of choice, avoiding meeting people and not developing social skills that would lead to an enjoyable social life and wonderful relationships).

Research has shown that animals and humans tend to take the smaller *immediate* reward, rather than waiting for a larger *delayed* pay-off.

Consider the example in Box 11.2. Maybe immediate, no-wait pay-offs are just more satisfying. Maybe 'a bird in the hand is worth two in the bush'. Maybe life teaches us that promises may be broken. In any case, being aware of the appeal and *excessive focus on the immediate pay-offs* can help us cope with the four situations above.

Where the immediate pleasures need to be decreased (1 and 2 above), one should avoid the situations and develop other incompatible responses, like assuming more of a responsible leadership role at work instead of playing around. One needs to keep eyes on the big, long-range consequences (see motivation in Chapter 4). Where one needs to tackle unpleasant immediate tasks (3 and 4 above), one should change the environment or oneself so that the necessary immediate behaviour is well rewarded, so, for problem 4, at the same time focusing on learning to enjoy, say, sport and studying. Again, keeping the future in mind can avoid major problems and achieve major goals. When we are fully aware of all the consequences of our actions, we can have more self-control and more pay-offs in the long run.

Regardless of the outcome of these many debates and questions about the technical term reinforcement, be assured that the outcome or consequences of a specific behaviour will in some way influence the occurrence of that behaviour in the future. Providing a material reward isn't always the best thing to do. But assuring that genuine satisfaction follows the desired behaviour will enhance your and others' learning and/or motivation.

As we conclude this discussion of learning, note:

- Learning processes are complicated, but there is a great deal of useful knowledge available in this area.
- Theories often fail to explain or predict real-life behaviour and the early theorists neglected many crucial causes of our behaviour.
- Learning theories and experimental researchers have seldom developed helpful treatment or self-help methods. Hundreds of therapy and self-help procedures already exist; they were mostly invented by suffering people and creative practitioners.

Table 11.1 summarises the ABCs of behaviour related to the type of conditioning.

Box 11.2: Short- vs long-term rewards affecting behaviour

Suppose someone offered you £8 immediately for an hour of work or £10 for the work if you would wait three days to the end of the week to be paid, which would you take? Most would take the £8 now. But suppose someone offered you £8 for the work in 30 days or £10 in 33 days, i.e. the same 20 per cent profit from the same three-day delay, which would you take? The 33-day offer, of course.

Table 11.1 Summary of the ABCs of behaviour

Type of conditioning	Antecedents	Behaviour	Consequences
Classical – Pavlov	1. Pair food and tone	Salivation	–
Classical – Watson	2. Pair rat and loud noise	Fear of rat	–
Operant – Thorndike	3. (Animal in cage)	Pull string	Get food and escape
Operant – Skinner	4. Animal in Skinner Box	Press bar	Food
Operant (job)	5. At work	Do work	Get paid
Self-reinforcement	6. Doing own project/study	Study more	Watch *The Simpsons* for 30 min
Avoidance	7. See a rat	Run away	Temporary relief of fear (but fear grows)
Avoidance learning	8. Child cries	Give into child	Crying stops but cries sooner and louder next time
Social learning	9. Observe model or receive instructions	Imitate model or use information	Success

The Meaning of Adult Education

> *Education conceived as preparation for life locks the learning process within a vicious circle. Youth educated in terms of adult ideas and taught to think of learning as a process which ends when real life begins will make no better use of intelligence than the elders who prescribe the system.*
>
> Eduard C. Lindeman, 1926

When teenagers discover this for themselves it is often too late – the adult world takes over, obliging them to fit into the pattern, follow the tradition of their elders and become elderly-minded before their time. Education within this vicious circle is not much fun but something to be endured because it leads to a goal. Sadly, there is no joy in the end if the means are irritating, painful and largely self-denying.

All too often, those that have 'completed' a standard regime of education leave school or university and turn to face in the opposite direction. Their view of education as a necessary annoyance for future generations will guide their children accordingly and so the cycle perpetuates. For them, while suffering 'education' as a means to getting a job, life will become ever more dull and boring, stereotypical experiences of his 'set'. Within a decade he will be out of touch with the world of learning, will not read much beyond the tabloids, will not engage in much of other media beyond the latest 'reality' nonsense or 'soap', and will be bound by the jargon of his job, regularly deriding those that seek better understanding and improvement. In short, he will have become a typical adult for whom the world of learning has slipped him by.

So, what can be done? Lindeman proposed a four-point solution which we would recognise as lifelong learning.

Lifelong Learning

First, it should be recognised that *learning is life*. Hence, if the whole of life is learning, then education can have no endings. Most great philosophical traditions, including those embodied in Gandhi, Tagore, Aurobindo and Krishnamurti, recognise a spiritual component to learning, teaching that knowledge is more than a way to get a job or score well on a standardised test, that it is the purpose for living, it is being human. No one needs adult education more than the university graduate, for they often make incorrect assumptions concerning the function of learning.

Secondly, lifelong learning is about non-vocational ideals. It is not enough to learn a speciality to do a job; learning must be about understanding the *meaning* of labour. However, true adult education begins where vocational education leaves off – its purpose is to put meaning into the whole of life.

Thirdly, the approach to adult learning is through *situations* not subjects. Traditional education is built around subject-specialists delivering the subject; students are secondary and required to adjust themselves to an established curriculum. In adult education the curriculum is built around the student's needs and interests. Every person finds themselves in specific situations with respect to their work – and other circumstances – that call for adjustments. Adult education begins at this point. Subject matter is brought into the situation and is put to work, when needed. Texts and teachers play a new and secondary role in this type of education; they must give way to the primary importance of the learner.

Fourthly, the most important resource is the *learner's experience*. If education is life then it follows that life is also education. All genuine education combines both doing and thinking in equal measure – together. In this way, life becomes rational and meaningful as we learn to be intelligent about the things we do and the things that happen to us. In this way we discover that the attractions of experience increase as we grow older. Thus, we should find cumulative pleasure in finding out the meaning of the events in which we play a role.

Lindeman proposed that we should encourage situations where 'friends learn from each other'; in his book he quoted Walt Whitman: 'learn from the simple – teach the wise'. He proposed that small groups of adults who want to keep their minds fresh and vigorous who begin to learn by confronting relevant situations, those that delve deep into their experience before resorting to texts and secondary facts, who are led in the discussion by teachers who are also searchers after wisdom, not fancy speeches, these groups constitute the setting for adult education, the modern quest for life's meaning.

People serious about learning are searching for the good life – they want to count for something; they want their experiences to become alive and meaningful; they want their skills and talents to be useful; they want to improve themselves as well as change the social order so that people can create a new environment where one's ambitions may be realised.

The place of qualifications

The First Steps into Learning research, commissioned by the Campaign for Learning and 'Learndirect', set out to explore what would motivate 'rejecters of learning' – the 16 per cent of the adult working population for whom learning holds little or no appeal – to take the first step into learning (*The Guardian*, 2005).

Respondents said they wanted choice about how, when and where they learn. They wanted flexibility, an alternative to traditional classroom learning and the opportunity to learn in bite-sized chunks as it suited them. They also wanted their learning to be relevant to their lives.

Many of those questioned were clear that if they were going to learn, they wanted to be able to get a qualification as a result, as qualifications were seen as a route to employment or a better job, to more money or a move to a better area. For many, qualifications were cited as the motivation to learn. Without a credit framework, the risk is that switched-off learners, who may only be motivated to learn by getting a qualification, will slip through the net.

Over the past four years, around 1.5 million people have taken a Learndirect course, of which three-fifths had done no formal learning for three years or more, and nearly 50 per cent claim they would not have started learning again without Learndirect. These impressive figures remind us that achievement can be measured in a range of ways – but not exclusively through qualifications.

Naturally, qualifications need to be to defined standards. The Management Standards Centre (MSC) is the government recognised standards-setting body for the management and leadership areas (for more information, see http://www.management-standards.org.uk/). Since 2003, the MSC has been engaged in a publicly funded project to develop a new set of National Occupational Standards (NOS) for management and leadership. The new standards, which were launched in November 2004, describe the level of performance expected in employment for a range of management and leadership functions/activities.

The national occupational standards for managers provide a useful benchmark for organisations of all sizes in the public, private and voluntary sectors, and can be downloaded free of charge from www.management-standards.org.uk.

Further details of qualification agencies in the UK can be found on the companion web pages.

University of the Third Age

September 2004 saw the 21st anniversary of the University of the Third Age (U3A). There are 544 autonomous U3As across Britain; none have teachers but instead have group leaders, who are sometimes, but not always, experts in the subject. Groups gather in a local hall or a member's home and devise their own course of study. They have over 140 000 members and numbers are growing at around 20 per cent a year.

Sadly, official approaches to lifelong learning seem to be focused on the young, giving them the skills that employers require. In 1996, 12 per cent of people aged 65–74 were learning; by 2005, the figure dropped to 8 per cent. All available studies suggest that retired people who keep their minds active by learning are fitter and healthier, and put off what the U3A calls the 'fourth' age of dependence. They are less likely to require expensive care, so providing learning opportunities for them saves the state money.

Continuing Professional Development (CPD)

CPD is a personal commitment to keeping professional knowledge up to date and improving personal capabilities. It focuses on learning and how people develop throughout their careers. Most people are probably already doing it, but by formally recording learning, individuals will show that they are actively committed to the development of their careers.

Being actively committed to CPD will:

- Enhance CVs
- Ensure professional recognition
- Showcase achievements
- Accelerate career prospects
- Enable people to command better salary and benefits
- Ensure greater job satisfaction.

Most members of professional bodies and the professions are expected to structure their learning and keep a record of their CPD.

It is a requirement that, as a professionally qualified member, each person provides evidence of CPD when making applications to upgrade membership within the professional body to the chartered level at such organisations as the Chartered Institute of

Marketing, Chartered Management Institute, and Chartered Institute of Personnel and Development.

There is a common principle on how individuals approach CPD, whether that is in terms of self-development or lifelong learning. It is about the learning and development that people undertake and the method they use to reflect on and record this learning.

The development record needs to reflect a range of all the learning and development opportunities that individuals have undertaken over the previous 12 months. Most professional bodies recommend around 35 hours, but this is only a guide. It is also recommended that people concentrate on the activities that make the most impact on the person and their job role.

Moreover, it is expected that future development plans are devised to cover each person's proposed action for the following 12 months, taking on board appropriate guidance given above.

Summary

In this chapter you have:

- Explored a selection of learning theories – classical and operant conditioning, and social/observational learning
- Been able to reflect on the place of lifelong learning for ageing demographics
- Explored the subject of adult education alongside work
- Recognised that nobody is too old to learn – especially in the 'Third Age'
- Seen the place of qualifications to support learning
- Considered the role of continual personal development as people move jobs and careers.

Questions

1. Consider your progress from secondary school to any other further education you have experienced. How did the approach to education differ? Which have you found most effective – and why?
2. Looking at how people in your organisation (or one with which you are familiar) learn, what are the most effective methods, giving reasons for your answer.
3. 'Diplomas' seem to be available on the Internet. Comment on the value of qualifications to your workplace (or one with which you are familiar).
4. What elements of 'operant conditioning' might have an influence on your desire to improve your ability to use information technology in the workplace?

References

The Guardian (2005) 7 September.

Lindeman, E. C. (1926) 'A Classic Statement on the Meaning of Adult Education', in *The Meaning of Adult Education*, Chapter 1, New Republic, New York.

Further Reading

Dotlich, D., Noel, J. and Walker, N. (2005) *Leadership Passages*, Jossey-Bass.

Reeve, F. (ed.) (2001) *Supporting Lifelong Learning*, Routledge Falmer.

12

Individual Learning Styles

Learn from the mistakes of others. You don't have time to make them all yourself.
From *It's a Wise Sage*, the Chartered Management Institute

Learning Outcomes

We have all learnt to do things but not all the same things, not all to the same extent and not all the same way – why is that? This chapter, and its companion web pages, take a broad view of some of the basics of learning theories to answer some of these questions. The chapter has been written to cover particular elements of the National Occupational Standards for Management and Leadership (*Managing Self and Personal Skills – Unit 3*; *Providing Direction – Unit 11*; *Working with People – Units 21 and 28*; and *Achieving Results – Unit 50*), and it covers some of the requirements of the Chartered Management Institute's Diploma in Management compulsory *Unit C41 – Developing your Management Style* (in respect of developing yourself), some of the compulsory *Unit C45 – Managing Performance* and most of the optional *Unit O42 – Developing Personnel and Personnel Performance*. This chapter will also be of value to those studying the CIPD Professional Development Scheme – particularly the *Leadership and Management* and *People Management and Development* modules, as well as people studying any of the CIPD specialist electives in *Learning and Development*.

By the end of this chapter you will:

- Recognise that any learning involves change and needs to be managed accordingly
- Understand that people go through various levels of competence as they learn new skills
- Consider a matrix of awareness of what people know or is known about them as a guide to learning
- Learn about four basic learning styles proposed as a cycle
- Learn a more complex model of learning styles to explain everyday observations about learning

- Realise that people have more than one intelligence that can be used as a route of learning
- Explore further approaches to learning based on pictures, words or practical application, and on thinking, feeling and doing
- Be able to evaluate learning through four stages.

A Process for Personal Change

In Chapter 11, we considered learning to be a change process – a change in behaviour. Unfortunately, for many people there is a resistance to that change as confidence blocks the development. This is best illustrated in the transition cycle; while the stages of transition were first documented in the 1960s when reviewing bereavement, they also have a place in our understanding of individual learning (Williams, 1999).

In the 1970s, it was realised that this transition process may be triggered by any major life event, good or bad, in work as well as personal life, e.g. in a new job or after redundancy. The same process also accounts for the 'survivor syndrome' – loss of morale in organisations a few months after large-scale changes, e.g. reorganisations, redundancies or acquisitions. When a major change in organisational practices is involved, individuals will go through a transition from one state to another where new behaviours have to be learnt. If you are of a 'certain age' and were in work at the time, recall the adoption of computerisation in your organisation.

The several phases of transition are shown in Figure 12.1. These involve predictable barriers to change, but can also lead to major opportunities for learning. The first reactions

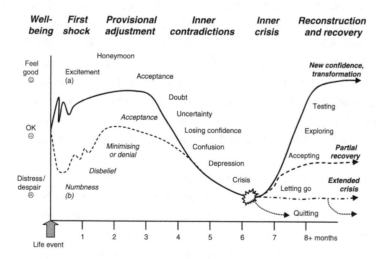

Figure 12.1 The transition cycle – a template for human responses to change. After Williams (1999).

depend on whether the event was good or bad. If it were seen as a positive change (the new computer system will reduce invoice errors and subsequent customer complaints), excitement would follow: 'Oh, good. Something is being done' (see (a) in Figure 12.1). If it were seen as a negative event ('You've all got to programme the Unix Platform system'), the reaction can be one of freezing, followed by denial or disbelief: 'It'll never work here; anyway, I wasn't employed to do that' (see (b) in Figure 12.1).

Whatever the type of change, after three to four months inner contradictions develop between the old view of the world, or what one expected to happen, and the new situation; this is triggered by acceptance that the person realises that a change (learning) is required – awareness of one's own shortcomings. The issues are usually too deep to recognise – for example, feelings of betrayal after redundancy if the person had given great loyalty to the organisation, or lost hopes for the future after separation or bereavement.

The person may become irritable, then anxious or confused, and lose confidence without knowing why – they will have a block to further learning. Stress and anxiety can develop into a personal transition crisis. If the contradictions are such that they affect deeply held beliefs, they may destabilise other parts of their life; trust betrayed in one situation may cast doubt on other relationships.

This is an important time for managers; the main hazards of the crisis phase result from severe stress and failing to recognise beliefs that are no longer valid. This tension can lead to loss of sleep and can include fatigue, errors of judgement, loss of strategic thinking, accidents and indiscretions or 'moments of madness' on the part of the individual. These put severe strains on work performance and personal relationships. There may be a strong urge to escape the situation – quitting jobs or relationships. If the situation is not recognised it may lead to nervous collapse needing several weeks of sick leave. If a whole team is in crisis this becomes evident in conflict and a 'blame culture' developing.

Note that the individual in this stage will make mistakes and have successes in attempting to become proficient in a new area of skill. This is the effective way of moving away from the crisis on the curve through to acceptance where learning can occur. However, the curve is not one simple progression from left to right. It does happen that individuals when experiencing the discomfort of a crisis will revert to denial: 'Oh, I can't do it; I probably won't have to anyway'. The positive and effective way of moving out of a crisis is into the exploring and testing stage.

At the organisational level, this stage is critical in terms of organisational change. It is the stage in which organisations undergoing significant change need to introduce and practise new techniques and methods of operation. It is the period when new strategies are implemented. In *In Search of Excellence* by Peters and Waterman (1988), the authors refer to this stage in their analysis of the characteristics of successful companies in Europe, Japan and the USA. One characteristic they found in the most successful companies that they have analysed is a culture that allows the individual the 'latitude to invent'. In these organisations, managers feel they have the opportunity to practise new techniques and methods of operating their part of the business without the restraining fear of recrimination for failure.

Driving out of crises, it helps if managers value good events before the change started and to reaffirm personal qualities and beliefs that are still important to individuals. This may happen in a 'defining moment', perhaps highlighting unfairness in working practices that have been unquestioned for too long. Defining moments may look like rebellion to managers, yet they may actually be valuable warnings in overstressed organisations – one employee may be expressing an underlying concern that affects the morale and performance of many others.

Breaking out of a transition crisis is therapeutic: an extended period of stress is released with a new sense of calm, well-being and energy. Once our mind is freed from strain it reorganises itself spontaneously within a few weeks. This recovery phase is an exciting process because we see the world more clearly. More accurate insights into the new reality help us to see new opportunities. Teams in recovery develop great energy and creativity. The recovery phase offers opportunities for personal development and starts a new life phase.

Awareness of Competence

The 'Conscious Competence' learning model or matrix helps explain the process and stages of learning a new skill (or behaviour, ability, technique, etc.). Of unknown origin, and originally showing four phases, more modern versions have a fifth stage or phase added. It is a useful model to illustrate the key phases that someone must go through before they reach higher levels of competence with a task. It is illustrated in Figure 12.2 and the learner or trainee always begins at Level 1.

Managers and trainers often assume that the trainees are at stage 2 and focus their efforts to getting them all to stage 3. All too often the trainer assumes that the trainee is aware that the new skills exist, and understands the nature, relevance, deficiency and benefit offered from the acquisition of the new skill. Unfortunately, if the trainee is at stage 1 – unconscious incompetence – they will have none or only some of these in place and will not be achieving conscious competence until they have become fully aware of their own situation and deficiencies. Trainees simply not seeing the need for training or any personal benefit coming from it may be a fundamental reason why so many training sessions fail. Indeed, some people resist progression even to this next stage; perhaps their confidence is holding them back. In these cases, it may be counter-productive to push them on through the stages – perhaps a person might be better suited to a different role, or permitted an adapted approach to the current role if appropriate and viable.

With such a simple model, a number of people have tried to add a fifth stage: the following are three such suggestions.

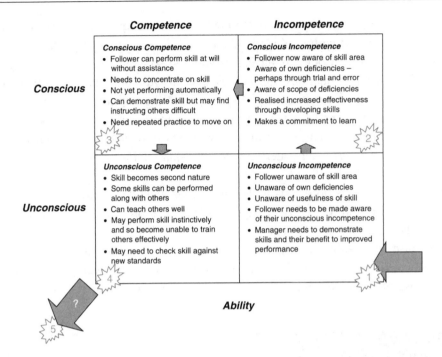

Figure 12.2 The 'Conscious Competence' learning model or matrix.

- *Conscious competence of unconscious incompetence* or an ability to spot unconscious incompetence in others – this ability to recognise and develop skill deficiencies in others is a different skill set altogether.
- *Reflective competence* – this is where someone becomes aware of their own unconscious competence, looking at themselves from the outside, digging to find and understand the theories, models and beliefs that inform what and how it is done.
- *Reconscious competence* – a stage where one is able to perform fluently, but also articulate what you are doing to yourself and to others. Some people never reach it – we all know experts that can't explain how they are doing what they are doing!

While it is not clear who originated the matrix – Confucius and Socrates have been cited as originators – it has similarities to the Ingham and Luft Johari Window (see below).

There are indications that the model existed in similar but different form. Various references can be found to an ancient Oriental proverb, which inverts the order of the two highest states:

- He who knows not, and knows not that he knows not, is a fool – shun him (unconscious incompetent)
- He who knows not, and knows that he knows not, is ignorant – teach him (conscious incompetent)

- He who knows, and knows not that he knows, is asleep – wake him (unconscious competent)
- But he who knows, and knows that he knows, is a wise man – follow him (conscious competent).

Johari Window

The Johari Window, named after the first names of its inventors, Joseph Luft and Harry Ingham, is one of the most useful models describing the process of human interaction (Luft, 1969). A four-paned 'window' (see Figure 12.3) divides personal awareness into four different types, as represented by its four quadrants or areas: open, hidden, blind and unknown. The lines dividing the four panes are like window shades, which can move as an interaction progresses and form a useful model for learning.

1. The 'open' or 'accessible' area represents things that both individuals know about themselves and that others know about them – e.g. name, job role, etc. The knowledge that the window represents can include not only factual information but a person's feelings, motives, behaviours, wants, needs and desires – indeed, any information describing who

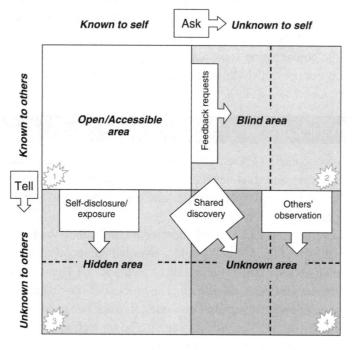

Figure 12.3 The Johari Window – after Joseph Luft and Harry Ingham.

they are. When we first meet a new person, the size of the opening of this first quadrant is not very large, since there has been little time to exchange information. As the process of getting to know one another continues, the window shades move down or to the right, placing more information into the open window, as described below.

2. The 'blind' area represents things that you know about the person, but that they are unaware of – e.g. a mark on the back of their jacket. This information is in their blind quadrant because you can see it, but they cannot. If you tell them that they have a mark on the back of their jacket, then the window shade moves to the right, enlarging the open quadrant's area. People may also have many blind spots with respect to many other much more complex things and exploring these is an essential part of the learning process.

3. The 'hidden' quadrant represents things that they know about themselves that you do not know. So, for example, they may not have told you what one of their favourite ice-cream flavours is. This information is in their 'hidden' quadrant. As soon as they tell you that they love maple-pecan flavoured ice-cream, they are effectively pulling the window shade down, moving the information in their hidden quadrant and enlarging the open quadrant's area. Again, there are vast amounts of information, virtually their whole life story, that have yet to be revealed to you. As you get to know and trust each other, they will feel more comfortable disclosing more intimate details about themselves. This process is called 'self-disclosure', and whether someone does this or not will depend on their trust in others and their own confidence – it clearly represents a potential barrier to learning.

4. The 'unknown' area represents things that neither they know about themselves nor you know about them. For example, they may disclose a dream that they had, and as you both attempt to understand its significance, a new awareness may emerge, known to neither of you before the conversation took place. Being placed in new situations often reveals new information not previously known to the individual or others (see Box 12.1).

Box 12.1: An example of 'shared discovery'

When the author conducted a Presentation Skills workshop for Accountants, he created a safe atmosphere of care and trust between the various participants. One of the delegates was usually terrified of speaking in public, but was surprised to learn that in such an atmosphere, the task was not so daunting.

Prior to this event, they had viewed themselves and others had also viewed them as being extremely shy. (They actually told a joke: when accountants talk to you, they usually look at their shoes, extrovert ones talk to *your* shoes!) Thus, a novel situation can trigger new awareness and personal growth. The process of moving previously unknown information into the open quadrant, thus enlarging its area, has been likened to Maslow's concept of self-actualisation. The process can also be viewed as a game where the open quadrant is synonymous with the win–win situation.

The Johari Window model of human interaction will be explored more in the section on confidence, as it impacts on the ability of someone to learn more about themselves and their skills and competencies.

Kolb Learning Styles

Kurt Lewin is probably best known in educational circles for his contribution to the experiential learning model and for his work with group dynamics.

His integrated four-step learning cycle begins with a concrete experience to validate and test abstract concepts. Observations and reflections are made, and abstract concepts and generalisations are then formed. Finally, the new concepts are tested in new situations. Lewin emphasised the here-and-now experience, followed by a feedback process based on observation and data collection.

These concepts are also applied to his work on group dynamics. His concept of T-groups (training groups – see Chapter 4) encourages group discussion and decision-making in order to solve problems. It combines the experiences of trainees with the conceptual models of the staff in a supportive environment. This methodology has played an important role in influencing organisational development, training and adult education in the later part of the 20th century.

David A. Kolb (with Roger Fry) created his famous model out of four elements: concrete experience, observation and reflection, the formation of abstract concepts, and testing in new situations. He represented these in the famous experiential learning circle (after Kurt Lewin) shown in Figure 12.4.

It is argued that the learning cycle can begin at any one of the four points – and that it should really be approached as a continuous cycle. However, usually the learning process begins with a person *doing* something (having a definitive experience – 1), then seeing the effect of the action in a given situation. Thus, the second step is to *reflect* (observation and reflection – 2) on these effects in the particular instance, so that if the same action was taken in the same circumstances it would be possible to anticipate what would follow from the action. In this pattern the third step is *understanding* the general principle (forming abstract concepts – 3) under which the particular instance falls. The fourth step is planning a *practical* approach to similar situations that will have predictable outcomes (testing in new situations – 4).

It is likely that an individual may develop generalisations of actions over a range of circumstances to gain experience beyond the particular instance and to develop an underlying general principle. Understanding the general principle does not imply, in this sequence, an ability to put the principle into words. It implies only the ability to see a connection between the actions and effects over a range of circumstances.

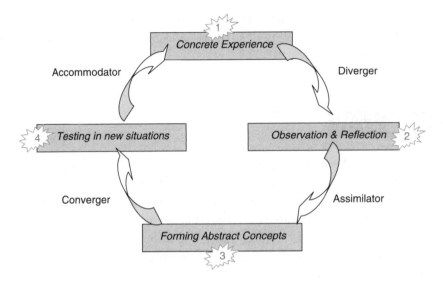

Figure 12.4 Adaptation of the Kolb learning cycle.

When the general principle is understood, the last step, according to David Kolb, is its application through action in a new situation within the range of generalisations. In some examples of experiential learning these steps (or ones like them) are sometimes shown as a circular movement, as in Figure 12.4. In reality, if learning has taken place the process should be drawn as a spiral. Any subsequent action following one 'circuit' is taking place in a new situation and the learner should now be able to anticipate the possible effects of their action.

Note two key points:

- The use of concrete, 'here-and-now' experience to test ideas
- The use of feedback to change practices and theories.

Individuals need to have experiences to learn and to undertake or receive feedback on their activity. In this way, Kolb wished to distinguish the process from cognitive theories of the learning process.

David Kolb on learning styles

David Kolb and Roger Fry (1975) argue that effective learning requires having four different abilities (as indicated on each pole of their model): concrete experience abilities, reflective observation abilities, abstract conceptualisation abilities and active experimentation abilities. Few can approach the 'ideal' in this respect and tend, they suggest, to develop a strength in, or orientation to, one of the poles of each dimension. As a result, they developed a learning style inventory (Kolb, 1976), which was designed to place people on a line between concrete experience and abstract conceptualisation, and active experimentation and reflective observation. Using this, Kolb and Fry proceeded to identify four basic learning styles.

Table 12.1 aims to summarise Kolb and Fry's views on learning styles and is adapted from Tennant (1997).

In developing this model Kolb and Fry have helped to challenge those models of learning that seek to reduce potential to one dimension such as intelligence. They also recognise that there are pros and cons associated with each style (and that being 'locked into' one style can put a learner at a serious disadvantage).

However, there are a number of problems with the model, explored on the companion web pages.

While there are problems, the model provides an excellent framework for planning teaching and learning activities, and can be used as a guide for understanding learning difficulties.

Table 12.1 Kolb and Fry's four basic learning styles

Learning style	Learning characteristic	Description
Converger	Abstract conceptualisation + active experimentation	▪ Good at practical application of ideas ▪ Able to focus on some reasoning of specific problems ▪ Not very emotional ▪ Probably has narrow interests
Diverger	Concrete experience + reflective observation	▪ Good imaginative ability ▪ Can generate ideas and see things from others' perspectives ▪ Interested in people ▪ Broad cultural interests
Assimilator	Abstract conceptualisation + reflective observation	▪ Very able to create theoretical models ▪ Excels in inductive reasoning ▪ More concerned with abstract concepts than people
Accommodator	Concrete experience + active experimentation	▪ Doing things is greatest strength ▪ Likely to take risks ▪ Spontaneous and does well when called upon ▪ Intuitive problem-solver

Jarvis Experiential Learning Model

Jarvis (1995) aimed to show that there are a number of responses to any potential learning situation. He used Kolb's model with a number of different adult groups and asked them to explore it based on their own experience of learning. He was then able to develop a model (Figure 12.5) that allowed different routes. Some of these are non-learning, some non-reflective learning and some reflective learning.

For a full description of the different types of learning, see the companion web pages.

While this represents a useful addition to our thinking about learning, a number of problems remain. There is still an issue around sequence – so many things may be happening at once, but Jarvis's model falls into the trap of sequential-stage thinking. As with Kolb's work there is a limited experimental base to support it. We can also ask questions as to whether these are different forms or routes, each learning process following different stages, or if they can be grouped together in a different and more compact way.

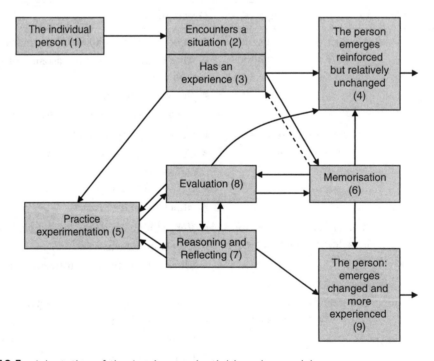

Figure 12.5 Adaptation of the Jarvis experiential learning model.

Howard Gardner's Multiple Intelligence

First published in 1983, *Frames of Mind* became a classical model both to understand and teach many aspects of human intelligence, learning style, personality and behaviour – in both education and in industry (Gardner, 1983). Table 12.2 illustrates Howard Gardner's model of the seven multiple intelligences in outline. While the table offers seven types of intelligence, Gardner toyed with three others that he did not develop as well as the others; this was not because he didn't feel they existed but that they were much more difficult to adequately and satisfactorily define owing, he said, to their complexity. Table 12.3 aims to summarise Gardner's suggested possible additional intelligences.

Naturally, many debate and interpret additions to the original seven, although *naturalist intelligence* does seem to be most popularly considered worth including. The original seven, it should be noted, are all relatively clear and easily understood, are measurable, and we can find many everyday examples to illustrate them. The additional human capabilities and perceptions are much more subjective and complex, may have cultural bias to them and, most importantly, suggest a degree of good or bad. The multiple intelligences are morally neutral – no type of intelligence is intrinsically right or wrong. In other words, intelligences are amoral – that is, neither moral nor immoral – irrespective of a person's blend of intelligences.

Table 12.4 expands the detail of the original seven intelligences, and suggests ideas for applying the model and its founding theory in order to optimise learning and training,

Table 12.2 Gardner's seven original intelligences

Intelligence type	Capability and perception
Linguistic	Words and language
Logical–mathematical	Logic and numbers
Musical	Music, sound, rhythm
Bodily–kinaesthetic	Body movement control
Spatial–visual	Images and space
Interpersonal	Other people's feelings and emotions
Intrapersonal	Self-awareness

Table 12.3 Possible extensions to Gardner's seven original intelligences

Intelligence type	Capability and perception
Naturalist	Natural environment
Spiritual/existential	Religion and 'ultimate issues'
Moral	Ethics, humanity, value of life

Table 12.4 Some detail of the seven original Gardner intelligences

Intelligence type	Description	Typical job roles	Related tasks, activities or tests	Clues to preferred learning style
1. Linguistic	Words and language, written and spoken.	Writers, lawyers, journalists, speakers, trainers, copywriters, editors, translators, PR and media people.	Write manuals; speak on a subject; edit a report; apply 'spin' to a story.	Words and language.
2. Logical–mathematical	Logical thinking, detecting patterns, scientific reasoning and deduction; analyse problems, perform mathematical calculations.	Scientists, engineers, computer experts, accountants, statisticians, researchers, analysts, traders, bankers, insurance brokers, negotiators, directors.	Mental arithmetic; create a complex process; analyse how a machine works; devise strategies.	Numbers and logic.
3. Musical	Musical ability, awareness, appreciation and use of sound; sees tonal/rhythmic patterns, sees relationship between sound and feeling.	Musicians, singers, composers, DJs, music producers, piano tuners, acoustic engineers, entertainers, environment and noise advisors, voice coaches.	Play a musical instrument; sing a song; review a musical work; coach someone to play a musical instrument.	Music, sounds, rhythm.
4. Bodily–kinaesthetic	Body movement control, manual dexterity, physical agility and balance; eye and body coordination.	Demonstrators, actors, divers, sportspeople, soldiers, fire-fighters, osteopaths, fishermen, drivers, craftspeople; gardeners, chefs, acupuncturists, healers, adventurers.	Demonstrate sports; create a mime to explain something, coach workplace posture, assess workstation ergonomics.	Physical experience and movement, touch and feel.

(Continued)

Table 12.4 Continued

Intelligence type	Description	Typical job roles	Related tasks, activities or tests	Clues to preferred learning style
5. Spatial–visual	Visual and spatial perception; interpretation and creation of visual images; pictorial imagination and expression; understands relationship between images and meanings, and between space and effect.	Artists, designers, cartoonists, storyboarders, architects, photographers, sculptors, town planners, visionaries, inventors, engineers, cosmetics and beauty consultants.	Design a costume; interpret a painting; create a room layout; create a corporate logo; design a building; pack a pallet for shipment, organise storage space.	Pictures, shapes, images, 3D space.
6. Interpersonal	Perception of other people's feelings; ability to relate to others; interpretation of behaviour and communications; understands the relationships between people and their situations, including other people.	Therapists, HR professionals, mediators, leaders, counsellors, politicians, educators, salespeople, clergy, psychologists, teachers, doctors, organisers, carers, advertising people, coaches and mentors; there is a link to what is now described as Emotional Intelligence or EQ.	Interpret moods from facial expressions; demonstrate feelings through body language; affect the feelings of others in a planned way; coach or counsel another person.	Human contact, communications, cooperation, teamwork.
7. Intrapersonal	Self-awareness, personal cognisance, personal objectivity, the ability to understand oneself, one's relationship to others and the world, and one's own need for, and reaction to, change.	Anyone that is self-aware and involved in the process of changing personal thoughts, beliefs and behaviour in relation to their situation, other people, their purpose and aims – in this respect there is a similarity to Maslow's Self-Actualisation level (see Chapter 4) and also to EQ (see above).	Consider and decide one's own aims and personal changes required to achieve them (not necessarily reveal this to others); consider one's own Johari Window and decide options for development; consider and decide one's own position in relation to EQ.	Self-reflection, self-discovery.

develop better learning interventions, and to assess learning and training suitability and, most of all, effectiveness.

Howard Gardner suggests that his multiple intelligences theory represents a definition of human nature, from a cognitive perspective, i.e. how we understand, how we are aware of things. This gives a guide to people's preferred learning styles, their behavioural and working styles, and their natural strengths. The types of intelligence that a person possesses suggest not only a person's capabilities, but also the approaches in which they prefer to learn and develop their strengths – as well as develop their weaknesses.

So, for example:

- A person who is weak spatially yet strong numerically will be more likely to develop their spatial ability if it is explained and developed by using numbers and logic, and not by asking them to pack a shelf in front of an audience.
- Someone who is strong musically but weak numerically will be more likely to develop numerical and logical skills through music, and not by being bombarded by numbers alone.
- A person who is weak bodily and physically yet strong numerically might best be encouraged to increase their physical activity by encouraging them to learn about the mathematical and scientific relationships between exercise, diet and health, rather than forcing them to box or play rugby.

We know that the risk of possible failure and being forced to act and think unnaturally can have a significant negative influence on our learning effectiveness. If we are happy and relaxed, however, we will learn more readily than if we are unhappy and stressed.

It is simple logic to recognise that a person's strength is also their learning channel, while a person's weakness is not a great learning channel for them. So, develop people through their strengths and we not only stimulate their development, we also make them happy (because everyone enjoys working to their strengths) and we also grow their confidence and lift their self-belief (because they recognise they are doing well themselves and they can get feedback that they are doing well too). Developing a person's strengths will increase their response to the learning experience, which helps them to develop their weaknesses as well as their strengths.

Gardner was at pains to point out that intelligence in itself is not a measure of good or bad, or of happy or sad. The different intelligences are not a measure or reflection of emotion type since, he argued, intelligences are emotionally neutral. No type of intelligence is in itself an expression of happiness or sadness, or an expression of feeling good or bad.

Gardner went on to propose that people possess a set of intelligences – not just one single scalable aspect of a person's style and capability type or level of intelligence. However, in the past and through to today in many quarters, intelligence was and is viewed as something measurable on a single scale: a person was – supposedly – to have a high, low or average intelligence, or a person would be considered 'intelligent' or 'unintelligent'.

Gardner demonstrated intelligence to be a mixture of several abilities (as we saw, he explains seven intelligences and suggests three others), all of which are of great value in life. But nobody excels in all. In organisations and life in general, we need people who collectively are good at different things. A well-balanced world, and well-balanced organisations and teams, are necessarily comprised of people who possess different mixtures of intelligences. This gives the group a fuller collective capability than a group of identically able specialists (see Chapter 6 on team roles).

Despite all that Gardner has taught us, organisations commonly still apply their own criteria (for example, IQ – 'Intelligence Quotient' – tests) to judge 'intelligence' and then label the individual either suitable or not. Adult people in work in business organisations are routinely judged by inappropriate criteria and then written off as being worthless by the employer. This type of faulty assessment is common during recruitment selection, ongoing management assessments, and matters of career development and performance review.

Many very successful people were judged to be failures at school – Sir Winston Churchill was a fine example. They were, of course, judged according to a very narrow definition of what constitutes intelligence. Everyone has a unique and different mix of intelligence types, and commonly the people with the least 'conventional' intelligence (as measured using old-fashioned narrow criteria) actually possess enormous talent – often undervalued, unknown and underdeveloped.

Managing people of mixed intelligences

Gardner, and others, pointed out that managing people and organising a unique mixture of intelligence types is a hugely challenging affair. It starts, however, with the recognition that people have abilities and potential that extend far beyond traditional methods of assessment, and actually far beyond Gardner's seven intelligences, which even he established are only a starting point.

We should not judge and develop people (especially children, young people and people at the beginning of their careers) according to an arbitrary and narrow definition of intelligence. Just because they are 'not like us' should not preclude them from our consideration, and they may have a place in a changing and developing organisation. We must instead rediscover and promote the vast range of capabilities that have a value in life, then set about valuing people for who they are, what they can be, and helping them to grow and fulfil their potential.

Gardner made clear at the outset that there could be additional intelligences worthy of inclusion within the model; thus, the model is extendable to modern ideas beyond those listed in his seven basic intelligences. As already discussed, defining additional intelligences is not easy. But they do exist, and people do possess capabilities, potential and values far beyond the seven original 'multiple intelligences'.

Gardner knew – as we can now recognise – that his multiple intelligences theory left some room to grow. So why is it that so many educators and organisations are still stuck on IQ and the 'Three Rs' (the hackneyed 'Reading, Writing and Arithmetic' – I have never understood these since they patently don't all begin with the letter 'R'). The seven intelligences are a more rational first step towards valuing and developing people in a more compassionate and constructive way.

VAK: Visual–Auditory–Kinaesthetic Learning Styles Model

Gardner's seven intelligences can be further explained and understood by looking at another classical intelligence and learning styles model, known as the Visual–Auditory–Kinaesthetic learning styles model or 'inventory', usually abbreviated to VAK and illustrated in Table 12.5.

The VAK concept, theories and methods (initially also referred to as VAKT, for Visual–Auditory–Kinaesthetic–Tactile) were first developed by psychologists and teaching specialists such as Fernald, Keller, Orton, Gillingham, Stillman and Montessori, beginning in the 1920s. Early VAK specialists recognised that people learn in different ways: suppose you were unsuccessful in trying to get a person to learn some software by giving them some instruction or by showing them what to do (visual), they might learn better by having a go themselves (kinaesthetic). The VAK theory is a favourite of the accelerated learning community, and continues to feature in the teaching and education of young people.

The Visual–Auditory–Kinaesthetic learning styles model does not overlay Gardner's multiple intelligences; rather the VAK model provides a different perspective for understanding and explaining a person's preferred or dominant thinking and learning style, as well as their strengths. Gardner's theory is one way of looking at thinking styles, VAK is another.

According to the VAK model, most people possess a dominant or preferred learning style; however, some people have a mixed and evenly balanced blend of the three styles. Some have suggested that since they relate to three of the senses – sight, sound and touch – taste and smell might also be involved in learning approaches.

Table 12.5 The VAK learning styles model

Learning style	Description
Visual	Seeing and reading
Auditory	Listening and speaking
Kinaesthetic	Touching and doing

The VAK learning styles model provides a very easy and quick reference inventory by which to assess people's preferred learning styles, and then, most importantly, to design learning methods and experiences that match people's preferences:

- *Visual* learning style involves the use of seen or observed things, including pictures, diagrams, demonstrations, displays, handouts, films, flip chart, etc.
- *Auditory* learning style involves the transfer of information through listening – to the spoken word, of self or others, of sounds and noises
- *Kinaesthetic* learning involves physical experience – touching, feeling, holding, doing and practical hands-on experiences.

One can easily evaluate people's preferred style through the use of some simple question-naires based, in part, on the language they might use to describe things. A simple example can be found with evaluating someone's opinion of a success:

- Visual – 'that *looks* successful ...'
- Auditory – 'that *sounds* successful ...'
- Kinaesthetic – 'that *feels* about right ...'
- Gustatory – 'the *taste* of success ...'
- Olfactory – 'the sweet *smell* of success ...'

Bloom's Taxonomy of Learning Domains

Dr Benjamin S. Bloom initially published his ideas in 1956 to define three learning 'domains' that he called cognitive, affective and psychomotor (Bloom et al., 1956). Bloom's Taxonomy was primarily created for academic education (hence the apparent complexity); however, it is relevant to all types of learning and can be simplified quite easily.

Taxonomy means 'a set of classification principles' or 'structure', and *domain* simply means 'category'. Bloom and his colleagues were academics, looking at learning as a behavioural science and writing for other academics, which is why they didn't call it 'Bloom's Learning Structure', which might have made more sense to business people.

While Bloom used rather academic language, the meanings are simple to understand:

- *Cognitive domain* – intellectual capability, i.e. knowledge or 'think'
- *Affective domain* – feelings, emotions and behaviour, i.e. attitude or 'feel'
- *Psychomotor domain* – manual and physical skills, i.e. skills or 'do'.

In each of the three domains Bloom's Taxonomy is based on the idea that the categories are ordered in ascending degrees of difficulty. Of fundamental importance, Bloom argued, was that each category (or 'level') must be mastered before progressing to the next level. As such, the categories within each domain are levels of learning development, and these levels increase in difficulty.

The simple matrix structure enables a checklist or template to be developed for the design of learning programmes, training courses, lesson plans and so forth. Effective learning – especially in organisations, where training is to be converted into organisational results – should necessarily cover all levels of each of the domains, where relevant to the situation and the person learning.

The learner should benefit from development of knowledge and intellect (cognitive domain), attitude and beliefs (affective domain), and the ability to put physical and bodily skills into effect – in other words, to act (psychomotor domain).

Table 12.6 provides a simple overview of Bloom's Taxonomy, developed by the author.

Bloom's Taxonomy is a useful reference model for anyone involved in teaching, training, learning and coaching – in the design, delivery and evaluation of these development methods. At its fundamental level, the Taxonomy gives a simple, quick and easy checklist to start to plan any type of personal development. It helps open up possibilities for all aspects of the subject or need concerned, and suggests a range of methods available for delivery of teaching and learning. As with any checklist, it also helps to reduce the risks of overlooking some vital aspects of the development required.

The more detailed elements within each domain provide additional reference points for learning design and evaluation, whether for a single lesson, session or activity, or training need, or for an entire course, programme or syllabus, across a large group of trainees or students, or a whole organisation.

Table 12.6 Adaptation of Bloom's Taxonomy of Learning Domains

Cognitive – knowledge	Affective – attitude	Psychomotor – skills
1. Recall data	1. Receive (awareness)	1. Imitation (copy)
2. Understand	2. Respond (react)	2. Manipulation (follow instructions)
3. Apply (use)	3. Value (understand and act)	3. Develop precision
4. Analyse (structure/elements)	4. Organise personal value system	4. Articulation (combine, integrate related skills)
5. Synthesise (create/build)	5. Internalise value system (adopt behaviour)	5. Naturalisation (automate, become expert)
6. Evaluate (assess, judge in relational terms)	6. Monitor (pros, cons)	6. Control (behaviour)

At its most complex, Bloom's Taxonomy is continuously evolving, through the work of academics following in the footsteps of Bloom's early associates, as a fundamental concept for the development of formalised education across the world.

However, as with so many of the classical models involving the development of people and organisations, one has a choice as to how to use Bloom's Taxonomy; it is no more than a tool – or more aptly – a toolbox. Tools are most useful when the user controls them, not the other way round!

Donald Kirkpatrick's Training Evaluation Model

Assessing training effectiveness often entails using the four-level model developed by Donald L. Kirkpatrick (Winfrey, 1999). According to this model, evaluation should always begin with Level 1, and then, as time and budget allows, should move sequentially through Levels 2, 3 and 4. Information from each prior level serves as a base for the next level's evaluation. Thus, each successive level represents a more precise measure of the effectiveness of the training programme, but at the same time requires a more rigorous and time-consuming analysis.

Donald Kirkpatrick has written several other significant books about training and evaluation, and has consulted with some of the world's largest corporations. His theory has now become arguably the most widely used and popular model for the evaluation of training and learning. Kirkpatrick's four-level model is now considered an industry standard across the HR and training communities.

The four levels of Kirkpatrick's evaluation model essentially measure:

1. *Reaction of trainee* – what they thought and felt about the training
2. *Learning* – the resulting increase in knowledge or capability
3. *Behaviour* – extent of behaviour and capability improvement and implementation/ application
4. *Results* – the effects on the business or environment resulting from the trainee's performance.

All these measures are recommended for full and meaningful evaluation of learning in organisations, although their application broadly increases in complexity, and usually cost, through the Levels from 1 to 4. It is worth recognising that as one evaluates at successive levels, the outcomes are less and less influenced by the training *per se*, as other factors affect what is being measured.

Table 12.7 summarises the basic Kirkpatrick structure, where more detail on evaluating learning at the four levels can be found.

Table 12.7 The basic Kirkpatrick training evaluation structure

Level	Evaluation type (what is measured)	Evaluation type and characteristics	Examples of evaluation methods and tools	Relevance and practicability
1	Reaction	Reaction evaluation – did the delegates have a good time? – i.e. how they felt about the training or learning experience	'Happy sheets', feedback forms. Also verbal reaction, post-training surveys or questionnaires	Quick and very easy to obtain. Not expensive to gather or to analyse
2	Learning	Learning evaluation – measures of the increase in knowledge – before and after training	Typically assessments or tests before and after the training. Observation or interview can also be used	Relatively simple to devise; easy for quantifiable skills. Less easy for complex learning
3	Behaviour	Behaviour evaluation – the extent of applied learning back on the job – implementation	Observation and interview over time are required to assess change, relevance of change and sustainability of change	Measurement of behaviour change typically requires cooperation and skill of line managers
4	Results	Results evaluation – the effect on the business or environment by the trainee	Measures are already in place via normal management systems and reporting – the challenge is to relate to the trainee	Individually not difficult; unlike whole organisation. Process must attributing clear accountabilities

Summary

In this chapter you have:

- Seen a model for change that managers can use to help people through their learning
- Seen that unless people move from a stage where they *didn't know they didn't know*, learning cannot occur
- Explored the Johari Matrix showing areas of self-awareness that may help to guide people in discovering more about themselves – and therefore learn
- Learnt about four basic learning styles – activist, reflector, theorist, pragmatist

- Explored a complex model (after Jarvis) to explain everyday learning experiences
- Recognised that people have more than one intelligence that can be used as a route of learning
- Explored further approaches to learning based on pictures, words or practical application (VAK model), and on thinking, feeling and doing (Bloom's Taxonomy)
- Seen how to evaluate learning through four stages – reactions of students to the training, learning achieved, transfer of that learning applied to the workplace, and results for the organisation.

Questions

1. Consider a significant personal event such as change of job, promotion, redundancy, etc. and describe the feelings you had over time as you began to cope. Do they mirror those described in the model for change in Figure 12.1?
2. Consider how you learnt to drive a car or use a personal computer. What experiences did you have and which did you prefer? From this, draw any conclusions you have in respect of either the 'Conscious Competence' learning model or Kolb's learning cycle.
3. Reflect on Gardner's multiple intelligence framework and consider your own preferences for learning. How could you use any observations to improve your learning in the workplace?
4. Given Kirkpartick's training evaluation model, how might you evaluate transfer of your people's learning from a course (e.g. tutor-led or distance learning) back to the workplace?

References

Bloom, B. S. et al. (1956) *Taxonomy of Educational Objectives: Handbook I, The Cognitive Domain*, David McKay Co Inc.

Gardner, H. (1983) *Frames of Mind: Theory of multiple intelligences*, Basic Books.

Jarvis, P. (1995) *Adult and Continuing Education: Theory and practice*, 2nd Edition, Routledge, London.

Kolb, D. A. (1976) *The Learning Style Inventory*, Technical Manual, McBer, Boston, MA.

Kolb, D. A. and Fry, R. (1975) 'Toward an Applied Theory of Experiential Learning', in *Theories of Group Process* (C. Cooper, ed.), John Wiley, London.

Luft, J. (1969) *Of Human Interaction*, National Press, Palo Alto, CA.

Tennant, M. (1997) *Psychology and Adult Learning*, 2nd Edition, Routledge, London.

Waterman, R. H. and Peters, T. J. (1988) *In Search of Excellence: Lessons from America's best run companies*, Reissue edition, Warner Books.

Williams, D. (1999) 'Human Response to Change', *Futures*, Vol. 31, No. 6, August, pp. 606–616.

Winfrey, E. C. (1999) 'Kirkpatrick's Four Levels of Evaluation', in *Encyclopaedia of Educational Technology* (B. Hoffman, ed.), San Diego State University.

Further Reading

In addition to the reference list:

Kidd, J. R. (1991) *How Adults Learn*, Prentice-Hall, Regents ESL.

13

Management Style and Ability Development

Most companies spend all their time looking for another management concept and very little time following up the one they have just taught their managers.

Kenneth Blanchard and Robert Lorber, *Putting the One Minute Manager to Work,*
Collins Willow, 1984

Learning Outcomes

From the earlier chapters we know that people learn in different ways but what can managers and others do to influence how people learn? This chapter, and its companion web pages, explore some of the theories of management as they impact on ability development of others. The chapter has been written to cover particular elements of the National Occupational Standards for Management and Leadership (*Managing Self and Personal Skills – Unit 3; Providing Direction – Unit 11; Working with People – Units 21 and 28;* and *Achieving Results – Unit 50*), and it covers some of the requirements of the Chartered Management Institute's Diploma in Management compulsory *Unit C41 – Developing your Management Style* (in respect of developing yourself), some of the compulsory *Unit C45 – Managing Performance* and most of the optional *Unit O42 – Developing Personnel and Personnel Performance*. This chapter will also be of value to those studying the CIPD Professional Development Scheme – particularly the *Leadership and Management* and *People Management and Development* modules, as well as people studying any of the CIPD specialist electives in *Learning and Development*.

By the end of this chapter you will:

- Consider whether managers are born or can develop (learn) their skills
- Explore what behaviours managers should focus on to be successful

- Consider whether it is better to have a range of styles to get work done through others
- Understand the importance of having a style to match the circumstances to help others improve their performance
- Review the differences between transactional and transformational leadership.

Early Theories

The debate over which management style is the most effective goes back as far as Confucius, who in 500 BC attempted to persuade the feudal kingdoms of ancient China that the effective leader should be 'humane, benevolent and just'. Not everyone was in agreement – Ch'in Shih Huang Ti, the first Emperor of China, some 200 years later disagreed and had 460 Confucian monks beheaded.

Over the centuries, the traits of the 'ideal' leader were considered. This 'Great Man' approach involved studying leaders of proven excellence and attempting to identify what they had in common. By the mid-1900s it was concluded that the qualities, characteristics and skills required in a leader are determined largely by the demands of the situation.

The work of Rensis Likert (see Chapter 4), in the Michigan studies, aimed to uncover what conditions would bring about the greatest workers' productivity. In some ways, this was similar to the intent and methods of the earlier Hawthorne Experiments (see Chapter 4). Both studies suggested that the physical elements of management seem to have little effect upon increasing motivation, ability and confidence that enhanced commitment. This was later demonstrated even more powerfully by Herzberg (Chapter 4) with his distinction between 'hygiene' and 'motivating' factors. The conclusion of these studies is that the way that the manager behaves has the most powerful effect on motivation.

The Michigan study concluded that managers can be either job centred or employee centred and that the latter were more effective. These studies' conclusions were further developed in the Ohio State studies that showed that the two ends of the Michigan continuum were not opposites but relatively independent of each other. The distinction created many models of management style, all largely based upon these insights.

Today, these independent variables are more often called a concern for production and a concern for relationships (further developed by Blake), or task orientation and relationship orientation (further developed by Reddin). However, when taken together they produce what are called 'management styles'. These will be explored as a preface to identifying a model for developing the ability of followers to be effective in their job role.

In the last 80 years or so in the literature on leadership there have been four main 'generations' of theory:

- Trait theories
- Behavioural theories

- Style – developing to contingency theories
- Transformational theories.

We shall review each in turn.

Trait theories

Warren Bennis (1998) concluded that leaders are people who are able to express themselves fully. They also know what they want, why they want it and how to communicate what they want to others, in order to gain their cooperation and support. They also know how to achieve their goals. Yet, what is it that makes someone exceptional in this respect? As soon as we study the lives of people who have been labelled as great or effective leaders, such as political figures like Nelson Mandela or Margaret Thatcher, it becomes clear that they have very different qualities.

Rather than starting with exceptional leaders, many tried to define the general qualities or traits they believed should be present. While some early trait research studies identified personality characteristics that appear to differentiate leaders from followers, others found no differences in characteristics between leaders and followers, or even found people who possessed them were less likely to become leaders than others. However, many popular books on leadership today provide lists of traits that are considered fundamental for effective leadership – John Gardner's (1989) is one example. Essentially, they say that if a person possesses these traits he or she will be able to take the lead in very different situations. While for some they are a guide (see Box 13.1), they do leave many questions.

The first problem is that those in search of 'traits' define a set of characteristics that make a leader – irrespective of the situation. (History suggests that this is not the case: while Churchill's qualities were exceptional in wartime, he lost the next peace-time election.) Was the situation not important? Secondly, many writers also tended to mix some very different qualities. We can see that some of Gardner's qualities, for example, are aspects of a person's behaviour, some are skills, while others are to do with temperament and intelligence. It is also a lengthy list – so what happens when someone has some, but not all, of the qualities? On the other hand, the list is not exhaustive, so what of other 'leadership qualities' that someone might have?

Some writers (Wright, 1996) tried looking at what combinations of traits might be good for a particular situation. While it does appear possible to link groups of personality traits to success in different situations, it remains open to debate.

There is a concern that many such lists have apparent 'maleness' (see Rosener, 1997). When men and women are asked about each other's characteristics and leadership qualities, both sexes tend to have difficulties in seeing women as leaders. However, whether the characteristics of leaders can be considered 'male' is questionable. Since it is hard enough to make a list of leadership traits that stands up to questioning, then the same certainly applies to lists of leadership traits specific to one or other gender.

Box 13.1: Gardner's attributes of leadership

John Gardner (1989) studied a large number of US businesses and leaders, and concluded that there were some qualities or attributes that did appear to mean that a leader in one situation could lead in another. These included, in no particular order:

- Physical vitality and stamina
- Courage and resolution
- Eagerness to accept responsibility
- Intelligence and action-orientated judgement
- Need for achievement
- Task competence
- Adaptability/flexibility
- Understanding of followers and their needs
- Capacity to motivate people
- Skill in dealing with people
- Self-confidence
- Decisiveness
- Trustworthiness
- Assertiveness.

Behavioural theories

Once traits had been explored, researchers turned to what leaders actually did – how they behaved – especially towards followers; they moved from *leaders* to *leadership*. This became the popular way of discussing leadership within organisations in the 1950s and early 1960s. Different patterns of behaviour were grouped together and labelled as 'styles' – perhaps the best known being Blake and Mouton's Managerial Grid (see Chapter 4). Various schemes appeared, designed to diagnose and develop people's style of working. Despite different names, the basic ideas were very similar. The four main styles that appear are:

- *Concern for task*. Here leaders emphasise the achievement of concrete objectives. They look for high levels of productivity and ways to instruct and organise people, and decide on activities in order to meet those objectives.
- *Concern for people*. In this style, leaders look upon their followers as people with emotions – their needs, interests, problems, development and so on. They are not simply units of production or means to an end.

- *Directive leadership.* This style is characterised by leaders taking decisions for others – and expecting followers or subordinates to follow instructions.
- *Participative leadership.* Here leaders try to share decision-making with others, encouraging people to develop their ideas and contribute.

Books and training materials often describe these two styles: concern for 'task' is set against concern for 'people' (after Blake and Mouton), and 'directive' is contrasted with 'participative' leadership (for example, McGregor's portrayal of managers as 'Theory X' or 'Theory Y' – see Chapter 4).

Many of the early writers that looked to participative and people-centred leadership argued that it brought about greater satisfaction amongst followers (subordinates). However, when researchers explored this there were many differences and inconsistencies between studies; it was difficult to say style of leadership was significant in enabling one group to work better than another. Perhaps the main problem, though, was one shared with those who looked for traits. The researchers did not look properly at the context or setting in which the style was used. Would the same style work as well in a criminal gang, a rugby team, and again in a hospital accident and emergency department? The styles that leaders can adopt are far more affected by those they are working with, the environment they are operating within and the nature of the task than had been originally thought.

Style theories

Researchers began to turn to the contexts in which leadership is exercised – and the idea that what is needed changes from situation to situation. Some looked to the *processes* by which leaders emerge in different circumstances – for example, in crises or where there is a stable business environment. Others turned to the ways in which leaders and followers viewed each other in various contexts – for example, in the army, political parties and in companies. The most extreme view was that just about everything was determined by the context. But most authors and writers did not take this route. They brought the idea of 'style' with them, believing that the style needed would change with the situation. Another way of putting this is that particular contexts would demand particular forms of leadership. This placed a premium on people who were able to develop an ability to work in different ways, could develop diverse people with a range of abilities and could change their style to suit the situation.

Contingency theories

What began to develop was a contingency approach. The central idea was that effective leadership was dependent on a mix of factors. For example, Fred E. Fiedler (1997) argued that effectiveness depends on two interacting factors: leadership style and the degree to which the situation gives the leader control and influence. Four things are important here:

- *The relationship between the leaders and followers.* If leaders are respected they are more likely to have the support of others.
- *The structure of the task.* If the task is clearly spelled out, defining goals, methods and standards of performance, then it is more likely that leaders will be able to exert influence.
- *The team.* As Adair pointed out (see Chapter 4), the leader also needs to consider the development of the team – even if briefing just one person, others may be influenced.
- *Position power.* If an organisation or group confers powers on the leader for the purpose of getting the job done, then this may well increase the influence of the leader.

Models like this can help us to think about what we are doing in different situations. For example, we may be more directive where a quick response is needed and where people are used to being told what to do rather than having to solve problems themselves.

People vs Production

As we saw in Chapter 4, with Jane Moulton, Blake developed the work of the Michigan and Ohio State studies and expressed his theory in the form of a grid (Figure 13.1). The vertical axis plots 'concern for people' while the horizontal axis plots 'concern for the task or production'. The detail of this grid can be found in Chapter 4.

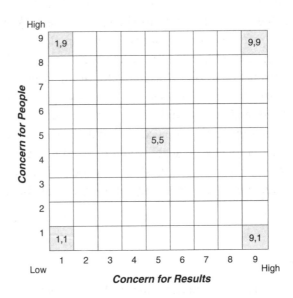

Figure 13.1 Adaptation of Blake and Moulton Grid Theory.

A dialogue explaining each area in more detail can be found on the companion web pages.

By evaluating a manager's style, Grid theory aims to make behaviours as tangible and objective as any other business asset. By studying each of the seven Leadership Grid styles and the resulting relationship skill behaviours, it is suggested that teams can examine, in objective terms, how a manager's behaviour helps or hinders them when developing their ability. Teams can explore types of feedback that work best for them and help to understand why. They can openly discuss how to improve decision-making and develop skills to resolve conflict. When discussing productivity, these and other subjects are usually considered 'off limits', but are the very subjects that usually get in the way of improving ability and productivity. The Grid approach aims to make these subjects not only 'discussable', but measurable in objective terms that generate empathy, motivation to improve and creativity in problem-solving.

Later developments of this work were situational – where the effectiveness of a management style depended upon the situation. The situation in the case of Hersey and Blanchard is characterised mainly by the task maturity (or ability) of the subordinates, their readiness to accept less control. In the case of Reddin, it is analysed in a more complex way and includes the expectations of the boss, co-workers as well as subordinates, the technology and the organisational culture.

These models will be developed further into Mackay's Ability Development Model in Chapter 14.

Authority vs Freedom

We discussed in Chapter 4 that Robert Tannenbaum and Warren Schmidt devised a simple continuum model that has been developed to a further level (see Figure 13.2). Fundamentally, it shows the relationship between the level of freedom that a manager chooses to give to a team and the level of authority used by the manager. As the team's freedom is increased, so the manager's authority decreases. This is a positive way for both teams and managers to develop.

Note that this model builds upon the early work of Lewin et al. (see Chapter 4); both 'autocratic' (left-hand side of model) and 'democratic' (right-hand side) styles are apparent, but *'laissez-faire'* is absent. The model emphasises that the dynamic interactions between managers and staff is all about transactions, be it tell, sell, consult or share. While share and consult interactions are nicer and more social than tell and sell, it is still about interactions.

When examining and applying the Tannenbaum and Schmidt principles, it is extremely important to remember that, irrespective of the amount of responsibility and freedom delegated by a manager to a team, the manager retains accountability for any catastrophic problems that result. Delegating freedom and decision-making responsibility to a team absolutely does not absolve the manager of accountability. That is why delegating, whether to

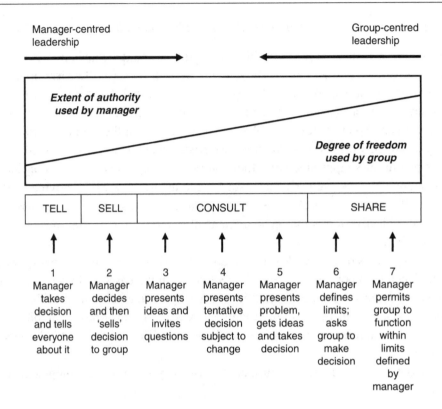

Figure 13.2 An adaptation of the Tannenbaum and Schmidt Continuum, showing the levels of delegated freedom, with some added explanation aimed at making it easier to understand and apply.

teams or individuals, requires a very grown-up manager. If everything goes well, the team must get the credit; if it all goes horribly wrong, the manager must take the blame. This is entirely fair, because the manager is ultimately responsible for judging the seriousness of any given situation – including the risks entailed – and the level of freedom that can safely be granted to the team to deal with it. This is not actually part of the Tannenbaum and Schmidt Continuum, but it is vital to apply this philosophy or the model will definitely be weakened, or at worse completely backfire.

More detail to Figure 13.2 to assist the practitioner can be found on the companion web pages.

Supportive vs Directive Behaviour

Chapter 4 introduced the Situational Leadership Model of Kenneth Blanchard and Paul Hersey that proposed that a manager's preferred style depends on the situation – in this case,

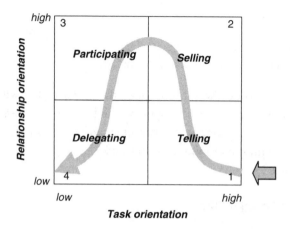

Figure 13.3 Adaptation of Hersey and Blanchard's Situational Leadership Model.

largely the 'maturity' of the followers – it is a valuable tool to consider how a manager can help improve a follower's ability to undertake a task and will be explored in more detail in Chapter 14.

Note from Figure 13.3 that the two dimensions are supportive behaviours and directive behaviours; each scale is relative (high or low), where 'low' just means less than average (it does not mean zero) while the high end of the scale means higher than average.

For the moment, it is worth exploring in simplistic terms each level in turn.

Level 1 – Telling/giving direction

- Follower: unable and/or unwilling
- Leader: high task focus, low relationship focus.

When the follower cannot do the job and/or is not motivated, then the leader takes a highly directive role, telling them what to do yet without a great deal of concern for their relationship. The leader may also provide a working structure, both for the job and in terms of how the person is monitored.

This is taking a particularly managerial stance, using whatever legitimate coercive power the leader has to make the person do the job that they do not want to do.

The relationship is less important here; first, the lower 'task maturity' of the person is assumed to lead to an attitude that does not respond well to a relationship-based approach, and second because the person may be replaced if they do not perform as required.

The style was recommended for dealing with new recruits to a job that just wanted clear instructions to do the job, or where the work was menial or repetitive, or where things had to be completed within a short time span. Subordinates are viewed as being unable and/or unwilling to 'do a good job'.

Level 2 – Selling/teaching

- Follower: unable yet willing
- Leader: high task focus, high relationship focus.

When the follower wants to do the job but lacks the skills or knowledge, the leader now turns on the charm more, acting in a supportive and friendlier manner as they help the follower to complete the task. Sometimes characterised as a 'training' approach, it is to be used when people are willing and motivated but lack the required 'maturity' or 'ability' to do the job to the required standard.

Level 3 – Participating/supporting

- Follower: able yet unwilling
- Leader: low task focus, high relationship focus.

When the follower can do the job, but is refusing to do it, the leader need not worry about showing them what to do, and instead is concerned with finding out why the person is refusing and thence persuading them to cooperate. It involves high support and low direction, and is used when people are able, but are perhaps unwilling or insecure (i.e. they are of 'moderate to high task maturity'). It is not a person's inability that holds them back at this level, so it is a manager's job to uncover the personal barriers to achievement of the objectives. Indeed, if a manager were to be too directive (suggesting that they thought the follower was unable to do the task), the follower's confidence might be undermined.

Level 4 – Delegating/giving freedom

- Follower: able and willing
- Leader: low task focus, low relationship focus.

When the follower can do the job and is motivated to do it, their 'task maturity' is such that the leader can basically leave them to it, trusting them to get on with the job. Note, however, the leader still identifies the problem or issue, but the responsibility for carrying out the response is given to followers. It does involve followers having a high degree of competence and maturity (i.e. people know what to do and are motivated to do it).

Effectiveness Orientation

Bill Reddin (1987) made the breakthrough to the next level of practical leadership theories. He is best known for the 3-D theory; in the mid-1980s it was the most powerful situational analysis of management of its time.

He developed the first relatively simple method of measuring what he called 'situational demands' – i.e. the things that dictate how a manager must operate to be most effective. His model was founded on the two basic dimensions of leadership identified by the Ohio State studies. He called them task orientation and relationships orientation. However, he introduced what he called a third dimension – effectiveness (see Chapter 7). Effectiveness was what resulted when one used the right style of leadership for the particular situation.

Reddin proposed and used an eight-box model of management behaviour (see Figure 13.4). Unlike some earlier writers (but like Blake), Reddin proposed that relationships orientation and task orientation are relatively independent – and that a manager can exhibit relatively high or relatively low degrees of each.

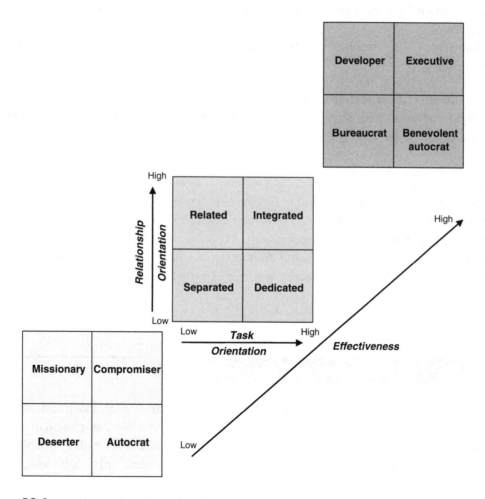

Figure 13.4 Reddin's 3-D style model. The complete 3-D style model consists of four basic styles, four more effective managerial styles, and four less effective managerial styles. The middle plane may be omitted once the basic style concept is understood.

Reddin's advance over Blake was his recognition that the same behaviour can be appropriate or inappropriate to the situation, and gave descriptions to the effective and ineffective styles. In fact, he showed that managerial behaviour can be positive or negative in any given situation. A major breakthrough of the theory was the acceptance that delegation was appropriate only in specific situations and that it was essentially hands-off in nature.

Reddin's three dimensions are:

- *Task orientation* – the extent to which a manager directs his (or her) subordinates' efforts towards goal attainment, characterised by planning, organising and controlling
- *Relationships orientation* – the extent to which a manager has personal job relationships, characterised by mutual trust, respect for subordinates' ideas and consideration for their feelings
- *Effectiveness* – the extent to which a manager achieves the output requirements of his or her position.

It is important to note that Reddin's research led him to the view that degrees of relationships orientation and degrees of task orientation were independent of effectiveness – that either could be correlated with success dependent upon the situation. As Reddin said:

> *Some managers have learned that to be effective they must sometimes create an atmosphere which will induce self-motivation among their subordinates and sometimes act in ways that appear either hard or soft. At other times, they must quietly efface themselves for a while and appear to do nothing. It would seem more accurate to say, then, that any basic style (of management) may be used more or less effectively, depending upon the situation.*

Transformational Leadership Style Inventory

James McGregor Burns (1978) distinguishes between transactional and transformational leadership; the work parallels other people such as Chris Argyris as it has a moral dimension.

Transactional managers 'approach their followers with an eye to trading one thing for another' while transformational managers are 'visionary leaders' who seek to appeal to their followers' *'better nature and move them toward higher and more universal needs and purposes'*. In other words, the leader is seen as a change agent.

Transactional leadership is recognised as good, effective and proper management based upon the techniques of management developed over the last 50 years. It recognises the need for and implements such processes as performance appraisal, performance-related pay, job descriptions, management by objectives, organisational process analysis and clarification, and job grading. It also recognises and uses praise, recognition and the delegation of responsibility. Such leadership puts into practice the thoughts of Herzberg.

One might argue that such leadership is rare enough. Indeed, if more organisations practised transactional leadership, the world would be a better, happier and more productive place. However, it is insufficient for James McGregor Burns. He argues that beyond this is transformational leadership.

Transactional leadership is still top-down. It is fair, process orientated, system driven, as objective as it can be but the decisions on goals and rewards are still made at the top and cascaded down. The ultimate aim of management by objectives, for example, would be that the objectives for every person and department in an organisation can be logically deduced from the objectives of the organisation as a whole. No such logical tree of objectives has ever existed, but that is the thinking behind MbO (management by objectives).

James McGregor Burns's view of transformational leadership is less about management by objectives and more about management by vision. One might think of a rank order of types of management, not what Burns says, but it places his ideas in perspective.

- Management by *command* – unsophisticated management in which subordinates are told what to do and have little say in what and when
- Management by *objectives* – process management in which subordinates are given goals and they decide how to achieve them
- Management by *communication* – sophisticated organisations in which skilled subordinates deduce their own goals by learning about the needs of the organisation
- Management by *vision* – in which management is about inspiring people to achieve what only they know they can achieve by concentrating on what is (just) possible.

Transformational leadership is about hearts and minds, about empowering people not controlling them; the main goals are summarised in Box 13.2. The word transformation means change, and transformational leadership is about empowering everyone in the organisation to learn, seek change and improvement, never to be satisfied with what is done today. It is based upon trusting skilled, dedicated, intelligent people doing what they have learned is best, taking responsibility immediately (indeed to seize it) and sharing leadership throughout the organisation. The leader's job is to facilitate increased learning, trust and understanding.

Burns's ideas now form the basis of the James McGregor Burns Academy of Leadership at the University of Maryland. When compared to Maslow, we can see that transformational leadership focuses on our higher aspirations (see Figure 13.5).

Box 13.2: The main goals of transformational leadership

- Transferring a vision
- Transferring an organisation
- Developing a collaborative culture
- Helping people develop
- Helping people solve problems more effectively.

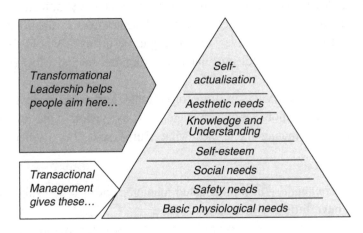

Figure 13.5 Transformational leadership focuses on higher aspirations.

Of all the models on offer, Paul Hersey and Kenneth Blanchard's classic study of situational leadership style is the most influential. There is a visible line of models and theories stemming from the Michigan studies, through the Ohio State studies, to Blake's grid through Hersey and Blanchard's situational leadership and then on to Reddin's 3-D theory. The development in the line is an increasing awareness of the importance of the situation in defining management style. (Hersey and Blanchard's situational leadership text, later made more digestible by *The One Minute Manager*, is fundamental in this sequence.)

Aside from their non-specific nature, there are some concerns with all such models – see the companion web pages.

Clearly, context is all – and the context of developing people depending on their particular situation will be explored in Chapter 14.

Summary

In this chapter you have:

- Explored trait theories that propose managers are born rather than can develop (learn) their skills
- Considered what behaviours managers should focus on to be successful
- Been introduced to the concept that managers need to behave on a continuum between autocratic and democratic
- Explored the importance of having a flexible style to match the circumstances to help others improve their performance
- Noted that flexibility is important but only if that flexibility proves to be effective
- Seen that transactional leaders trade one thing with another to reach particular aims, whereas transformational leaders act as change managers.

Questions

1. Describe your manager or one that you have known. How would you describe their style? What evidence supports your analysis?
2. Describe your best boss – which you've had or could have. Describe your worst boss – which you've had or could have. Compare your answers with others and explain any differences.
3. What would you want of a manager in the first few days of starting a new job? Compare and contrast that with what you want from them after you have been in the job for several months.
4. Considering the culture of your organisation and the prevailing style of senior management, discuss the appropriateness of that style, basing your observations on any theory that you have read about.

References

Bennis, W. (1998) *On Becoming a Leader*, Arrow, London.

Burns, J. M. (1978) *Leadership*, Harper Collins, New York.

Fiedler, F. E. (1997) Situational Control and a Dynamic Theory of Leadership, in *Leadership: Classical, contemporary and critical approaches* (K. Grint, ed.), Oxford University Press, Oxford.

Gardner, J. (1989) *On Leadership*, Free Press, New York.

Reddin, W. J. (1987) *How to Make your Management Style More Effective*, McGraw-Hill.

Rosener, J. B. (1997) Sexual Static, in *Leadership: Classical, contemporary and critical approaches* (K. Grint, ed.), Oxford University Press, Oxford.

Wright, P. (1996) *Managerial Leadership*, Routledge, London.

Further Reading

In addition to the references listed:

Lubit, R. H. (2003) *Coping with Toxic Managers ... And Other Impossible People in the Workplace*, Financial Times Prentice-Hall.

Stout Rostoon, S. (2002) *Accelerating Performance: Powerful New Techniques to Develop People*, Kogan Page.

Watkins, M. (2003) *The First 90 Days: Critical Success Strategies for New Leaders at All Levels*, Harvard Business School Press.

Wills, M. (1993) *Managing the Training Process*, McGraw-Hill.

14

Mackay's Ability Development Model

Obviously, you have to get rid of the good people as soon as possible or they will make you miserable ...

Scott Adams, the creator of The Dilbert Principle

Learning Outcomes

This chapter, and its companion web pages, pull together a range of theoretical approaches to ability development, giving a highly practical model for managers. The chapter has been written to cover particular elements of the National Occupational Standards for Management and Leadership: *Providing Direction – Lead People 9*; *Facilitating Change – Foster Innovation 14*; many sections of *Working with People*; and *Achieving Results – Unit 50*, and it covers some of the requirements of the Chartered Management Institute's Diploma in Management compulsory *Unit C41 – Developing your Management Style* (in respect of developing the trust and support of others), some of the *Effective Communications* elements of compulsory *Unit C44*, some of the compulsory *Unit C45 – Managing Performance* and most of the optional *Unit O42 – Developing Personnel and Personnel Performance*. This chapter will also be of value to those studying the CIPD Professional Development Scheme – particularly the *Leadership and Management* and *People Management and Development* modules, as well as people studying any of the CIPD specialist electives in *Learning and Development*.

By the end of this chapter you will:

- Have looked at how much a manager might influence a person's ability development
- Be able to consider both the task being done and the person doing the work – and explore the interaction of the two variables
- Have looked at four levels of ability and what to do at each level
- Have been introduced to a practical model for ability development

- Begin to uncover a way of evaluating your management style, its flexibility and its effectiveness in developing the ability of others.

Background to the Ability Development Model

Theories of management, motivation and leadership abound; most of them focus on getting work done through other people. When one distils each theory down to the fundamentals, there is no escaping the fact that they all, to a greater or lesser extent, have to do with the *people*. That is, the people whose responsibility it is to initiate the process of activity and the people whose responsibility it is to undertake the activity. For our purposes here, we'll call the first 'leaders' and the second 'followers'. In this way, we'll break down the hierarchical basis of many views of the management function, where 'I am the boss, you do as I say or else' tends to prevail.

In today's organisations we often find people have a leadership role for a given task, where they may or may not have a hierarchical control or sanction over others involved in the work. This is particularly true in a project management or matrix management environment, or where an individual 'does work' for a number of people.

The purpose of this chapter is to provide a background to the situational Ability Development Model (ADM) developed by the author and marketed through Duncan Alexander & Wilmshurst. It uses as its basis the Hersey and Blanchard Situational Leadership Model discussed in Chapter 13.

Managers may evaluate their ability development style through the use of a questionnaire. It should be realised that, clearly, it is not possible to develop situations that accurately reflect true-life experiences that one might most easily relate to in the workplace, although the author has made an attempt to provide sufficient variety to illustrate the concept of the ADM.

See the companion web pages for more information on the use of questionnaires.

Questionnaires

In the ability development elements of the questionnaire, a number of scenarios have been devised where readers are asked to consider each situation on its merits and from the 'clues' in the mini case-scenario decide on what they would do, if anything, as a consequence. A selection of them has been reproduced in this chapter to illustrate key ideas.

Naturally, five or six lines of text do not represent the full understanding that an individual 'leader' may have of their 'followers'. Therefore, in practice, a person developing a group or individual will have a much better understanding of how they might deal with a given situation. However, the questionnaire is designed to provide enough information to guide the individual on choosing the most *effective* approach to ability development in the given situation.

Alternative responses

Having considered their likely action, respondents to the questionnaires are then asked to choose which of the four alternative actions (a–d) most closely matches their likely approach to ability development. Again, since the world does not easily divide itself into four separate alternatives, respondents are asked to identify with the one approach that *most closely* resembles what they might actually do. (The reader is invited to be aware of their 'theory-in-action' and 'espoused theory' at this point – see Chapter 15.)

In scanning the alternative responses, delegates can see that they vary on the amount of involvement, direction and control they have with each situation, and on the amount of dialogue they may choose to have with the follower. The alternative style responses will be discussed further below.

Task Ability Control Orientation

Task ability behaviour is the extent to which the 'leader' engages in defining the task, telling the what, when, where, why and how of a job – and if there is more than one person, who is to do what in:

- Goal setting
- Organising
- Deciding time limits
- Directing
- Controlling.

When a 'leader' is trying to get work done through a follower, there is a varying amount of attention that must be given to how the task should be done. Let us illustrate this with a case study (see Box 14.1).

In this situation, the leader needs to be much more 'task ability orientated' because the follower's ability to do the job to the required standard cannot be left to chance; in this situation, the follower's *task maturity* – for this task – is low.

Dropping someone 'in the deep end' to 'learn on the job' means that the leader must be prepared for the follower to make errors, since they can only 'best guess' what is required. The new recruit would not feel too good about herself struggling to undertake her first tasks, her confidence will be undermined and, before long, her motivation towards her new employer will decline.

If someone does not know how to do a particular task and are ticked off for getting it wrong when they 'have a go', their motivation to try again will be compromised. So, the leader needs to address the follower's *ability* before they can be expected to perform.

Box 14.1: Helping a new recruit with basic tasks in the first days in a new job

Jan is an outgoing and personable administrator who has recently joined Duncan Alexander & Wilmshurst as an Office Manager. She has good keyboard skills, shorthand and an organised approach to general office duties.

Suppose, early on her first day, one of the Partners asks her to do a couple of letters for him. Now, he could hand her some handwritten notes, a dictation tape or ask her to take some shorthand. Having done that, he could just leave her to get on with it. He may think he is being highly effective as he can now get on with his own work. However, he has not clarified how he wants the letter to be laid out on the headed paper, what typeface the firm uses – is it the Microsoft Word 'Times New Roman' default, 10 or 12 point? How does he sign himself? When would he need the letters back – immediately, by lunch, or would before the evening post be OK? What about franking and the mail room? He, or someone else in the organisation, would have to explain more concisely what is required.

Now, while Jan is tenacious and willing to do her best, the lack of direction is doing nothing to help her find her feet in the new job. Treated like this, she can soon become disenchanted with her new employers.

He needs to give Jan better instructions – clear and straightforward instructions – not too detailed at first: that may only serve to confuse or overload. It is not very helpful if the Partner spends four hours explaining in intricate detail all abut the job on the first morning, it is too much too soon.

Let us now consider Jan several weeks into her new job, where she has been able to become proficient at handling general correspondence (see Box 14.2).

Box 14.2: Helping a new recruit several weeks into the job with basic tasks

Jan has been working for Duncan Alexander & Wilmshurst for several weeks now. She has developed a clear understanding of how the Partner works with the key accounts and the varied work of the firm. She knows pretty well all there is to know about general correspondence, electronic and paper filing, and outgoing mail and, indeed, has been making positive, practical suggestions on how office administration might be improved. Just imagine how she would respond now if a Partner in the firm gave her some correspondence to do and started to explain how she should lay out letters and what the company house style is!

In this situation, for that task of general administration and correspondence, she is being over-supervised, which will have the same detrimental effect on her as being left to 'sink or swim'. The leader needs to be much less task ability orientated and less directive because – for this task – Jan has demonstrated her *task ability maturity*. Indeed, if she comes up with a bright idea on how to improve office procedures (which she actually did recently to reduce the time it takes, by 10 per cent, to generate an invoice) that makes sense to the Partner, what does she want from him? Not being told how he would do it and his intervention to make sure his ideas were followed; her ideas are probably better than his anyway! She wants very little from him save his support and sanction to go ahead; in other words, for him to act as a mentor – a 'wise counsellor', available as required.

So, as far as the task ability orientation of a leader is concerned, there is a need for the leader to be sensitive to the individual's position (task ability maturity) on the continuum between 'high task ability orientation' (where the leader needs to be very directive to get the task done to the required standard) and 'low task ability orientation' (where the 'leader' should not get too involved, since the follower is quite capable of doing the work to the required standard unsupervised).

We can see here a scale of ability, but this is only one of the factors. Motivation and Confidence are also important issues. If Jan were not motivated to do a job, the Partner would need to address this directly and deal with the problem (see Chapter 9 for a similar approach). Equally, if Jan was anxious about a part of her job and would not do it because she was not confident of getting it right, then again, the Partner would need to address her confidence (see Chapter 19 for a similar approach). When she is both motivated and confident, the Partner would need to give much less attention to these issues.

Clearly, from the leader's point of view, it is in their interests to get the follower from the high task ability orientation to the low task ability orientation end of the continuum represented in Figure 14.1.

In order to progress a follower along the continuum, the leader needs to use differing styles to assist the person in their development or task ability maturity. As we have seen, the leader may need to be aware of a number of models of learning as they take the follower along the continuum, such as those outlined in Chapter 13. In this model, we propose four different approaches to assist the follower with developing their task ability maturity, of which more later.

So far, our 'leader', the Partner in the example, has been very 'transactional' in their approach (see Chapter 13). They have not given much attention to the *person* doing the task – the thoughts, feelings and context of the 'follower' – save for recognising that when there is low task ability maturity (Box 14.1), the person needs clear *instructions* (because anything less is going to leave too much to chance, which will compromise our follower's motivation and confidence) and where there is high task ability maturity (Box 14.2), the

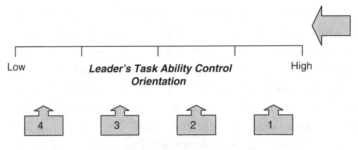

Follower's Level of Task Ability Maturity

Figure 14.1 The task ability orientation continuum. A new recruit, for example, would start at the right-hand side and the leader would need to take them through four stages to improve their task ability maturity until the follower is at the left-hand end, where they are fully competent and the leader needs to do little to assist them with the task. Individuals may appear anywhere on the continuum from time to time and indeed can slip back to a lower level of ability owing, for example, to increased complexity in the workplace.

follower needs *support* but otherwise little intervention from the leader (because anything more is going to undermine the follower's confidence and probably, too, in time, their motivation).

Let us turn to the working relationship between the leader and follower.

Relationship Orientation

First, a definition: relationship orientation is the degree to which the 'leader' engages in two-way or multi-way communication, giving 'socio-emotional' support by facilitation inter-actions, active listening and providing feedback to the 'follower'. This means considering the human dimension of the person undertaking the work.

As with task orientation, there is a range of approaches that the leader can take. Their approach will depend on the situation presented by the follower when undertaking the task. The degree to which the leader engages in relationship-orientated approaches will range from lower than average (and that does not mean zero) through to higher than average – the height or degree to which this approach is taken being dependent on the follower's needs and their relationship with the leader.

Again, this orientation can best be illustrated by example (see Box 14.3).

Now, let us consider the situation of our new recruit, Jan, a couple of days into the job, where Jan is about to make what she thinks is a useful suggestion about how to improve her effectiveness in her administrative duties (Box 14.4).

Box 14.3: Managing the relationship with a new recruit on the first day into a job

Let us take Jan, our new recruit. On day 1, when she is 'learning the ropes', it is not particularly helpful if the 'leader' engages in too much open dialogue, asking 'How do you feel we might do the job better or, 'what do you think about...?.' It's too soon. As said earlier, Jan just needs clear instructions so she can get on with making an early impact.

Followers need leaders to ensure that they have made themselves clear – that they seek to be understood rather than force the 'follower' to understand. In this situation, the follower is unlikely to respond to too high a relationship orientation – it is too early.

Only when Jan has got more comfortable with her basic tasks will she feel more like 'opening up' to discussion and dialogue about her job.

Box 14.4: Managing the relationship with a new recruit when she makes a suggestion just days into a job

Let us take Jan, our new recruit, a couple of days into her new job. The Partner mentions that he is open to ideas: 'How do you feel we might do the job better?'

She had been told to 'file as you go' with client correspondence – much as one might do in a law or accounting firm. However, from her point of view, this means that she makes several journeys each day to the central client filing to the same file. She comes to the Partner and suggests keeping filing in a 'filing tray' on her desk and filing 'once a fortnight or so when the tray is full'.

Now, unfortunately, this is not a good idea (as anyone picking up the file would not have the latest details to hand and, with so many files open, it could lead to chaos across the firm). Hitherto, Jan has not had the opportunity to see things from the wider firm perspective and other people's involvement with a given client. Her task maturity is developing but is not yet very high.

The Partner could just tell her to follow usual office procedures – the job would be done properly: but what of the person, how might she feel about this approach?

Here, the Partner needs to consider how Jan might respond when she has come up with an idea that has been quashed. He now needs to consider more the person doing the task – she needs him to be acting in a supportive and friendlier manner as she needs help to improve her task maturity.

How the leader handles someone that is making progress in their task ability maturity needs careful consideration. Simply coming back with detailed instructions only addresses the task ability orientation, not the person doing the task. The leader's style needs to change in order to help the follower improve their ability further – the follower needs *training*. In other words, the leader and follower need to open a dialogue to explain further about the task in such a way that the follower feels they personally are more involved and asking questions, i.e. taking an active part, in their development.

This leader style is now one of a *trainer* giving more full details of the task, showing the wider picture of the job, reinforcing the follower's approach to ideas yet still keeping some control on how the task will be managed. The leader is still likely to monitor the situation to ensure that the task is carried out properly, but may start to guide the follower in evaluation parameters, i.e. more advice about what constitutes a job well done.

In this way, the follower has learnt a valuable lesson: the leader knows all the answers! When they have a concern or question about how they may improve their effectiveness, the follower knows that they only need ask their leader for direction and further 'on-the-job' training. However, there are problems: for the follower to learn about the whole job, they will have to have every idea reinforced by the leader and the leader will be interrupted every time there is a query. This could be a block to both the leader's and follower's progress – the leader is not being left alone to get on with their own work (and will probably be working into the night when the office is quiet when the follower has gone home!) and the follower won't take action and move on until the leader takes a decision.

Let us now consider another scenario between Jan and the Partner a few weeks into the job (see Box 14.5).

Box 14.5: Managing the relationship with a new recruit when she asks for guidance a couple of weeks into a job

Let us consider Jan, our new recruit, a couple of weeks into her new job. She knows that the Partner has an 'open door policy' and he is happy for her to pop in for guidance. She has been thinking about a change to office procedures and wants some help.

The Partner is aware that Jan frequently comes up with some good ideas but feels that she could think them through a little more to see the best way forward, but she does not 'take the initiative' sometimes. He is frequently interrupted during the day and has been giving 'on-the-job' training for some while now.

Jan comes into the Partner's office and has a query on a simple bookkeeping matter, part of her regular administrative duties. He can clearly see the right option and is tempted to explain what to do to get her on her way so he can get back to his work. However, he realises that he needs to change his approach.

This time he asks her what the options for dealing with the query are. She says, 'That's what I am here for! What do *you* think?' Undeterred he continues, 'OK, so what about cash flow – getting the money in?' With this prompt, she suggests, 'Well, I could do "a" or "b", possibly "c"'. 'OK, what'll the client think about "c"?' he asks. Jan dismisses 'c' as a non-starter. He continues, 'That'll leave "a" or "b"; which one will get the money in quickest?'

With this prompting, Jan realises her best option. The Partner asks, 'If I weren't here, how would you check this one through?' Jan concludes, 'I'll run it past Alyson in our Accounts Department first and check with Dorothy in accounts at the client end too'.

In this scenario, the Partner has not been functioning as a 'trainer' but more as a 'coach', getting Jan not to 'do as I do' but to 'think as I think'. While the interaction may take a little longer than taking charge of the task and training her on what to do, Jan has been coached into approaching the problem from a wider perspective. The Partner has helped her improve her task ability maturity and she can consider using the same approach to some of her other ideas – in this way she will be able to come to him with solutions rather than just a series of problems.

In order to develop a follower in their task ability maturity, the leader needs to consider their interaction and provide continued 'socio-emotional' support, engaging them in a dialogue about their thought process, *coaching* them into providing the solution to the problem. If the follower comes up with the right way forward, or can see through their own analysis how a job might best be done, they will be able to improve their ability without persistent recourse to further 'training' from the leader. Their commitment to the solution would be that much higher too.

Once the follower has been able to demonstrate higher levels of task ability maturity, it is time for the leader to 'let go'. At this stage, the follower is going to need less help and support – again emphasising that this does not mean they don't get any support – from the leader. Let us finally consider how the Partner might deal with the relationship orientation as far as the idea that Jan had to improve efficiency of office procedures (see Box 14.6).

Box 14.6: Helping a new recruit who identifies a useful business improvement several weeks into the job

Jan has been working for Duncan Alexander & Wilmshurst for several weeks now. She looked at the process the firm employed to generate a client invoice for one of the Partner's to deliver an open course (that is, 'open' to the public – as opposed to in-house) training event on behalf of one of their clients. She recognised that waiting for the Partner to open his e-mail and confirm the fees for the training introduced a delay in the process, whereas having the fee-note routed direct to her would mean she could generate the invoice including the expenses without his involvement. He didn't really

(Continued)

Box 14.6: Continued

need to approve the invoice either as her relationship with all clients' account departments was such that she would deal with any queries on 'standard' training events at the usual venues.

She came up with an idea that made sense to the Partner. He had no need to explore in more detail how she would implement the idea, how she would feel about dealing with this or that problem, given what he knew about her highly competent interpersonal skills and attention to detail.

She requires little of the Partner but his support and trust.

So, at the top end of the 'task' range, when the follower's task ability maturity is its highest, followers appreciate being 'left alone' to get on with their jobs without too much involvement from their leader. In other words, provided they are aware of their leader's support and encouragement, they will maintain their task ability.

Remember, a person's task ability maturity will be specific for a given task; if they attain Level 4 for one task (such as general correspondence in our example), the follower is going to be at Level 1 for a new telephone system. For this task – managing calls with a new phone system – the follower is going to need clear instructions from someone or risk losing callers. They may move from this level to Level 2 and so on quite quickly, nonetheless.

Let us put these two dimensions – concern for task (the person's task ability maturity) and concern for the person (degree of socio-emotional support and two-way interaction) – into one model (see Figure 14.2), the Ability Development Model (ADM).

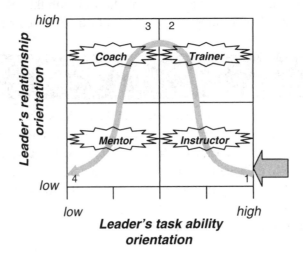

Figure 14.2 Mackay's Ability Development Model (ADM).

Adapting to the ADM

By taking each level along the task ability maturity scale, we can identify practical approaches to developing people that fits with the Ability Development Model.

Level 1 – give clear *instructions*

At this level, the 'leader' identifies that they need to take some decisions to ensure that the job gets done. This may be because the 'follower' does not know how to do the job to the required standard. The leader has identified something in the 'task ability maturity' of the follower that they need to address.

In terms of the task ability orientation, the leader will have to engage in defining roles for the individual or team, explaining the who, when, what, why, where and how of the task. If there is more than one person involved in undertaking the task, the leader will need to direct who has to do what in goal setting, organising the group, deciding time limits, and generally directing and controlling the group. They may need to help the 'follower' identify that their task ability maturity is low and that they can see the value in doing the task to the required standard.

The leader will also have to monitor progress, as the follower will need appropriate feedback to improve.

At this level, the leader's style is one of telling or taking the role of *instructor*.

- *Level 1 ability*. Give people clear instructions to get the job started and monitor closely.

Level 2 – give *training* on the detail of the task

Here, the 'follower' has demonstrated their ability to do the task to some degree and has shown that their ability is getting into shape. However, while they have moved some way along the Task bar, indicating that the 'leader' needs to be slightly less focused on the basics of the job in hand, the task will by no means be completely satisfactory in every respect. At this stage, the follower will indicate a need to enter into dialogue with the leader to get assistance to understand the job better. This behaviour on the part of the follower should tell the leader that they would benefit from a different style in order to gain the help they need to do the task more completely and effectively.

So, in general terms, the follower is only moderately able to do the task, but has indicated that they are ready for further help and guidance to do the job better. Thus, the leader adopts a more interactive style and explains more about the task. Moreover, if the leader showed some appreciation that the follower had clearly been thinking how to improve their productivity, the follower would be more likely to consider further interactions and training opportunities from the leader.

Again, the 'leader' will need to identify what controls need to be in place to ensure the standard of work is appropriate and monitor to some degree, but the follower may begin to undertake some self-evaluation.

At this level, the leader's style is one of *explaining the way* to do the task or taking the role of *trainer*.

- *Level 2 ability*. Give training on why the right way of doing things is best and clarify monitoring parameters.

Level 3 – involve in discussion as a *coach*

When a 'follower' has shown that they are improving their ability to undertake a given task, they will still need to interact with the 'leader'. This is because, although they are becoming more competent, the leader still cannot leave them to their own devices because the finer points of a task may not be undertaken correctly. At this stage, a follower may come to the leader to ask their advice on how to do a particular part of the job.

Now, if the leader is too task ability orientated and explains what they would do in a given situation, and why, all the follower has learnt is how the leader would solve that particular problem – and also that the leader is a great problem-solver. Next time, with a similar query, it will be so easy to ask the leader – the follower doesn't have to take any risk and does not have to do too much thinking.

Do you want a team of 'solution seekers' (who keep asking your solution to problems) or a team of 'problem-solvers' (who are able to think like you do, not just do as you do)?

At this level, the leader and follower engage in joint problem-solving rather than the leader always taking the lead. In other words, the leader asks the appropriate questions, such as 'What options have you got...?' or 'What do you think is the best way of dealing with it...?', or 'What about: cash flow/the impact on the client/effect internally on that department, etc?' The leader can also get the follower to identify what the evaluation parameters might be so they can largely monitor conformance themselves.

It may be that, in this situation, the follower actually has all the ability in the world to undertake a task, but there is some other underlying factor preventing them from performing. This is where socio-emotional support is so crucial. Again, telling someone else what the leader would do to get the task done may not be what the individual needs, but a discussion of the issues that are getting in the way of the task being done. At this level, leaders need to be prepared for internal relationships to be at conflict or something outside of work affecting an individual's motivation or confidence. It may not always be ability that is necessarily lacking at this level.

At this level, the leader's style is one of participating or taking the role of *coach*.

- *Level 3 ability*. Coach people to challenge their own thinking, asking 'why' more than telling 'how'. Identify how the follower can evaluate their own conformance.

Level 4 – *mentor*; act as wise council

Here, the 'follower' is able to do the job with little intervention from the 'leader'. The leader has confidence in the ability of the follower and demonstrates through trust and assurances that the individual's ability is valued.

The leader cannot pass down the responsibility for the task – ultimately they will always remain responsible for the outcome of the follower – but they can give the follower the authority to do a given task.

Developing trust gives the follower further motivation to do the task. They may have found their own intrinsic reward in doing the task or recognise that the task being completed is valued by the organisation at large, and they will keep their motivation to complete the task to the defined standard.

Finally, they are in no doubt about their own task ability maturity. Provided no one adversely affects their MAC Factors, all they need from the leader is occasional reinforcement of their personal contribution. Over-supervision or too much 'just checking' from the leader is not needed, and indeed may damage the relationship and undermine the follower.

At this level, the leader's style is one of delegating or taking the role of *mentor*.

- *Level 4 ability*. Ask them for solutions and look to outcomes rather than challenge their process.

Evaluating a Scenario

In the following scenario, taken from one of the specific style evaluation questionnaires developed by the author, consider the situation and look for clues as to what level the person is on their task ability maturity continuum, Levels 1–4. Then look at the four alternative approaches to deal with the problem – what would you do?

Recently, the firm has begun to get involved in more consultancy work and you have asked one of the assistants to make her own suggestions on scheduling the extra activity. Now you find that there are complaints from the staff that she will not do the job. You had selected her because her past job performance had been excellent, she was reliable and she worked well within the firm. It seems she is reluctant to solve the problem of how best to schedule the extra work. You would:

a. Explain how you would resolve the scheduling problem yourself while making sure to encourage her input into solving the problem.
b. Let her know about the complaints raised against her but leave her to resolve the scheduling problem, letting her know you are there to support her.

c. Act quickly to resolve the scheduling problem and ensure that your measures are implemented.

d. Discuss the amount of work with the assistant and try to find out why she is not able to do the task on time. However, you would not tell her what to do.

The clues to this person's task ability maturity are that *'her past job performance had been excellent; she was reliable and she worked well within the firm'*, suggesting Level 4, but she has 'slipped back' along the continuum in as much that *'that there are complaints from the staff that she will not do the job'* and is now at Level 3. So, it is not her task ability maturity that is completely compromised – something or someone is getting in the way for the task being done.

- If you did 'c' and put matters right, her confidence is likely to be knocked rock bottom and her motivation to do the task pushed low, too. Fear of a reprisal is not a good motivator in the long run. She does not need telling how to handle the basics of the job anyway!
- If you did 'b' and just let her know about the complaints you will have done nothing to help her personal situation. She knows you are there to support her but haven't actually done anything about it.
- If you did 'a' you would at least have invited her to give some input into solving the problem and her socio-emotional concerns – perhaps an internal conflict in the firm – may have surfaced. However, being too task ability orientated may have compromised her willingness to discuss matters with you as she may feel that you don't value her task competence.
- 'd' is the preferred option as it does not undermine your belief that she can do the task but does give her opportunity to open up about another problem outside the task ability axis. Trusting her task ability will serve to maintain a relationship of trust between the two parties and she is more likely to turn to you for socio-emotional support.

This has shown two key parameters of the model, as outlined below.

Task ability maturity is a two-way process

It is not a one-way street. People do forget and slip back along their task ability maturity continuum; the other factors of Motivation and Confidence have an impact on Ability, as all three 'MAC Factors' are interrelated. Addressing one of the factors can have an influence on the other two. Just because someone forgets a finer point of a task they have been doing for a while, the 'leader' does not have to go right back to square one and control the basics all over again.

Situational effectiveness is clear

Situational effectiveness is easy to comprehend. In the scenario above, the further away we are in our ability development style from what the 'follower' *needs*, the less our effectiveness. Equally, the closer we are to matching the *current* needs of the follower, given their *immediate* situation (not what they *used* to be like), the more effective we are.

We can evaluate an effectiveness score simply. In the above scenario, which ideally called out for a 'leader' to 'coach' to solve the problem, we could 'score' the responses according to Table 14.1.

Sometimes even the most aware practitioner can make mistakes (see Box 14.7 for an admission of guilt!).

Table 14.1 Evaluating the effectiveness of each style – according to the demands of the 'follower' in the scenario in this chapter

Response	Style	Score	Commentary
c	Instructor	−2	Simply giving instructions on what to do will get the job done but will compromise the relationship, so is less effective
b	Mentor	−1	The mentoring offered support but the 'leader' did not apply it appropriately, weakening the relationship
a	Trainer	+1	Functioning as a trainer is not 'wrong'; it allows for personal matters as input into problem-solving, it is just less effective
d	Coach	+2	The most effective – it opens dialogue over the problem and does not undermine the person's ability

Box 14.7: Taking a minute to think before acting is far more effective

Back in 1997, my then PA had been working for Duncan Alexander & Wilmshurst for a short while; she showed good ability developing finance control activities in addition to her other duties. She had been on a foundation Excel™ course run by Business Link recently. She was then able to design new spreadsheets using Microsoft™ Excel and was developing new formats for tracking revenue and expenditure – now that a decent accountancy firm had been found to replace the part-time bookkeeper we had engaged. For elementary income and expenditure purposes she was, for all intents and purposes, at Level 4 for spreadsheets.

One morning she was working on a new spreadsheet when I was just about to leave the office for a client meeting. She wanted to write the formula for VAT percentages in a new spreadsheet cell and asked, 'Oh, how do you do percentages?'

(Continued)

Box 14.7: Continued

I could not remember off the top of my head but know that if I am working on a new spreadsheet I would 'copy and paste' any function from an existing sheet. Rather than ask her a simple question, 'Can you paste it from an existing spreadsheet?' so that she would think like me (i.e. coach her on how to solve the problem, Level 3), I reached across her, took the mouse and said, 'Oh, give it to me; it's easy. Watch!' (Level 1). I left for my meeting feeling really happy with myself for solving the problem for her.

I had cause to telephone the office from the car on another matter and got an unusually short riposte from my PA. After the call I thought something was not quite right, so telephoned again to enquire what was wrong. I was told in no uncertain terms by her that she had felt humiliated and looked a right dunce in front of others in the office.

If I had just taken a minute and thought about her situation a little more, I would have realised that her personal confidence and self-esteem were particularly low (owing to her lousy treatment at home from her husband) and that my being highly 'task ability' focused was not going to be effective. I had compromised our working relationship; it took a while to win back her trust.

For a further evaluation of your situational task ability maturity style, consult the companion web pages.

Summary

In this chapter you have:

- Looked at how a manager might influence a person's ability development
- Explored how to consider both the task being done and the person doing the work – and explored the interaction of the two variables
- Looked at four levels of ability and what to do at each level – instruct, train, coach and mentor
- Been introduced to a practical model for ability development
- Begun to uncover a way of evaluating your management style, its flexibility and its effectiveness in developing the ability of others.

Questions

1. Consider someone within your workgroup that you know well. For their allocated tasks, identify where they are on the Ability Development Model for each task.

2. Considering your own competence on tasks within your job description. Evaluate your task ability maturity (see Figure 14.1) for your principal tasks.
3. Thinking of your line manager, or a manager that you know well, evaluate their dominant style when helping their people with their work. How flexible do you feel they are and are they effective when they do flex?
4. Image that you have a colleague who is a manager at your level that is unable to 'let go', who spends too much time checking-up on their very competent and talented people, and therefore has to spend time catching up on their own work – often late in the evening. How would you help them develop their coaching and mentoring skills?

Further Reading

Blanchard, K. and Johnson, S. (1983) *The One Minute Manager*, William Collins.
Hersey, P. (1999) *The Situational Leader*, Pfeiffer & Co.
Mackay, A. R. (2007) *Recruiting, Retaining and Releasing People*, Butterworth-Heinemann.
Smart, B. D. (2005) *Top-grading: How Leading Companies Win by Hiring, Coaching and Keeping the Best People*, Portfolio.

Part 4

Confidence Building

15

Self-esteem

The task of leadership is not to put greatness into people but to elicit it, for the greatness is there already.

John Buchan

Learning Outcomes

Without it we become paralysed – it is as simple as that! This chapter, and its companion web pages, explore self-esteem from a number of perspectives. The chapter has been written to provide support to many elements of the National Occupational Standards for Management and Leadership: *Providing Direction – Lead People Unit 9*; many sections of *Facilitating Change*; many sections of *Working with People*; and of *Achieving Results*; and it assists with some of the requirements of the Chartered Management Institute's Diploma in Management compulsory *Unit C41 – Developing Your Management Style* (in respect of developing the trust and support of others), some of the elements of compulsory *Unit C44 – Effective Communications*, some of the compulsory *Unit C45 – Managing Performance* and most of the optional *Unit O42 – Developing Personnel and Personnel Performance*. This chapter will also be of value to those studying the CIPD Professional Development Scheme – particularly the *Leadership and Management* and *People Management and Development* modules.

By the end of this chapter you will:

- Have looked at self-esteem from a number of perspectives
- Know how to evaluate self-esteem
- Understand some of the causes of low self-esteem
- Have explored Transactional Analysis as an aid to interpersonal communication
- Know how to assist in developing self-esteem in yourself and others
- Have explored emotional intelligence and its link with self-esteem.

What is Self-esteem?

Definitions of self-esteem vary considerably in both their breadth and psychological sophistication. Intuitively, we know that high self-esteem means that we feel good about ourselves and our inherent worth. More specifically, it means we:

- Have a positive attitude
- Evaluate ourselves highly
- Are convinced of our own abilities
- See ourselves as competent
- Are in control of our own lives
- Feel able to do pretty much what we want
- Compare ourselves favourably with others.

Conversely, we also know what it means to experience diminished self-esteem: self-depreciation, helplessness, powerlessness and depression.

Note that there are differences between self-concept and self-esteem:

- *Self-concept* is the totality of a complex, organised and dynamic system of learned beliefs, attitudes and opinions that each person holds to be true about his or her personal existence. Paraphrasing Charles Handy (1989), he said:

> *As we grow older we tend to fix on a self-concept which we then tend to find ways of protecting that selection by surrounding ourselves with people whose self-concept is roughly the same and who confirm ours as being sensible. Thus, we go to live among similar kinds of people, select newspapers that reflect our values, join clubs and go on holidays where our chosen self-concepts will not be challenged. Criticism of our chosen self-concept can be ignored, either by rejecting the source of it, or by physically avoiding the chance of incurring it, e.g. by not mixing out of one's chosen group. But a different and/or traumatic experience can often cause us to revise our ideal self-concept.*

- *Self-esteem* is focused upon feelings of personal worth and the level of satisfaction regarding one's self. There is: (1) a *cognitive* element describing 'self' in specific terms, e.g. power, confidence; (2) an *affective* element or degrees of positive or negative views, e.g. high or low self-esteem; and (3) an *evaluative* element related to some objective and standard, e.g. what a graduate with a first-class honours degree should be able to do.

Nathaniel Branden (1990) provides an interesting view of self-esteem. He proposes two interrelated aspects:

- A sense of personal efficacy (self-efficacy) or confidence in a person's ability to think and act
- A sense of personal worth (self-respect) or an affirmative attitude towards a person's right to live and to be happy.

Fundamentally, self-esteem can be defined as *'the disposition to consider oneself as competent to cope with the challenges of life and to be deserving of happiness'*.

Why is it Important?

The importance of self-esteem can be considered from several perspectives.

First, it is important to normal, psychological development. To cope adequately with the challenges of growing and developing, people need to believe they have the capacity to achieve what they want to and that they are deserving of happiness and joy in life. Lacking a belief in either of these, they may be productive in an external sense, but are probably less effective and innovative than they would be if they possessed high self-esteem. They may not be able to reach higher levels of motivation (see Chapter 9) or ability (see Chapter 14).

The effects of self-esteem may also be recognised in planning a career and decision-making. For a person to make a non-traditional career choice, e.g. a female entering engineering, or to go against family pressures, requires someone to have a belief in their ability to make appropriate plans and decisions even though important others in their immediate family and social group disagree with them.

Trying to register for advanced placement classes or applying to a highly competitive university may also challenge the self-esteem of an individual. Most people have experienced times when they were on top, when they were at their 'peak performance'. These 'peaks' illustrate that when people believe in themselves (have high self-efficacy), they believe they can accomplish almost anything. They are expressing a self-esteem that motivates, excites and empowers them. It is this expression of strong self-esteem at a critical stage in their lives which can help a person to become more of what they are capable of becoming.

It has also been suggested that high self-esteem gives a person protection against the 'downs' in the roller-coaster of life. Rejections, disappointments and failure are a part of life's rich tapestry. Life is not always fair – even our best efforts are not always successful. But high esteem can assist a person in 'weathering the storm,' to look beyond immediate setbacks.

Current management literature is filled with descriptions of the type of people who will function well in our 'information' society. Descriptions of these people are replete with statements regarding the need in an information age for workers who can make independent decisions, take risks, vigorously pursue new ideas and untried approaches, and act on their own initiative. These traits are characteristic of persons with high self-esteem, of those who are confident of their abilities and gain pleasure from acting on them. These traits also assume an economic importance because they lead to more effective and productive employees. Organisations with productive employees are successful in the competitive marketplace and earn greater profits.

Specific characteristics of self-esteem

An analysis of current research suggests a number of significant findings and generalisations about the importance and effects of self-esteem upon youth and adults. Self-esteem has been described as a 'social vaccine', a dimension of personality that 'inoculates' people against a wide spectrum of self-defeating and socially undesirable behaviour (California Task Force to Promote Self-esteem and Personal and Social Responsibility, 1990).

The findings of the above-mentioned analysis are summarised on the companion web pages.

Evaluating Self-esteem

There are many examples in the literature and on the Web illustrating methods by which one can evaluate a person's self-esteem. They vary in degrees of sophistication and one hardly needs to consider the questionnaires, as for many it is fairly obvious when self-esteem is compromised; nonetheless, they do aim to give individuals a method of self-appraisal. Figure 15.1 is one developed by the author and gives a series of statements that the respondent is asked to evaluate their level of agreement.

Table 15.1 is an outline of what your score means.

The Cause of Low Self-esteem

Say you are in fulfilling employment for several years and your family life is going well, then you lose your job; it may be devastating, initially, but once you are over the shock you will have a good chance of finding the resources to cope. However, on the other hand, if you have to move house when you receive your redundancy notice, and then hear the next day that a parent has terminal cancer, recovery is bound to be much more difficult. Sometimes life just throws an unbearable amount of trouble at us, all at once, and we have to mobilise all the support we can from friends, family and community to help us survive it.

There are other causes too, which are explored on the companion web pages.

	Statement	True	Partly True	Partly False	False
	Score:	5	4	2	1
1	I generally feel as competent as my peers				
2	I feel that I have quite a lot to offer an employer				
3	I don't worry what others think of my views				
4	I rarely feel guilty asking others to help				
5	I make friends easily				
6	Being myself is important				
7	I don't need others' approval to feel good				
8	I deserve love and respect				
9	I enjoy socialising				
10	I admit my mistakes openly				
11	I am optimistic about my future				
12	If I fail, it is due to circumstances, not my ability				
13	I rarely dwell on personal setbacks for very long				
14	Other people are not luckier than me				
15	I don't need others to tell me I have done a good job				
16	I don't feel guilty about doing what I want				
17	I accept myself as I am and am happy with myself				
18	I never hide my true feelings				
19	I feel valued and needed				
20	I can accept criticism without feeling put down				
	Total of each column × score:				
	Sum Overall Total (%):				

Figure 15.1 Self-assessment questionnaire; answer each as honestly as you can. Totalling each score will give you a percentage measure for your self-esteem.

Table 15.1 Self-assessment questionnaire evaluation

Score	Evaluation of self-esteem
80 or more	High – you probably feel very comfortable facing life's challenges and can probably assist others in your organisation to develop their self-esteem, but do be aware that overconfidence can have its pitfalls!
79–60	Good – you are pretty confident and will readily develop strategies to improve your confidence. There is a guide in this chapter with ideas that are worth sharing with your workgroup.
59–40	Moderate – your self-esteem may be holding you back yet, again, you will find it fairly easy to improve. You may have been hard on yourself so why not discuss your thoughts with someone that knows you well and whose confidence you trust?
39 or less	Poor – not to worry; you're not alone and have probably been too hard on yourself. Anyway, organisations need a diversity of people and they are lucky to have you! You'll find plenty of ideas in this chapter to help develop your self-esteem. You can do it!

How does childhood experience affect self-esteem?

Children tend not to have much power or status in our society, and therefore may still be subject to many common experiences that can undermine their self-esteem. These include, in particular, violence, loss and neglect.

Why keep 'low esteem' workers?

Managers might want to simply dismiss employees with low self-esteem, but recognising the importance of diversity for innovation, there is a place for such people. Many creative and innovative employees are sensitive and introspective. Unlike their more extroverted colleagues, they do not get quite as much feedback from others and, as a result, they can suffer more from lower self-esteem.

Organisations with a premium on creativity cannot afford to hire only clones of their most outgoing employees. Extroverted people can also experience low self-esteem as the competition among employees to excel and the sheer pace of change is bound to tax everyone's self-esteem. As a result, fear of change based on lower self-esteem could cut across all levels and personality types within an organisation. See how to manage change when there is low confidence in Chapter 18.

How to Deal with Bullying in the Workplace[1]

Frequently, bullying and harassment are often obvious, but sometimes people are unsure whether or not the way they are being treated is acceptable. If this applies to you there are a number of things to consider, including:

- Is there an organisational statement of standards of behaviour that you can consult – and has what has happened fallen outside those parameters?
- Has there been a change of management or organisational style to which you just need time to adjust – perhaps because you have a new manager or work requirements?
- Can you talk over your worries with a colleague first, then consider a personnel manager or union representative if there is one, your line manager/supervisor (if they are not the cause), or a mentor whom you may find share your concerns?

It may be that you could ask for changes to your workload or working practices to enable you to cope better with undue pressure from a manager to produce results. If you are certain that you are being bullied or harassed, then there are a number of options to consider, and these are briefly set out in Box 15.1. You should take any action you decide upon as quickly as possible.

---

[1] See also Mackay (2007), which has a section on dealing with bullying in the workplace.

Box 15.1: What to do if you feel you are a victim of bullying

First of all, do remember that disciplinary procedures may be used for disciplinary action against someone who makes an unfounded allegation of bullying or harassment. However, if you feel that you have a genuine case, the following paraphrases excellent advice from ACAS:

- Naturally, avoid being alone with the bully.
- Try to talk to colleagues to find out if anyone has witnessed what has happened to you, or if anyone else is suffering.
- Keep a diary of all incidents – records of dates, times, any witnesses, your feelings, etc. Keep copies of anything that is relevant – for instance, annual reports, letters, memos, notes of any meetings that relate to your ability to do your job. Bullying and harassment often reveal themselves through patterns of behaviour and frequency of incidents. Keep records and inform your employer of any medical help you seek.
- Let your union or staff representative know of the problem, or seek advice elsewhere, perhaps from a Citizens Advice Bureau, an ACAS enquiry point or one of the bullying helplines that are now available by phone and on the Internet – try http://www.acas.org.uk/index.
- If you are reluctant to make a complaint, go to see someone with whom you feel comfortable to discuss the problem. This may be your manager or someone in personnel (particularly if there is someone who specifically deals with equality issues), your trade union representative or a counsellor if your organisation has suitably trained people available.
- Tell the person to stop whatever it is they are doing that is causing you distress, otherwise they may be unaware of the effect of their actions. Be firm, not aggressive. Be positive and calm. Stick to the facts. Describe what happened.
- If you do decide to make a formal complaint, follow your employer's procedures, which should give you information about whom to complain to and how your complaint will be dealt with.
- If you find it difficult to tell the person yourself, you may wish to get someone else – a colleague, trade union official or confidential counsellor – to act on your behalf.
- If you cannot confront the bully, consider writing a memo to them to make it clear what it is you object to in their behaviour. Keep copies of this and any reply.

(Adapted from the ACAS advice leaflet – http://www.acas.org.uk/index)

If you have a union representative or other adviser, ask them to help you state your grievance clearly, as this can help in its resolution and reduce the stress of the process. Most employers have a grievance procedure that will be used to handle your complaint, and some organisations have special procedures for dealing with bullying or harassment. After investigating your complaint, your employer may decide to offer counselling or take disciplinary action against the bully/harasser in accordance with the organisation's disciplinary procedure. Remember the advice in Box 15.1 – disciplinary procedures may be used for disciplinary action against someone who makes an unfounded allegation of bullying or harassment.

As discussed in Mackay (2006), as part of the Employment Act 2002, the government introduced standard internal systems for dealing with dismissal, and discipline and grievance issues. These systems require employers and employees to follow a minimum 'three-step' procedure – involving a statement (setting out in writing the grounds for action or grievance), a meeting between the parties and the right to appeal. The new provisions apply to all employers, no matter how many employees they have. For further information visit the Employment Relations section of the Department of Trade and Industry website at www.dti.gov.uk/er.

Transactional Analysis or the 'OK Corral'

Eric Berne developed Transactional Analysis (TA) as an approach to psychoanalysis and therapy in the early 1950s, but it was taken up by commercial organisations in the 1960s as they tried to improve the ways people in general interacted. It defines some basic 'ego states' and 'life positions' that individuals can adopt, and uses those to describe how transactions then occur between two people. The idea is that if you know your own state, and can determine the other person's state, you can use your behaviour to influence the interactions between the two of you – and in turn assist in developing someone's self-esteem.

Ego states

Berne defined three basic personalities or 'ego states', each with characteristic attitudes, feelings, behaviours and language. Two of the states subdivide into two further facets (see Table 15.2)

Life positions

The other building block of TA is the view we have of ourselves in relation to other people around us. There are four 'life positions', shown as a grid that became known as the 'OK Corral' (Figure 15.2). The quotation in each box typifies the attitude of each life position.

People will move around the grid depending on the situation, but have a preferred position that they tend to revert to. This is strongly influenced by experiences and decisions in early life:

Table 15.2 The three personalities or ego states

State	Subdivision	Characteristic
Parent	Critical Parent	■ Makes rules and sets limits ■ Disciplines, judges and criticises
	Nurturing Parent	■ Advises and guides ■ Protects and nurtures
Adult		■ Concerned with data and facts ■ Considers options and estimates probabilities ■ Makes unemotional decisions ■ Plans and makes things happen
Child	Free (Natural) Child	■ Fun-loving and energetic ■ Creative and spontaneous
	Adapted Child	■ Compliant and polite ■ Rebellious and manipulative

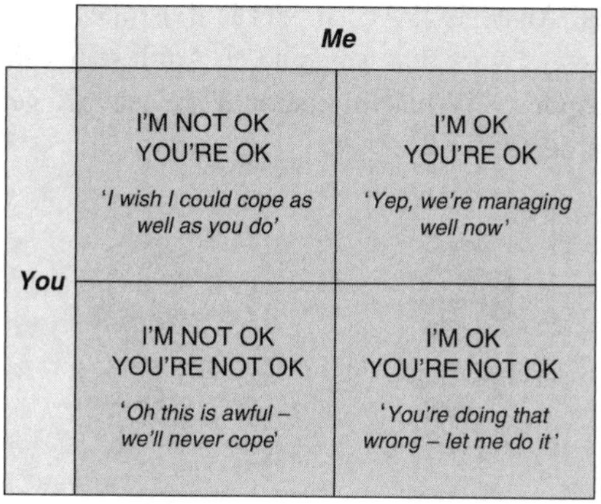

Figure 15.2 The 'OK Corral' life positions.

- *'I'm OK, you're OK'* people are in the 'get along with' position. They're confident and happy about life and work, and interact by collaboration and mutual respect, even when they disagree.
- *'I'm OK, you're not OK'* people are in the 'get rid of' position. They tend to get angry and hostile, and are smug and superior. They belittle others, who they view as incompetent and untrustworthy, and are often competitive and power-hungry.
- *'I'm not OK, you're OK'* is the 'get away from' position. These people feel sad, inadequate or even stupid in comparison to others. They undervalue their skills and contribution and withdraw from problems.
- *'I'm not OK, you're not OK'* is the 'get nowhere' position. These people feel confused or aimless. They don't see the point of doing anything and so usually don't bother.

Interactions or transactions

The central concept of TA is that transactions between people can be characterised by the ego state of the two participants. What's more, the ego state adopted by the person who starts the transaction will affect the way the other person responds.

Let's look at an example of two people leaving for a meeting. Mr Smith says 'what time shall we leave?' and Mr Jones replies 'after lunch at 2.30'. This is a simple Adult-to-Adult transaction.

However, if Mr Smith adopts a Child state, 'We'll have to leave soon for that meeting, we're bound to get stuck in traffic', it will tend to produce a Nurturing Parent response from Mr Jones: 'Don't worry, they've finished resurfacing the bypass, we'll leave at 2.30 and have plenty of time'.

This model shows how the transaction 'balances' between the two people: if one drifts into Child that will encourage the other to move to Parent, and vice versa. The preferred state for most business transactions is Adult-to-Adult, but it's acceptable to move to another state as long as one is aware of it and is ready for the changed response from the other person. The Transactional Analysis 'PAC' model is illustrated in Figure 15.3.

Of course it doesn't always work that way, and an Adult state can sometimes be met with, say, a Critical Parent response: 'What time should we leave?' gets 'Why are you asking me? You're driving, you decide!'

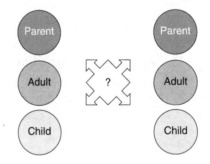

Figure 15.3 Adaptation of the Transactional Analysis 'PAC' Model.

Strokes

We all need and look for care, attention, love and recognition from others, and in TA, a 'stroke' is defined as a unit of recognition. With children, strokes are obviously sought and given: they show off their new toy, or misbehave to get attention, and know the adults will respond right on cue. But grown-ups do the same: working hard, deliberately making mistakes, arriving late or simply arriving home and sighing 'You won't believe what happened on the train this evening!'

Strokes can be positive or negative, and it's generally better to give a negative stroke than none at all (because that may be taken as negative anyway). But in many business organisations, strokes are subject to a set of unwritten rules. For example:

- Most positive strokes are false ('plastic')
- Don't ask for positive strokes – certainly not directly
- Don't give positive strokes freely
- If you give positive strokes, make them conditional
- Don't miss a chance to give a negative stroke
- Never give a physical stroke – by touching someone.

The result is a cold, unfeeling environment where normal human emotions are mostly suppressed. Even in 'warm' organisations where it's OK to express feelings, strokes are still subject to certain norms – such as not giving them to people above you in the hierarchy.

In the absence of a free exchange of strokes, people manipulate others in order to get the strokes they crave, and start playing games.

Games

The complexity of the TA model leaves it open to manipulation, or 'games'. You adopt a Parent state to make them do something for you, or a Child state because you want someone's help. But often the games end up damaging the relationship, and the type of game someone plays is influenced by his or her life state.

Examples of games players include:

- The Persecutor – 'See what you made me do . . . ?' 'If it weren't for you . . . '
- The Rescuer – 'What would you do without me . . . ?' 'I'm only trying to help . . . '
- The Victim – 'Poor old me . . . '; 'This always happens to me . . . '; 'Go on, have a laugh at my expense . . . '

There are more themes to the TA model but every day there are complex transactions that fit the model. Many effective leaders – especially those who are seen as 'good with people' – apply the TA principles, often without being aware of it. Even though TA has fallen out of fashion, it is just as applicable today as it ever was. If you are really interested in how people interact – and not just wanting to hone your interpersonal skills – then TA is worth exploring.

Improving your Self-esteem

If you want to improve your self-esteem or improve yourself in any way at all, you first need to find the inner desire and will to do it. Low self-esteem feeds on negative messages and thoughts, so don't indulge in self-criticism. Why are you joining the other side to wage war against yourself? Silence your inner judge.

The companion web pages have some general tips that are a start on the road to more positive approaches.

Self-motivation

This is central to everything positive that we want to do in life – perhaps it is even more important than self-esteem! Why? Because if we want to improve self-esteem or improve in any way we first need the inner desire and will to do it. While we may look for others to encourage us, we cannot always rely on them to do it; while we may be fortunate to have someone at work or socially who will always 'pull us through', we can become a burden on them – how can we cope if they are not there?

We need self-motivation to:

- Plan a new or altered direction in life
- Take up a new activity, hobby or challenge
- Be enthusiastic about life and living
- Have the courage to see things through despite setbacks or negative comments from others.

This is not an exhaustive list because self-motivation is so important and individual in every aspect of life. How can we get going if we lack self-motivation? How can you become motivated again? Try the following 10-minute exercise.

Develop your 'chuffed chart'

Think about what you really enjoy doing, maybe something you want to take up or a hobby you've always wanted to devote more time to. What's stopping you? Think about giving it priority, to start doing what you love doing. Very few people on their death bed wished they had spent more time in the office!

Make a list of things you'd like to improve on and how you are going to do it.

Review all the successes you've enjoyed in every area of your life, totally forget any negatives, just positive successes here!

Draw your version of your personal 'chuffed chart' over the last five or so years (see Table 15.3). What were you doing five years ago? What has changed for you since then?

Table 15.3 List your personal achievements over the past five or so years and make some plans for the next 12 months

Area of achievement	Last few years	Plans in next 12 months
Personal – non-work	Now married to right person!	Build gazebo
Career	Formed business partnership, worked in Manhattan	Become coach on MBA programme
Material wealth	Bought KMX 125 (motorcycle) for lads	Repairs to 300-year-old cottage!
Health	Ran half-marathon in 2 hr 4 min	Beat last year's time – under 2 hr!
Learning	Midlands II RFU Referee	*Reader's Digest* French – complete!
Cultural	Performed at local concert	Visit Corsica, Rome and Istanbul

Consider what has made you particularly happy ('chuffed') or sad over the past few years. Now focus on the good things; write a bullet point or two against each of the topics given in italics in Table 15.3 that are important to you – that you, personally, feel good about. They don't all have to be work related and they don't have to be big things – particularly 'material gain': it does not have to be that you have bought an Aston Martin 'Vanquish' (I wish!), but maybe a new DVD player or digital camera that you are having some fun with. Some examples are given in the table. Figure 15.4 gives a graphic example.

Having done that, consider the next 10 years – if that is too far ahead, think about the next 12 months. What are you going to reflect on that you feel good about one year from now? Again, Table 15.3 gives some examples.

If you are planning to share that future with someone dear to you, get them to do the same exercise on their own, then swap lists: can you help them to achieve theirs and can they help you achieve yours?

Improving Others' Self-esteem

As we established, high self-esteem can never be given to a person by another person – like their manager – or their organisation. It must be sought, 'earned' by the individual for him or herself.

So, as a manager, what are the options? The experience of many counsellors would favour a discussion that explores a client's overall self-esteem (enhancing his or her generic self-esteem), but also focuses upon blockages which retard the expression of the person's high self-esteem in specific areas.

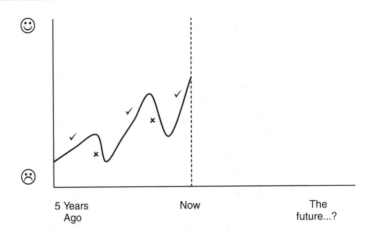

5 Years Ago   Now   The future...?

Figure 15.4 A personal 'chuffed chart' over the past five years, noting some 'ups' and 'downs' – list the 'ups' in a table such as that shown in Table 15.3.

Our best option is to consider guiding the person towards some of the self-help materials; among the most popular (judging by book sales) would be Stephen Covey's (1999) *Seven Habits of Highly Effective People*.

A fuller description of Covey's Seven Habits can be found on the companion web pages.

Stephen Covey's Seven Habits are a simple set of rules for life – inter-related and synergistic, and yet each one powerful and worthy of adopting and following in its own right. For many people, reading Covey's work or listening to him speak literally changes their lives. This is powerful stuff indeed and many suggest it is highly recommended.

This 'Seven Habits' summary is just a brief overview – the full work is fascinating, comprehensive and uplifting.

In his more recent book, *The 8th Habit*, Stephen Covey introduced (logically) an eighth habit, which deals with personal fulfilment and helping others to achieve fulfilment too. The book also focuses on leadership. Time will tell whether *The 8th Habit* achieves recognition and reputation close to Covey's classic original Seven Habits work.

Emotional Intelligence

Recent discussions of emotional intelligence (EI) proliferate across the American landscape – from the cover of *Time*, to a best-selling book by Daniel Goleman, to an episode of the *Oprah Winfrey* show. But EI is not some easily dismissed new 'psycho-babble'. EI has its roots in the concept of 'social intelligence', first identified by E. L. Thorndike in 1920.

Psychologists have been uncovering other intelligences for some while, and grouping them mainly into three clusters:

1. *Abstract intelligence* – the ability to understand and manipulate with verbal and mathematic symbols
2. *Concrete intelligence* – the ability to understand and manipulate with objects
3. *Social intelligence* – the ability to understand and relate to people.

Thorndike defined social intelligence as 'the ability to understand and manage men and women, boys and girls – to act wisely in human relations'. He also included inter- and intra-personal intelligences in his theory of multiple intelligences. These two intelligences comprise his social intelligence. He defines them as follows:

Inter-personal intelligence *is the ability to understand other people: what motivates them, how they work, how to work cooperatively with them. Successful salespeople, politicians, teachers, clinicians, and religious leaders are all likely to be individuals with high degrees of interpersonal intelligence.*
Intra-personal intelligence *is a correlative ability, turned inward. It is a capacity to form an accurate, veridical model of oneself and to be able to use that model to operate effectively in life.*

Emotional intelligence, on the other hand, 'is a type of social intelligence that involves the ability to monitor one's own and others' emotions, to discriminate among them, and to use the information to guide one's thinking and actions'. According to Salovey and Mayer (1997), EI subsumes Gardner's inter- and intra-personal intelligences, and involves abilities that may be categorised into five domains:

- *Self-awareness* – observing yourself and recognising a feeling as it happens
- *Self-regulation* – handling feelings so that they are appropriate; realising what is behind a feeling; finding ways to handle fears and anxieties, anger and sadness
- *Self-motivation* – channelling emotions in the service of a goal; emotional self-control; delaying gratification and stifling impulses
- *Empathy* – sensitivity to others' feelings and concerns, and taking their perspective; appreciating the differences in how people feel about things
- *Handling relationships* – managing emotions in others; social competence and social skills.

Self-awareness (intra-personal intelligence), empathy and handling relationships (inter-personal intelligence) are essentially dimensions of social intelligence.

Why is emotional intelligence important?

Researchers investigated dimensions of EI by measuring related issues, such as social skills, interpersonal competence, psychological maturity and emotional awareness, long before the term 'emotional intelligence' came into use. Social scientists are just beginning to uncover the relationship of EI to other phenomena, e.g. leadership, group performance, individual performance, inter-personal/social exchange, managing change and conducting performance evaluations. Thus, it is suggested, emotional intelligence, the skills that help people harmonise, should become increasingly valued as a workplace asset in the years to come.

It had become recognised in the late 1990s to be of growing importance to commerce: people that rise to the top of their field – whether in psychology, law, medicine, engineering or banking – are not just good at their jobs. Such people are affable, resilient and optimistic.

In other words, it takes more than traditional cognitive intelligence to be successful at work. It also takes 'emotional intelligence', the ability to restrain negative feelings such as anger and self-doubt, and instead focus on positive ones such as confidence and congeniality. The theory first captured the public imagination a number of years ago with the release of Daniel Goleman's (1995) book. This text stirred controversy when Goleman claimed that people endowed with emotional skills excel in life, perhaps more so than those with a high IQ. Goleman drew his propositions from behavioural, brain and personality research by such psychologists as Peter Salovey and John Mayer, who first proposed the model of emotional intelligence.

In a more recent book, Goleman (1998) focused on the need for emotional intelligence at work, an area often considered more head than heart. Not only do bosses and corporate leaders need high doses of emotional intelligence, but every people-orientated job demands it too, Goleman argued. Also, whereas IQ is relatively fixed, emotional intelligence can be built and learned, he claimed. Companies can test and teach emotional intelligence, as many employers began to do in the 1990s.

However, while some psychologists view Goleman's proposition as an encouraging prescription for building career skills, others say its validity remains unproven. Some of the theory's critics question the way emotional intelligence is defined and claim it cannot be taught. Others maintain that cognitive and technical skills ultimately qualify people for the best jobs and help them excel at those jobs.

Emotional intelligence defined

At issue for many of the theory's critics is the way Goleman defined emotional intelligence. John Mayer, a University of New Hampshire psychologist who was one of the first to coin the term, defines it more narrowly than Goleman. For Mayer, emotional intelligence is the ability to understand how others' emotions work and to control one's own emotions.

By comparison, Goleman defines emotional intelligence more broadly, also including such competencies as optimism, conscientiousness, motivation, empathy and social competence.

According to Mayer, these broader traits that Goleman relates to emotional intelligence are considered personality traits by other theorists. For example, psychologist Edward Gordon says that emotional intelligence deals largely with personality and mood, aspects of the individual that cannot be so readily changed. Gordon claims that improving employees' literacy and analytical skills, not their emotional skills, is the best way to boost job performance. 'Work success is mostly cognitively driven,' says Gordon. 'Emotion by itself won't get you very far.'

Responding to such charges, Goleman says cognitive skill 'gets you in the door' of a company, but emotional skills help you thrive once you're hired. To illustrate Goleman's point, psychologist Steven Stein, a marketer of tests that assess employees' emotional intelligence quotient (EQ), cites the example of a Harvard business graduate who received numerous job offers from companies clamouring to hire her. However, due to a lack of emotional intelligence, the woman continually sparred with her employers and couldn't keep any of the jobs.

Studies of close to 500 organisations worldwide, reviewed by Goleman in his book, indicate that people who score highest on EQ measures rise to the top of corporations. 'Star' employees possess more interpersonal skills and confidence, for example, than 'regular' employees who receive less glowing performance reviews.

'Emotional intelligence matters twice as much as technical and analytic skill combined for star performances,' he says. 'And the higher people move up in the company, the more crucial emotional intelligence becomes.'

EQ at work

Bosses and leaders, in particular, need high EQ because they represent the organisation to the public, they interact with the highest number of people within and outside the organisation, and they set the tone for employee morale, says Goleman. Leaders with empathy are able to understand their employees' needs and provide them with constructive feedback, he says.

Different jobs also call for different types of emotional intelligence, Goleman says. For example, success in sales requires the empathic ability to gauge a customer's mood and the inter-personal skill to decide when to pitch a product and when to keep quiet. By comparison, success in painting or professional tennis requires a more individual form of self-discipline and motivation.

And there are gender differences in emotional intelligence as well, says Stein. After administering EQ assessments to 4500 men and 3200 women, his organisation found that women scored higher than men on measures of empathy and social responsibility, but men outperformed women on stress tolerance and self-confidence measures. In other words, says Stein, women and men are equally as intelligent emotionally, but they're strong in different areas.

Teaching emotional strength

Patterns of emotional intelligence are not fixed, however. So men and women can boost their all-round EQ by building their emotional abilities where they lack them, claims Stein.

Working with psychologists and executive coaches, for example, women can hone their assertiveness skills and learn such stress management techniques as meditation, yoga or jogging, says Stein. Men can learn the importance of listening to co-workers and customers, reading their moods and winning their trust – all increasingly important aspects of leadership, teamwork, and customer and co-worker relations, says Stein.

Indeed, notes Goleman, the real value of the growing work on emotional intelligence is its implications for workplace training.

'IQ is relatively stable throughout life but much of emotional skill is learned,' says Goleman. 'There's a huge market for psychologists as executive coaches, helping people in the workplace build their emotional competencies.'

Summary

In this chapter you have:

- Looked at self-esteem from a number of perspectives
- Been able make an objective measure of self-esteem
- Explored some of the causes of low self-esteem – including childhood experiences
- Explored Transactional Analysis as an aid to interpersonal communication: parent–adult–child
- Considered how to assist in developing self-esteem in yourself and others
- Explored emotional intelligence and its link with self-esteem.

Questions

1. Consider Handy's view of the self-concept. Discuss the implications for an organisation with people with a wide variety of differing self-concepts.
2. Consider the culture of your workplace and identify any likely causes that might adversely affect someone's self-esteem.
3. Imagine that you suspect someone you know has low self-esteem. Identify possible communications from them that support your suspicions and relate them to your understanding of Transactional Analysis. What can you do to help them?
4. Give your self an informal appraisal of Covey's Seven Habits of effective people. What can you do to improve your effectiveness?

References

Branden, N. (1990) What is self-esteem? Paper presented at the first International Conference on Self-Esteem, Oslo, Norway, August (ERIC Document Reproduction Service No. CG 022 939).

California Task Force to Promote Self-esteem and Personal and Social Responsibility (1990) *Toward a State of Self-esteem*, California State Department of Education, Sacramento.

Covey, S. (1999) *Seven Habits of Highly Effective People*; see http://www.more-selfesteem.com/books1.htm.

Goleman, D. (1995) *Emotional Intelligence: Why it Can Matter More than IQ*, Bantam.

Goleman, D. (1998) *Working with Emotional Intelligence*, Bloomsbury.

Handy, C. (1989) *The Age of Unreason*, Business Books Ltd.

Mackay, A. R. (2007) *Recruiting, Retaining and Releasing People*, Butterworth-Heinemann.

Salovey, P. and and Mayer, J. (1997) *Emotional Development and Emotional Intelligence*, Basic Books.

Further Reading

Covey, S. (1999) *Seven Habits of Highly Effective People*; see http://www.more-selfesteem.com/books1.htm

16

Assertiveness

The meek will inherit the earth – if that's OK with everyone else.

Anon

Learning Outcomes

This chapter, and its companion web pages, explore assertiveness and offer a range of practical tactics to deal with difficult situations at work. The chapter has been written to provide support to many elements of the National Occupational Standards for Management and Leadership: *Managing Self and Personal Skills*; *Working with People*; and of *Achieving Results*, and it assists with many of the requirements of the Chartered Management Institute's Diploma in Management compulsory *Unit C41 – Developing your Management Style*, some of the elements of compulsory *Unit C44 – Effective Communications*, some of the compulsory *Unit C45 – Managing Performance* and most of the optional *Unit O42 – Developing Personnel and Personnel Performance*. This chapter will also be of value to those studying the CIPD Professional Development Scheme – particularly the *Leadership and Management* and *People Management and Development* modules, as well as people studying any of the CIPD specialist electives in *Learning and Development*.

Naturally, it will have application in all walks of life, too.

By the end of this chapter you will:

- Be able to define assertiveness
- Understand a popular 'instrument' for assessing conflict style
- Know the differences between submission, assertiveness and aggression
- Consider a set of 'workers rights' for application at your place of work
- A '4A' approach for managing difficult people at work
- Have access to ways of dealing assertively with customers – and still keep them.

What is Assertiveness?

Being assertive is something we normally consider confident people do naturally. That does not mean being pushy or selfish in order to get one's own way – assertive behaviour is positive and brings results in dealings with others. Not being assertive can cultivate low confidence, low self-esteem and worse. Assertive people will be confident to stand up and be counted, will put their opinion forward and stand by it. They will not be quiet and get ignored. Normally, because of the perceived risk involved in expressing an opinion openly – rather than keeping quiet – a certain level of confidence is required. To conquer shyness or become more effective socially a person needs to be more assertive.

Simply put, assertiveness is asking for what you want or speaking up for yourself when you feel strongly that you have something to say, without putting someone else down.

Learning to act and speak in a more assertive way could help overcome several obstacles in life, such as shyness, low self-esteem and a lack of confidence. If you are trying to improve your confidence or that of your people, then assertiveness training could help.

Being assertive is important to individuals because:

- *Career.* Those who are passive at work are often undervalued and ignored for promotion. It is those who put themselves forward and ask for responsibility who get it. Being more assertive will bring better opportunities and more job satisfaction.
- *Success and ambitions.* Setting a goal needs assertiveness with others who may try to dissuade or stand in the way. Again, being assertive just means someone declares an intention to do something and claim a right to be what they want to be.
- *Self-esteem.* Passive people who don't feel they have spoken up for themselves in any situation not only could lose out but will feel terrible inside. This feeling may reduce confidence and, in time, could even lead to depression.
- *Relationships.* Expressing feelings and being able to ask for what one wants makes for happier relationships and a happier partner.
- *Family.* It is important to compromise whether as a son, daughter or parent, but it is also important to be assertive in decisions where people need to state what they want. Women especially often need to be more assertive or the demands on them can be unbearable.
- *Friendships.* Any friendship should be on an equal footing. When one person starts to demand too much of the other it is time to reassess that friendship. Being assertive and telling friends honestly is very important and being passive is a recipe for disaster.

Assertiveness is a positive quality as long as assertiveness does not hurt anyone else and as long as wishes are stated calmly and confidently – that is, not acting selfishly. We all have a right to be ourselves and do what we feel is right – without compromise to others. Selfishness is when someone doesn't care about others, only themselves. Being assertive is all about respect for one's self that is reflected outwards and respect for others as having equal rights.

Thomas–Kilmann Conflict Mode Instrument

Developed by Kenneth W. Thomas and Ralph H. Kilmann, it is a widely used, self-assessment instrument measuring an individual's behaviour in conflict situations. The basis of the model uses two dimensions of behaviour – the first being degrees of 'assertion' from submissive through to assertive, the other 'assisting' running from uncooperative to cooperative. The model can be represented as in Figure 16.1 and has five conflict handling modes:

- *Competing* – the goal is 'to win'
- *Avoiding* – the goal is 'to delay'
- *Compromising* – the goal is 'to find a middle ground'
- *Collaborating* – the goal is 'to find a mutual gain–gain solution'
- *Accommodating* – the goal is 'to yield'.

The basis of the instrument is a questionnaire that gives respondents pairs of statements where they have to choose the one they most agree with; an example is shown in Table 16.1.

More detailed descriptions can be found on the companion web pages.

The instrument's non-evaluative approach helps participants understand how often they use each of the five conflict handling modes, and learn about the most appropriate uses for each mode and how to increase their 'comfort level' for less-used styles.

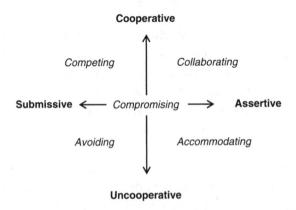

Figure 16.1 Adaptation of the Thomas–Kilmann conflict mode instrument

Table 16.1 Examples of paired Thomas–Kilmann instrument statements

Choose either A or B, whichever best reflects your situation	
A. There are times when I let others take responsibility for solving the problem.	**B.** Rather than negotiate on the things that we disagree on, I try to stress those things upon which we both agree.
A. I try to find a compromise solution.	**B.** I attempt to deal with all of his/her and my concerns.

Aggressive and Submissive Behaviour

When someone stands up for what they want but shows little or no concern for the effect they are having on others they are being aggressive. This can have long-term and potentially quite serious effects, both for the individual concerned and everyone around them. These include:

- Health problems such as ulcers, hypertension, migraine, exhaustion.
- Feelings of guilt or regret.
- A breakdown of communication.
- A loss of trust and respect.
- Isolation from colleagues and friends.
- Short-term and long-term damage to projects, resulting from:
  - Shortage of information. People are unwilling to confront the aggressor with the truth because they know how they are most likely to react.
  - Shortage of specialist knowledge. They haven't given people a genuine opportunity to contribute.
  - Limited access to the grapevine.
  - An inability to call in 'favours'. They don't help anyone, so why should anyone help them?
- Short-term and long-term damage to career prospects.

If someone regularly uses aggressive behaviour, they may reap short-term rewards, such as getting their own way or achieving power over others. The downside is that people will seek to avoid them and, wherever possible, they will make sure that they are excluded from developmental projects that require a creative and organic approach. Ultimately, people will work against them.

Alternatively, submissive behaviours can be equally serious, and include:

- Health problems, such as depression, lower back pain, digestive problems, insomnia.
- Feelings of anger, frustration and self-pity.

- A downward spiral of low confidence and low self-esteem.
- The loss of respect.
- Breakdown of work relationships as people realise that they are able to take advantage of the individual – and then they may feel guilty.
- Short-term and long-term damage to projects, resulting from:
  - Missed deadlines. An inability to say no means that the person (and their team) takes on unrealistic amounts of work and then are unable to complete on time.
  - Soaring costs. If people aren't able to deal with aggressive colleagues, spending can quickly get out of control, or they can find themselves burdened with many 'nice' but expensive and unnecessary resources.
  - Poor teamwork. An inability to take a firm line with aggressive colleagues may lead to squabbles, arguments, confrontations and, ultimately, a total breakdown of working relationships on the team.
  - Ill-conceived ideas. Because people find themselves unable to control aggressive colleagues they could find themselves held responsible for an outbreak of expensive mistakes resulting from people realising they can be as outrageous and experimental as they like.
- Short-term and long-term damage to career prospects.

If someone regularly uses non-assertive behaviour they may often reap short-term rewards, such as avoiding unpleasantness or keeping everyone happy. The downside is that they will become increasingly frustrated and anxious as people begin to assume that the other person will agree to their demands. The person will feel that they are losing control, and that their preferences, opinions and ideas carry little weight with the team.

The Rewards of Assertive Behaviour

The benefits of assertive behaviours include:

- Fewer stress-related health problems.
- Improved self-confidence, self-esteem and self-respect.
- Increased respect from others.
- Improved work relationships as people begin to:
  - Gain confidence in the person's honesty and openness.
  - A realisation that the individual says what they mean and means what they say.
  - Instil confidence in others as they recognise that they are a 'safe pair of hands'. They know where they stand.
  - Feel free to make suggestions and offer up creative ideas. People willingly share information.

- Short-term and long-term benefits for projects include:
  - Consistent achievement of objectives. Because all agreements are realistic, deadlines are met and spending remains within budget.
  - Improved teamwork. The aggressive people realise that they will not be able to intimidate, the non-assertive people recognise they will be listened to. Everyone begins to understand that assertive people are prepared to discuss, negotiate and – where necessary – compromise.
- Short-term and long-term career benefits.

People begin to realise that assertive people have the confidence to voice their opinions and ideas reasonably and calmly. They come to see them as someone who will not be intimidated or manipulated, who will work at creating harmonious relationships, and who operates with a high degree of firmness, integrity and honesty.

Assertive Behaviour in Action

So, how does one become assertive? It does not happen overnight and, as said, can take training to change behaviours sufficiently consistently. Being assertive involves operating from a position where the person recognises that they have:

- The right to be heard and so does everyone else
- The right to hold your own views, opinions and beliefs, and so does everyone else
- Something to contribute and so does everyone else
- The right to disagree and to say 'no', and so does everyone else.

The aggressive position is, generally, 'I alone have these rights', while the non-assertive or submissive position is 'Everyone has these rights – except me'.

Assertive communication

Assertive communication consists of three simple steps:

- *Step 1*. Listen and acknowledge that you have heard and understood the other person's point of view. Ask open questions if more information is needed.
- *Step 2*. Express, clearly and calmly, your own position and feelings.
- *Step 3*. Make constructive suggestions about what could or should happen next.

The three steps involved in assertive communication are now described in more detail.

Demonstrate you've heard and understood

Make a clear and simple statement that acknowledges whatever has been said. This is important because, if you are dealing with an aggressive person who feels that what they have said has been ignored or brushed aside, then they will become even more aggressive. Non-assertive people will have great difficulty in repeating their question or request, but will inwardly burn with anger and frustration. This can prove to be an explosive combination that may ignite sometime in the future, when you are least expecting it.

Express own feelings and views – find out more, if needed

Be direct and honest, and don't be frightened to use 'I' and 'my' statements like:

- 'I'd like it if ...'
- 'I think that ...'
- 'I feel ...'
- 'In my opinion ...'
- 'My view is that ...'.

Don't jump to conclusions and be prepared to take the time to find out more. Ask open – how, why, what, when and where – questions like:

- 'How do you think we should deal with this?'
- 'What, in your view, is the main problem?'
- 'What changes would you like to see?'
- 'What would your approach be?'

Even if someone's opinions are diametrically opposed to yours, do remember that they have the right to hold their own opinions. But also remember that being assertive is about maintaining your own position, even when someone is being aggressive and pushing you hard.

Make constructive suggestions on what next

Often, it's not enough just to say 'No' or 'That's not what I want'. Be prepared to make suggestions or offer alternatives. For example:

- 'My view is that we have to proceed very carefully with this; however, we could think about ...'
- 'I feel that right now would be the wrong time to launch a new campaign. Even so, I recognise your concern, and it would be helpful to know if you think there is another time, later this year, when we could introduce these new ideas ...'

- 'I'm very concerned that you have not been able to meet the deadline we agreed. The key step we need to take now is to create a plan to finish the job by the weekend. What do you suggest?'

Assertiveness and core statements

Working out a 'core statement' can be a very useful exercise when you know, in advance, that you have to:

- Confront someone and explain your dissatisfaction
- Stand firm to your point of view in the face of strong opposition
- Ask for something you want
- Refuse a request.

To create a core statement, simply focus on your objective. Think about what you want to achieve as a result of the communication. There follows some examples of core statements that match the list given above.

Confront someone and explain your dissatisfaction

- 'I'm extremely concerned by your sales figures to date and I need to see an improvement by the end of the month.'
- 'I feel that the way you answered questions at that meeting was inappropriate and unacceptable because you used out-of-date statistics. I would like you to update your information and then arrange another meeting so we can go through the data again.'
- 'I've noticed that your team is not producing the results that we agreed would be a minimum acceptable level of performance. I'd like you to prepare a report, by Wednesday, outlining the steps you will take to improve performance.'

Stand firm in the face of strong opposition

- 'I understand your concerns, but I am convinced, having seen the lab report, that we have no alternative but to abandon the project.'
- 'I can see this is important to you but, in my opinion, the plan won't work because there isn't enough in the budget to cover all the additional costs.'
- 'I can see why you think we ought to wait but, in my opinion, if we're going to do this, we need to do it now before we lose our competitive edge.'

Ask for something you want

- 'I recognise that money is tight, but I really need another member of staff if we're to reach the targets we've agreed.'

- 'I know there have been difficulties in the past, but I really need to spend some time in the Amsterdam plant if I'm going to find a solution to the problem.'
- 'I can see why you don't want another delay but, in my opinion, further tests are absolutely necessary because I need to make sure that the network will support the software.'

Your core statement should be your bottom-line, ideal outcome. Of course, as part of the process of searching for a win–win outcome you may have to negotiate and, to some extent, compromise. But, at the very least, if you give your core statement some serious thought before the encounter, you will have a clear idea of what you want the outcome to be.

Saying 'No!'

Many people have great difficulty with refusing requests and saying 'No!' An aggressive refusal to a reasonable request can cause terrific resentment: 'I only asked if I could move my desk and she went ballistic!' A non-assertive refusal can leave the other person wondering whether the answer was yes or no: 'I went in, asked if I could change the rota, he rambled on for nearly 20 minutes and I've come out of his office and I still don't know. What a waste of time!'

People often mistakenly believe that if they say no, people will:

- Get angry and cause a scene
- Feel resentful and, at a later date, take some kind of revenge
- Spread gossip and rumour about the refusal
- Perceive the person saying 'no' in a very negative way.

Robyn,[1] a Senior Receptionist, explains:

> I just hate having to say 'No'. I always feel guilty and I always think that people will feel angry or let down if I refuse a request. So I can never really win. If I say 'No', I feel guilty or anxious . . . and I always seem to spend ages apologising. If I say 'Yes', I often feel irritated or frustrated because, afterwards, I wish I'd had the courage to say 'No'. It's hopeless.

If you are caught in a similar spiral, the key points to remember are:

- When you say 'No', you are merely refusing the request and not rejecting the person.
- Refusals can be simple, open and honest statements.

---

[1] Robyn was a delegate on one of the many Client Care courses run by the author.

274

There are a number of assertive responses that one can give to ensure that you stand your ground yet do not come across as aggressive.

Five such examples are given on the companion web pages.

Assertive body language

When practising assertiveness, you need to make sure that your attitude, words and non-verbal communication all match. Body language is a powerful form of communication. If, for instance, you say something like 'I'm not prepared to support you on this one', while at the same time smiling a sickly smile and wringing your hands, then your listener will know that he has got you in a tight corner.

There are a number of body language signals you can give to show that you are prepared to listen, but you really do mean what you say. These include:

- Standing or sitting upright and straight.
- Not fidgeting. By keeping your movements to a minimum you will give an impression of calmness and authority.
- Looking the other person squarely in the eye without staring. Staring is aggressive, and being unable to make eye contact is often perceived as non-assertive, or even shifty.
- Matching the expression on your face to the words you are using. A stony, impassive face can be aggressive, and a hesitant or fixed smile can be perceived as inappropriate and non-assertive.
- Maintaining an even, well-modulated tone of voice. Shouting or speaking very softly and very slowly through clenched teeth are aggressive techniques. Non-assertive people often speak hesitantly and allow their words to trail away at the end of sentences.

Assert your Rights at Work

As we have already mentioned, everyone (that means you and the rest of the world) has certain rights. An example developed by a workgroup in consultation is shown in Box 16.1, you may find it helpful, as part of your assertiveness strategy, to photocopy the list and keep it beside your desk as a constant reminder – or better still, get it raised at the next workgroup meeting and amended as *your collective* way of moving the dynamics of the group forward to a more comfortable style.

Box 16.1: An example of your workgroup's agreed rights

You have the right to:

- *Say No*
- *Express your views, opinions and beliefs* (even if they are different from the mainstream)
- *Ask for what you want* (while recognising that you might not always get it!)
- *Change your mind* (in the light of new information or circumstances)
- *Make mistakes* (because everyone does)
- *Not know or understand* (because you can't be expected to know and understand everything)
- *Make your own choices* (because you know what you need and what suits you best)
- *Be yourself.*

Dealing with Difficult People at Work

There is no such thing as difficult people, but their behaviour might be! Despite our best efforts, there are times when we need to resolve conflict with people at work. A simple model of dealing with such situations is shown in Figure 16.2.

Assess

Assess the task – recognising the presence of strong emotion, start by actively listening and gathering information about the nature of the problems created by the difficult person. Gather data – it doesn't matter how stormy the conversation gets, since you don't have to say much. The merit of silence is that you don't do immediate damage to the relationship.

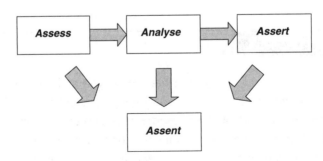

Figure 16.2 The '4A' Model for dealing with conflict at work.

Invite more rhetoric – '*Have you said all you want to say?*'

Alternatively, widen the catchment area – '*Have I made you angry in any other way – is this about lots of other things?*' Be permissive; let the other person vent their passion.

Mutual respect provides the basis for stable human relationships. This implies respect for the dignity of others and respect for you being expressed with a simple combination of firmness and kindness.

Analyse

Analyse the task. Try to read the 'family feel' of the problems involved. We all tend to treat the workplace in some sense like home. Since all bad behaviour begins as an attempt to solve problems, you need to see what the difficult person is really trying to achieve in order to know how to respond.

Consider Transactional Analysis of the behaviour (see Chapter 15). Is there an underlying attempt to overthrow 'parental' authority? Is the behaviour childishly calculated to elicit sympathy or attention? Is there a 'sibling rivalry' at work, expecting you to prefer one employee or colleague to others? And where does the behaviour of the difficult person interlock with your own vulnerabilities?

Assert

Assert yourself with a problem person by presenting the vital facts non-critically – '*I'm finding this situation intolerable*', '*I feel it would be more helpful if . . .*', '*It's very distracting for me when you . . . but I feel we really can work together as a team when you . . .*', '*I want to hand this project over to you for the next two months and this is the sort of outcome I'd like to see . . .*'.

This doesn't mean you have to remain emotionally neutral or bland. Nothing is more provocative to a raging colleague than an assumed expression of smiling indifference. It's bad for them, bad for you and bad for the quality of communication. Getting on the same wavelength may well mean giving voice to your own sense of irritation. The secret is how you convey this frustration. '*I'm actually extremely angry about the whole thing*' can be spoken in loud, emphatic staccato words without violating the principles of assertion theory. Mirroring the mood of the other person can help bring you closer together.

Keep your body language open. This helps you receive information and persuades the other person to offer it. You may additionally mirror or copy some of the gestures being given out as a means of furthering rapport. As the other person starts to unwind, it's helpful for you to keep pace.

If they indicate an appeal by using wide-open hands, perhaps you can send back the same message. Gestures reinforce a message. So, if you seriously want to prevent someone from interrupting you, hold up your hand like a police officer stopping a stream of traffic. This is far more effective than saying: '*Fine . . . I haven't finished yet!*'

Avoid being deflected by diversionary appeals. You should also feel confident enough to point out that the office isn't the family therapy centre and that no one else enjoys the way the individual is currently behaving. You must keep fairness in mind and give the other person the initial benefit of the doubt.

It may be necessary to offer models of alternative conduct for the difficult person because they may not know how to behave in the office environment or what is really expected of them. Never shrink from stating a personal assessment (prefacing the remarks with a formula such as '*My feeling is . . .*') and never accept personal denigration ('*You're entitled to your views as to my ability but I am not willing to accept the terms you have used – can we start again on a different basis, in new language, or shall we return to this another time?*').

Remember, the person with the most behavioural flexibility is the one most likely to control the interaction.

What sort of response can you give to this person to make them feel more accepted and personally secure? Always bear in mind that the meaning of the communication is the response you provoke. Even if you are misunderstood, that misunderstanding is the outcome! If you don't like the outcome, you must try to generate a different response.

Assent

Finally, win Assent and gain a commitment towards a positive outcome. Can the employee, colleague or customer suggest ways in which they could be helped to alter their actions or behaviour?

It is always better to get a solution from the person by whom it has to be applied. The idea makes sense to them, since they thought it up. It belongs to them, so they have a stake in its success. And they learn from their own thought processes something of the nature of problem-solving. Taking ready-made solutions from others only teaches obedience.

Conclude with a deal and confirm it in writing if necessary.

Assertive Customer Complaint Handling

Refer to Corsan and Mackay (2001) on this topic.

Those in customer-facing situations may appreciate having the guide on the companion web pages.

Summary

In this chapter you have:

- Met a definition of assertiveness
- Explored the Thomas–Kilmann 'instrument' for assessing conflict style
- Explored the differences between submission, assertiveness and aggression
- Seen an example of 'workers' rights'
- Observed a '4A' approach for managing difficult people at work – assess, analyse, assert, assent
- Seen a reference on how to deal assertively with customers – and still keep them.

Questions

1. Two assertive people are unable to reach agreement in a discussion at work. How might you mediate to reach agreement?
2. Discuss with your workgroup an appropriate set of 'rights' for the way that you wish to work together.
3. Suppose someone was being aggressive towards you at work. What approaches might you take to resolve the situation?

Reference

Corsan, J. R. and Mackay, A. R. (2001) *The Veterinary Receptionist*, Butterworth-Heinemann.

Further Reading

Back, K. (2005) *Assertiveness at Work*, McGraw-Hill.

Paterson, R. J. (2000) *The Assertiveness Workbook: How to express your ideas and stand up for yourself at work and in relationships*, New Harbinger.

17

Achievement

The greater danger for most people is not that our aim is too high and we miss it, but that it is too low and we hit it.

Michelangelo

Learning Outcomes

Perhaps achievement is more than Woody Allen suggested: '20 per cent talent, 20 percent luck and 60 per cent just turning up!' This chapter, and its companion web pages, explore achievement from a number of perspectives. The chapter has been written to provide support to many elements of the National Occupational Standards for Management and Leadership: *Managing Self and Personal Skills*; *Providing Direction – Lead People Unit 9*; many sections of *Facilitating Change*; many sections of *Working with People*; and of *Achieving Results*. It also meets many of the requirements of the Chartered Management Institute's Diploma in Management compulsory *Unit C41 – Developing your Management Style*, some of the elements of compulsory *Unit C44 – Effective Communications*, much of the compulsory *Unit C45 – Managing Performance* and most of the optional *Unit O42 – Developing Personnel and Personnel Performance*. This chapter will also be of value to those studying the CIPD Professional Development Scheme – particularly the *Leadership and Management* and *People Management and Development* modules, as well as people studying any of the CIPD specialist electives in *Learning and Development*.

By the end of this chapter you will:

- Have explored the basics of achievement
- Compared and contrasted optimism and pessimism
- Considered the Management Achievement Model – Mach One
- Have explored more theories about achievement and its central role in inspiring self-confidence
- Considered issues on being motivated to study.

The Fundamentals of Achievement

Today, more and more people are functioning like singles tennis professionals or golfers. Few spend their careers as a 'team player' for a large multinational; most people will be 'free agents', competing from one event to another, or contracting services for the length of a project, to solve a problem, or for a limited period of time. This means they have to be at the top of their 'game' all the time. In the past, most people either worked on a farm or worked for a large corporation, where it was possible to have a bad month, or even a slow year, and still get by. Today, almost nobody in business has that luxury.

For more and more people, the challenge is, like the tennis star, to sharpen their skills and show up, have a little practice, and then they get one chance to perform. If they don't perform they go home. No win, no glory – and no cheque! It's a wonderfully free, individualistic and exciting world, but it can also be brutally honest and ruthlessly humbling. So, what are the fundamentals of achievement? There are four such fundamentals.

First fundamental: do what you are good at

It has never been easier or more important to do what you love and what you are designed to do! Most of us no longer have to do work we are not suited for. Some say that the road to greatness, wealth and personal satisfaction lies in taking the path of least resistance.

Everyone is more likely to be motivated in their job if there is a good match to the portfolio of activities they really want to be doing. On the author's Motivation, Ability and Confidence Building workshops, delegates spend a few moments developing their dream portfolio.

'*You are to assume that you have won the lottery and never need to work for money again. In the table below, list the activities that you currently do that you will keep, and which you would drop. Then in the final column, list those new activities that you would like to work on.*' (See Table 17.1 for an example.) Most people consider their work environment, but the exercise need not be limited – a 'whole life' view can be very illuminating.

Table 17.1 Example of step 1 of the 'dream portfolio'

Activities that you will keep:	Activities that you will drop:	New activities that you would like to work on:
■ Developing new courses ■ Meeting new clients ■ Working with young professionals . . .	■ Overnight travel midweek, without my wife ■ Boring administration	■ E-commerce ■ Training new tutors

Then delegates are asked to put their first list aside. They then think about their skills and talents. '*What are you really good at, or do you feel that you might be with appropriate training? Produce a list of skills.*' (See Table 17.2 for an example.)

Finally, delegates are asked to use the skills listed in step 2 to act as a filter for the dream portfolio in step 1. '*Use this refined portfolio to compare with your job. Are there activities in your job role not in your portfolio that could be passed on to someone else? Is there something that you are not doing that could be a good match for your portfolio? Don't go for major changes initially – look for some quick hits, but plan to make bigger changes later.*'

Table 17.3 is an example of this third step. Note that it would only work if there was someone else who might reasonably take on the 'not wanted tasks' and did not feel that these were being 'dumped' on them. Indeed, there may be someone who might actually enjoy that type of work as an extension of their responsibilities or greater involvement.

Getting a better match to what a person really wants to be doing is a great motivator and can help define new achievements in the job. Occasionally, this exercise results in someone realising that they want to be working for a different department or different organisation. It might seem dangerous in those circumstances, but bear in mind that it is probably better for both the person and their firm to leave highly motivated than downright fed up!

This may be a fun exercise, but if someone can make something happen as a result of it, it will be very motivational. Beware, though, if you use it, of alerting someone to the

Table 17.2   Example of step 2 of the 'dream portfolio'

What are you really good at?	What might you be really good at – with appropriate training?
■ Presentations – design and delivery ■ Writing – articles, course materials ■ Dealing with people . . .	■ Information technology

Table 17.3   Example of step 3 of the 'dream portfolio'

Activities in your job role that could be passed on to someone else:	Activities that you are not doing that could be a good match for your portfolio:
■ Expenses claims ■ Car administration – tax, insurance, MOT, servicing	■ Developing press releases ■ New articles for web pages ■ Delivering courses via webcam

differences between their portfolio and reality, then doing nothing to help them to bridge that gap. In the examples given in Tables 17.1–17.3, there are some things that might be difficult to achieve – such as always travelling midweek with their wife – but they might be able to delegate some of their administration to free up time to get publicity developed for the firm. The opportunity for some e-commerce and web-based activity could also be investigated. The 'dream portfolio' might be a useful preamble for a person's appraisal too.

Second fundamental: do it very, very well

There is no substitute for skill. In any profession, and in almost any situation, the top 20 per cent will do well. If you know what you're doing, if you show up, if you get the job done (and if you have a great coach!), sooner or later you'll win. If you don't love what you do enough to practise and develop your skills, ask yourself, 'What's wrong?'

Third fundamental: patience

Not everything is achievable immediately and what is worth having is worth striving for. Provided people can see that they are making progress towards a goal, perseverance will be reinforced and a little tenacity will be seen to prevail.

Fourth fundamental: luck

Super achievement involves the mystery called 'luck'. Many motivational speakers focus only on their 'secret of success', claiming they have the 'law' of money or the 'law' of success on their side. By definition, you can't count on luck to make up for lack of talent or lack of preparation. And there's no use blaming 'bad luck' for poor choices or stubbornness or bad judgement. Success comes from acknowledging luck, then going about your business the best way you know how. Many people have been credited with the following quote, although it was Ben Hogan who said it first:

> *Funny thing, the more I practise, the luckier I get!*

To achieve remarkable things, follow your talents and passions, work extremely hard at something you love so much you just can't help yourself, be patient and persevere. Lady luck shines most on those who work the hardest at what they do best!

Optimism and Pessimism

Psychologist Robert Holden[1] suggests that 'if someone is happy they are probably in denial and that deep down there is probably some pain and suffering to work on'. Most people, when asked how they are, will say: 'Mustn't grumble, bearing up, can't complain, not bad...'. Much of the workforce deals with the bad things in life: doctors and veterinary surgeons look for illness (not wellness); journalists the latest doom, gloom and scare story; the police for crimes; insurance assessors seek out disasters; health and safety executives the dangers – and managers...?

Happy events, good deeds, people's achievements and heart-warming stories are only given the merest glance, while acts of generosity are viewed with cynicism – 'no one does something for nothing'. However, Mr Holden is convinced that identifying the things that bring us success is a better approach to achievement in life and work than focusing on problems. Unfortunately, childhood teaches us not to boast and that pride comes before a fall, and that happiness is no more than a short step to smugness; all these qualities can be related to complacency and our achievements slip into the background of continued struggle. The warning is that 'the caution that informs our perceptions can be self-fulfilling... be careful what you look for – you might just find it... if you look for problems, you will find them'. Conversely: 'a focus on success is more likely to generate positive results...'.

The Mayo Clinic in the USA over the last 30 years found that optimistic people had a much lower risk of premature death than those who were pessimistic (*Financial Times*, 2004). While pessimism may be a workplace risk, this is not so for the legal profession. Structural pessimism among lawyers lends a professional advantage, where casting a cynical eye over a legal document is best equipped to uncovering hidden catches. Unfortunately, the same cynicism also breeds neurosis and anxiety about long-term success. Perhaps this is why the Law Society and Bar Council, uniquely among the professions, funds a charity (LawCare) dedicated to helping lawyers overcome stress, depression, and alcoholism and drug abuse.

While the study calls for a transformation of attitudes and management approaches in law firms so that people turn pessimism into cautious optimism, many do not want to change. Part of the problem, according to Holden (see earlier footnote), is that we spend too much time rushing about in a manic society that confuses what he calls 'hurry sickness' with genuine achievement. Why do we have to rush so fast, fast-tracking a career that takes a trainee to the top by the time they are 40 only to be discarded by the system in their prime?

Why have a 'to-do list' packed with trivial items? Why not have a shorter 'to-achieve list' – identifying those things that we want to *achieve* where we are most *adding value*?

---

[1] Founder and Director of 'The Happiness Project', addressing a conference of HR managers – see http://www.happiness.co.uk/.

Peter Drucker said, 'There is nothing so useless as doing efficiently that which should not be done at all.' But we are committed to 'doing' rather than 'achieving', as if by doing we will win the rat race. However, as Lily Tomlin, the US comedian and actress, observed: 'The trouble with the rat race is that if you win, you are still a rat'.

So, the pressure on billable hours in law firms remains. Doctors still largely focus on cures rather than prevention; newspapers continue to publish bad news because we want to read it.

Perhaps it is time, as Mr Holden suggests, to start a conversation about what we want to achieve in society that will equate with achievement, success and happiness at work. Is achievement and success a 70-hour week, a bigger salary, the number of people you manage? Has it something to do with your daily e-mail count or the size of your departmental budget? Perhaps it is a long marriage, a clean licence and a knighthood? Or could it be something as simple as an optimistic state of mind, accessible to all.

Managerial Achievement (Mach One)

The Mach One system ('M Ach' is short for *M*anagerial *Ach*ievement) is based on the experience of managers and their thinking about the critical dimensions of high achievement, as well as the findings of management research. The challenge facing all managers, therefore, is to attain a high level of results in the critical areas of their jobs by effectively utilising the limited resources available to them. Mach One is simply a system for increasing managerial achievement. So, management achievement is defined as:

- A question of *how* managers manage, not *what* they manage
- Being directly related to the specific behaviour of the manager
- The result of doing the right thing, at the right time, in the right circumstances
- A matter of determining which areas of their job are the most important – that is, knowing what results are critical and where effort is most likely to produce high pay-offs, and then deciding how to manage these areas most appropriately.

But managerial achievement is beyond simply setting priorities and determining what results are important. Automation and computerisation help to increase output, but without Motivated, Able and Confident people, no organisation can survive the pressure of competition for long.

Mach One has two main dimensions. It focuses on:

- The manager's job and the important results that must be achieved within it
- The behaviour the manager exhibits in getting the job done.

Within these two elements, Mach One focuses on how managers take decisions, communicate with employees, motivate them, improve their ability, build their confidence, build teams and lead them – all are interrelated components that lead to achievement.

Further descriptions and illustrations of this model can be found on the companion web pages.

As a final comment on Mach One, it has proven to be a rather complex model and has not found continuing favour in the development of modern managers, although there are many committed consultant practitioners who value the use of Mach One. The model is not particularly intuitive and is not easy for managers to visualise in training and development environments – as a result, its effective use back in the real world is much less likely.

Theories about the Desire for Achievement

The desires to succeed and to excel are called achievement needs, and achievement motivation is basic to a 'good life' where achievers, as a whole, enjoy life and feel in control. Being motivated keeps us productive and gives us self-respect, but where and how achievement needs are learned are complex, intriguing and important questions. They are important for both teachers and tutors in school and colleges, but are equally important in the world of management. There are a number of different academic approaches to understanding the 'theory of achievement' that are addressed in this section to guide the busy manager.

Needs theory and achievement

David McClelland et al. (1953) and John Atkinson (1981) have contributed greatly to this area of study. They began by developing a measure of the need to achieve in a test where subjects were asked to make up stories about pictures; they found that persons with high achievement needs can be identified by the stories they tell – namely, more stories about striving for excellence, overcoming obstacles or accomplishing some difficult goal. Other researchers (Jackson et al., 1973) suggested that achievement needs are made up of several factors, where someone wants to:

1. Gain approval from experts – peer recognition.
2. Make money – largely to acquire material possessions.
3. Succeed on our own – independence.
4. Gain respect from friends – social standing.
5. Compete and win – overcoming others.
6. Work hard and excel – largely an intrinsic reward.

Thus, one high achiever might strive primarily to build a reputation among their peers, while another person, equal in overall need to achieve, would concentrate on gaining respect and status from friends, and so on, depending on their past experience of what a certain achievement had given them.

So, how do we learn to have a high or low need for achievement? It comes partly from our childhood, where some authors suggest that a high achieving male tends to have rejecting parents who expect him to become independent early, make high demands on him, reward his success and/or punish unsatisfactory behaviour (which increases the fear of failure). Rather surprisingly, it was found by Byrne and Kelley (1981) that both loving-accepting (undemanding?) and dominant (over-controlling?) fathers tend to have less ambitious sons. However, sons of managers and owners have much higher needs to achieve than sons of fathers with routine jobs.

However, what of females and their need for achievement? Weitzman et al. (1972) discovered that most children's books described boys as active, effective and achieving, while girls were described as watching the boys, being a boy's helper or just tagging along. An experiment showed that sexist stories actually had an immediate impact on the behaviour of nursery school children. Girls were more active and persistent in their work if they had heard stories picturing girls that way. This is just one minor example, but it is generally recognised that our needs, goals and self-concepts come from thousands, maybe millions, of experiences.

In general, teachers believe that high achievers have respectful, praising, optimistic, supportive, hard-working parents who are themselves learning and success orientated. These parents expect each person in the household to do their share of the chores and to follow reasonable rules. They talk with each other about their work and studies.

For managers' purposes, these childhood experiences or the lack of them may be of interest, but they occurred in the past and therefore are unchangeable (although a person might change their reaction to their past). What can you do to influence your people now that enables them to be highly motivated and achievement orientated? How can you encourage them to be so intent on reaching a distant goal that nothing, within reason, gets in the way?

Experience shows that it is much more complicated than just a person's single need that makes them do something; although it is a large part of it if we can understand their fundamental needs and can do something about them. Borrowing a lot from learning theory, there are three factors determining achievement behaviour.

Motives

Within our people a large number of competing motives or needs are striving for expression at the same time, such as the need for money, the need for achievement, the need for close relationships, the need for power and the need to be cared for by others. Besides the conflict among many motives, the theory assumes there is a conflict between the hope of success and the fear of failure, i.e. an approach-avoidance conflict over each goal. The fear of failure can keep us from learning or trying something new at work, just as the fear of rejection can keep us from getting emotionally involved with someone.

The strength of the approach and avoidance tendencies is determined by the relative strength of the need to achieve and the need to avoid failure (or success), plus the next two factors.

Expectations

What someone expects to happen if they follow a certain course of action is their expectations. They observe the situation and, based on their past experience, estimate the likelihood of success and the chances of something bad happening, depending on what they do. Having some hope of achievement is necessary, but it is not a simple situation – a highly motivated achiever may utilise complex optimistic or pessimistic cognitive strategies, as discussed in attribution theory later in this chapter. For now, we can consider different approaches of two types of 'high achievers' to a workplace presentation:

- *'Illusory glow' optimism.* Here, an optimistic, high-achieving person may seek out work colleagues who value and reinforce their successes at work; he or she frequently relives a fantasy of their past accomplishments and dreams of the future, and they may relax with friends before an important presentation. Such a person nurtures and protects their self-esteem and confidence. They expect to do very well, they work very hard, they enjoy their successes and, if they should fail, they automatically and immediately apply an 'I couldn't help it' defence of the ego – and optimistically take on the next challenge.
- *'Defensive' pessimist.* Here, the high-achieving person will be defending their self-esteem before the presentation, not afterwards. Such a person expects to do poorly or, at least, anticipates a variety of possible stumbling blocks. He or she works very hard, preparing especially well for the anticipated problems and difficult questions. They use the high anxiety and stress of the presentation as a motivator, not as something to avoid, and then take an 'I expected it' attitude towards the rare failure that does occur – and with anxious excitement systematically attack the next challenge. (This strategy is very different from the pessimistic person who 'bad mouths' him or herself after a failure: 'I'm such a fool,' 'I couldn't be bothered', etc. and often giggles at themselves. Such a pessimist is likely gradually to lower their expectations and goals, and perform more and more poorly until eventually becoming a total pessimist who has no hope, expects to fail and therefore doesn't try.)

Both the 'illusory glow' optimist and the 'defensive' pessimist are challenged by hard tasks; achieving is important, gratifying and absorbing for them; they see themselves as having considerable control over the situation and stick with the task, even though it is hard and occasionally disappointing. Compare these achievers with the underachievers described later.

Incentives

The *incentive* a person feels depends on how attractive the possible outcomes are to them personally (relative to how unattractive the possible risks are to them). Each major task, such as winning new business, learning to design spreadsheets, completing a stocktaking to writing recommendations for Just-in-Time Inventory Management, asking the boss for a raise, getting a Certificate in Supervisory Management through to an MBA, going round the world on two wheels, or raising three children, provides an enormous range of possible pay-offs, some more appealing to one person than the next. The more likely a person feels they are to succeed in the task, *and* the more appealing, important, the right thing to do, exciting or wonderful the eventual goal to them, the more drive and enthusiasm they will have about the activity.

In summary then, how motivated someone is depends on:

1. The strength of fairly consistent motives or needs inside of them.
2. Their expectation of what outcomes certain actions will produce.
3. How badly at this time they want a certain pay-off over all the other wants they have and over the risks they face.

The needs, expectations and incentives are mostly learned; together, these factors (our motivation) largely determine what we do and how far we get in life – however we choose to 'measure' how far we have come. Although the past experiences related to these factors are unalterable, the factors that influence our lives so enormously can be changed by us – that's the beauty of being human!

So, what can you do to keep people striving for special goals? The following is a range of suggestions to bring up in conversation with them:

- Break their major goals into manageable daily tasks and get them to set aside the time
- Ask them to uncover pleasure from the work and reward their progress
- Remember their past successes and get them to imagine how good they will feel when they accomplish their goal
- Also get them to imagine how bad they will feel if they just give up or make a mess of the tasks
- Use peer group pressure, to get them to focus on trying to improve on their best efforts thus far, to arouse interest
- Seek encouragement and find 'heroes' to inspire them.

Remind them, as Mark Twain said: 'Don't go around saying the world owes you a living. The world owes you nothing. It was here first.'

Attribution theory and achievement

Another related theory to help us understand behaviour and motivation, like Graham's procrastination (see Chapter 11, Box 11.1), is 'attribution theory'. In the 18th century, Hume (1739) argued that assuming there are causes for everything that happens is an inherent part of observing the world, because it makes the world more meaningful. Humans want to know. For instance, if someone bumps into you at work, you wonder why. You may assume he or she is aggressive, clumsy, flirting, that you are in the way, etc. Obviously, what you assume is the cause of the bumping makes a big difference. Likewise, Graham might ask himself, 'Why do I put off studying?' And answer, either 'because I am a poor learner' or 'because it is boring'. He *attributes* his procrastination to his slowness or to the dullness of the reading. These kinds of assumptions about causes (we seldom know for sure the real causes) will certainly influence how we behave and how we feel.

So, why are some people highly motivated to achieve and others not? According to attribution theory a high achiever will:

- Approach rather than avoid tasks related to succeeding because he or she believes success is due to high ability and effort that they are confident of. Failure is thought to be caused by bad luck or a poor manager/customer, i.e. not their fault. Thus, failure doesn't hurt their self-esteem but success builds pride and confidence.
- Persist when the work gets hard rather than giving up, because failure is assumed to be caused by a lack of effort which he or she can change by trying harder.
- Select challenges of moderate difficulty (50 per cent success rate), because the feedback from those tasks tells them more about how well they are doing, rather than very difficult or very easy tasks which tell them little about their ability or effectiveness.
- Work with a lot of energy because the results are believed to be determined by how hard one tries.

Conversely, the unmotivated person will:

- Avoid success-related chores because he or she tends to (a) doubt their ability and/or (b) assume success is related to luck or to 'who you know' or to other factors out of their control. Thus, even when successful, it isn't as rewarding to the unmotivated person because they don't feel responsible, it doesn't increase their pride and confidence – good feedback from a manager is crucial (see Chapter 18).
- Quit when having difficulty because they believe failure is caused by a lack of ability which they can't do anything about – to develop someone's ability in the most appropriate style (see Chapter 14).
- Choose easy or very hard tasks to work on because the results will tell him or her very little about how poorly (presumably) they are doing – again, good feedback and reviewing of work is fundamental (see Chapter 18).

- Work with little drive or enthusiasm because the outcome isn't thought to be related to effort – so a manager needs to develop their motivation using the appropriate style (see Chapter 9).

Motivated underachievers

Sometimes an underachiever with a 'work problem' is not unmotivated, but in fact is highly motivated to perform poorly and not get promotion because they want to avoid success! Why and how would anyone choose to perform badly at work, which is clearly connected with what one does for most a lifetime? Because they are afraid of achievement and want to avoid responsibility.

The underachiever unconsciously utilises excuses to explain why he or she is doing poorly and why it isn't their fault. They say, 'They didn't explain what they wanted' or 'Everyone else doesn't bother – why should I?' or 'My mates had all kinds of things planned for me the night before the presentation'. The trouble is they believe they want to succeed and they believe their own excuses; this self-deception is 'the crap gap'. They also believe that the situation is beyond their control, that they are innocent victims of circumstances. They aren't uncomfortable enough to fight their way out of the gloomy situation they are in.

Since the underachiever is afraid of achieving, the usual efforts of managers – for example, offering rewards, threatening sanctions and being assigned a terrific 'buddy' in work – are ineffective because these methods don't deal with the self-deception and the fears. They don't want to look honestly and carefully at themselves, their motives, their values or their future. Why not? Because being successful and realising that one has the ability to perform well at work, tidy their work area, claim their own expenses on time, choose a meaningful career, work full-time (whatever the goal) means the person is ready and able to 'grow up' – to 'be on his or her own', to be responsible, to be independent and to keep on taking care of him or herself for the rest of their life. On the other hand, being unable to manage your life (without it being your fault) keeps others from expecting you to be mature and capable. Growing up is scary for some adults and some don't want to do it (on a conscious and/or unconscious level) – the Peter Pan Syndrome.

Since this kind of underachiever is not aware of this self-deception, it may be hard for them to help themselves.

To see how a manager can help close the 'crap gap', the difference between what the employee thinks they want ('good job performance') and their actual behaviour (mostly avoidance of all responsible behaviour through the use of excuses), a nine-stage process has been devised and is included in the companion web pages.

This process has been adapted and condensed down into the chapter on Confidence Development (see Chapter 19).

Hopefully, some people will be able, without their manager's intervention, to see that they are lying to themselves by the use of excuses. Then, by consciously taking control of their work (stopping the self-conning), some people can help themselves. Others will not be able to see why they are underachievers but they will realise they are not performing up to their potential; an option may be for them to seek professional help.

Besides the 'attitude problem' type (about 50 per cent of all underachievers), dealt with above, there are several other kinds of underachievers, usually related to moderately serious psychological disorders requiring professional treatment. These include:

- Anxiety disorder
- Sociopathic disorder (lack of conscience, manipulative)
- Identity disorder (confusion about life goals)
- Defiant disorder.

Some have suggested the workplace indifference of some people as being due to cultural differences, e.g. if a person assumes that only white middle- and upper-class people care about getting good appraisals and promotion, and if they aren't in that social-economic group or hate that type of person, then it becomes difficult for them to take work seriously. Of course, there are those who become offended or resentful due to a personality clash and say, 'I won't work for you'. There may be many ways to be unmotivated. In any case, a wasted mind is a terrible loss to the organisation, but it is even more serious for their life when it is their mind that is wasted.

Social-cognitive approach to achievement

Managers may be able to define two basic types of workers: (a) learning orientated – those wanting to learn and gain competence; and (b) image orientated – those wanting to look smart and/or avoid looking stupid. All people want to build their self-esteem, but we try to do it in different ways. While oversimplified, there are groups of findings roughly associated with these two types. Understanding these types may help managers help staff and, indeed, managers help themselves.

- *Learning orientated.* These people see intelligence as changeable ('I can learn to use the software' or 'I can get more efficient'). They enjoy learning, often fascinated with specific parts of their job, getting the designs approved, solving customer enquiries, banking the cheques. They see low performance at work as due to a lack of effort or a poor strategy, which they can change. Pride is based on the amount of effort they put in, not on looking smart. They work hard. Being unchallenged is boring and offers no chance to test or prove themselves. Thus, even if they don't feel they are really bright, they will take on tough, challenging intellectual tasks, risking failing on an assignment. Are men mostly like this?

- *Image orientated.* These people see intelligence as permanently fixed. They consider it very important that others see them as smart or, at least, not stupid or naive. Since doing well is assumed to be due to brains and not effort, there isn't much need to work hard. In fact, if a person has to work hard to learn something, that suggests they aren't very smart. And, if they do poorly, there isn't anything they can do about it. They were born that way. Naturally, such a person would avoid difficult challenges if doing poorly seemed likely (is this especially true of bright women?). They tend to be less curious, less interested in new ideas and in learning about themselves. Their pride is based on good impression management, not on honest, careful estimates of their ability. They avoid testing their limits. Thus, the person's level of confidence is shaky – one foul-up at work, one criticism of them, one foolish statement by them raises their own doubts about their intelligence. Even high achievers fall into this trap; their worry about their image reduces the intrinsic satisfaction they get out of achieving something new.

Managers must attempt to build the self-esteem and confidence of their people, sacrificing perhaps implanting knowledge. Three popular principles guide many managers: give lots of positive reinforcement, expect people to do well (self-fulfilling prophesy) and build the person's self-esteem. All sound commendable but all may be harmful in certain circumstances. For example:

- Expecting and rewarding success on easy tasks does not encourage a person to tackle hard tasks
- Being 'successful' on easy tasks doesn't build self-confidence – it makes people feel less able to tackle the more challenging
- People that know their limits aren't being tested
- People are being misled if they are subtly being told that it is easy to succeed at work – at a certain level it might be true, but not compared to when a person strives and achieves something worthwhile.

Become Motivated to Study

Many managers may be using this text as a module reader for a management qualification; the author, having tutored many people and having studied himself over the years, knows personally how challenging this can be. To become motivated to learn while in work, particularly through distance learning, you must:

1. Learn to genuinely enjoy reading, studying and using the information (usually telling others about it).

2. Negotiate support at home and at work so that you can willingly take on tough assignments, realising that you will occasionally not do well or not get assignments completed on time.

3. Feel competent and be taught or tell yourself that doing poorly on an assignment or an examination basically means that you need to work harder, achieve focus or take a different approach, or all three.

4. In most cases, believe the information learned is worthwhile (at least for gaining the qualification).

So, if you were an undisciplined person, like Graham (Chapter 11, Box 11.1), how could you become motivated to study and gain self-confidence?

■ *Learn 'I am responsible'* – that the more you study, the more you learn and the better your grades are (as well as, quite possibly, your performance at work). Thus, you begin to feel more responsible for what you get out of your course. How exactly can you do this? (a) Keep records of how much you study and compare your grades when you have studied a lot with times when you study very little. (b) Prove to yourself that you are in control of your learning, no one else, not the tutor, not the assignment, not luck.

■ *Learn 'I can be in control'* – that you are capable of directing your life. How? (a) Schedule more study time and reward your promptness and increased effort. (b) Carefully measure the greater efficiency you achieve, e.g. how much more of the last few paragraphs do you remember when studying intensely? (c) Remember: doing poorly simply means you should try harder. Take pride in your self-control.

■ *Learn 'I have ability'* – that you have more ability than you previously thought. How? (a) Have more success by developing skills, like reading and assignment writing skills. (b) Get more information about your ability, such as assignment feedback or a respected person's honest opinion. (c) Increase your feelings of competence.

■ *Learn 'I value learning'* – that you can value studying and success in your course more. How? (a) Write down all the benefits of doing well in each assignment. (b) Remind yourself that each successful step in each module means three things – you are earning a chance to continue, you have what it takes to succeed and you have done something worthwhile. (c) Make use of what you learn, e.g. tell others, interact with others who can add to your knowledge, apply the knowledge in other module workshops or at work, etc.

■ *Learn 'I may deceive myself'* – that you, like others, are capable of remarkable self-deceiving and self-defeating thought processes which interfere with many important activities in your life, ranging from doing your best in assignments to your golf handicap or asking the smartest person for a date. How? (a) Observe your attributions, especially your excuses, and double-check their accuracy. (b) Overcome your fears by doing whatever scares you (if it is safe)! (c) Attend closely to your self-concept, including self-efficacy and attitudes about changing, and find the best views for you – review Chapter 15 on self-esteem too.

You need to realise that change is possible before you can change and that the more effort you put in, the more you learn; the more you learn, the more able you are to do well. We all remember a tutor telling us how they nearly failed yet they were able to 'pull through' with a little appropriate application. But why don't the hundreds of 'you-can-change-your-life stories' told by friends and colleagues or on TV or in films have the same effect on all of us? One possibility is that our belief in our own self-control is very situation specific, i.e. the success story of an average-turned-super insurance salesperson would probably not inspire a public sector manager to study harder.

Finally, studies of academically gifted women often find that they 'drop out' of college or distance learning management programmes. At the very least, almost every very bright woman finds it necessary to frequently deny or hide her intelligence. Men and women find highly able women threatening. One may think sexism is in the past, but being superior is especially hard for women. Chapter 4 in Mackay (2007) aims to help gifted women who want to achieve their potential and return to work.

Summary

In this chapter you have:

- Explored the basics of achievement – do what you are good at, do it well, and have patience and a little (self-made by practice) luck
- Compared and contrasted optimism and pessimism – and found that perhaps we should review what we mean by 'success'
- Considered the Management Achievement Model – Mach One
- Explored more theories about achievement and its central role in inspiring self-confidence – including ideas about the need to achieve, the influence of others on our success, issues surrounding 'motivated underachievers' and social group influences
- Considered issues on how to be motivated to study.

Questions

1. Run through the exercise in the first section of the chapter to see if there are even small areas of your job that you can delegate to others to make space for doing more of what you enjoy. What possibilities have you uncovered?
2. Among your work group discuss what you individually and collectively consider as success. Compare these findings with measures your organisation employs (see the balanced scorecard for ideas in Chapter 8).

3. Imagine that one of your workgroup has lost their way a little and does not seem to have their usual 'energy' for work; being a good colleague and friend they turn to you for advice. Given they say they have no health or family worries, what advice would you give?

4. In order to boost your motivation to study, review the final section of the chapter and write some positive notes where indicated on your personal situation. Compare these with others in your study group.

References

Atkinson, J. W. (1981) Thematic Apperceptive Measurement of Motivation in 1950 and 1980, in *Cognition in Human Motivation and Learning* (G. d'Ydewalle and W. Lens, eds), pp. 159–198, Lawrence Erlbaum Associates, Hillsdale, NJ.

Byrne, D. and Kelley, K. (1981) *An Introduction to Personality*, 3rd Edition, Prentice-Hall, Englewood Cliffs, NJ.

Financial Times (2004) 30 September, p. 13.

Jackson, D. N., Ahmed, S. A. and Heapy, N. A. (1973) Is Achievement a Unitary Construct?, University of Western Ontario, *Research Bulletin No. 273.*

Mackay, A. R. (2007) *Recruiting, Retaining and Releasing People*, Butterworth-Heinemann.

McClelland, D. C., Atkinson, J. W., Clark, R. A. and Lowell, E. L. (1953) *The Achievement Motive*, Prentice-Hall, Englewood Cliffs, NJ.

Weitzman, L., Eifler, D., Hokada, E. and Ross, C. (1972) Sex-role Socialization in Picture Books for Preschool Children, *American Journal of Sociology*, Vol. 77, pp. 1125–1150.

Further Reading

Chandler, S. (2004) *100 Ways to Motivate Yourself: Change Your Life Forever*, Career Press.

Tracy, B. (1995) *Maximum Achievement*, Simon & Schuster.

18

Building Confidence Through Constructive Feedback

When you end a reprimand with a praising, people think about their behaviour not your behaviour.

Kenneth Blanchard, co-author of *The One Minute Manager*

Learning Outcomes

Why do some managers find it so difficult to give (or receive) good feedback? This chapter, and its companion web pages, are designed to help. The chapter has been written to provide support to key elements of the National Occupational Standards for Management and Leadership: *Working with People – Units 26 and 27*, and it meets many of the requirements of the Chartered Management Institute's Diploma in Management compulsory *Unit C45 – Managing Performance*, some elements of compulsory *Unit C44 – Effective Communication*, and much of the optional *Unit O42 – Developing Personnel and Personnel Performance*. This chapter will also be of value to those studying the CIPD Professional Development Scheme – particularly the *Leadership and Management* and *People Management and Development* modules, as well as people studying any of the CIPD specialist electives in *Learning and Development*.

By the end of this chapter you will:

- Understand the central role managers have in enhancing and maintaining people's confidence
- See how doing so links with their own self-confidence
- Have discovered a range of ideas for giving and receiving feedback
- Have explored the differences between criticism and constructive feedback
- Know how to break bad news (tough decisions) to people
- Know what pitfalls managers should avoid in their dialogue with staff.

Why Build Staff's Confidence?

> *One of a manager's most important responsibilities is increasing subordinates' self-confidence; employees then have a more optimistic – but realistic – view of their skills and talents.*
>
> James Tingstad, 1991

By increasing your staff's self-confidence you will get more than psychic rewards. If employees feel good about themselves, then productivity and morale both improve. There are a number of reasons for this:

- Confidence is contagious – people who feel good about themselves are likely to increase the self-confidence of those around them. Self-confident people are respected by colleagues and management, and they return that respect.
- Self-confident people are decisive rather than tentative – they focus on their work responsibilities instead of worrying about the reactions of others.
- Self-confident people are optimistic about reaching their objectives.
- Self-confident people are expressive – they forge ahead instead of waiting for someone else to show the way. They are risk-takers, and taking risks is crucial in technical organisations. People who lack self-confidence, on the other hand, tend to be like sheep – followers – rather than focus on progress.

A caution about overconfidence: people must accurately perceive their abilities so they will accept tasks that are appropriate to their skills. Managers play an important role in working with staff, to assign tasks so individuals can determine for themselves which challenges they can best handle. Note the guide presented in Chapter 14 to taking a flexible approach to developing people – tasks, each according to the individual's task maturity.

Given that improving self-confidence among staff is a vital responsibility for a manager, there are five key activities for achieving it.

Accepting

Accept people for themselves, not just their actions. People who feel valued as individuals, rather than just because their work is constantly monitored, will be more secure and less intimidated by small, everyday mistakes. So, personal security cultivates innovation. Secure employees develop a realistic form of self-confidence, since they are more likely to recognise their deficiencies and admit them to others.

As mentioned above, look to Chapter 14 to develop your flexible style in managing people with differing levels of competence – particularly those who are willing, have most of the ability to do a job unaided but need you to give them a guide. These people need a coach, not a trainer.

It is difficult to maintain an accepting attitude in the midst of others' mistakes, but it will make you a better manager. By and large, remember that parents are forgiving of their offspring's misdemeanours! Look to Transactional Analysis to understand Parent–Child interactions (Chapter 15).

Praising

Good managers take the time to listen to their staff and are concerned about their people's self-esteem. Managers that are too insensitive, too busy or too concerned with their own egos to praise subordinates miss a significant opportunity to develop their people – effective managers have effective staff.

So, to deliver effective praise, note the guide given here or, for a more comprehensive review, see Chapter 15. Praise should not be limited to the annual appraisal either (covered in Chapter 6 of Mackay, 2006).

- So as not to be counter-productive or scorned, deliver praise that is truly deserved.
- The most genuine form of praise is a spontaneous comment.
- Never suppress the urge to praise.
- So the recipient knows exactly what is being praised, make your comments specific.
- Expand a specific comment into general praise: 'You handled that customer well; you controlled your temper even though she was being unreasonable and you also managed to calm her down. Well done.'

There are many options to praise people by recognising them as individuals or members of a group. Suggestions on how to find non-cash rewards can be found in Chapter 7, Box 7.2. Usually, the problem is not an inability to find the proper reward vehicle, but rather the manager's reluctance to praise.

Appreciating

Appreciation is similar to praise, but while praise acknowledges that the employee has excelled at some skill or task, appreciation explains what the employee's *effort* has done for you personally, another individual, the team or workgroup, another department, or the company as a whole.

To appreciate, show your staff how their achievements have benefited you personally (as well as the company), and make it clear that you appreciate their efforts. (If you really have trouble appreciating your people, ask yourself whether you can meet your job or career objectives without them.)

The value of appreciation is largely determined by the giver, whereas the value of praise is determined by whether the recipient feels it is deserved. Managers should show appreciation when it is due – otherwise, managing becomes manipulating.

Show appreciation through personal comments and notes, but make it sincere: 'The Head of Department just commented on my monthly report and said it was very useful to her – I did say that that was partly due to your great contribution. Thanks!' You will also find that appreciation will be reciprocated, resulting in a far more pleasant and productive work environment. Receiving a note of thanks from a member of staff is among the most rewarding events for a manager.

Encouraging

An employee needs encouraging most when they have made a mistake. This is when you can help the employee admit errors and learn from them: one word of encouragement during a failure is worth a whole book of praise after a success (see Box 18.1).

Beware: the greatest threat to self-confidence is criticism – even a single remark. Box 14.7 in Chapter 14 showed that when someone is unsure, taking a minute to think before acting is far more effective and far less damaging. While some believe 'constructive' criticism improves performance and cultivates personal growth, criticism is almost always destructive. Regression, not growth, is the most likely consequence of criticism. We will explore the difference between constructive criticism and constructive feedback – a subtle change but a world of difference.

The only kind of criticism you should encourage among subordinates and yourself, and the exception in most work environments, is self-criticism. Secure and self-confident group members, who see each other as friends, are more likely to self-criticise. Because morale and status are threatened, external criticism tends to stifle self-criticism and can inhibit personal development.

Box 18.1: If someone fails when they should have known better

If someone fails when they should have known better, should the manager explain again very carefully how the task should be done? It is tempting to say 'yes'.

However, some people experience failure not because they do not know what to do, but because they are insufficiently confident to try. If the manager explains again very carefully how the task should be done, the manager is reinforcing this lack of confidence by implying that the employee is not ready to achieve. If the manager recognises that someone does know what to do but is apprehensive, then the manager should work to build the person's confidence, not their knowledge.

If the manager frequently finds fault, then group members will become defensive and lose self-esteem. They may tend to hide their mistakes or blame someone – anyone – but themselves. Therefore, they will be more likely to look to someone else to put matters right – rather than take the initiative themselves. What is needed is less managerial criticism coupled with increased managerial praise and encouragement.

Reassuring

Reassuring is defined as 'restoring assurance or confidence to an individual' and is directed to someone who generally feels inadequate. (This differs from encouraging, which is a response to something specific, like a mistake.)

Pretty well all people have feelings of personal inadequacy and doubt at some stage, so most people need reassurance. People like to be praised for what they do well, but they need reassurance in areas where they are less confident. It is important that people realise they are making progress in developing a skill, that any problem is not perhaps so bad in the context of the wider picture, or that no one is perfect (see Box 18.2).

The more important a person is to us, the more we need signals from him or her that our relationship is healthy and productive. Therefore, managers must frequently reassure, particularly in research and development or IT, where the disappointments commonly outnumber the successes. Recall the OK Corral (Figure 15.2 in Chapter 15).

Beware, a beneficiary might feel patronised if reassurance is overdone. Reassurance requires empathy – an identification with the other person's point of view and feelings: 'I know things look pretty tough now. I felt like that until the revised software was released and we got things running smoothly again'.

On the most effective and productive teams, leaders and their people have a realistic appreciation of their self-confidence. Individuals' self-confidence can easily go up or down

---

Box 18.2: 'Oh, I love the sound of breaking glass . . . '

A young chemistry student was always accidentally breaking laboratory glass. Neil Haddon, his Chemistry Master, made him Glass Monitor for the rest of the year, responsible for cleaning up and washing all glass at the end of each lesson. The gesture was either designed to put him right off the subject or to make a difference to the student – in the event, he overcame his heavy-handedness, and went on to study Organic and Physical Chemistry as part of his Applied Sciences Degree from Leeds University, graduating with full Honours in 1977. Perhaps the Master knew that more than glass was at stake!

That boy was the author – thanks, Neil . . .

and managers can make an impact on sustaining it. The entire team will find their jobs more enjoyable – and managers will be ready to tackle the toughest problems.

A Manager's Self-confidence

A study by George O. Klemp Jr and David C. McClelland (see www.theworking manager.com), *What Characterizes Intelligent Functioning Among Senior Managers?*, examined the attributes that distinguished successful senior managers from their average counterparts, through a method called *job competence assessment*. The results of the study indicated that there were eight competencies which differentiated between top senior managers and their average counterparts. These competencies fell into three categories:

- Intellectual
- Influence
- Self-confidence.

The last competency appearing in the study was self-confidence. 'This important competency might well have been listed first, because we found it to be so prevalent among the outstanding senior managers.'

These people, although recognising difficulties, never expressed any doubt that they would ultimately succeed. In the behavioural interviews, they displayed strong self-presentation skills and came across as very much in charge: they acted to make the interviewer feel comfortable, and they responded quickly and confidently to the request in key situations. By contrast, the average senior managers were more tentative, saying such things as, 'To this day I don't know whether I made the right decision'.

The report went on to say, '. . . outstanding managers expressed self-confidence by seeing themselves as prime movers, leaders or energisers of the organisation, being stimulated by crises and other difficult problems, rather then distressed or overwhelmed by them'.

Tips for Giving and Receiving Feedback

Feedback is all about communicating openly about someone's performance or the effect on other people and is therefore a vital part of your job as a manager. It is essential that you create a general atmosphere of habitual occurrence, not just the dreaded annual appraisal!

Giving or receiving feedback is not always easy but, if done properly, the rewards can be great: open communication plus clear understanding leads to continuous improvement. By following a few simple ideas, you will be able to give people effective feedback and reap the rewards.

These checklists are summarised on the companion web pages and cover:

- *Positive feedback*
- *Corrective feedback*
- *Helpful feedback*
- *Unhelpful feedback*
- *Giving feedback*
- *Receiving feedback.*

Feedback is a gift: you choose what you wish to do with it!

Criticism vs Constructive Feedback

Imagine the scenario – you have been away for your desk for a short while and on your return you see a handwritten note from the boss, *'My office – 10 o'clock, need to talk to you'*. On a scale of 'chuffedness' are you high or low? There is no context and you have no idea why they want to see you. Generally, most people would say that experience suggests that given a choice between a 'talk' with the boss and 'root-canal work', it is the dentist's chair every time! The problem is that when we have been on the receiving end of one-to-one feedback, it has tended to go something like Figure 18.1.

The dialogue goes something along these lines:

(a) 'Thanks for coming in. Good to see your report yesterday, I must get on with sorting the new developments you flagged up . . .'

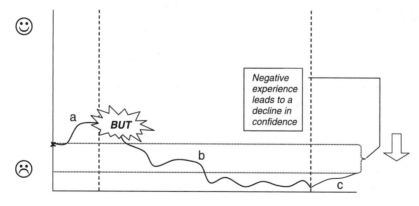

Ten minute chat...

Figure 18.1 The 'bitter sandwich' – the effect when criticism (b) is sandwiched between positive comments (a and c).

So far so good; then a small conjunction enters the conversation, a joining word... BUT ... isn't it curious, we all know the word:

(b) 'But... about that e-mail to finance... blah-de-blah-de-blah... quite honestly, if you... blah-de-blah-de-blah... and I think you should... blah-de-blah-de-blah... and if you don't... blah-de-blah-de-blah...'

And down the 'chuffed chart' we go. Then we get to the end of the conversation with the boss and they say:

(c) 'I am glad we've had this conversation...' (who's glad? certainly not those on the receiving end) '... now we know what is required, we'll have no more of it, I am sure you can do that. OK?'

This approach is one of the classic 'bitter sandwich' – the bad part is sandwiched between two good bits. However, given the experience where their confidence has taken a knock, the next time there is a one-to-one with the boss, the guard is up again, staff are defensive and less likely to look to ways that they might improve – just ways to avoid a verbal earbashing.

So, how can managers give feedback that is constructive rather than destructive – damaging confidence – and keep staff open to improvement? The concept is simple yet needs planning to become effective in practice. Rather than link criticism between two pieces of praise, link the positive introduction with 'AND', offering the appropriate level of guidance according to the situation. The dialogue would then follow something like Figure 18.2, thus:

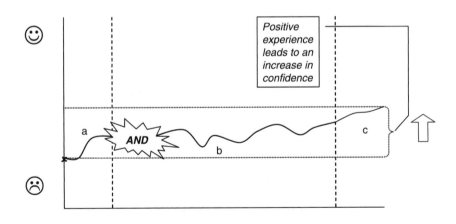

Ten minute chat...

Figure 18.2 The 'better sandwich' – the effect of linking good behaviour in one area (a) with expected behaviour (b), before finishing with reinforcement (c)

(a) 'Thanks for coming in. Good to see your report yesterday, I must get on with sorting the new developments you flagged up . . . '

Then linking with the word AND:

(b) 'And if you gave the same attention to detail in your e-mails to finance as you have in your report, I am sure you could achieve the same positive outcomes. Now, how are we going to make sure that this happens?'

Note the 'we' word. Sometimes, the manager may have a responsibility to address some problems that are getting in the way of the person's performance. Given that they are not as defensive they might come back with: *'If we could just make sure that I get support with some of the office administration, I wouldn't have to fire off an e-mail in haste – I could give my communications the attention they deserve.'*

While the person might not be exactly jumping up and down, punching the air with glee, at least their confidence has been maintained and a more open dialogue has been exchanged. The manager might not have been aware of the problem highlighted above but at least they know where the problem lies.

Then we get to the end of the conversation with the boss and they can now say:

(c) 'I am glad we've had this conversation . . . ' (and both parties probably are glad that they have) '. . . I'll speak with the Admin' Supervisor and you'll give yourself time to check your e-mail before hitting the "Send" button! I am sure you can do that. OK?'

While this approach is not going to be the panacea for all ills, it does show how linking positive behaviours in one area with what is required in another can maintain an individual's confidence. When they next have an opportunity for a one-to-one with the boss, perhaps staff will not have the same sense of dread they may have had before. It does take a while for such positive reinforcement to achieve this sort of culture change, but it is worth starting the journey.

How to break bad news

Sometimes the unwelcome messages have to be given – main backers pull out, revenue not as forecast, an aggressive takeover – and someone has to do it. The following is a guide:

■ *Deliver it face to face.* E-mail, voice mail, memos and noticeboards are not the media. Whether to individuals or small groups, it must be done face to face as people must be given the opportunity to respond and ask questions.

- *Beware the 'grapevine'.* Most organisations have an informal communications system that is very efficient but not usually accurate or effective. Remember, the certainty of despair is a lot easier to deal with than the despair of uncertainty, so get the right messages out there sooner rather than later.
- *Choose your timing carefully.* Publish the information internally just ahead of external announcements so that people do not hear their bad news from the media. Listed companies have to tell shareholders first so planning is key; senior teams might be briefed after the markets close in the evening and cascaded the following morning if key workers are not overlooked. (The author, having been made redundant just after one Christmas, would have preferred to have heard a month earlier so as to manage private expenditure more appropriately!)
- *Plan for normality.* Unless the whole business is compromised, it is worth ensuring that contingency plans keep things smooth while the urgent matters are dealt with.
- *Be honest.* If the news is 'dressed up', people might see through it, fear the worst and rumours will start. Confidence will get a double dose of depression.
- *Don't get overly emotional.* While bursting into tears might be empathetic with someone's plight, it does not give them support. Displays of extreme emotion can get in the way of the message; showing you are affected is acceptable if it comes naturally.
- *Take ownership.* While one might not agree with the decision, it is not very mature to slag off the people that made the tough decisions. Express your disappointment, acknowledge that it was a tough decision and hard on some people, but (assuming you were properly briefed) explain that you can see why it was made.
- *Support people.* To many, bad news is hard to take; people will go through the transition cycle (see Figure 12.1 in Chapter 12). Let people get over the shock and then follow up with briefing sessions; consider offering helplines and counselling sessions too.

Daft Things Managers Should Not Say

What things should you never, ever say to your people? A selection of comments that, directed to an employee, can only do harm to your business, is given below.

- *'Just make it happen.'* This remark conveys both condescension and laziness in just four words. You are treating your employee like a fool and avoiding any responsibility for getting things done. If there's a problem with something you've requested, ask your employee to give you the details; from there, work together to address it.
- *'You need to work smarter, not harder.'* This is more Dilbert than Drucker! However, it has an element of truth to it – we all need to direct our working energies in the most efficient and effective way possible. But this is a worn-out cliché that lacks any

genuine guidance and has long since lost even a shadow of impact. Instead, opt for real details when urging your people to use mind instead of muscle. For example, give people SMART[1] objectives in the first place – and brief professionally at the outset – to show real involvement and direction, not lame lip service. See Chapter 7 of Mackay (2007) for a clear approach to *briefing* your people.

- *'That's a no-brainer.'* This is particularly inappropriate in a professional setting and definitely not 'politically correct'. First, everyone – our chocolate labrador Rhia being the obvious exception – has, in fact, a brain. Second, every task, no matter how simple or menial, involves some cerebral activity. To suggest one or the other is insulting and demeaning, and isn't likely to motivate employees to new heights of performance. Try 'I thought that too' or some other form of confirmation that will be a lot more uplifting.

- *'Well, duh.'* See above. This is a particularly insulting, demeaning version, not to mention sophomoric. Leave this one to the hooded and tongue-studded teenagers at the shopping mall.

- *'I don't want to hear any excuses.'* While no one wants to put up with an employee who seems to have a convenient rationale every time something goes 'pear shaped', this is a harsh form of confrontation that does little more than back someone into a corner with an accusing finger armed and ready. Instead, try to give your people a chance to explain what happened with a focus on fixing what went wrong – not merely attaching blame. You never know, you might be part of the problem!

- *'You're lucky I don't fire you.'* If you want a person to develop a robust case for bullying at work, this is the right way to start. We all make mistakes, but threatening a person with dismissal is not merely ineffective and disheartening, it usually comes across as pretty idle. If you have scared them, they will retreat into a shell, or they will be laughing under their breath while you appear a fool. So, don't lose your temper but review what may have gone wrong and discuss ways to improve employee performance.

- *'I've got my eye on you.'* Unless you have a glass eye this is yet another comment that's needlessly intimidating. If someone is not performing effectively, talk to them, direct them how to improve and monitor them appropriately with candid, upfront reviews.

- *'I don't pay you to think.'* Henry Ford said that with every employee comes a free brain. Any manager who ever says this ought to pay someone to think, because they are certainly not up to the task themselves. Instead, let your people know that, in fact, you welcome their thoughts and feedback. Innovation is the way forward. In the end, you may get something that will help your business grow and your employee has the satisfaction – perhaps in more than one form – that they have contributed something of value.

---

[1] See Chapter 1 for a definition of this acronym.

Summary

In this chapter you have:

- Seen the central role managers have in enhancing and maintaining people's confidence
- Seen how doing so links with their own self-confidence
- Discovered a range of ideas for giving and receiving feedback
- Explored the differences between criticism and constructive feedback
- Seen a checklist on how to break bad news (tough decisions) to people
- Explored pitfalls that managers should avoid in their dialogue with staff.

Questions

1. You have been unfortunate enough to have had some misplaced criticism from a senior manager in another department that others in the organisation have overheard. What strategies will you take to deal with the matter?

2. Suppose you have a member of your workgroup who appears capable and willing but is very cautious to the point that they won't attempt new tasks for fear of 'getting it wrong'. Who do you feel initially might be best placed to assist this person – their line manager, the rest of the group, a close colleague, or are they best left to work through it themselves? Support your decision with reasons.

3. Someone who is usually very able and willing has made a mistake in an internal report they published last week and their confidence has taken a bit of a knock. Who do you feel initially might be best placed to assist this person – their line manager, the rest of the group, a close colleague, or are they best left to work through it themselves? Support your decision with reasons.

4. You have been asked to advise your workgroup that there are going to be some redundancies in your area in three months time, but the details have yet to be confirmed.[2] Write some notes preparing for a team meeting you are to give on Monday.

References

Mackay, A. R. (2007) *Recruiting, Retaining and Releasing People*, Butterworth-Heinemann.
Tingstad, J. E. (1991) *How to Manage the R&D Staff*, AMACOM Press, New York.

---

[2] While not best practice, a client organisation did just that!

Further Reading

Garber, P. and Garber, P. R. (2004) *Giving and Receiving Performance Feedback*, Human Resource Development Press.

Mackay, A. R. (2007) *Recruiting, Retaining and Releasing People*, Butterworth-Heinemann.

19

Mackay's Confidence Development Model

I didn't fail. I just discovered another way not to invent the electric light-bulb.
Thomas Edison, after trying 9999 ways to perfect the electric light-bulb

Learning Outcomes

This chapter, and its companion web pages, pull together a range of approaches to confidence development, giving a highly practical model for managers. The chapter has been written to cover particular elements of the National Occupational Standards for Management and Leadership: *Providing Direction – Lead People 9*; *Facilitating Change – Foster Innovation 14*; many sections of *Working with People*; and *Achieving Results – Unit 50*. It also covers some of the requirements of the Chartered Management Institute's Diploma in Management compulsory *Unit C41 – Developing your Management Style* (in respect of developing the trust and support of others), some of the *Effective Communications* elements of compulsory *Unit C44*, some of the compulsory *Unit C45 – Managing Performance* and most of the optional *Unit O42 – Developing Personnel and Personnel Performance*. This chapter will also be of value to those studying the CIPD Professional Development Scheme – particularly the *Leadership and Management* and *People Management and Development* modules, as well as people studying any of the CIPD specialist electives in *Learning and Development*.

By the end of this chapter you will:

- Have looked at how much a 'leader' might influence the development of a person's confidence
- Be able to consider both the task being done and the person doing the work – and explore the interaction of the two variables
- Have looked at four levels of confidence and what to do at each level

- Have been introduced to a practical model for confidence development
- Begin to uncover a way of evaluating your management style, its flexibility and its effectiveness in developing the confidence of others.

Background to the Confidence Development Model

Assuming that we were born sound in mind and limb, our parents helped us learn to walk. If you have children, you have probably enjoyed the process yourself. Picture the scene: you find a carpeted area and get the child to stand unaided next to the sofa. The child takes a few stumbling steps to your outstretched arms: 'Come to Daddy/Mummy' as appropriate – then 'oops', over they go. Then what do you do, 'Oh dear! Never mind; up you get and try again.' This scenario bears some analysis.

What we don't do is find some stone flooring – learning to walk over flagstones is not the best location! We don't take away our offered hands at the last minute. We don't yell at them for their failure: 'Look, I told you how to do it, now get back there and do it properly.' No? Why not? Because we intuitively know that we need to build a child's confidence alongside their skills. We can't expect one without the other.

When the child grows and gets into the 'terrible twos or threes', the approach changes – parents are much more directive and can sometimes forget their child's vulnerabilities. (Just listen to how some parents speak to their small child in the trolley as they go around the local supermarket!) As time goes on and the child becomes a youngster, teenager and then young adult, the confidence development element of the older/wiser person declines and may even go into reverse, where some individuals actively undermine their follower's confidence, having their own agenda in mind – not the follower's best interests.

Why do some managers behave in this way? Ann McDonald of the Centre for Personal and Professional Development (reported in *Professional Manager*, November 2005, p. 25) says:

> *One is lack of self-esteem, a feeling of not being good enough. The second is fear of not achieving what is expected. Either of these can provoke a response that damages others, a controlling behaviour that turns the victim into the abuser. Managers who are confident and authentic don't behave in a toxic way.*

Chapter 17 took a brief look at parental influence on a youngster's need for and pursuit of achievement; as managers we pick up the threads of this experience and aim to make improvements in the workplace. As we have seen, theories of motivation and ability development abound; all of them to varying degrees focus on getting *tasks* done through other *people*, but very little of that investigation looked at confidence building alongside motivation and ability development.

The purpose of this chapter is to provide a background to the situational Confidence Development Model (CDM) developed by the author and marketed through Duncan Alexander & Wilmshurst. It is built on a background of building a person's confidence through various levels of involvement with others, getting feedback on achievement and building their own self-esteem through the process, ultimately becoming sufficiently independent to function on their own.

Through experience it has become apparent that no one individual will have the same degree of confidence all the time with all their tasks. Moreover, different people doing the same job need different approaches to achieve the same confidence with a task as the next person. It all depends on what their situation is at the time, and the effective manager is able to recognise the dynamics of the situation and respond accordingly.

This variability may leave the practising manager or other 'leader' bewildered about how to address a particular set of circumstances. It is not enough to be flexible, one has to flex in the right manner to be effective. Naturally, a starting point will be an understanding of one's current or preferred style when trying to create the right environment in which a staff member or 'follower' might evolve greater confidence to tackle a task and achieve a given outcome, and whether that style has flexibility and is effective when flexed.

'Leaders' may evaluate their confidence development style through the use of a questionnaire. It should be realised that, clearly, it is not possible to develop situations that accurately reflect true-life experiences that one might most easily relate to in the workplace, although the author has made an attempt to provide sufficient variety to illustrate the concept of the CDM.

See the companion web pages for more information on questionnaires.

Questionnaires

In the confidence development elements of the questionnaire, a number of scenarios have been devised where readers are asked to consider each situation on its merits and from the 'clues' in the mini case-scenario decide on what they would do, if anything, as a consequence. A selection of them has been reproduced in this chapter to illustrate key ideas. They relate largely to Western-style enterprises in both the private and public sectors, commercial and not-for-profit, to large and more modest concerns alike.

Naturally, four or five lines of text do not represent the full understanding that an individual 'leader' may have of their 'followers'. Therefore, in practice, a person aiming to develop the confidence of a group or individual will have a much better understanding of how they might deal with that given situation. However, the questionnaire is designed to provide enough information to guide the individual on choosing the most *effective* approach to confidence development in the given situation.

Alternative responses

Having considered their likely action, respondents to the questionnaires are then asked to choose which of the four alternative actions (a–d) most closely matches their likely approach to confidence development of the individual in the situation given. Again, since the world does not easily divide itself into four separate alternatives, respondents are asked to identify with the one approach that *most closely* resembles what they might actually do. (The reader is invited to be aware of their 'theory-in-action' and 'espoused theory' at this point – see Chapter 11.)

In scanning the alternative approaches, respondents must assess the issue that is most likely to deal with the follower's anxieties, self-esteem and concerns, and therefore build their confidence in the given situation. The alternative style responses will be discussed further below.

Task Confidence Control Orientation

Task confidence control orientation behaviour is the extent to which the 'leader' takes an active role in developing the confidence of the 'follower' when undertaking their tasks, or if there is more than one person, the degree to which the 'leader' controls factors such as:

- Setting feedback parameters – who from and how obtained
- Controlling limits to the activity – particularly frequency of feedback
- Building one-to-one or team dynamics
- Establishing self-evaluation
- Allowing self-direction.

When a leader is trying to get work done through a follower, there is a varying amount of attention that must be given to help the individual find confidence in undertaking the task. Let us illustrate this with a case study (see Box 19.1).

In this situation, the leader needs to apply more 'task confidence control' because the follower's confidence to do the job to the required standard cannot be left to chance; in this situation, the follower's *task confidence* – for this task – is low. Leaving someone in this situation alone to find their own confidence in their assigned tasks when they are clearly not comfortable about it will not work – in fact, it is likely that, left for too long, this person making an error in one part of their work may lead to others in the organisation doubting their abilities in other areas. So, the leader needs to address the follower's *confidence* before they can be expected to perform.

Box 19.1: A new recruit lacking confidence with part of their work

Alexander is a graduate of sports science and has been recruited to Duncan Alexander & Wilmshurst on a short-term contract working to develop 'Life-Coach' training programmes. He is a very likeable person, is quite capable within his specialism and gets on well with others in the firm. However, he is worried about his first venture into the commercial world – he doesn't want to foul up in his first proper job! After a few days on board, he is having a problem with IT – he did not do so well at school in IT and always preferred more tangible things – like a rugby ball!

He is really enthusiastic about the project; he has demonstrated that he has a number of good ideas and can put them across well in discussion and appears confident in meetings in the firm as the project is being outlined and planned. He has shown confidence in delivering a short presentation on some of his ideas – he says he is used to speaking out through coaching sports teams, having done so at college.

When he comes to using a computer (where he'll need to be getting his ideas together so he can update the company web pages in time), he is hesitant. He has shown that he knows what to do but avoids the work with all sorts of excuses – he says he'll probably accidentally delete the DAW web page rather than update it and look a fool!

Clearly, this is not a situation where the Senior Partner responsible for IT can leave Alex to struggle on his own; he has had plenty of training and shows that he can do the IT part of the job – he just is not confident at it on his own.

In this scenario, the person lacks confidence – so who is best placed to help them find it, perhaps the Senior Partner? No, the follower may not feel too comfortable with this, being unsure about showing themselves up in front of the 'Top Team' at this stage. How about the rest of the workgroup? Maybe too many people to see them make a mistake? So, who is left? In this situation, they will probably prefer to 'sit next to Nellie' or find a 'buddy' – someone with whom they work with that they get on with, have trust in their discretion not to gossip about them, and who knows their way around the job. Let us suppose that this is a function where Jan, our administrator in Chapter 14 who has got her job – including that of IT support – managed competently. Knowing her way around Dreamweaver®, she is able to give one-to-one constructive feedback to the follower and offer them a safe environment to develop their confidence. Given such an opportunity, it will not be long before Alex is able to build his confidence alongside his developing skills.

Other than setting up the colleague to help the follower build his confidence, the degree to which the manager gets themselves or others closely involved with the person is relatively low at this stage; if they don't 'shape up' they will have to 'ship out' – although this should not be used as a warning or threat to anyone with low task confidence!

Let us now consider the follower (Alex) several weeks into his time at the firm, where he has been able to achieve more things than were expected from the life-coach/web page development project (see Box 19.2).

Now, clearly, the follower's confidence has not leapt from the situation in Box 19.1 to the situation in Box 19.2 overnight. Much work has had to be done in developing that confidence in parallel with their ability. However, it is clear that, in this second situation, the follower is very confident about the project overall and has gone beyond the expected parameters. If the leader applied the same style as before to affect the follower's confidence, what would happen?

If the leader were to make sure that they checked it through with their colleague first, one-to-one, tell the follower how much others are sure they can do the work and express their own confidence in the person, their task confidence control would have been too high and heavy-handed – it would most likely have the opposite effect and undermined their confidence, knocking them back. 'Why is everyone so keen to back me up – don't they think I can do it? Perhaps I can't – I'd better check.' As the follower's task confidence maturity is high in this situation, they do not need external influences; the leader can relinquish considerable confidence control and not intervene to try to boost their confidence – simply add their own thanks and acknowledgement when the time is right.

So, as far as the task confidence orientation of a leader is concerned, there is a need for the leader to be sensitive to the individual's position – task confidence maturity – on the continuum between 'high task confidence orientation' (where the leader needs to identify, control and implement a plan to develop the person's confidence to help them get the task underway) and 'low task confidence orientation' (where the leader need not get too involved, since the follower is quite confident in bringing their own innovation to the work unsupervised).

Box 19.2: Confidence of a new recruit several weeks into a project

Alexander has been working for Duncan Alexander & Wilmshurst for several weeks on the 'Life-Coach' project. He has been able to draw on former tutors from Loughborough University and brought in Dave Aldred – England Rugby's kicking coach – to chat with the Partners over lunch. Dave's agreed to do an introduction for the Life-Coach section of the DAW web page – Alex offered to amend the design and launch the piece through Dreamweaver®.

The rest of the team are enthused about the innovation and can see a developing business opportunity. Alex has been invited as a speaker at a seminar on *Life-Learning from Sports Coaches* at the Business Design Centre, Islington. He has also organised a team at DAW to 'fun-run' the London Half-Marathon to raise funds for Macmillan Cancer Relief.

The Partner overhears others in the firm thanking him for the developments and saying how much he has enjoyed putting his ideas into practice.

We can see here a scale of confidence control, but this is only one of the factors. Ability and motivation are also important issues. If Alex were not able to do the web development part of the project, the Partner would need to address this directly and deal with the problem (see Chapter 14 for a similar approach to ability development). Equally, if Alex was not motivated about a part of his job ('I don't like sitting at a computer – I am much more of a "doing" than "thinking" type of person') and would not do it because he was not motivated to give the web development part of the project the attention it deserves, then again, the Partner would need to address his motivation (see Chapter 9 for a parallel approach to motivation development). Assuming that he is both able and motivated, the Partner would need to give much less attention to each of these issues and focus on the confidence aspect.

Clearly, from the leader's point of view, it is in their interests to get the follower from the high task confidence orientation (where they need to provide help and support to guide the follower in developing their confidence) to the low task confidence orientation end of the continuum (where the follower becomes largely independent and self-confident) represented in Figure 19.1.

In order to progress a follower along the continuum, the leader needs to use differing approaches or styles to assist the person in their task confidence maturity. As we have seen, the leader may need to be aware of different approaches to build a person's confidence as they take the follower along the continuum, such as outlined in Figure 19.1. In this model, we propose four different approaches to assist the follower with developing their task confidence maturity, of which more later.

So far, our leader, the Partner in the example, has been very 'superficial' in their approach to the person – at first (Box 19.1) they just set them up with one person to help them build

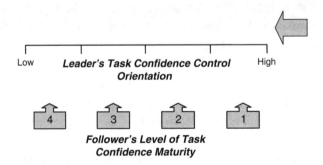

Figure 19.1 The task confidence control orientation continuum. A new recruit, for example, may start towards the right-hand side and the 'leader' would need to take them through four stages to improve their task confidence maturity until the 'follower' is at the left-hand end, where they are fully self-confident and the leader does not need to address their confidence. Individuals can appear anywhere on the continuum from time to time and may slip back, losing confidence owing to some event that knocks their self-esteem – for example, a bullying individual or an angry customer.

their task confidence maturity in the one area of their job where they lacked confidence,[1] then they left them to their own self-confident, almost 'extroverted' way (Box 19.2) and did little to intervene.

Where there is high task confidence maturity, the follower would appreciate acknowledgement but otherwise little intervention from the leader (because anything more is going to undermine the follower's confidence that they can achieve particular goals – i.e. confidence to deliver what was required or ability to do the task – and probably, in time, their motivation).

Let us turn to the working relationship between the leader and follower.

Relationship Orientation

First, a definition: relationship orientation is the degree to which the 'leader' engages in two-way or multi-way communication, giving 'socio-emotional' support by facilitation interactions, active listening and, in terms of confidence development, developing levels of feedback for the 'follower'.

As with task ability and task motivation orientation, there is a range of strategies or approaches that the leader can take. Their approach will depend on the situation presented by the follower when undertaking the task. The degree to which the leader engages in relationship-orientated approaches will range from lower than average (and that does not mean zero) through to higher than average – the height or degree to which this approach is taken being dependent on the follower's needs and their relationship with the leader.

Again, this orientation can best be illustrated by example (see Box 19.3).

Now, let us consider the situation of our new recruit, Alex, a couple of days into the job, where he has been confident to get going with the web development but does not seem to be confident to show to others what he has done and get on with other parts of the work (Box 19.4).

How the leader handles someone that is doing some of what is required of them, with some confidence, but is not sufficiently assured to do other things alone, perhaps coming up with some excuse or another not to do them, needs careful consideration. The leader needs to consider the follower's confidence maturity.

Simply getting someone else to give them one-to-one feedback relies solely on the leader influencing the allocation of a succession of individual 'hand-holding' helpers. The follower will remain shy in this context and will not 'open out'. This is not an effective way of running an organisation and misses the opportunity to involve the group in developing the

---

[1] Note, for some individuals there may be more than one area of doubt in the follower's mind about their own abilities – their perceived ability to cope, rather than an actual lack of know-how.

Box 19.3: Confidence control with a new recruit on the first day into a job

Let us take Alex, our new recruit. On the first day, when he is exploring the parameters of the 'Life-Coach' project, it is not particularly helpful if the Partner overseeing the project engages in too much open dialogue, asking 'How do you feel we might use the web page strategically?' or 'What do you think about our firm and e-commerce?' It's too soon. As said earlier, Alex just needs to build his confidence in this part of his role and contribution so he can get on with meeting the requirements of the project. We saw that assigning Jan to provide that reassurance was all that was needed.

Followers need an individual to relate to so that they can 'try out' approaches to a job knowing that their fragile self-esteem over one part of their work is not going to be undermined by 'someone taking their arms away or yelling at them' as they try to walk – that person needs to feel confident as soon as possible and not be bullied or shown up in front of a group of work colleagues or the boss. In this situation, the follower is unlikely to respond to too high a relationship orientation from the manager – it is too early.

Only when Alex has become more confident with his web-page development will he feel more like 'opening up' to discussion and dialogue about his contribution with more people or the boss.

Box 19.4: Confidence control with a new recruit when they are still not doing things they are capable of, and should do, a few days into a job

Let us consider Alex, our new recruit, a couple of days into his new job. Jan has been providing some one-to-one feedback and encouragement in his web development work. He seems to be building his confidence and Jan has found that he is capable of taking over these parts of her job, leaving her to concentrate on the financial and client care aspects of her administration function.

She finds that the main parts of the project are under way but that there are some other fundamental activities that Alex doesn't seem to be confident to undertake: he is reluctant to show what he has done to others and he will not work alone on other aspects, yet appears quite capable of doing so. He always seems to be hesitant unless she is sitting next to him. This is a little frustrating for her as she has other things to do than hold his hand on this one – she needs to let go.

The Partner could just tell Alex, as before, that he needs to sit next to Duncan or Andrew to build his confidence one-to-one. Would this high level of confidence control have the desired effect? It might, although since the Partner knows he is confident with most other things in the contract, he is unlikely to develop full confidence maturity sitting next to a succession of 'buddies'.

So, what of the person, how might he feel about his confidence in the context of the firm?

Here, the Partner can relinquish some of the one-to-one input into confidence development and bring in peer-group influences.

While Alex may feel secure in his role, what about his sense of belonging to a peer group that values his contribution? He needs help to develop his own confidence maturity in the role.

follower's confidence maturity further. The leader needs to address both the task confidence orientation *and* the person doing the task. The leader's style needs to change to help the follower improve their confidence further – the follower needs to build their confidence and see their role develop from an individual one-to-one context into a team function. In other words, the leader needs to encourage the follower to seek group acceptance of their new ideas in such a way that the follower feels they personally are more involved in a group setting.

The leader can do this by getting others to take an active part in the process of confidence development of the follower. This leader's style now gives an insight into the knock-on effect of the follower's activity as a team function, showing the wider picture of the job, reinforcing the follower's contribution to the whole. It may be that the follower's work does not have a direct impact on another department, it just means that they seek group approval of their work. The individual that was doing the hand-holding can be instrumental in introducing the person's work to a wider audience and is ideally placed to reinforce the value of the follower's contribution.

The leader is still likely to monitor the situation to ensure that the correct confidence-building messages reinforce the person's self-confidence properly and may start to guide the follower in becoming aware of it, i.e. listening more to others' approval and engaging in more dialogue, and being ready to take further ideas. Naturally, organisational culture plays a part in ensuring other people's contribution to the whole is acknowledged appropriately. If there are any criticisms of the individual and their confidence is knocked, the manager needs to be on hand to deal with the criticism and assist the individual's self-confidence only if a problem occurs. Therefore, the manager is still towards the higher end of the task confidence maturity orientation, having to manage the group's dynamics.

In this way, the follower has discovered something valuable: the fact that others can give feedback and support for their contribution to the team effort; it is also fulfilling a sense of belonging, however temporary in the case of the contract worker in our scenario. The follower can also begin to deal with any adverse comments as their self-esteem improves.

But there are problems: for the follower to build their confidence from a team they have to have their confidence reinforced by a number of individuals, their 'buddy' and particularly the rest of the team. This requires the manager to relinquish some control of the confidence development from one person, where they have most control, to the group, where they have less. This could be a block to both the leader's reputation and the follower's confidence building – the follower might not feel confident if their contribution is not valued as expected or that, while appreciated, nobody let them know. If this happens, the leader might have to go back to square one and find another individual to provide the confidence development which, it is suggested, might have only a limited and short-term effect.

There are other issues to consider that will be addressed further in this chapter.

Let us assume that the team gives positive feedback on his contribution to the business; Alex is developing more confidence in the web development part of the job, so now let us move things forward a few weeks and consider another scenario (see Box 19.5).

Box 19.5: Confidence maturity development with a new recruit when his confidence could be compromised a couple of weeks into a job

Alex, our new recruit, is a couple of weeks into his web development project. He knows that others are quite impressed at what he has done thus far on the project and he has been getting some positive feedback from both the Partner and some of her colleagues in the firm. While still recognising that he is on a short-term contract, he went drinking with Andy who was working on another IT project and was involved with the rest of the staff when they went ten-pin bowling.

However, he was aware that one or two people didn't quite see what all this sports coaching had to do with business consultancy, especially the marketing research team, who were quite scathing about his efforts – behind his back. The Partner has become aware of the criticisms and speaks to Alex about it.

This time she knows his confidence is building well but wonders if Alex knows of the criticism and how he would react if – or more likely when – he finds out. So, during one of their regular project updates she asks him, 'So, how are the new developments on the project going down with the others?' 'Oh, OK' is his non-committal answer. Undeterred she continues, 'OK, so what about the market research team – what did they say at the presentation you gave yesterday?

With this prompt, she considers the reaction. 'Well, not a lot really. Just a few bemused looks and a few whispers; there'll be an opportunity in it for them but that's someway down the line.'

With clarity of the specific issue as it might affect him raised, the Partner can then invite Alex to reflect on any possible criticisms and what he might do about them. 'How do you think you'd deal with any objections they raise or questions about the place of the project in their area of work?' 'Well, I could show them the long-term benefits in more detail, I suppose. Or, since they are in market research, one of those Mintel studies on the place for life-coaching in the workplace.'

In this scenario, the Partner has not been giving confidence-boosting comments herself or getting tangible responses from others for Alex; she has opened him to strategies that he can use to strengthen his own self-confidence in handling criticism, dealing with objections and thereby directing him to build his own self-worth – building his confidence maturity along the way. While the interaction may take a little longer than taking charge of the confidence building and telling Alex how much he and his work is valued and sorting out the market research team for him – he knows that and he has been through this stage already – this approach is likely to have a more lasting effect.

It is important at this stage that Alex 'fights his own battles' and develops his own task confidence maturity.

In order help a follower develop their task confidence maturity, the leader needs to consider their interaction and provide continued 'socio-emotional' support, engaging them in a dialogue about their thought process, inviting them to think about their own reaction to criticisms when undertaking a particular piece of work and strategies to deal with it. If the follower comes up with recognising they can build their own confidence, they will be able to improve their self-esteem without persistent recourse to further input from the team or from the leader. Developing their own self-confidence would have more impact on them and be longer lasting too.

Once the follower has been able to demonstrate higher levels of task confidence maturity, it is time for the leader to 'let go'. At this stage, the follower is going to need less guidance or feedback – again emphasising that this does not mean they don't get any support – from the leader. Let us finally consider how the Partner might deal with the relationship orientation as far as the work that Alex is doing with Dave Alder, the kicking coach, and the new web pages is concerned (see Box 19.6).

So, at the top end of the 'confidence' range, when the follower's task confidence maturity is its highest, followers appreciate being 'left alone' to innovate on their own, being creative without needing too much involvement from others, save the appropriate bit of interest and nod of appreciation. In other words, provided they are aware of others' support and encouragement, they will maintain their task confidence.

Remember, a person's task confidence maturity will be specific for a given area of work; if they attain Level 4 for one task (such as web page developments in our example), the follower is going to be at Level 1 for a new project or a significant job change. For a new project – say, developing a new training package – the follower may slip back some way along the task confidence maturity continuum. They may move back in stages or go right back to square one and need the leader's intervention to assign a 'buddy' again.

Box 19.6: Self-confidence from a new recruit who identifies a useful business opportunity several weeks into the job

Alexander has been working for Duncan Alexander & Wilmshurst for several weeks on the 'Life-Coach' project. He has been able to draw on former tutors from Loughborough University and brought in Dave Aldred – England Rugby's kicking coach – to chat with the Partners over lunch. Dave's agreed to do an introduction for the Life-Coach section of the DAW web page – Alex offered to amend the design and launch the piece through Dreamweaver®.

The rest of the team are enthused about the innovation and can see a developing business opportunity. Even the marketing research team found a report from the Chartered Management Institute on life-coaching to add more credence to the development. Alex has been invited as a speaker at a seminar on *Life-Learning from Sports Coaches* at the Business Design Centre, Islington. He has also organised a team at DAW to 'fun-run' the London Half-Marathon to raise funds for Macmillan Cancer Relief.

As mentioned earlier, the Partner overhears others in the firm thanking him for the developments and Alex saying that he was confident that the firm's profile in selected business sectors would be enhanced by some of the new associations. He requires little of the Partner in this situation, but her thanks would always be appreciated.

Let us put these two dimensions – concern for task (the person's task confidence maturity) and concern for the person (degree of socio-emotional support and two-way interaction required) – into one model (see Figure 19.2), the Confidence Development Model (CDM).

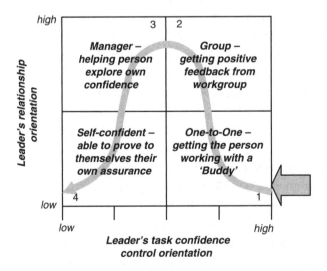

Figure 19.2 Mackay's Confidence Development Model (CDM).

Adapting to the CDM

By taking each level along the task confidence maturity scale, we can identify practical approaches to helping people develop their own confidence that fits with the Confidence Development Model.

Level 1 – *one-to-one* 'buddy' system of feedback

At this level, the 'leader' identifies that they need to take control of the person's most fundamental confidence level to ensure that the job gets done. This may be because the 'follower' is not at all confident to do their job, or a large part of their job description's duties, for fear of making a mistake or appearing foolish. The leader has identified something in the 'task confidence maturity' of the follower that they need to address.

While not giving a person too much responsibility as a first choice, the person needs to feel that it is OK to make a mistake (within certain parameters) and is not exposed to ridicule by peers too soon either. If they work with the leader directly, he or she can provide the feedback. If they work as part of the department, a 'buddy' is assigned to provide the positive encouragement. The leader may need to help the follower identify that their task confidence maturity is low – perhaps that their excuses for not doing it are no longer valid – and that they can see that a helping hand is there, in confidence, from another person.

The leader will also have to monitor progress as the follower will need appropriate feedback to build their confidence – in other words, the leader or the assigned 'buddy' can catch them doing it right.

At this level, the leader's style is one of establishing *one-on-one* support work.

- *Level 1 confidence.* Set controls on the basic level of one-on-one feedback to build confidence and to get the job started and monitor closely. Also give positive feedback where possible. Monitor and support the 'buddy' as appropriate.

Level 2 – encourage *group support* and positive feedback

Here, the 'follower' has demonstrated their confidence to do the task to some degree and has shown that their confidence is developing. It has to be said that most people start their jobs at least at this level and it is only the most vulnerable individuals who drop below this level in their task confidence maturity. While most followers will be at or have moved some way along the confidence bar, indicating that the 'leader' needs to be slightly less focused on the basics of confidence, not everyone will by any means be completely confident in every respect for all tasks.

At this stage, the follower will quickly indicate a need to gain confidence by sharing their experiences with their work colleagues. This behaviour on the part of the follower should tell the leader that they would benefit from a different style in order to gain the confidence they need to do the task more completely and effectively.

So, in general terms, the follower is only moderately confident to do the whole task but has indicated that they are ready for their further contribution to be recognised more widely. Thus, the leader encourages a more interactive style from the group and develops a team approach of acceptance and constructive feedback. Therefore, the leader is aware of the context of a person at work and their adapting to a mutually supportive working environment.

Again, the leader will need to identify what controls need to be in place to ensure the feedback from the group is positive and appropriately supportive and monitor to some degree, but the follower may begin to undertake some self-evaluation of their feedback from the team.

At this level, the leader's style is one of developing *group feedback* from the workgroup, thus relinquishing control of some of the confidence-building factors.

- *Level 2 confidence*. Explore team dynamics to encourage others to give positive feedback and assist the follower in monitoring positive feedback.

Level 3 – the *manager* helps explore confidence building

When a 'follower' realises that their confidence is developing and they are feeling positive about the situation, they will indicate a higher level of confidence maturity and will need somewhat less intervention from the 'leader', which does not mean none at all. This is because, although they are becoming more confident, the leader still cannot leave them to their own devices because they will not be totally self-assured, especially if criticised directly or behind their back.

They may not be ready to bring their full confidence to the work they do. At this stage, a follower may undertake the majority of their job but still indicate a lack of confidence in their decision-making, unsure of their own self-reliance in all aspects of the task.

Now, if the leader is too task confidence orientated and gives them direct confidence-building feedback on how much the team/organisation regard their contribution, these approaches will not work in the long run. Next time they are unsure through a lack of confidence in some area, the follower will need direct support all over again.

Do you want a team of 'dependent energy-sappers' (who keep asking for others to give them assurance) or a team of 'energisers' (who are able to feel good about themselves – and in turn will make others feel good about themselves too)?

At this level, the leader and follower engage in a discussion to explore the follower's feeling of self-worth and their own perspective of themselves. In other words, the leader asks the appropriate questions, such as 'How do you feel about any challenges?' or 'What do you think others think of you?', or 'What are you going to do to deal with criticism, etc.?' The leader can also get the follower to identify how they will recognise how well they are contributing on their own and then they can largely monitor achievement themselves.

It may be that in this situation the follower actually has all the ability in the world to undertake a task, but there is some other underlying factor preventing them from getting on with it alone. This is where socio-emotional support is so crucial. Again, telling someone else to give them encouragement as a team member may not be what the individual needs, but a discussion of the issues that can help them find their own self-worth – especially when no one is looking! At this level, leaders need to be prepared for any ability shortfall and that followers can actually do the tasks. Equally, there may be something outside of work affecting an individual's motivation or confidence. It may not always be purely confidence that is necessarily lacking at this level.

At this level, the leader's style is one of the *manager* helping others find their own self-confidence from within.

- *Level 3 confidence.* The manager helps people to establish their own self-confidence, asking 'How will you handle criticism?', and helps identify how the follower can reaffirm their own self-reliance to others and the organisation.

Level 4 – *self-awareness* of their confidence

Here, the 'follower' is confident to do the task with little intervention from the 'leader' or any-one else. The leader is assured of the follower's confidence and demonstrates this with trust and does little to intervene, save for acknowledgement and approval when the time is right.

Developing trust gives the follower further confidence to continue where they have found self-fulfilment in their achievements; they may have the confidence to bring their energy to innovate and discover that the task can be done more efficiently or more effectively than first thought.

Finally, they are in no doubt about their own task confidence maturity. Provided no one adversely affects their MAC Factors, all they need from the leader is occasional reinforcement of their personal contribution. Over-supervision or too much 'just checking you are OK' from the leader is not needed and indeed may damage the relationship and undermine the follower.

At this level, the leader's style is one of allowing self-confidence to endure in the person with the job – finally letting go for this task.

- *Level 4 confidence.* Reinforce success and ask them for innovative solutions, asking 'why not' rather than challenge their ideas.

Potential Criticisms of the Model

There are a number of areas where the model might be criticised. Bearing in mind that it follows the same pattern for ability and motivation task maturity development, there are naturally some parallels and some areas where the model might not appear to suit every situation when a person's confidence to do a piece of work is compromised to varying degrees. Let us address some issues:

- *What if a leader and a follower are working together?* When, say, a secretary is working directly for one person (a fairly rare occurrence today, but one where many can understand the dynamics), what role does the manager have in building a low level of confidence? In this situation, the business relationship may be one where the manager can give the secretary one-on-one feedback for many of their duties and so build confidence. However, as far as the myriad of office duties is concerned, the manager is unlikely to have either the time or the know-how to give feedback to the secretary on every last bit of detail to build confidence effectively across all secretarial tasks. Assigning an appropriate 'buddy' here would help share out the confidence building. The manager has the majority of control as they will have selected – and possibly developed – the buddy.
- *Can't the leader provide second-level confidence building and not a group?* Again, while a manager might be involved in this confidence-building process, there are two reasons why this might not be the most effective approach. The first is that a follower might not yet have the confidence to open up fully to the manager, as they may fear people in authority, may not be as willing to show them their doubts and may be anxious as to what this may mean come appraisal time. The second reason is that in order to achieve a sense of belonging – the second-level motivator in the Motivation Development Model – peer-group acceptance is more powerful at this early stage. Giving people the opportunity for 360° feedback that is positive and constructive is a powerful way to develop low confidence. Clearly, the manager is still fairly directive at this level of confidence, either to guide the follower to seek team approval or ensure that the team gives the reinforcement required.
- *What if the group gives poor feedback and damages confidence at Level 2?* Here the manager's involvement and control from the sidelines rather than objectively and directly to the follower is so important. Organisational culture clearly has an effect but, again, acceptance by the group will be so important at some level to get the person to build their confidence. The manager might be involved to deal with any disharmony 'in the ranks' and ensure that any mavericks and potential interpersonal conflict is addressed. Only then can the follower move on. If the follower is unaffected by peer criticism, their confidence is pretty robust and they may be on to Level 3 or 4 already.

- *Wouldn't it be more logical to develop confidence through buddy, manager, then group?* The group have a role earlier, as said, in developing confidence at the second level, where the manager has a duty to control to some degree. The manager is best placed to have some close involvement with the person at Level 3 (high relationship orientation) but is less directive (low) on controlling task confidence maturity. This is because they are aiming to help the person onto Level 4. The manager's role is to help give socio-emotional support to the follower, allowing them to think through strategies to deal with personal criticisms or doubts about their work; it is a stage of helping the person let go of other's help and standing on their own two feet.

Evaluating a Scenario

In the following scenario, taken from one of the specific style evaluation questionnaires developed by the author, consider the situation and look for clues as to what level the person is on their task confidence maturity continuum, Levels 1–4. Then look at the four alternative approaches to deal with the problem. What would you do?

After a recent departmental meeting you asked one of the team to produce a newsletter for business clients. After an initial investigation, he was so enthusiastic about the newsletter that you gave him the freedom to work on the project with Helen – a Partner – to develop his own ideas but keep within budget and with limited involvement from you. Initially, this person worked well with the other Partners on the project and produced a good first issue, but recently he has delayed publication of the second issue in the series. You would:

a. Not intervene, as you expect that in time the situation will improve.
b. Intervene quickly, set your own schedule and encourage them to follow your guide.
c. Get the person involved in a discussion on the project, but you would try not to be too directive.
d. Get them to collect all group ideas from others in the firm that are reasonable and then get them to ask for group feedback on the second issue.

The clues to this person's task confidence maturity are '*that this person worked well with the other Partner on the project*', suggesting confidence growing from Level 1 and that '*recently he has delayed publication of the second issue in the series*' so that confidence has not grown from there to any degree. So, there is nothing to suggest they are unable to do the task, having provided '*a good first issue*' and they were motivated, '*enthusiastic about the newsletter*'.

- If you did 'a' and left it alone, nothing would improve and the person would not get confident on their own – they need help!
- If you did 'c' they might not be too open with you – they have not got the second issue published and may be in denial about their lack of confidence. They may blame others for their lack of achievement.
- If you did 'b' you would at least have got the second issue published and they may get some confidence from your intervention. However, you may be suggesting that they are not competent and undermine their confidence, so not the most effective.
- 'd' is the preferred option as it does not undermine your belief that they can sort out the problem and you will be getting them to draw on the group for support. Assuming their ideas are reasonable, and their suggestions get published in the second issue, the group are going to give positive feedback to the person involved. In this way, the individual can broaden their feedback to more than just one person and build their confidence in the process.

In summary, it is important to remember the following two key parameters of the model.

Task confidence maturity is a two-way process

It is not a one-way street. People do lose their way and slip back along their task confidence maturity continuum; the other factors of Ability and Motivation have an impact on Confidence, as all three 'MAC Factors' are interrelated. Addressing one of the factors can have an influence on the others. Just because someone isn't confident about some small part of their job from time to time, the 'leader' does not have to go right back to square one and control the confidence basics all over again.

Situational effectiveness is clear

Situational effectiveness is easy to comprehend. In the scenario above, the further away we are in our confidence development style from what the 'follower' *needs*, the less our effectiveness. Equally, the closer we are to matching the *current* needs of the follower, given their *immediate* situation (not what they *used* to be like), the more effective we are.

We can evaluate an effectiveness score simply. In the above scenario, which ideally called out for a 'leader' to 'develop group dynamics', we could 'score' the responses according to Table 19.1.

For a further evaluation of your situational task confidence maturity style, consult the companion web pages.

Table 19.1 Evaluating the effectiveness of each style – according to the demands of the 'follower' in the scenario in this chapter

Response	Style	Score	Commentary
a	Self-aware of confidence	−2	They cannot be left alone or nothing is going to happen and they may retreat into a shell
c	Manager exploration	−1	The manager may not be able to open discussion as the 'follower' may fear the manager's reaction
b	One-to-one feedback	+1	While one-to-one starts the process again, and they get confidence accordingly, confidence may be undermined
d	Develop group support	+2	The most effective – it develops wider feedback and they probably build their confidence in other areas too

Summary

In this chapter you have:

- Looked at how much a manager might influence the development of a person's confidence
- Been able to consider both the task being done and the person doing the work – and explore the interaction of the two variables
- Looked at four levels of confidence and what to do at each level – 'buddy', group, manager and self-awareness approaches
- Been introduced to a practical model for confidence development
- Begun to uncover a way of evaluating your management style, its flexibility and its effectiveness in developing the confidence of others.

Questions

1. Consider someone within your workgroup whom you know well. For their allocated tasks, identify where they are on the Confidence Development Model for each task. Can you explain any differences?
2. Considering your own tasks within your job description, evaluate your task confidence maturity (see Figure 19.1) for your principal tasks.
3. Thinking of your line manager, or a manager that you know well, evaluate their dominant style when helping develop the confidence of their people. How flexible do you feel they are and are they effective when they do flex?

4. Imagine that you have a colleague who is a manager at your level that is 'a bit of a bully', in as much as they are often undermining the confidence of their very competent and talented people, who therefore are not very forthcoming in suggesting organisational improvements. How would you help the manager before they create a problem involving a genuine case of grievance from one of their people?

Further Reading

Blanchard, K. and Johnson, S. (1983) *The One Minute Manager*, William Collins.

Hersey, P. (1999) *The Situational Leader*, Pfeiffer & Co.

Lubit, R. H. (2003) *Coping with Toxic Managers ... And Other Impossible People in the Workplace*, Financial Times Prentice-Hall.

Part 5

Looking Forward

20

Times are Changing

There is nothing more difficult to plan, more doubtful of success, nor more dangerous to manage than the creation of a new system. For the initiator has the enmity of all who would profit by the preservation of the old institutions, and merely lukewarm defenders in those who should gain by the new ones.

Machiavelli

Learning Outcomes

Some wise sage said that the only constant in business is change – the good news is that this chapter, and its companion web pages, are here to help! The chapter has been written to cover particular elements of the National Occupational Standards for Management and Leadership: *Providing Direction – Map the Environment Unit 5, Lead People Unit 9*; most sections of *Facilitating Change*; many sections of *Working with People*; and selected parts of *Achieving Results – Unit 46* regarding understanding markets. It also covers some of the requirements of the Chartered Management Institute's Diploma in Management in as far as *change* is involved in all compulsory and optional units to some degree. This chapter will also be of value to those studying the CIPD Professional Development Scheme – particularly the *Leadership and Management* and *People Management and Development* modules, as well as people studying any of the CIPD specialist electives in *Learning and Development*.

By the end of this chapter you will:

- Understand what change is in an organisational context
- Explore a model for tracking environmental change
- Understand the sort of resistances to change that can occur internally
- Review a range of approaches for dealing with resistance to change
- Explore a checklist of activities to manage organisational change
- Know how to plan an effective change programme
- Consider a range of issues to enable people to remain motivated through change
- Learn about how to get others involved in the change process.

Change Defined

The Concise Oxford Dictionary defines 'change' as *'making or becoming different'*. While this may be too vague, most management dictionaries or glossaries of terms rarely attempt to tackle a definition. For managers, managing change involves accomplishing a transition from a current state to a new state and handling the problems which arise in getting there. However, as we shall see, it is best not to consider change as a destination but as a revised way of working to deal with the changing world.

Change to meet the demands of all stakeholders will result as a consequence of the interaction between equipment (technology), processes (working procedures), organisation structure and people. A change to one of these four elements will inevitably lead to changes to the others, because the organisation is a living, evolving, integrated system.

'Times are a-Changing'

Charles Handy (1989) observed that if one were to take a frog, sitting in water at 4°C, it would be quite comfortable. Cold-blooded animals over winter at that temperature are found at the bottom of ponds. Now, if the water were to warm up slowly – about one degree an hour – the frog would not notice the change. In fact, the water could eventually boil and at no time would the frog be distressed and try to jump out. (Please don't try this at home!)

The point of all this is that the frog was insensitive to its changing environment and died as a consequence. So, do you have any potential 'frogs' waiting to be boiled in your organisation, too stuck in the mud to notice the changes around them?

It seems that there are far too many senior people unwilling (or too arrogant) to explore the changes around them – perhaps being too busy with today's problems to notice the changing temperature. But things are changing.

A business with a marketing policy (and all firms have one, whether they recognise it or not) is dealing all the time with a whole series of changing variables. Among them are the following:

- *The general economic situation.* Boom or recession, growth or stagnation, a developed or an underdeveloped economy, these factors will have a profound effect on what is possible and on how firms can operate. Cost of housing, personal debt levels and interest rates are just a few of the potential influences.
- *Customer needs.* The social climate will affect the needs customers feel to be important, as will the level of development of a society. Other stakeholders will be important too.
- *Competition.* What competitors are doing will profoundly affect what is possible.
- *Technology.* The introduction of a new technology, such as electronics or IT, will completely change the existing situation and how we work.

- *Legislation.* Governments are increasingly intervening in the operation of the marketplace and hence changing the commercial environment. For example, changes to Legal Aid practices have had a profound effect on British law firms.

These and other factors change all the time, both independently of each other and in reaction to each other. The external environment is constantly changing and the acronym PEST is used as an analytical tool to help think through changes in our markets by looking at:

- Political decisions
- Economic changes
- Sociological developments
- Technological changes.

During a recent management seminar run by the author, groups of junior solicitors (within 36 months, Post Qualification Experience) identified issues and actions for their firms, summarised in Table 20.1.

Table 20.1 took 15 junior lawyers under an hour to compile and present. While not a comprehensive list, it identifies important issues that affect the way that a firm operates.

Table 20.1 PEST issues and actions identified by junior solicitors in early 2006

PEST factor	Possible action by the firm
Political	
■ Legal Services Commission	■ Keep up to date – plan changes
■ Lexcel/IiP Standards	■ Be aware of requirements and implement
■ Audits	■ Random internal audits to check compliance
■ Downsizing/right-sizing	■ Restructure so that all feel involved – inform everyone
■ Money laundering/data act	■ Review systems and procedures, training, appoint specialists
■ Market competition	■ Work harder on providing better value than the competition
■ Fixed/capped costs	■ Work harder to work smarter, manage client care on costs
Economic	
■ Increased mortgage rates	■ Consider movement to other markets – remortgage, insolvency
■ Increased National Insurance	■ Cut the fat!
■ Inflation	■ Delegate basic admin' tasks to 'proper' support staff, focus on chargeable work
■ Interest rates increase	■ Tighten up policies on aged debt/disbursements
■ Global recession	■ Maintain flexibility to take advantage of opportunities in regional or national markets

(Continued)

Table 20.1 Continued

PEST factor	Possible action by the firm
Social	
■ Flexible working hours	■ Introduce scheme, define parameters, increase client availability of our services
■ Commuting time	■ Consider remote working, using IT, improve access, improve client service
■ Working parents	■ Careful consideration, flexible working as above, involve staff and clarify options
■ Team building	■ Need to improve firm morale, help people feel they have a voice and are valued. Run staff audit
■ Maternity/paternity	■ Consider locums, options for part-time to attract and keep good people
■ Lawyer recruitment	■ Need to provide attractive social policy to attract and keep the best
■ Internal social support	■ Organised through work area, young particularly at work for long hours
Technological	
■ The paper-free office	■ Training for all staff, review IT packages, learn from best practice
■ Mobile phones	■ Used to increase information flows to/from clients. SMS messaging off e-mail?
■ Widespread client base	■ Telephone conferencing, video link, link to social issues of flexible working
■ Reduce costs/increase efficiency	■ Consider option for better information management and use of intranet for standard forms, electronic library, precedents, save space
■ Lawyer accessibility	■ Balance use of IT to manage client contact and allow time to do the work – support staff have vital role

Not one person had ever been asked their opinion of the issues that affect their future in their firm. Most had no idea if their firm was taking any action on few, if any, of the possible initiatives proposed.

Collectively, the PEST issues have a kaleidoscopic effect, which means that the total legal and business environment constantly changes. Firms must be aware of these changes and react to them. Going on doing as we have always done must lead sooner or later to a situation where we apply yesterday's answers to today's problems, and disaster must follow.

Because running a successful and developing business is concerned with what people will do tomorrow, it is always subject to risk and uncertainty. (Risk means that we know that certain actions may have a number of different outcomes, and we have to calculate the odds in favour of the outcome we desire; there are other areas where we just do not know – that is uncertainty.) There can never be total knowledge about the future; we can, however, make sure that we do know what the present situation is and where events appear to be leading. Information is a precious commodity in all business activity, and nowhere more so than in leading a business.

The factors listed above are often referred to as the non-controllable variables – those that firms and individuals cannot control but have to build into their business planning. The marketing mix contains the controllable variables, which can be changed to provide us with the appropriate response.

We can view the management of any business as a constant series of actions and reactions between clients and the organisations trying to satisfy their needs. The clients make their needs and/or problems known, the organisation makes it their business to receive that information. The organisation uses its resources (money, materials, skills and ingenuity) to develop ways of satisfying the needs. Organisations must then communicate the existence of the 'solutions' back to the customers, whose needs created the 'problems' (Figure 20.1). Clients will gladly pay for solutions to their problems or satisfaction of their needs.

So, if clients are living and working in changing circumstances, then their needs and problems are changing too. How can we risk standing still believing that we have no need to change – or are we just frogs and we haven't noticed it getting warmer?

Why Do Organisations Have Such a Problem with Change?

We saw in Figure 12.1 of Chapter 12 that people go through a transition cycle as they battle with change, since their confidence – their perceived ability to cope – is compromised. But there are a number of problems arising out of individuals' low self-esteem and low level of confidence in handling the change because of the effect the change is perceived to have on them. Four underlying reasons for resisting change are:

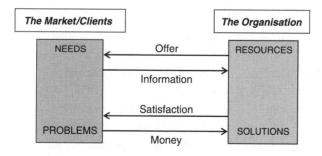

Figure 20.1 The marketing process – from Wilmshurst and Mackay (2002).

- *Parochial self-interest*. If a person has invested in a particular 'status quo', they are often the least likely to want to change it. They may feel that they will lose something of value – like working with their 'clique' or on their 'pet' projects.
- *Misunderstanding*. Here the person does not trust the source of the reasons for change and feels powerless to do anything about it. The 'grapevine' is probably working overtime!
- *Different assessments of the situation*. Often, the more junior people in an organisation have a perception of the situation that they feel is different from the instigators of change. As we saw earlier in the chapter, junior people are not often consulted about the influences on organisations.
- *Low tolerance for change*. This is where someone feels that their self-esteem will be particularly compromised – like losing the position of power conferred on them as being the one with particular skills essential to the old ways of working.

These reasons for resistance are summarised in Table 20.2, showing the likely outcome and reaction to the change.

The lower an individual's self-esteem, the more they will tend to blame themselves rather than the organisation for their inability to adjust to change comfortably. If they tend to berate themselves for perceived failings then they will punish themselves even more viciously as they perceive their discomfort with a particular change initiative. A downward spiral may then set in, consisting of alternating decreases in their adaptability and their self-esteem. In the worst eventuality, they may hang on quite rigidly to familiar routines or become too depressed to function at all.

For organisations that manage change skilfully, it can become the driving force that perpetuates success and growth, with every change presenting a new opportunity to increase efficiency or to build the business. But all too often, change fails, as organisations fail to rise to the challenges it brings.

Change efforts of the past decade have appeared under many banners, including TQM (Total Quality Management), Business Process Re-engineering, and so-called

Table 20.2 The likely outcome and reaction to various reasons for resistance to change

Reason	Outcome	Reaction
Parochial self-interest	Expect to lose something of value as a result	'Political' behaviour
Misunderstanding	Misinterpretation; low trust and lack of trust	Rumour
Different assessments of the situation	Perceives changes unfavourably; may have different information	Open disagreement
Low tolerance for change	Fears that may not possess skills/aptitudes	Excuses; face-saving behaviour

'right-sizing/restructuring' that many firms instituted as jargon for cost-cutting measures to stay in business!

In most cases, the primary drivers of the proposed change are the demands of an evolving marketplace, which may include everything from the emergence of new technologies and swings in the economic cycle to the rapid movement to a global economy. Naturally, the influences may be more parochial and include a dramatic increase in the number and quality of new competitors or shifts in the behaviour of existing competitors.

For many organisations, a typical change management programme follows a predictable pattern:

- Senior management announces a new corporate quality/engineering process improvement programme
- Company-wide half-day training workshops are arranged to bring everyone up to speed
- Cross-functional committees are quickly set up to meet and discuss 'the way forward'
- Resources are reallocated, desks duly moved, PCs plugged in at a new abode
- Somewhere along the way, the reasons and focus for change get lost!

The causes of failure of corporate change efforts are varied, but the vast majority come from within the company:

- *Misunderstanding of what change is*. Change is a journey, not a destination; where change is viewed as an event, it will be just a single event.
- *Lack of planning and preparation*. Management may suffer from tunnel vision, looking only to the end result, oblivious to the steps required to get there.
- *Change programme has no clear vision*. If you don't know where you're going, how can you expect to get there?
- *Goals are set, but too far in the future*. Employee enthusiasm can hardly be expected for a seven-year change plan without recognition of short-term wins.
- *The quick-fix option*. Change means more than a quality poster, T-shirt, coffee mug, half-day seminar or management message in the company newsletter.
- *Poor communication*. Giving information gradually is risky – the grapevine may get there before you.
- *The legacy of previous change*. The result of years of streamlining and right-sizing may well be a sceptical, risk-averse culture that is incompatible with the innovative spirit central to change.
- *'The way we do things around here'*. Especially where the organisation has enjoyed success in the past, managers may believe it is because of, not in spite of, the way they do things; they may fail to realise the success stemmed from, for example, a wide open marketplace, a new product idea or favourable exchange rates for exports.

- *Fear of failure*. Managers may begin to ask themselves: will business suffer short-term? Will share price plummet? Will workforce morale wane? Worst of all, will we be blamed?
- *Employee resistance*. For example, inertia from middle managers with 15 years tenure and two ranks to go before retirement.
- *Disregarding the domino effect*. One of the most common organisational mistakes, for instance, is to implement programmes without altering the reward systems to support the new performance-driven, team-orientated environment, leaving staff with no incentive to transform their behaviour.
- *Ill-prepared employees*. Typically, organisations raise the hurdles, but fail to provide the training or skills necessary to clear them; encouraging employees to adjust to change requires more than the physical relocation of their PC and in-tray.

Reviewing Chapter 15 will guide managers on how to improve an individual's self-esteem – but what of strategies of organisational change?

Dealing with Resistance to Change

Methods for dealing with resistance to change are many, but they fall into six categories listed here. As we go down the list the cost of implementation *decreases* while the speed with which change can be implemented *increases*. Those at the top tend to have a more lasting effect and reduce the resistance to the change initiative.

- *Education and communication*. By bringing all affected by the change on board in the consultative process, managers have more opportunity to achieve 'buy-in'. It is important in this process to find those 'change managers' who are confident and who will champion change in the organisation.
- *Participation and involvement*. If there are others in the organisation who have significant power to compromise the change initiative and where those driving change do not have all the information they need to progress, this approach gives others opportunity to integrate their ideas into the change programme and improve their confidence that they will be able to function effectively.
- *Facilitation and support*. This is the 'softly-softly' approach, recognising that many key individuals lack confidence about the need for change and their role in the process; they are suffering a lack of confidence and as a result need a helping hand.
- *Negotiation and agreement*. If the group has a particular power to resist the change and where some individuals will clearly lose out, careful negotiation will be required so that a mutually satisfactory agreement can be sought.
- *Manipulation and co-option*. This is a relatively inexpensive approach but one that can easily backfire. It will deal promptly with any resistance but will leave resentment.

■ *Explicit and implicit coercion.* While fast and effective in achieving change in a short time, recriminations from the disaffected can result. One's legal position must be clarified prior to any action.

The various approaches, where they are commonly used, and their pros and cons are summarised in Table 20.3.

One simple model for visualising an employer's activity required to achieve various levels of impact on employees when aiming to reach commitment in a change initiative is

Table 20.3 Six key strategies for change

Approach	Commonly used in these situations	Advantages	Drawbacks
Education and communication	Where there is a lack of information or inaccurate information and analysis	Once persuaded, people will often help with the implementation of the change	Can be very time-consuming if many people are involved
Participation and involvement	Where the initiators do not have all the information they need to design the change, and where others have considerable power to resist	People who participate will be committed to implementing change, and any relevant information they have will be integrated into the change plan	Can be very time-consuming if participators design an inappropriate change
Facilitation and support	Where people are resisting because of adjustment problems	No other approach works as well with adjustment problems	Can be time-consuming, expensive and still fail
Negotiation and agreement	Where someone or some group will clearly lose out in a change, and where that group has considerable power to resist	Sometimes it is a relatively easy way to avoid major resistance	Can be too expensive in many cases if it alerts others to negotiate for compliance
Manipulation and co-option	Where other tactics will not work or are too expensive	It can be a relatively quick and inexpensive solution to resistance problems	Can lead to future problems if people feel manipulated
Explicit and implicit coercion	Where speed is essential and the change initiators possess considerable power	It is speedy and can overcome any kind of resistance	Can be risky if it leaves people mad at the initiators

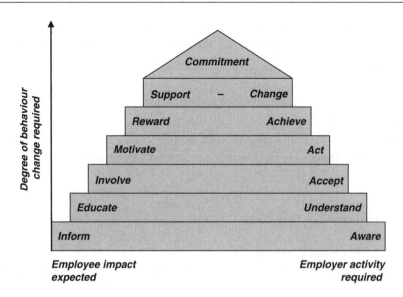

Figure 20.2 Employer's activity required to achieve higher levels of impact on employees to reach full commitment to a change initiative.

represented in Figure 20.2. The greater the degree of change required in the employees, the more time and energy required by the employer to achieve the given impact.

Managing Organisational Change

There are a number of definitive strategies for dealing with organisational change but whatever strategy is chosen, finding your 'change champions' is a key first step.

When considering change there are those whose confidence is low and so may have a poor attitude to change; they can entrench their position, holding onto the past where they feel more comfortable – their self-esteem intact. Others with more confidence may be looking forward to the change and be more robust in their attitude.

When it comes to dealing with change, there is another dimension – that of energy. When these two – attitude and energy – combine we have different people-types depending on where they are between these two dimensions (see Figure 20.3).

- *Good eggs.* Clearly, these are those who have both the energy for change and the right attitude; they are your change champions. A friend Chris Mullen, who has remained with Unisys for nearly four decades, said recently of his longevity in a firm at the forefront of technology: 'You need three things – you have to understand the business, understand where it is going and be leading the changes.' A 'good egg' if ever there was one!

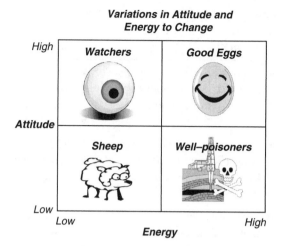

Variations in Attitude and Energy to Change

Figure 20.3 The two dimensions of people's approach to change – attitude and energy.

- *Watchers*. There are those who are keen for the change to go ahead – they just want someone else to drive it forward. Give them a role and they will probably follow the change champions if they are shown the way.
- *Sheep*. There are those who make things happen and those who wonder what happened; sheep are in the latter category. They will most likely come along to a safe place once it is all over.
- *Well-poisoner*. There are those who have all the energy to make things happen, but unfortunately have a poor attitude to the change, so will do all in their power to compromise initiative. They are likely to be a little cynical to say the least. Participation and involvement may be a solution (see Table 20.3), but remember, 'it is the herd that moves the horse'. Get a sufficient body of people behind you and well-poisoners become isolated, so their attitude may change – or they leave.

Once your change champions have been identified it will be important to develop an appropriate strategy to manage the change process. This text is not a specific guide to change management – see the Further Reading list for some suggestions – but the following represents five key strategies summarised in Table 20.4. Note that they mirror Tannenbaum and Schmidt's continuum (see Chapter 4), giving varying levels of freedom to the group in implementing the change strategies.

- *Directive*. Giving little room for freedom on the part of the staff. Unless there is genuinely little room for manoeuvre – such as when implementing new legislation or adopting particular directives – the approach may be met with resistance. Help, support and training of the appropriate sort may be needed to manage the individual's confidence through the process.

Table 20.4 Five key strategies: their approach with examples

Change strategy	Approach	Examples
Directive	■ Imposition of change by management which could bypass recognised bargaining	■ Imposition of pay settlement ■ Work practice changes backed by ultimatum ■ Need to follow new legislation, etc.
Negotiating	■ Recognised legitimacy of other bargaining groups ■ Concessions possible on implementation	■ Productivity bargaining ■ Agreements with suppliers on quality
Normative	■ Seeks overall attitudes/values about change ■ Often uses external change agents	■ Quality commitment ■ New Values Programme ■ Teamworking ■ New culture ■ Employee commitment
Analytical	■ Based on clear definition of problem ■ Collection and study of new data ■ Use of experts	Project work, for example: ■ On new pay systems ■ Staff utilisation ■ New information systems
Action-centred	■ Start with general idea of problem ■ Try out solutions and modify in light of effects ■ More involvement of those affected than in analytical work	■ Absence reduction programme ■ Some quality approaches

- *Negotiating.* Settlement should achieve a gain–gain situation where both parties come away feeling that they have a mutually satisfactory agreement.
- *Normative.* The aim here is to win the 'hearts and minds' of the people involved, and is one where respected external advisors can add credibility to the initiative and give confidence to the organisation as the change is implemented.
- *Analytical.* Both management and staff can be involved in drawing together further information to support a given direction for change; again, external advisors may assist in the data collection to underpin the need for change.
- *Action-centred.* This involves a much more collaborative effort on the part of all individuals, but will only be effective if management agree to buy in to the outcomes – they are the ones who need confidence with this approach.

How to Plan an Effective Change Programme

For anyone planning to implement change within their organisation, this checklist provides a range of issues that need to be considered. It covers any type of change programme and aims to guide the planning process by covering the basic building blocks of change.

Whatever the pace of change within our organisation, the fact is that change is omnipresent in the world around us: one only has to look at their mobile phone. Did you even have one five years ago? What features has it got today? And it is not just technological change. All organisations need to be aware of political, economic, social, environmental and technological changes as they affect the way the business operates. Its staff, its customers – in fact, all its stakeholders – are affected.

The following represents a guide for managers planning their change initiatives:

- *Think the change through.* Read the 'gurus' on change management – they have a wealth of good ideas. While it will take a day or two – the changes you are facing will take longer and the path will be particularly bumpy – especially if you get it wrong.

  Look at your prospective change from a broader view before getting too focused on the detail. As Stephen Covey (1989) says: start with the end in mind.
- *Prepare the right change culture.* Consider the suggestions in Table 20.5.
- *Select a 'change champion'.* Change programmes benefit from a 'champion' to galvanise the plan and the action. The champion's credibility is of paramount importance, as is sufficient seniority and a proven track record. The champion must also be lively, energetic, passionate and committed – if you are not the right person to be leading change, recognise it now!

Table 20.5 How to prepare the culture for change

Get the culture right	Support change	Help people
■ Share information widely ■ Allow for suggestions, input and differences from widespread participation ■ Break changes into manageable chunks and minimise surprises ■ Make standards and requirements clear ■ Be honest about the downside	■ Recognise current value systems ■ Create a blame-free culture of empowerment and push down decision-making – but clarify decision boundaries ■ Break down departmental barriers ■ Design challenging jobs ■ Free time for risk and innovation ■ Focus on the interests of all stakeholders	■ Recognise staff needs and dealing with conflict positively ■ Be directional without being directive ■ Involve everyone ■ Earn commitment and trust ■ Develop relationships ■ Understand how teams work ■ Recognise one's limits and others' strengths

Consider the four types of person you may have around you in Figure 20.3. Your change agents are 'good eggs' and will take up the challenge, the 'watchers' will go with them albeit more slowly, the 'sheep' will be the last to go but they'll get there in the end. Your 'well-poisoners' have 'seen it all before' and know that 'it'll never work here', and need particular care to make sure they don't poison the well for others. Harness their energy by letting them drink from the clean pool of success that you can show in small stages.

- *Select the right team for change.* Get a team of 'good eggs' with a mix of technical competencies and personal styles, not necessarily all at senior levels. Most members should be respected individuals from within the organisation, not outsiders. You need 'movers and shakers' whose commitment is not in doubt, but temper them with a few known mavericks with a reasonable attitude rather than someone who will trip up your best intentions to show how clever they are. All should have earned respect within the organisation and be widely trusted and credible.

Remember that some people fear the change through a poor self-esteem, feeling that their skills and aptitudes will be redundant as the change takes effect in the evolving organisation.

- *'Sell' the case for change.* Show people what the organisation will look like as the culture change programme develops. Consider structures and culture – what will be the best structure to add value across the organisation? How will the best work together? What will the implications be?

You might know why the organisation needs to change but you need to persuade others; everyone must be convinced of the urgency of the need. You might need some market research to build your case which marshals both quantitative and qualitative arguments. Spell these out in terms of business objectives linked to a vision of how much more all stakeholders will benefit if the change is successful.

In reality, persuading people of the need for change can be a complex and sensitive business; no one likes surprises that might significantly and adversely affect their livelihood. Consider bringing someone in from the outside to act as a catalyst, but manage this with care and sensitivity. There is no substitute for people 'owning' the change programme. Get a group of staff to identify the drivers of change themselves – they'll see and understand the need for change.

- *Define the scope of change.* Consider its coverage and limits rigorously. To be fully effective, change needs to operate in six dimensions (see Table 20.6). Compare the six items listed to the McKinsey 7S Model (Chapter 4); consider that the seven areas are like compasses – all need to be in the same direction to be successful (see Figure 4.6 in Chapter 4).

- *Analyse your management competencies.* Change programmes will not be successful unless senior managers are fully committed to them. Is your management team signed up to change? Address honestly the position of those who are not change agents. Consult with senior managers to identify further change factors, see Box 20.1 for some ideas.

Table 20.6 Compare the dimensions of change that need to be congruent for success

Six dimensions for change	McKinsey 7S Model
■ Markets and customers	1. Structure
■ Products and services	2. Strategy
■ Business processes	3. Systems
■ People and reward systems	4. Style of management
■ Structure and facilities	5. Skills – corporate strengths
■ Technologies	6. Staff
	7. Shared values

Box 20.1: Key factors in mapping change

- *Leadership*. Does the leader set an example and foster learning and development?
- *People*. Do people think naturally about what's coming next? Or will the next change be met with the same old shock and horror?
- *Control*. Do measurement and procedural control stifle creativity?
- *Integration*. Do we have a business of people in separate boxes or do we mix across areas and responsibilities?
- *Processes*. Which are the key activities that give us our strength?

- *Identify the positive and negative forces*. There will be forces driving and restraining change – identify both sets. Aim to reinforce the drivers, or add new ones, and to weaken or lessen the restraining forces through education. This is often a slow process, but it can be helped by frank discussion and particularly by positive success.

    Table 20.2 identifies common reasons for resistance to change, linking their outcome and reactions.
- *Draw up an outline plan*. Plan for change in the way you would for any major project. Cover:
    - *Vision*. What is the 'big idea' behind the change? What is the organisation striving to achieve? This must be clear and compelling.
    - *Scope*. What needs to change if the organisation is to realise its vision?
    - *Time frame*. What will change when, and in what order? Radical change takes time, especially if attitude change is involved.
    - *People*. Who will be most affected by change and how? Who will play prominent roles in implementing change (the change agents)?
    - *Resources*. How much will the change cost? Will there be offsetting benefits?
    - *Communications*. Will you need new mechanisms and structures to communicate with front-line employees?

Table 20.7 Dos and don'ts for effective change

Do	Don't
■ Think outside the box: remember Albert Einstein, who cautioned that the thinking that brought the problems is unlikely to be the thinking that will solve the problems ■ Use diversity: find out the opinions of others and 'outsiders': within the organisation and tap the views of customers, suppliers and other stakeholders ■ Go large: many change programmes fail to deliver the expected results because their ambitions are too narrow or not radical enough ■ Be patient and persistent: change takes time	■ Forget to see the wood for the trees: keep the overall vision in mind ■ Underestimate resistance to change: expect it and cost-in extra training and other resources like communications ■ Skimp on resources for training or communications ■ Start a major change programme until you have the absolute support of the top management team ■ Push resistance: it will only push back against you; instead listen and persuade

- *Training*. Have you allowed for the training of managers and front-line employees in both hard and soft skills associated with change?
- *Organisation structure*. Will changes be needed, for example towards a flatter structure?
- *What will the change programme cost?* It can be expensive, particularly if it is associated with plant closure or redundancies. Recognise this and draw up a separate budget. Don't underestimate the 'softer' costs of training or the communications the programme will require.
- *Explain the change programme to line managers*. Use the plan to outline the likely impact of the programme on structures, people, processes and market offering. Seek feedback and suggestions, and use them to refine the plan and build consensus in favour of change.
- *Communicate*. The key to successful change. Communicate continuously with stakeholders (employees, customers, suppliers and owners) as you develop and build the programme. Build trust about the likely extent of change. Beware the grapevine – do not allow rumour to circulate; be honest. Also, review Table 20.7 for dos and don'ts for effective change.

Motivating People Through Change

Today's markets are ever more turbulent, society is changing, technology advances, so it is ever more important for organisational success to motivate employees and use human assets to the full. However, although we have had a century or so of theory and practice to call on, managers are often perplexed about motivation considering there is no ready solution. Indeed, as many a manager looks for the 'quick-fix', the more baffling motivation appears. We know individuals are motivated by different things and in different ways, and recognise that there are times when delayering and the flattening of hierarchies can create insecurity and uncertainty, and lower staff morale. There are also more staff on limited-term contracts or work part-time, and who are usually especially hard to motivate.

During times of particular change, staff may feel that their existing skills will no longer be valued in the new ways of working, which leads to a lack of confidence and lowering of self-esteem. Thus, motivating people through periods of particular change needs careful managing.

There are some obvious advantages of motivating people with few negatives, although there are many barriers to be overcome. These may include unaware or absent managers, poor working environments, out-of-date equipment and entrenched attitudes such as 'We don't get paid any extra to work harder' and so on.

With a positive motivation philosophy and practice in place, productivity, quality and service should improve because motivation helps people towards:

- Achieving goals
- Gaining a positive perspective
- Creating the will to change
- Building individual abilities and self-esteem
- Managing their development and helping others
- Developing a team approach
- Fostering a positive vision of the future.

Change motivation checklist – a guide for managers

The following should spur some thoughts:

- *Read Chapter 4.* While these theories date back over the past several decades, they are still valid today. A basic understanding of their main principles will be invaluable for building a climate of honesty, openness and trust.
- *Consider what motivates you.* Think what factors are important to you in your working life and how they interact. What has motivated you and demotivated you in the past? What motivates your family and friends? Is money really a powerful motivator? Real responsibility, positive support when things go wrong, satisfying a need for meaning, belonging, achievement and developing can all be equally, or even more, important.

    Understand the differences between real, longer-term motivators and short-term spurs. If you do not find your firm providing a new microwave in the kitchenette, the cash behind the bar at the local pub every third Thursday or even private healthcare as a motivator then perhaps your people will not either.

    Ask what people want most from their jobs – some may want more responsibility, more financial incentives, better working conditions and a choice of remuneration benefits. In performance appraisals, attitude surveys and informally, ask what motivates them – you may be surprised.

- *Management by walking about*. Catch someone doing something right – and tell them! Ensure that you do it genuinely, don't go overboard or appear to watch over shoulders. If you can see how their work could be improved, rather than shout it out, encourage them to find their way instead. Set an example and earn respect; you do not have to be able do everything better than your staff. Make sure staff know what levels of support they may expect.

- *Remove demotivators*. See Herzberg Two-factor Theory (Chapter 4) – and deal with those that can be quickly and easily; others require more planning and time to work through. If you can find out what is frustrating people you have a ready-made and keen appetite for change. That you are concerned to find out what is wrong and are prepared to do something about it is, in itself, motivating.

- *Show support*. Whether you have a 'gotcha culture' that penalises error and jumps on mistakes or one that views mistakes as learning opportunities, your staff need to understand the kind and levels of support they may expect. How far can they bend rules or use initiative to step outside established procedures and yet receive the support they will need? Support is often the hurdle at which motivation practice and the relationships being built can falter.

- *Money does not always motivate*. And they will claim that their fringe benefits are an incentive. Money actually comes low down in the list of motivators (are you still really motivated a month or two after a pay rise?). Fringe benefits can be effective in attracting new employees but rarely motivate people to use their potential more effectively.

- *Take action*. Having listened to staff, do something to improve present policies and attitudes, consulting fully with staff and unions. Consider policies that affect flexible working, reward, promotion, training and development, and participation.

- *Get on and manage change*. Use the checklist earlier in the chapter. Adopting policies is one thing, implementing them is quite another. With entrenched poor motivation the whole style of management needs to be reviewed. It is a natural human instinct to resist change even when it is beneficial – especially if confidence is low. The way change is implemented is crucial to success or failure through its own power to motivate or demotivate. A flexible style of management is required depending on the motivation, ability and confidence of the people to undertake the required change. More than this, if one uses the wrong style for the situation, the effects can be quite damaging. If you:

  - Tell people what to do (instruct or deliver a monologue) – you may overlook the hopes, fears or expectations of your people or the fact that they know full well what is required (perhaps better than you!).

  - Wax lyrical (try to persuade people) – your overpowering reasons will fall on deaf ears if your people are ahead of you anyway. Moreover, if they have some ideas of their own and *you* don't listen, you will soon have a disgruntled team of people.

- Consult – it will soon become obvious if you have made up your mind anyway. It may be less effective if you 'consult' when people want freedom to get on and do the job; your intervention may undermine their confidence or suggest that you don't trust them.
- Look for real participation – sharing the problem-solving and decision-making with those who are to implement the change, you can begin to expect commitment and ownership along with the adaptation and compromise that will occur naturally. However, if your followers are inexperienced or uncertain and looking to you to lead, that you are 'sharing' may give them cause to doubt your strength of leadership.

- *Recognise learning preferences*. All change involves learning. People rarely learn computing solely by reading a manual or attending a course; they learn by practice and experience. Think back to how you learned to use a computer; some prefer to try things out first (plug 'n' play) then reflect afterwards (where has my work gone), while others find it useful to read and reflect before practising.

Chapter 12 explored learning and developing abilities; as a reminder it is sufficient to recall that Honey and Mumford (1982) distinguished four basic styles of learning:

- *Activists* – like to get involved in new experiences, problems or opportunities and are not too happy standing back, observing and being impartial.
- *Reflectors* – like to take their time and think things through; they don't like being pressured into rushing from one thing to another.
- *Theorists* – are comfortable with concepts and theory, and don't like being thrown in at the deep end without apparent purpose or reason.
- *Pragmatists* – need a link between the subject matter and the job in hand, and learn best when they can test things out.

Given that we learn with different styles, preferences and a mix of approaches, remember your people will respond best to stimuli and suggestions that take account of the way they learn best. Trying to develop people against their grain will usually only succeed in demotivating them.

Table 20.8 Dos and don'ts for motivating staff in a time of change

Do	Don't
<ul><li>Recognise that you don't have all the answers</li><li>Take time to find out what makes others tick and show genuine care</li><li>Lead, encourage and guide staff, don't force them</li><li>Tell your staff what you think</li></ul>	<ul><li>Make assumptions about what drives others</li><li>Assume others are like you</li><li>Force people into things that are 'good for them'</li><li>Delegate work, but delegate responsibility</li><li>Neglect the need for inspiration and excitement</li></ul>

- *Provide feedback.* Explored in more detail in Chapter 18, feedback was seen to be one of the most valuable elements in the motivation cycle. Explain to people how their developments, performance and accomplishments are progressing. Offer comments with accuracy and care in consideration of the next steps or future targets.

Table 20.8 suggests some dos and don'ts for motivating staff in a time of change.

How to Get Others to Participate – A Guide for Change Agents

One of the enduring frustrations is that there may have been a management initiative to review ways of improving the effectiveness of the organisation – perhaps on an 'away-day' – but all the momentum dies when faced with the reality of the workplace. The hoped-for changes just don't seem to happen. There are many reasons for this: apathy, dislike of change, fear, the perceived difficulties in implementation, lack of knowledge of how to do things differently – all rank high as obstacles. Add to this existing work overload and lack of clear measures of improved performance and one has a recipe for 'business as usual'.

In order to get 'follow-through' one does need commitment to the process – and this requires 'ownership'. If individuals don't see the need for change, they won't.

In any new initiative, consider the price and the prize – what is the cost vs benefit? As a change agent, you may have to alter the balance of these levers. You may need to go to the heart of the matter to identify the rationale behind what is needed. You will have much more success convincing those around you if you too are convinced about what is needed. Take a positive attitude to resistance. Change is unlikely to be worthwhile without it.

Enhance the perception of the goal by focusing on the direct benefits for those around you in terms that they will appreciate. Is it that they will be part of an effective team, have less hassles in their working day or something more tangible? You may be able to reduce the perceived price by finding ways to illustrate how easy the adjustments are to make, build people's confidence and get them involved in developing the practicalities of the change.

When an away-day has generated a 'laundry list' of ideas – nice to haves – it is no surprise that few actually happen in the cold light of a busy working day. It is better to aim for a few rather than a long list, perhaps no more than 10 things that a group may attend to – perhaps fewer. Aim to get a name and a time for completion against each item; aim for short time periods and easy gains. This will build confidence and momentum for larger and longer tasks. Remember to get the group to review progress regularly and highlight appreciation for those who have some success against the action list. For those who have reasons rather than results, aim to involve them in problem-solving initiatives to devise a methodology for moving things forward. If little has happened because the task was considered too big, get it broken down into bite-sized chunks and develop a schedule around that. Remember to enlist others' help if possible to share the load.

If all else fails, consider rewards for those who apply themselves to making things better – or sanctions for those that don't cooperate.

Summary

In this chapter you have:

- Reviewed what change is in an organisational context
- Explored the PEST model for tracking environmental change
- Examined the sort of resistances to change that can occur internally
- Reviewed a range of approaches for dealing with resistance to change
- Explored a checklist of activities to manage organisational change
- Examined how to plan an effective change programme
- Considered a range of issues to enable people to remain motivated through change
- Learnt how to get others involved in the change process.

Questions

1. Review recent initiatives in your organisation – or one with which you are familiar – and critically evaluate how successfully the people were managed. What would you recommend is done differently in the future?
2. Explain why removing the resistance to change is generally more successful than increasing the forces pro-change.
3. It is said that 'it is the herd that moves the horse'. Describe strategies in your organisation – or one with which you are familiar – that would demonstrate that this is not a cliché.
4. Complacency is a human fallacy – explain how you would knock senior management out of their complacency to recognise that internal changes will be in the long-term best interest of the organisation.

References

Covey, R. S. (1989) *The Seven Habits of Effective People*, Simon & Schuster.

Handy, C. (1989) *The Age of Unreason*, Business Books Ltd.

Honey, P. and Mumford, A. (1982) *Manual of Learning Styles*, Peter Honey Publications, Maidenhead.

Wilmshurst, J. and Mackay, A. (2002) *The Fundamentals and Practice of Marketing*, Chapter 1, Figure 1.5, Butterworth-Heinemann.

Further Reading

Carnall, C. (2002) *Managing Change in Organisations*, FT Prentice-Hall.

Holbeche, L. (1998) *Motivating People in Organizations*, Butterworth-Heinemann, Oxford.

Hussey, D. E. (1998) *How to be Better at Managing Change*, Kogan Page, London.

Kotter, J. P. (1996) *Leading Change*, Harvard Business School Press.

Mackay, A. R. (2007) *Recruiting, Retaining and Releasing People*, Butterworth-Heinemann.

Moss-Kanter, R. (1988) *The Change Masters: Corporate Entrepreneurs at Work*, Unwin Paperbacks, London.

Price Waterhouse Change Integration Team Better Change (1995) *Best Practices for Transforming your Organisation*, Irwin Professional Publishing, New York.

Smith, S. (ed.) (1997) *Create That Change: Ready-made tools for change management*, Kogan Page, London.

21

The Future of Work

Reviewing a book about the future is as dangerous as writing one, since neither the assertions nor the criticisms of them can be proved.

Hermann Hauser, *Management Today*, December 2003, p. 30

Learning Outcomes

Let's talk about the future – as that is where I plan to spend the rest of my life! This chapter, and its companion web pages, have been written with tomorrow in mind to cover particular elements of the National Occupational Standards for Management and Leadership: *Providing Direction*; most sections of *Facilitating Change*; and many sections of *Working with People*. The chapter also provides a resource to many of the requirements of the Chartered Management Institute's Diploma in Management and the CIPD Professional Development Scheme in as far as 'managing in the future' is the basis of all professional management qualifications.

By the end of this chapter you will:

- Have had a short review of the past as a prediction for the future
- Know something about information technology and its influence in the workplace activity, particularly e-collaborating
- Recognise that e-learning is making inroads and also consider how to help it find its place
- Discover the importance of flexible working
- Know some of the pitfalls of working from home and how to manage a virtual team
- Review interim working and discover its attractions for many people
- Have considered future trends in work and children, pensions, incapacity benefit and older workers
- Have looked further at women in work in the future
- Understand the importance of a work/life balance and approaches to achieving it
- Know what is meant by work with meaning.

Tracking Future Trends

Any view of the future will be someone's personal selection of often contradictory predictions made by distinguished people in different fields. From such ramblings will be a picture that will be as much influenced by the writer's ability to comprehend complex technological issues as by emphasis on one scenario over another.

As author, I have tried to be as objective as possible in selecting ideas for this final selection for the text, recognising that the predictions might not be right, or if they are, will anyone take any heed of the warnings or opportunities identified? History suggests not.

Given that many of the current changes in the business environment were predicted well in advance, how can we excuse the fact that we are continually caught out by changes in the world around us? There have been any number of 'surprises' that have wrong-footed some of Britain's major industries. These include:

- Legislation on business largely compromises business rather than *enables* business
- The growth in information technology does not mean we have more leisure time
- A diet consisting mainly of fat, sugar and salt is bad for children
- Bank customers prefer to talk to human beings face to face in a branch
- Financial services people working on commission have not generally had the customer's best interests at heart when selling products that mature in 25 years' time
- Low-cost airlines have altered holiday and leisure behaviour
- The population of Europe has been ageing demographically.

Since all of these issues have been precisely pointed out by trend analysts (see Hayward, 2004), why have they all been cited as reasons for commercial underperformance and consumer dissatisfaction?

Here are some further 'surprises' yet to hit the headlines:

- Governments cannot continue to spend more than they earn each year – neither can consumers.
- With waste sites filling and resources becoming scarcer, unnecessary packaging will have to be reduced.
- Within a generation, the concept of finishing 'work' and spending 20 or more years in full retirement will be unheard of.
- Ever increasing rates of staff turnover at all levels in organisations and continued outsourcing of services abroad will severely diminish customer satisfaction.
- The current welfare state in the UK is unsustainable as the increasing numbers of people in retirement or on other benefits, aligned with the growing numbers of civil servants employed to administer it, outstrips the number of people in work to pay for it.

- The continued pressure to reduce costs will lead to a reduction in the quality of food and goods.
- Some lesser educated indigenous people of Western Europe will not do some fundamental work that Eastern European, Asian or Chinese will be only too happy to do (or the services that can will be outsourced overseas) to the detriment of Western society – someone working in a call-centre in Lahore does not pay UK income tax and national insurance.

So, why don't businesses heed the warnings? As suggested in Chapter 20, there is a lot going on in the business environment but not much action. There are three reasons for this.

First, *inflexibility* – many companies are inflexible and unable to respond appropriately or quickly to changes, assuming they notice them in the first place. Companies need communication channels to permit messages about changes to affect their tactical and strategic responses to the influences. There are some other problems the author has witnessed in organisations of late:

- The data about the need for changes so often do not rise above administrative levels.
- Data are collected and filtered so that they only reinforce decisions already made in a self-congratulatory way, rather than challenge the status quo.
- Even if the information reaches decision-makers, they often don't know what to do with it, as their organisation structure is not able to respond to change in the most effective way.
- 'Another reorganisation' is often a lame attempt at progress.
- Customer feedback (complaints or praise) and staff opinions are rarely systematically tracked; if they are, the results are frequently only given lip service.

Remember the 'boiled frog' example in Chapter 20.

Second, there is a worrying *lack of competence* – despite considerable salaries and people's best intentions, many organisations and senior people in them are unable to comprehend the information they are given. While there is a glut of data available to executives, the 'wheat and chaff' are not separated, analysis-paralysis is rife, few data are digested, less are understood and very little acted upon. The more a person sees, the less they understand. Moreover, the feeling is that if someone understands, they haven't grasped the whole picture; the sheer size of the task means that it is harder and harder to assess what is really important.

In an age where the corporate philosophy is to 'get closer to the customer' (see page 3 of your company's annual report), it appears that as organisations get bigger, they get more bureaucratic and more anonymous, yet still they continue to grow.

Third and most worrying is *short-term self-interest* – too many senior people in organisations ignore obvious signals of the future because of their cynical self-interest. Who cares about the long term when the average Marketing Director is in place for only 18 months and the average employee in the UK has been in eight different jobs by the age of 32? Add to this that it seems that the current business culture rewards failure (Equitable Life directors or Roger Holmes and others at Marks & Spencer), who cares about the long term? Even if someone noticed the future trends, they probably don't plan to be around to deal with the consequences.

Why are organisations surprised when consumer trust and respect for the financial services industry, the oil industry, the food industry, the media, transport infrastructure, the government and its politicians are so fragile when they all have so obviously not responded to the signals consumers have been giving them about their products, services and their behaviour?

The consumer response has been to lower their loyalty; the next generation of consumers (your employees) is being brought up to switch brands and suppliers at the drop of a hat, to be as short-term and expedient as the companies they deal with – and this is being seen in the workplace too. This is altering the dynamics of commerce, taking away the inertia of core business that allowed trends to be ignored yet companies still to prosper.

For long-term corporate health, a longer-term perspective in thinking and acting is fundamental. The data are available; action is required to sustain us into a more secure future – beyond the next 18 months, that is! The more senior a person is in an organisation, the more he or she should be focusing on the future. It is crucial that relevant knowledge management is in place to track what is changing and what is not (and what ought to change), and that this is effectively exploited. The effectiveness of senior managements' strategies will depend on their ability to ask the right questions and how they have been listening to, and acting on, the answers.

So how do you protect yourself in an ever changing world (and help your staff cope too)?

Box 21.1: Foresight's view of the next 50 years

A government think-tank, Foresight, published its 50-year predictions in January 2006. With four scenarios outlined, the world of work will become very different than it is today. So, will we be going to an office building at all, and if we do, will it be by horse following a global energy crisis? Will the transport infrastructure change as much as suggested to cope with congestion and climate change? Will there be sophisticated urban colonies where most people will live with more local food supplied by the rural hinterland? It is suggested that 'pay as you go' road pricing will be a country-wide by 2015 – it was being trialled in 2006 in central London. Some of the report's critics said that much of the report was just 'pie-in-the-sky' imagination and unlikely to be realised – just as 'flying' personal cars predicted 50 years ago are not a feature of today's society.

The first step will be to stop relying entirely on the judgements of other people and start being a trend-spotter yourself. Keeping one's eyes and ears open (to view one's own situation as an outsider might) will be crucial, finding a few moments every now and then to look beyond the daily challenges to get a sense of what is going on beyond the horizon. Perhaps this means finding dedicated time and space to see the broader perspective. Look behind the work that you are doing and challenge the assumptions that underpin what you do. Look for what others might not have seen, a better way to achieve the objectives, perhaps redefine the objectives. Build a network to keep abreast of what others in your profession are doing and thinking. Box 21.1 gives one resource's view of the future.

However, it is not enough to see the future – you need to be prepared to be part of it. While it is easy to be comfortable in a given role or function, suppose someone else decides to shift your comfort zone? Two fundamental approaches will increase your ability to cope:

- *Self-belief*. Trust yourself and have the confidence that you can make the right choices in the long term, even against short-term setbacks.
- *Justify your employability*. You have to make sure that you reinvest in your learning. If an organisation is not willing to make sufficient investment, as the saying goes: *if it is going to be – it is down to thee*!

The Growth of Legislation

In the last section we identified future trends that had been largely overlooked by businesses. As Patience Wheatcroft, Business and City Editor of *The Times* observed in *Management Today*, in November 2005, Lord Turner of Ecchinswell produced a report on the state of the UK pension system, yet some 18 months later, when this text was being written, what has been done to implement his proposals?

While some pension issues may be too far ahead for most politicians now in power to address, with some companies collapsing and members of their pension schemes losing their pension entitlement, the UK government launched the Pension Protection Fund. Companies are likely to have to pay £1 billion into the fund in the first year and the bill will keep rising.

But the new regulation on pensions is but the tip of a massive iceberg of legislation in the past few years; we have a whole gamut of new regulations that companies must pay for (see Box 21.2).

Manchester Business School estimated that the cost of new regulations introduced since 1988 is over £20 billion (*Management Today*, 2003), with a further £10 billion for the minimum wage and £4 billion for the increases in employers' National Insurance Contributions. New parental employment rights alone could add a further £300 million a year.

There are further measures likely to be welcomed by families – from increases in statutory maternity leave, maternity pay, unpaid maternity leave to the introduction of paternity

---

Box 21.2: A selection of the new legislation affecting British business since 1988

- 48-hour working week
- A reduction in the qualifying period for unfair dismissal
- A new public interest disclosure act
- A higher cap on unfair dismissal payouts
- The introduction of European-style working councils
- New range of restrictions on the dismissal of striking staff
- Restrictions on repeated fixed-term working contracts
- A working family tax credit – paid through company payrolls
- The minimum wage
- A new right to take time off to study
- Changes to student loan regulations
- Enhanced trade union recognition
- The right to accompaniment to company hearings
- The creation of complex stakeholder pensions.

---

leave, possibly transference of unused maternity leave, up to 13 weeks unpaid paternity leave, and a new right to adoption leave – all paid for in some way by employers. But what of those employees who don't have children – they have to fit the bill (via taxation and lost income from stretched employers) and provide cover while colleagues are away.

The cumulative effect of these legislative changes for business, especially small businesses, could be devastating. There is more in the pipeline from Brussels with new rules on worker consultation (yet to be fully clarified), rules on employing temporary agency staff, new discrimination legislation and much more.

All of this is on top of a rising tax burden (windfall taxes, £5 billion pension levy, extra oil taxes, National Insurance, carbon emissions, etc.), an ageing population moving out of full-time employment and an increase in state employment with proportionally less people working in the private sector.

As reported in *The Independent* (25 January 2006), the Institute of Fiscal Studies concluded that, despite recent increases in taxation (mainly on companies), the Chancellor (Gordon Brown) will have to raise taxes still further to fund his long-term spending commitments.

Ruth Lea, director of the Centre for Policy Studies, observed that there has been a range of complicated regulations from the EU on anti-discrimination measures, working time, working conditions, and information and consultation procedures (*The Daily Telegraph*, 2006). She went on to say that 'the EU, intent on creating a socialist workers' paradise, continues to harass the UK about its opt-out from the compulsory maximum 48-hour week and is undoubtedly going ahead with implementing the employee-friendly Charter of Fundamental Rights'.

It is not any easier for the individual 'man in the street'. In the lead editorial of the same newspaper, it suggested that there has been a 'surreptitious' creation of a DNA database, an 'explosion' of anti-terrorist legislation, increases in the 'discredited' methods of stop and search by British police, and the proposal for a 'compulsory' national ID scheme. The editorial suggested that we might have to justify our existence to the state, rather than the other way round, the country becoming less free, but less safe as well. Something has got to give!

Information Technology and Working Practices

Mobile technology is already revolutionising working life – and whatever one writes about it is out of date as soon as it is published. But imagine the scenario: you are sitting in a virtual office with a virtual representation of yourself and your colleagues around you. Someone in another office across the world has hard copy of a document that they want you to comment on so they insert it into a slot and, instantly, the same image is there for you and everyone else to view.

Not so amazing; you probably have had a fax machine sitting quietly in the corner of your office and virtual images are part of gaming technology already. But with computing capabilities doubling every 18 months or less, we will see 'digital dust' monitoring your stress levels and rescheduling your work for you, chairs with electronic monitoring of your posture to spot when you need a check-up, and a digital 'helper' to update you automatically on the actions that it has taken on your behalf. See a glossary of terms in Box 21.3.

'In the future we will see intelligent agents acting as personal assistants, sifting and dealing with information, while digital dust will mean that even the tiniest thing can be connected', according to John Ames, managing consultant to BTexact Technologies, the R&D arm of BT (*Professional Manager*, 2003). It is likely that the manager of the future is someone who has a personal area network wherever they are, always connected to the Internet.

Box 21.3: A selection of technology for mobile communications (see more information through your favourite search engine)

- *ADSL/WiFi/3G/GSM/GPRS/xDSL*. Different forms of broadband connectivity, each for different environments and applications.
- *Convergence*. A group of technologies to integrate voice and data services, permitting easy access to e-mail and redirecting voice mail to PDAs.
- *Dial-up*. A slow method for connecting to the office that requires the opening of a telephone line between the two sites. Insecure, it is only for back-up.

(Continued)

Box 21.3: Continued

- *Encryption*. Essential security technology that scrambles data over wireless networks; the greater the encryption, the slower the transmission.
- *IM*. Instant messaging permits something you type onto a PC to be instantly seen on another.
- *PDA*. Personal Digital Assistant or hand-held computer; ranges from a BlackBerry to a Palm Pilot.
- *SMS*. Short Message Service used for text from e-mail to mobile phones and back. Used by traders wanting prices, procurement managers closing deals and service organisations keeping clients informed.
- *Voiceover IP (VoIP)*. Voice and data transmission travelling over telephone wires, but the information is in packets – like the Internet. Benefits include cost reductions ('always on', like the Web), mobile connectivity (logging on is simply 'plug-and-play') and better call quality (termed hi-fi telephony).

Over 50 per cent of managers in larger businesses are estimated to be using Personal Digital Assistants (PDAs) – hand-held mobile devices that can access the Internet and act as a basic personal organiser by setting up diary appointments. Most modest mobile phones have an appointment/calendar function with an alarm. While the limit is the size of the screen, voice entry is just around the corner.

Although the ability to access e-mail during down-time spent travelling or waiting for meetings can bring vast time savings and speeds of response to busy managers, there is a worrying trend. HP called it 'infomania' – an obsessive desire to receive and respond to e-mail communications however trivial: laptops on the beach, PDAs at breakfast while on weekend retreats. Moreover, there is a risk of alienation of many people working remotely too much – both from the employee feeling isolated not having the direct human contact and the manager fearing they are losing control of their staff. Personal contact is vital and managers must make time to get together and speak to people – have that coffee in contact with other people, not just in the company of your e-mails.

Telephones

Looking recently for a new mobile phone for my wife, I was surprised to find that the 'feature-driven' displays showed devices that had built-in cameras and a torch, ready to download videos and music, play games, and watch news and sports clips – the clam-shell designs would have come in handy at the winter festive season: they are strong enough to crack walnuts. The shop assistant missed the irony when I asked if these devices could be used to make and receive telephone calls!

Every 3G device contains an application unmatched by any other consumer electronics gadget – you can make telephone calls with it. Wireless telephony brings in annual global revenues exceeding £1000 billion – perhaps that is the 'killer application'. Indeed, there are good reasons why 3G capacity could be used more to provide cheap calls – even substituting for calls over fixed-line connections that we are seeing BT offer already – than any other small-screen entertainment services on which many operators are focused. Not only could this bring in more revenue, it could help operators defend against emerging competition from Internet technologies such as Wi-Fi and WiMax, a long-range broadband technology.

Back in 2004, Vodafone launched 3G in the UK with subscription packages that included both entertainment and cheaper calls. Who can blame them; they spent £13 billion on acquiring 3G licences earlier in the new millennium. However, as long as voice tariffs remain high, operators face a long-term threat from wireless calls being routed over the Internet via Wi-Fi or WiMax, not over their networks. Indeed, BT Group incorporated Wi-Fi technology into mobile phones, allowing Voiceover Internet Protocols to be made from 25 000 Wi-Fi hotspots.

So, what of this for the business manager? Recognising that e-mail or text dialogue is not as powerful as voice communications, encourage text messaging only for finite one-way messages where a response by text is not required but a call. It is those people who can undertake a conversation with confidence and clarity that people will want to do business with. Recommend the use of text sparingly – we risk having a generation of today's teenagers entering the workplace in a decade or so who not only have poor written communication skills, but are also lacking in the ability to express themselves in conversation.

MP3 theft

Apple's iPod and MP3 players are increasingly popular as mobile entertainment and storage devices – indeed, many mobile telephones have an MP3 facility to download music and film. The original 150 000-word text for this book and its companion web pages travelled with me on trains and planes while it was being developed – all saved on a 256 MB memory stick no bigger than a disposable gas cigarette lighter.

Gloriously fast and easy to use, they can be plugged into a PC and used to copy data, often bypassing firewalls or password protection. Therefore, they pose significant potential risks for companies. Disaffected employees could use such MP3s to download numerous files of their employer's confidential information and intellectual property with the intention of selling it to a competitor, moving to that competitor, or starting up their own business.

So, what can employers do to protect themselves from such abuse and what does the law offer as protection? Start with clear confidentiality, anti-competition and IT policies that are reflected in the text of staff contracts. The use of storage devices and other media, including CDs and floppy discs, needs to be properly controlled, possibly prohibited in sensitive areas, with clear and strictly enforced guidelines on employees taking information away to work in home PCs. Get good legal advice to draft precisely restrictive contractual clauses that can be enforced in the courts to clamp down on misuse of sensitive data and damaging competitive activity by current or former employees, or contractors and consultants.

Mobile communications

Mobile working has been around for a long time – wireless-capable laptops and smart phones are easy and relatively cheap to acquire. However, the everyday nature of access to e-mail, diary functions and the ability to book a holiday on the move hides the fact that the truly mobile business needs more than the latest flashy gizmo for key people. There are two routes to becoming 'mobile'.

There is ad hoc. Here someone gets a new device or management gets a brainwave and purchases some new kit, but shrinks away from the cost and complexity of the support systems and training necessary to make it work effectively. Faced with a fear of not seeing junior staff at their desks in the morning and losing control, managers get cold feet and try to grab back the reins.

The 'official' route involves a more thorough approach: management makes a value judgement; laptops, mobile phones and PDAs are acquired along with the essential in-house organisational and security systems; the people to be mobilised are trained and equipped to work out of the office. Concomitant with this tangible activity is the hope for increased corporate productivity rising alongside employee freedom, with individual effectiveness growing alongside a better work/life balance. There is also the potential to save money and streamline processes by improving the surrounding management systems.

Of major concern is that the former ad hoc approach is more common. While there are theoretical benefits of allowing people to work remotely, nearly one-third of mobile workers report losing money through missing messages and more than half have missed a meeting (*Management Today*, 2005). In order to become fully mobile, organisations need everything from secure, always available IT connectivity to the transformation of the work culture and management processes. Experience suggests that the former cannot be relied on or the latter achieved. Four case studies to illustrate how firms are grappling with the problems are given below:

- Siemens Communications equipped 110 000 people in the UK civil service with an IP profile – a mobile computer identity that travels with them around the organisation. This means that whether they are working from home, in a different office or move to another department, the individual can immediately log on without having to gain special access or be allocated a new ID by the IT department.
- Continental Airlines has mobilised cabin crews and pilots with wireless PDAs to help them share flight information more effectively. Naturally, the major concern is security following the atrocities of 9/11, particularly as all employees have access to operational

data, passenger and flight plans. So, replacing their four icons on their desktops for differing remote access, Fiberlink provided a secure, easy-to-manage, one-click remote access solution.

- With more than 600 field-service technicians making over 2500 service visits a day throughout the UK, the imaging and copier technology distributor Ikon was looking for a mobile solution. An application from Dexterra allows data on products, customers and problems to follow the mobile people making their service calls. Moreover, the new system means that the average parts order takes seconds rather than five minutes, saving 15 700 person-minutes each day and more than £40 000 per year in telephone costs.
- While these types of mobile communication are relatively straightforward, the bank Kleinwort Benson's Channel Island division required something different. They have many high-net-worth clients that value 'personal home visits' from fiduciary managers, investment staff and client advisors. Although they need a central system that is flexible, it must also be global and secure. Their solution was to opt for a system from OpenHand that was more secure than BlackBerry PDAs; these carry risks from theft and data hacking, while OpenHand keeps information centrally and more secure, plus the e-mail function can operate with different network standards, so maintaining service standards globally.

So, many companies are going mobile to achieve differing ends, and it seems that mobile technology (devices, connectivity and manageability) is developing rapidly yet has already outstripped organisational ability, or willingness, to use it. Security is paramount, which leads to a question of management. This is a major consideration, since mobility changes the nature of organisations. Businesses should implement an effective wireless asset management (WAM) strategy and treat wireless assets like any other. However, management is also about people – managers and employees.

Mobility shows up bad management – the productive knowledge workers who thrive on mobile working practices will inevitably gravitate towards better managed, better mobilised companies. Dickensian management will be exposed and results-orientated management will be rewarded.

Pros and cons of e-collaborating

IBM and the Economist Intelligence Unit interviewed over 350 remote workers across Europe, and discovered that nearly half feel they lack access to what might be called corporate social capital – chatting over lunch and informal office networks. (When the author's firm were called in to do a staff audit of a business with high staff turnover, they discovered that the loss of a staff canteen in their smart new office building contributed to a feeling of isolation from the 'grapevine', yet all staff still populated one building, albeit distributed by department on selected floors of a massive eight-floor complex.)

People need informal collaboration to get ahead and to form relationships with colleagues. Workers can feel alienated and under-appreciated when working away from the office because of a lack of appropriate management support, technologies, skills and performance measurements necessary to work effectively and productively.

Mobile technology can assist with some of the problems of remote workers. Hi-fi telephony – which uses broadband technology to facilitate phone conversations in pin-sharp CD quality stereo – helps people connect more effectively, communicating emotionally and factually. At another level, some companies use instant messaging and video-conferencing to have virtual coffee breaks – regular times when mobile workers can meet online to exchange ideas and chat informally.

However, deeper cultural problems remain for managers. If employees think that what counts is 'presenteeism' – simply being seen to be at work – then they will grow more anxious about more remote working practices such that the improved work/life balance and improved productivity might not be realised. Conversely, if managers can learn to trust and empower employees to be more self-directing, relinquishing micro-management control over them – and be seen to do so – mobility can begin to reap rewards.

The technology for e-collaborating is the easy part – you probably have an office suite of software that allows one document to be amended by a group of people, storing a version that tracks each person's changes in a different colour. Bulletin boards have been around for a while: a series of e-mails, some with documents attached, are presented in a conversational structure where onlookers can add their own dialogue. They have their limits as they are not in real time (although useful across time zones) and they are passive, requiring an individual to seek out the board or they might miss something. At the other extreme is the Net meeting, where people are connected in real time; the dialogue can be text (confusingly called 'chat'), spoken voice or video link. Some Net meeting software offers shared white boards appearing on each collaborator's screen, and they can host other software. The ultimate is bespoke collaboration software, working in tandem with office suites to provide collaborative support in a unified environment.

For the future, a clear trend is an increasing ability to make electronic collaboration more like the real thing. This might involve, for example, small pictures of each group member when they are logged on (perhaps live video images), which can be clicked on to initiate a quick chat or dragged together to form informal meetings. A further enhancement is to make it easier to collaborate with the right people. Software could monitor your type of work to build a profile of the topics dealt with; then, when you need to collaborate with a specific resource, the system puts you in touch with the right person – and you control the profile that you want the system to track or advertise a specialism without identifying yourself to the person asking for help.

Whatever the technology, it is developing the right 'culture' that must take the top spot for managers to get right. See Box 21.4 for sources of collaboration browsing.

Electronic communities need to be voluntary rather than imposed. At ICL, the Fujitsu-owned British company, they major on their support for collaboration, with over

350 electronic communities within the organisation – groups using a dedicated part of the company's intranet, bulletin boards, shared documents and Net meeting groups. They provide a new community with the tools to add discussion forums, Net meetings and shared documents, and to manage intranet content; all this is pushed out to the communities themselves so that they take ownership. With the massive amount of information flowing, it would be a nightmare to manage centrally, so people have to be encouraged willingly to share knowledge.

In such environments, chatting needs to be encouraged; managers need to remove the initial suspicion, educating the organisation into realising that the exchange of information is an essential activity for a modern business.

When setting out to improve e-collaboration, take each stage in turn:

- Explore the capabilities of your office suite of software first.
- Then, without investing more, look to see what can be achieved from your intranet, from web discussion forums and from Net meetings.
- Once you have explored the pros and cons of your situation – as each business differs – approach collaboration vendors to get them to show you how and if they can add value for each level of extra expenditure (see Box 21.4 for some ideas).

Box 21.4: Sources for collaboration browsing – find more information through your favourite search engine

Office suites
Lotus – www.lotus.com
Microsoft – www.microsoft.com
WordPerfect – www.corel.com

Net meetings
Microsoft – www.microsoft.com
Netscape – www.netscape.com

Collaboration companies
eRoom – www.eroom.com
ICL – www.icl.com
Lotus – www.lotus.com

E-learning

On the back of increased efficiency and lower cost per learner, corporations are pursuing the installation of e-learning systems. Given that e-learning is a technology-driven solution, it is all too easy to assume that the solution lies in the technology. However, all too often, when learning systems have been installed they have had a negligible response. Imagine the classroom analogy – a major event is organised with a popular keynote speaker, all the visual aids and a fine lunch prepared, but no one turns up as you did no marketing. The high visibility of failure of instructor-led training (ILT) pushes marketing of the event to the fore; with technology-based training (TBT) it is often overlooked but perhaps needs to be more important.

The literature shows some successes – but these are for self-selecting, highly motivated people who are generally technologically aware. With a mixed ability organisation in the real world, the introduction of e-learning will involve not only telling people that it is there, but also how and why to use it. Successful e-learning systems involve organisations that invest heavily in the culture shift in perception, they take time and they involve people at all levels from the outset. It requires the top people getting face to face with people to let them know how important the change of approach is and what the individual and collective benefits are – and that message needs to be sustained. Managers need to 'talk the talk' *and* 'walk the walk'.

Classroom-based training is the traditional approach, bringing people together in an appropriate environment and allowing people to focus on their own learning, but it is limited by time and travelling in congested cities. E-learning, delivered to the desktop, has its attractions. Online tutoring and peer-group interaction, via e-mail and chat rooms or video-conferencing, may be the way forward but there are costs: online networks, courseware, and the cost of monitoring and evaluation. Some firms are literally taking to the road and delivering their training through e-learning from mobile vehicles that can add the people element that aims to achieve the all-important winning of hearts and minds of the learner. Tesco has used mobile training vehicles from PC Coaching to entice customers into seeing what e-commerce can do for them, aiming to increase the number of online shoppers. But it is not just the UK that is developing e-learning.

Norway has invested in a programme to improve the IT skills of 4 million people. Established by the 'The Competence Network of Norwegian Business and Industry', the instillation of the Saba e-learning infrastructure is the first time that a country has modelled the practices of successful global corporations to provide greater training and skills aimed at improving customer, partner, employee and supplier productivity. The system links employees throughout the country, providing flexibility, speed of delivery of training solutions and the ability to integrate multidiscipline learning applications – all on a platform that is accessible to all who desire, or require, training. More than 40 content providers have come together on the platform to offer training and re-education skills that will not only reduce the time-to-competency of Norway's workers, but also, it is hoped, reduce the amount that companies, governments and schools spend on training.

While the global corporate and government spend on learning is estimated to be more than $300 billion, it is growing – with more and more on e-learning. However, as most readers probably admit, when they have a problem with something they don't understand, they would still prefer to turn to a friendly face to help them out.

Flexible Working

Ten years ago it was predicted that by today the plc was going to be history, replaced by global chains of IT-enabled, flexible workers. If the 'firm' was the organising economic unit of the 20th century, the 'network' was to provide the economic architecture of the 21st. Yet it seems that in most areas of economic life we remain non-networked – glued to old-style organisations, big brands and standard jobs. While some capitalist dynamics have seen some major shake-ups, not least in finance itself, ordinary economic processes and social systems have not. The 'network economy' is a term that has been used to describe a range of separate issues such as 'globalisation', the impact of IT, corporate organisation and labour market change.

So why have traditional companies not lost out to networked economies? There are two reasons:

- Employees like to belong and feel part of a community. An organisation provides the solidarity that most people welcome – Maslow's sense of belonging. While they may not be as sexy, they are more secure.
- A company offers brand value that even a network of highly talented individuals cannot. No one ever got fired for buying IBM or hiring McKinsey. The brand from an established organisation provides security for cautious purchasers.

From an economic standpoint this leads to gross inefficiencies – consider advertising agencies. Big firms need big brands so they invest in grand offices, generous hospitality, sponsorship and so forth – all of which needs to be paid by the big-brand client in higher fees, yet no one will get fired for engaging a big agency. However, most creative people in advertising agencies don't like the large agency mentality so they go solo, but without the big agency name behind them they can struggle.

While IT has revolutionised capital markets, its potential to reconfigure the world of work remains almost entirely unrealised. We have not been turned into networked knowledge workers; many of the jobs created as a result of computer technology are less knowledge-based than pre-industrial farming – particularly in contemporary service jobs.

Empirically, the network economy is as much a mirage as the new economy. Networking offers us so much that the opportunity should not be ignored, but the difference between networking and not working is one vowel.

There are some high-profile organisations that have embraced networking with open arms. BT has 63 000 people in some form of flexible working and over 12 000 employees working from home. Legislation and concerns about logistics seem to worry managers – they see flexible working as just another problem rather than an option that can be a motivational, performance-enhancing and overhead cost-saving opportunity.

Of course, it would help if transport, industry, environment and educational officials worked together to create a framework that is good for the economy, good for the environment and reflects an increasingly integrated lifestyle – rather than penalise people for commuting at peak times, which deals with the symptom of congestion and not the cause. Workers are moving around too much because organisations enforce work patterns where everyone has to be there at the same time to get work done. Why struggle to get into work to e-mail the person next door or phone and leave a message to someone stuck in traffic?

In a recent report from the CBI, nearly one-half of organisations said that transport problems were having a detrimental impact on profitability, 40 per cent reported that their business growth was held back and 33 per cent said that transport problems were having a notable effect on investment in their business (*Professional Manager*, 2006). The survey reported that many organisations have tried to address the problems – 57 per cent have introduced more flexible working and nearly a half has altered delivery schedules or logistics. However, 93 per cent of employers and 86 per cent of staff believe that these measures alone cannot overcome the problems and extra transport infrastructure investment is necessary.

If everyone who went into an office to sit at a workstation and use their phone, e-mail and a PC worked remotely just one day a week it would reduce their commuting by 20 per cent at a stroke. While this approach would not work for manufacturing, plumbers or retailers, it would work for knowledge workers.

The benefits of flexible working include:

- Employee attraction and retention
- Employee motivation and loyalty
- Increased productivity
- Increased health benefits with reduced stress and a better work/life balance
- Reduction in cost and time commuting
- Reduced absenteeism
- Less office costs.

The business issues that need to be considered before adopting flexible working include:

- Impact on teamworking
- Communication issues
- Coordination of resources
- Employee disenfranchisement and loss of identity
- Fewer informal communications
- Resentment from employees not flexi-working
- Performance management.

On the issue of motivation, a recent report from the Chartered Management Institute suggests there is a link between adopting modern work patterns, business performance and motivating employees (see www.managers.org.uk). The study found that one-half of organisations that were growing and dynamic offered facilities for regular flexible working, while only 36 per cent of the declining organisations offer it. The study also found that options for flexible working were one of the top 10 factors that influenced managers to join their current employer. Respondents indicated that they could cope with the long working hours culture if they had some flexibility about when and where they put in the hours. Box 21.5 summarises some ideas for introducing flexible working.

Managers need to ensure that staff have the appropriate information to do their job, as many flexible workers cite isolation and lagging behind others as the biggest drawbacks to doing their job properly. Managers need good communication, trust and sound objective setting as the key skills to manage flexible workers; they also need greater than usual skills in motivating, ability development and confidence building, along with good planning and team-building skills. Managers therefore need to manage much more by outputs and results, rather than by inputs and the time people put in. Organisations need to look to the training and coaching given to managers to build their skills in these areas for flexible working to reap its potential benefits.

Box 21.5: Key thoughts when introducing flexible working

- *Look for mutual gain.* There could be gains for the organisation in terms of opportunity to broaden customer access to the service by longer opening, cover over lunchtimes, even easier access to the staff car park, better morale and better recruitment and retention; there are many benefits for staff, including a better life/work balance, easier commuting and a greater sense of ownership of their job.
- *Keep flexible.* Every organisation and all staff are different, so start by finding out what staff want and how the organisation might meet those needs – parents might want time off in holidays, single people may prefer later hours or a sabbatical for travelling.
- *Set clear guidelines.* Avoid resistance through line managers being unclear about what is possible. Consider flexitime, annualised hours, a compressed working week, job-sharing options or term-time working, and ensure managers apply the options objectively and consistently.
- *Plan flexibility.* In customer-facing jobs shifts must be covered, but in an office environment, managers need to plan ahead and ask for staff to play their part of the deal by being responsible in keeping to agreed arrangements.

(Continued)

Box 21.5: Continued

- *Think outside of the box.* Use flexible working as an opportunity to review current working practices. While this can uncover jobs that suit flexible working, if their job does not easily lend itself to flexible working consider moving someone (rather than sidelining them).
- *Take legal advice.* There is a raft of legislation, including the Employment Act, that you need to make sure you comply with; sound legal advice is good security against problems.
- *Walk before running.* Start with small groups as a 'test' rather than convert the whole organisation; use them as role models and iron out any glitches. Make sure that there are no 'favourites' and keep people informed about trials.
- *Measure the outputs.* Monitor key areas such as absenteeism, morale, staff turnover and key performance indicators to establish a case for flexible working, looking for a sound cost/benefit case.

Working from Home

There are already 8 million people working from home and a further 2 million working from home at least one day a week (report by Standard Life, 2006). It is expected that this figure will rise to 12 million by 2020 with 'demuting' as a significant trend. However, not all organisations have adopted the practice, with one-third of employers reported as not making any provision for home working (Workplace Survey, 2003 – see www.managers.org.uk).

While one can work very well at home without interruptions, less gossip, and no time-consuming and energy-draining commute, the human instinct is to form teams and stick with like-minded others. We did it at school; we do it as adults at work; 'day-bugs' were frowned upon as an inferior species by boarders – even if we consistently won the inter-house competition. Working from home means that people miss out on the all-important informal information networks.

Moreover, many homes have children or animals, sometimes both, and they don't mix well with the committed home worker. Finding a truly comfortable space separate from your daily life can be a big problem – sat in the third bedroom on your own all day is maybe not quite what you had in mind! If it is not soundproofed, it means it's the garden shed for you. Don't be too dismayed, you'll be in the good company of George Bernard Shaw, Roald Dahl and Daphne du Maurier – they all worked in a shed. And don't answer the front door. This is not so much a security issue but it is so easy to get distracted by double-glazing salespeople, political and market research canvassers, delivery drivers wanting you to take something because your neighbours are 'at work', charity collectors, relatives and friends 'just passing', and meter readers. Then there is the temptation to sort the garden/garage/house before settling down to a coffee and biscuits – then there is the kitchen to clear, put on some washing, feed the cat – and now it is time to collect the children.

From a management perspective, there are two crucial issues:

- Measurement – are they actually working?
- The usefulness of technology – who is it best suited for?

When it comes to home workers, not all jobs are the same. At the fundamental level are 'white-collar', process-driven activities like call-centre operatives. Here it is about software-driven processes undertaken over the Internet. Wherever your people are (Aberdeen or Andover, London or Lahore), these people do easily managed activities; the technology to quantify what they do is straightforward.

At the other end of the spectrum you have highly motivated knowledge workers who adapt well to the technology and prefer to be measured by results (outputs) rather than do work that can be realistically measured on a daily basis. Measurement of daily activity is a moot point – when did you last look over the shoulder of a talented web designer or copywriter?

For the middle group, it is more difficult. Unusually, they need more supervision as their work is neither routine nor project based and their problems will probably be more complex to manage. Add to this that everyone is their own systems administrator – they have to save and back up their own work, be their own security, and deal with many everyday system problems; someone cannot come running along the corridor to sort a defunct mouse!

However, the technology is getting better. At the author's consultancy we have virtual IT support from someone who can navigate the LAN, sort technical problems and 'see' what the people are doing to sort technical problems. We have software to manage collaborative projects with Associates and can engage talented people wherever they are to provide creative and competitive solutions to client problems.

There are a few things worth reminding prospective or current home workers. They need to call up a greater degree of self-management and discipline than comparable people in the workplace. They have to compartmentalise their working time and place to keep the two separate. Many home workers actually put in more hours than their workplace colleagues – upsetting their work/life balance when they took flexible home working to help deal with an imbalance. When a home worker spends 10 hours a day in the company of their PC and e-mails, in time they may not have the rich fund of stories with which to entertain friends.

For the employer, most want creative, problem-solving team players; while solitary confinement may boost the balance sheet, it is probably not the best answer. Moreover, many firms have dress-down workdays; few people have the acting skills to remain professional when dressed in a kimono!

Top 10 tips for home working can be found in Box 21.6.

Box 21.6: Top 10 tips when working from home

- *Get the right tools*. This means computing with broadband, printing and facsimile – and a telephone line separate from the domestic line.
- *Get the right space*. Separate home and work as much as possible physically and set times for work and play.
- *Keep in touch*. Make sure that the office knows that you are there; also, keep in touch with chat and gossip as much as possible; informal networks are crucial.
- *Develop a routine*. Develop a structure for the day and make sure your partner and/or family respect the fact that you are working and don't take advantage of you being around.
- *Identify black holes*. Analyse your time and work out where you waste time, then eliminate that black time from your day.
- *Get others to buy in*. Make sure friends and family know that you being at home does not mean that you are available for a chat or chores.
- *Beware the guilt trips*. While you can take advantage of some flexibility, don't beat yourself up over taking time off provided you are achieving the outputs you need to achieve.
- *Develop allegiances*. Seek out others who are also home workers to learn from them and gain a sense of identity; they are a valuable source of moral support and problem solving.
- *Don't let it fester*. If you feel that there is a problem with head office, get on to it immediately – clarify it and stop the problem escalating. Perhaps organise a face-to-face meeting if you don't have access to video-conferencing tools.
- *Spread the word*. Become an advocate of home working both within your organisation and outside; the more people do it, the more you will become the 'norm'.

Managing virtual teams

How do managers build and maintain virtual teams of people that they don't see every day and how does this differ from face-to-face working?

Of course, managing 'virtual' people is nothing new. Any national sales manager will have had experience of managing groups of people necessarily spread across the country, whether the people themselves worked at a remote site – like a network of restaurants – or a team of people making sales calls in a geographical region. Managing overseas operations is similar, save for differing distances, possibly time zones and frequently languages. However, today, as we have seen, there are many more people working from home, often on their own, with no particular need to go out and make personal calls on customers or suppliers or travel into a place of work where they regularly meet others. It is managing these people that will be our focus.

As with any communication, the media and the message are the crucial dimensions to explore. Those that have been effective face to face cannot assume that they will be effective in a virtual environment. It is essential that the leader establishes and maintains 'influence' in the group, yet must remember that 'power-playing' will have little or no value in virtual teams – it may be severely damaging.

Three 'rules' for managing virtual teams can be found in Box 21.7.

Media

Managers' first need to understand the media employed to communicate with their people and recognise patterns of usage. Some media allow communications in 'real time' – that is, 'live' (such as the telephone) – allowing a richness of content. Others such as e-mail and an intranet have a time delay – as does an SMS communication to a mobile device (phones, etc.). A manager needs to decide which is best for a given purpose given the time zone and any organisational boundaries.

When people have time to consider their response without the immediacy of 'live' communications, there is opportunity to develop clarity and richness in the message. This will be particularly useful in managing cross-cultural groups, where team members are using a common language that may not be their 'mother tongue'. Conversely, those methods that require immediate 'real-time' interactions do speed up dialogue and can shift delays. Remember, using a conference call or a video-conference, with software that can facilitate immediate data transfer, can achieve rapid consensus on critical decisions.

One of the obvious differences in virtual working that computer-based media facilitates is that the team member can literally disengage from the technology without the leader or the other team members knowing immediately.

Message

With the nuances of the media, leaders need to consider their messages carefully, so that a mutual trust is developed between the parties. To this end, managers need to try to capture, in virtual working, the 'social' nature of the organisation. This does not mean sending jokes around or inviting people to play virtual games. Managers need to find ways to stimulate relationships online and develop mutual understanding.

Box 21.7: Three 'rules' for managing virtual teams

1. Make sure that you invest time into 'building' the team through online socialising – there is a human behind the message.
2. Online leadership requires a careful consideration of the media and the message – aim to be more of a coach rather than dominate all the time.
3. Your leadership authority will be different online – work to establish trust and mutual respect for all.

Virtual working has the advantage of being largely free of race, age and gender disadvantages. Thus, the leader – whether imposed or elected – needs to minimise explicit directive behaviours, since any hierarchies can fade online. Looking at the three Development Models in the MAC Factors (Motivation in Chapter 9, Ability in Chapter 14 and Confidence in Chapter 19), one can see that with a virtual team, a manager needs to have a lower task control orientation in any of the three key factors. A leader will find more success in a democratic approach of shared control and consensual decision-taking, particularly in the early stages of a new virtual project group.

The leader's role in this situation is more subtle; the 'conversation' (either in real time or delayed) is more subtle, focused on the business processes and allowing 'buy-in' to ideas to achieve a solution rather than direction on what to do. Hence, the effective virtual leader adopts the role and style of a coach – in this way helping the group establish clear procedures and goals, modelling desired behaviours and actions, and asking appropriate questions – just as we saw in the 'Level 3' styles of each of the three Development Models.

Disengagement

As the virtual environment gives the leader little early warning of people withdrawing temporarily or completely from the group, it requires clearer and more structured processes with clear roles and a careful consideration of the communication technologies and patterns of use than with face-to-face environments. Also, managers need to consider how to maintain business processes, decision-taking and the progress towards objectives if the technology should fail.

As with a face-to-face group, a clear set of objectives needs to be agreed by each individual; a clear set of working protocols, and clear individual tasks and responsibilities, will all assist the virtual team. However, in some more complex virtual working environments, to reach a clear summary the leader may need to interlace the communication threads and develop a consensus, ensuring that any patterns, interpretations and conflicts are resolved to ensure agreement. While interpreting an individual's contributions may not seem to be a new task, dealing with online 'silence' must be dealt with, requiring subtlety and emotional intelligence.

When there is mild conflict in face-to-face situations, appropriate humour and irony may help to resolve the problem – these may lead to quite the opposite in a virtual environment; deepening misunderstanding and resentment may develop, leading to more disengagement. Thus, decisions are likely to be delayed, buy-in may not be unanimous, and frustration can prompt ill-considered reaction from leaders and team members. The manager needs more patience; critical paths need to reflect the nuances and decision-making may need to wait for a face-to-face opportunity.

Good news is acceptable online, bad news is not – especially when delivered to a mobile phone – which is not secure anyway!

Working Part-time

So, someone in your department asks you if they can go part-time. How should you respond? Clearly, if you ignore the request, you'll be inviting trouble. The individual may leave – if that is what you wanted, all to the good? Maybe not! After all, before they leave they are a major source of discontent and that dissatisfaction can spread. If they do leave you'll have to accept that their knowledge and know-how leaves along with their contacts, plus you will have the cost and effort of hiring a replacement – and the stress on those (probably mostly you) who 'cover' key tasks until a replacement is found.

One of the first steps will be to enquire gently why they are aiming to go part-time. Child and parent care are two obvious examples, but think about those who are aiming for extended study periods. While child/parent care may be lower on your list of good reasons to accept a case for part-time working, a high proportion of those who study an MBA leave their companies within 18 months of completing a qualification.

While you may be able to sympathise with a person's need for a better work/life balance, you probably have your needs too. Naturally, one might view with suspicion those who want to start their own business to supplement their income or those who just want more time for themselves – their loyalty might be in question.

Ask them what is in it for the organisation? Your primary concerns will be logistical: how does the person aim to achieve in four days or fewer what they did in five? If they will not be able to do it all, who can? You might have to consider if there are others with spare capacity who can handle additional tasks and responsibilities. Get them involved in thinking through the departmental impact and make a robust case before deciding – they might come up with some surprises to assist your decision; if they can't, it softens your refusal.

Naturally, many roles do not lend themselves to part-time working, particularly daily customer-facing functions – that is, unless there is someone to provide competent support or a job-share scheme.

There are some head-of-department roles that can be successfully handled in fewer than five days a week. Mia Kennedy, the strategic planning director of AMV BBDO, the UK's largest advertising agency, was able to move to a three-day week after the birth of her first child. It required a highly organised approach and a really efficient PA, ensuring that she was involved in the important things where she could add most value, but delegating other areas where her direct involvement was not vital. It required good 'lieutenants' who needed support in developing their management skills. Obviously, she needed to be very diligent and make the most of the time she was in the office, and used travel time for business reading to keep up to date and a PDA BlackBerry to manage her electronic communications.

When it comes to your staff, as with any negotiation, work out what they want and what they are willing to trade with their employer. What concessions are they willing to concede and what value are they to the organisation. For example, are they willing to take a salary *pro-rata* as the savings may be helpful? Would they be willing to trial it for, say, three months, with an objective review? Do be careful not to use the ultimate sanction and 'let them go', as they might have a case for unfair dismissal (see Mackay, 2006).

Interim Working

For many looking for long-term security, flexible working and a choice of assignments, they turn their backs on a permanent job and become an interim manager. Here, the person gets involved in specific projects on behalf of a client organisation with defined parameters and deliverables. Some assignments still entail long hours and often nights away from home, but the option of taking time out between clients more than compensates for any negatives.

The author, having been made redundant three times in six years in the 1980s/1990s, confirmed that companies often do not take a caring, paternalistic attitude – one just accepts the financial reality of the global marketplace, where companies have to flex to meet rising or falling demand. With thousands of final pension salary schemes being shut down, more and more employees realise that they have to put 'number one' first. Moreover, the transition into interim work is easier for managers in the mid-2000s because they are already working in bite-sized chunks on a project basis, often with different teams of colleagues.

As one interim manager commented (*Professional Manager*, 2004):

> *I am not tempted by the money; it is wonderful being free to express my views to clients without fear – as an outsider I have no axe to grind, there is relatively little stress, no psychological contract, you have objectivity and no baggage.*

Research by human resources consulting firm Chiumento (*Professional Manager*, 2004) among interim managers found that 17 per cent chose that route seeking a better work/life balance (see later in this chapter).

The current trend is for client firms not to consider individuals under 35 years old, as they tend to be viewed by some as interim people and not interim managers. The Institute of Interim Managers (IIM; see www.ioim.org.uk and www.interimmanagement.uk.com) has seen an increase in younger members in their mid thirties and forties in recent years – that category making up nearly one-quarter of their membership. It needs to be recognised that there will be periods of feast and famine; one cannot expect assignments to appear when wanted and, like buses, several may come along at once. This can put pressure on the financial front and the uncertainty can put a strain on personal relationships at home. However, there has been an increase in younger women entering the interim market and they can be particularly good at it – they tend to be more focused than men on the challenge of the role itself, rather than the status of a title or climbing the corporate ladder.

People embarking on interim management need to recognise that it requires considerable self-discipline to put in the marketing effort during 'rest' periods. The interim manager needs to keep in touch with their clients, set themselves targets and take the time to invest in themselves.

Family Fortunes

In a study sponsored by nine investment banks, Shell and the Metropolitan Police (*The Daily Telegraph*, 2005), it was found that most female bosses (about 70 per cent) think that women's need to balance work and family is a barrier to career progression, while most male managers (more than half) disagree. This suggests that female managers are more downbeat than their male colleagues about the obstacles to equality that exist at work.

Women managers are more critical of the behaviour of senior leaders in relation to equality and are less convinced of their commitment to the ethos. Other studies have shown that many managers consider maternity leave to be a 'serious risk' for their business – particularly small to medium-sized enterprises. Given the UK government's Parental Rights Bill extends maternity rights from six to nine and ultimately 12 months leave, the concerns of business managers deepen. Moreover, the then Trade Secretary unveiled plans to allow mothers to transfer 'spare' maternity rights to the child's father if she chose to return to work within the year (Work and Families Bill, 19 October 2005). Clearly, with many parents working for different organisations, dividing the allowance between them would be complex and potentially unenforceable. While such measures are welcome as they raise the profile of 'family-friendly' approaches to management in organisations, there are costs both to organisations and taxation – and there are concerns in other quarters too.

Employers need to make sure that they not only cover staff on maternity or paternity leave, but also that they are aware of and respect employees' legal rights. In Britain in 2003, some £4.3 million was awarded by employment tribunals, which grew to £6.2 million in 2004.

Children

While the combination of tax breaks, tax credits, higher child benefit and free pre-school education, expanded maternity, paternity and parental leave is good for parents, is it best for children? Some 'tough' questions raised by Richard Reeves (2005), writing in *Management Today*, included:

- How do we really want children to be raised – by their parents or by professional and semi-professional childcare workers?
- Why should parents – especially affluent ones – receive tax handouts partially paid for by the childless?

- What are the real costs to business and national competitiveness of high levels of support by parents?
- Are we all prepared to pay for it?

He went on to argue that children's needs are best served by parents as a first resort, yet official attitudes seem to favour dawn-to-dusk childcare based around schools. Rather than restructure working lives or the labour market to meet the needs of children, he feels that children's pattern of life is altered. While expected to adapt to the needs of the market economy when still in short trousers, far from adopting a family-friendly economy it seems we are adapting economy-friendly families. Surely the gains of a stable, loving start for our children is worth the costs – even, dare one suggest, a degree of personal sacrifice – otherwise, we will have lost the right to consider ourselves a civilised society.

Pensions

Perhaps children of today need to be brought into 'economic line' as early as possible, since it is suggested that a child born today is likely to live to 100 and will need to be 'in work' for more than 40 or so years to support such longevity – and staying in one organisation will be almost unheard of. In the past, retirement funds were expected to provide for individuals a few years into retirement. The contributions from the unfortunates that died a couple of years after retiring provided for the others that survived. Equally, it is predicted over the next decade that there will be 0.8 million less 16- to 34-year-olds in work making National Insurance Contributions.

Some interesting, and worrying, statistics emerged from The Prudential:

- A quarter of people between 55 and 64 feel they cannot retire at 60 (women) or 65 (men) because they do not have a big enough pension or sufficient savings.
- A third of women think they will have to work beyond the state pension age.
- More than a million people are currently working beyond the state pension age.
- By 2015, 2.5 million people are predicted to be working beyond the state retirement age.

With Britain's pension industry's £130 billion shortfall, it can only be filled by increasing the retirement age and giving better tax breaks to people who save for private schemes (*Evening Standard*, 2005). Most firms believe that it will take more than a decade to repair the damage to pension funds caused by the abolition of tax breaks and poor stock market performance.

Older workers

A labour market report published by the Department of Work and Pensions and the Office for National Statistics (see www.statistics.gov.uk/focuson/olderpeople, accessed March 2006) revealed that one in five 'older workers' over 50 is self-employed, compared to only 14 per cent of people aged 25–49. The report showed that the employment rates of men and women aged between 50 and state pension age in Great Britain were 72 and 68 per cent respectively in Spring 2004, compared with 64 and 60 per cent in 1994.

With an ageing workforce, there needs to be a culture shift in how managers and employees view 'older people' generally – particularly in as far as it affects the organisation and the contribution these people make to the workplace. Naturally, many will be looking for part-time work and they may be more flexible than employees with young children.

For all employees throughout their working lives – and the older person today – retraining will be mandatory to maintain employability; tomorrow's worker may have more than one 'career' and will work for many more organisations. Career breaks to raise children will be less 'damaging' as new careers in middle age with mature students in further education become more commonplace. Older workers will have much to give, whether in commerce, industry, social services or charities.

Self-*motivation*, lifelong learning enhancing *ability* and developing the *confidence* to face the challenges of new technology and changing working practices will be necessary to provide financial security, maintain intellectual capacity and physical well-being into the latter parts of a century lifespan.

Incapacity benefit

One problem that has to be addressed is that far too many families – 2.7 million British claimants – have become dependent on incapacity benefits. A green paper (January 2006) disclosed that the sick and disabled could be paid about £20 a week less than at present unless they took advantage of a £360 million package of help, advice and rehabilitation.

But why have so many people fallen into a poverty trap? Why do they prefer a mix of benefit and black economy to the little-respected dignity or low-paid straight (i.e. taxable) work? It has been suggested that, much of the time, people stay on benefits even though they have sporadic work because they need security as well as money (Orr, 2006), not just because staying on or around the poverty line is predictable.

Unfortunately, many of the services available are not as attractive as they might be for getting people back to work.

- Job Centres, for example, tend to get the least attractive jobs as they have a reputation for attracting the least dynamic job seekers.
- An out-of-work person inspired by a 'small business advisor' will have to provide financial resources for the assistance before claiming reimbursement from the state against receipts.
- Do banks lend generously to the long-term unemployed?

Box 21.8: The real benefits of being in work

1. *Structure and purpose.* Our education system develops a sense of a 'nine-to-five, five days a week' working culture. Work continues to provide a shape to the day, the week and the month, while being out of work leaves the person with poor time management and extended, restless sleep patterns.

2. *Man is a complex, social animal.* Work provides an expanded friendship network, colleagues providing a source of support and interest, conversation and shared feelings. Home workers miss it, the unemployed can't find it – they are left feeling isolated, forgotten and friendless.

3. *Social identity.* For men especially, you are what you do, which explains all the fuss over job titles. Many people define themselves in terms of the exact job they do and who they work for – being on benefit may have lost its stigma but it implies another loss.

4. *Sense of achievement.* Work often channels our skills and talents; the most satisfied at work are artists, potters and gardeners, because so much of them is in their work.

5. *Physical and mental agility.* Research shows that maintaining both wards off disease, both physical and mental; being on benefit is not stimulating.

(After Adrian Furnham, Professor of Psychology at University College London)

Sadly, one-third of new claimants on incapacity benefits claim depression; recovering depressives cannot be pushed too hard, too fast. Life can be very hard for many people, they become wounded and damaged, and need understanding from compassionate managers. Box 21.8 summarises the real benefits of being in work but remember: there are good jobs and bad ones. Badly paid, antisocial, low-status, menial labour is unlikely to provide many benefits – it may be that many people on incapacity benefit today were in this type of employment.

The Future for Women in Work

While the chapter on women returning to work in Mackay (2007) looked at organisations making provision for today's returners, what of tomorrow? There are a number of issues affecting the future of women in work.

Many of the jobs that women do now, in shops and offices for example, will either not be there or will have changed out of all recognition in the coming years. Just look at the current increased popularity of shopping online, the growth of technology in the workplace and the outsourcing of key skills overseas. Organisations need to address how best to anticipate and prepare for this situation. Moreover, there are clear indications that there are fewer jobs in women's traditional work areas such as clerical/secretarial work and sales assistants, yet an increase in managerial and professional levels. Women need to become aware of where new opportunities lie, so that they can build on their existing skills during any break in employment to give them the best chance of making a valuable contribution to the workplace on their return.

We have seen statistics showing that women are having their children at a later age, so it follows that they will be returning to work older – yet with more years of earlier experience. Organisations need to harness this experience and counter issues of women returning and ageism.

While this chapter has reviewed the changing and increasing variety of work arrangements, particularly in the 'knowledge' and service sectors, how do businesses and women's organisations ensure that women do not have a disproportionate share of the less well paid and less secure part of a two-tier workforce?

There is a need to build 'return to work' strategies and advice into future educational programmes for mature women students – and to make them available to all women, irrespective of ethnicity, before a course starts so that they have the best informed choice before enrolment.

The pattern for the majority of people over their longer working lives will become more fragmented – episodes of work interspersed with breaks for caring responsibilities, education and so on are forecast to become the norm. In these circumstances, it will be even more difficult for employers to justify the disparity in pay between the genders. At the same time, a competency approach is moving towards pay and rewards for achievement in place of time served; this means that all organisations' pay strategies really must reflect fair pay for work done.

With such widespread changes in working practices, being a 'returner' will become less exceptional; this means that organisations need to consider how 'exit', 'keeping in touch', 'training and modernisation of skills', as well as 're-entry' processes are made widely available to all returners, irrespective of gender.

Since women are well placed to benefit from the structural changes taking place in the world of work, have particular lifestyle needs, are more comfortable with variety and are generally less committed to positions of 'status' at work, organisations must be ready to make changes to their employment policies and practices to capitalise on the benefits that women offer.

Work/Life Balance

In March 2000, the Prime Minister launched the government's Work/Life Balance campaign. Its purpose was to 'help parents balance their work and family responsibilities' and its solutions included 'the reform of the ways in which the tax and benefit system supports families with children and those on a low income'. It was therefore a 'work/*family* life' balance campaign. Much of this chapter has addressed some of the issues that enable the policy to work and considered some of the concerns – but what of those working people who don't have children or whose children have 'flown the nest'? Should not organisations consider them? Are they not also allowed a work/*personal* life balance or don't they want one?

The newspapers and management journals are full of stories about working hours getting longer, difficulties in commuting adding to the hours, job security being non-existent, targets getting tougher, we are all teetering on that work/life balance, just managing to save ourselves from plunging into divorce, alcoholism, impotence and financial ruin if we don't 'keep our noses to the corporate grindstone'.

Sadly, it is not quite as it seems and we need to 'wake up and smell the coffee' on this one. A 2004 Web@work survey revealed that over 50 per cent of US workers spend between one and five hours online each day for personal reasons. In one month in 2002, 7.9 million workplace Internet users viewed online dating sites. Also in the USA, 35.2 per cent of the workforce received more than five personal e-mails a day and 10.3 per cent received over 20.

In the UK, some employees' Internet use is limited by their ability to get into work: two-thirds of UK young professionals admitted in one survey that they had called in sick due to hangovers at least once in the preceding month. In another study, it was discovered that 9 million 'questionable' or 'suspicious' requests for sick notes are made each year to UK doctors – 9 million represents one-third of the UK workforce! When it comes to a 'sickie', Monday and Friday are the most popular (23 and 25 per cent respectively), while Wednesdays only account for 8 per cent – it must be severe toxicity from being at home. There are many thousands of chat rooms, web logs and sites on the Internet set up specifically for the millions of people that spend hours not working at work (Bolchover, 2005).

So why don't people admit their poor 'work/life balance' is largely of their own making? Most employees are in mass denial:

- We have bored junior staff pretending to all around them that they are occupied and motivated for fear of losing their jobs.
- Middle managers are too busy forming political alliances with those in power above them to worry too much about their underlings.
- Senior managers are blissfully unaware of the grassroots disquiet, surrounded by yes-men (but fewer yes-women), their heads swelled by the advances of ambitious middle managers and filled with the latest management text drivel about how easy it is to get to the top.

As Sir Winston Churchill observed: 'Men occasionally stumble over the truth, but most of them pick themselves up and hurry off as if nothing has happened.'

Perhaps we should seek the truth and look at it a while! One truth is that there are many sad cases of 'presenteeism' in the workplace, but with Blackberry and Palmtops on the beach we now also have 'virtual presenteeism'.

The sad fact is that, despite the suggestion that people are at work far too long – and perhaps the fact that British workers spend more time at work than any other European counterpart yet their productivity is not the highest suggests that they may have a point – people do 'work' long hours. At least, they are 'at work' for a long time. In the same study mentioned earlier in the chapter, it was found that one in five managers were working for more than 60 hours a week. The report recommended that companies 'identify role models for work/life balance'. In particular, firms should consider a 'mentor-buddying scheme' for those wanting to change their working patterns to 'guide them through making a business case and negotiating with their manager, and providing them with work advice about how to make a new work schedule work for them and their team'.

Achieving the balance

It may be that you are quite happy working 15 hours a day, five or six days a week. But remember all those clichés – very few people on their deathbed wished they had spent more time in the office. If you really feel that no other aspect of your life is suffering because of your work, you have probably got your work/life balance right.

But if, like most of us, you sometimes feel torn between finding time for your business and the other things – and people – that are important to you, then your work/life balance is something you need to work on. This is particularly true if you feel that some areas of your life are actually suffering because of your working hours.

Ask yourself the following questions. Do you:

- Feel stressed most of the time?
- Find it difficult to delegate work tasks to others?
- Feel guilty about not being able to 'do it all' – even when you know your expectations of yourself are unreasonable?
- Find it difficult to 'switch off' from work?
- Feel that your relationships with your family/friends are suffering because of the time you spend working?
- Find it difficult or impossible to fit leisure activities into your schedule?

If you have answered 'yes' to any of these, you need to start thinking about improving your work/life balance. Perhaps use your diary and record those other non-work activities that you have undertaken; then, after a month, review your activity and work out what proportion of time you have had for the other things in life – like family, friends, exercise, hobbies, yourself. Then you will be better able to decide what areas you need to change.

If you own your own business, the idea of completely changing the way you work can seem impossible. Instead, to improve your work/life balance, try focusing on specific areas and improving them, one at a time. Aim towards:

- Recognising your own limitations. You have to understand that you can't do everything perfectly and that the in-tray will never be completely empty – adjust your expectations accordingly.
- Doing that which makes most money first, then meet your legal obligations – question the need to do the rest.
- Separating work and home – e.g. not taking your work home with you, leaving work by a certain time, not working weekends.
- Scheduling and taking holidays.
- Taking commitments to family and friends seriously.
- Delegating work – hiring the right people, developing them and managing them appropriately.
- Learning time and stress management techniques.
- Setting aside 'me' time – this is time for you and you alone.

Box 21.9 has some further suggestions on how to gain a better work/life balance but still manage your career upwards.

Box 21.9: Top 10 tips for managing a career and getting a work/life balance

- *Blur the boundaries.* Make work part of your life rather than a separate entity.
- *Manage expectations.* If you are going to be working late, be honest and let people know in advance, then aim for payback.
- *Keep a clear head.* Make a 'to-achieve' list before you leave work and leave it there. Then think ahead towards your destination.
- *Show your humanity.* Show other people in each part of your life that you have another side; 'take five' and share your day and experiences, then move on – you don't want to be a bore.
- *Set challenging goals.* You have these at work, so why not set a personal challenge that motivates you? Learn to play the piano or run a marathon – and get in to it.
- *Talent transfer.* Use your skills in one area of work to enrich another. Good at organising – organise your son's rugby tour. You can write reports – do one for your residents' association.
- *Get focused.* Charming people have time for others; copy them and get the same reputation. At work, focus on your staff, not the weekend dinner party; at home, focus on your partner, not the sales meeting.

- *Set a reasonable pace.* Busy times need your full effort for best effect, but schedule time to recharge the batteries; aim to smooth the flow.
- *Call time-out.* A change is a good as a rest, so schedule something out of work and rethink what and who is really important to you.
- *Share goals.* Look at what you want to achieve and how well you are doing; use the guide in the chapters on self-esteem and achievement.

Work/life balance and your staff

Staff who do not take their leave can also be vulnerable to burnout, and lack of holiday can cause low morale and resentment. Therefore, it makes sense to encourage staff to use their holiday entitlement as well as take any other statutory leave they may have. Only allow weekend working for special circumstances when there are particularly important projects in progress or you are in seasonally busy periods, and always make sure 'time off in lieu' is taken. Provided you have an efficient system of planning for leave, this should not cause your business any major problems.

Good practice will include:

- Reminding staff to take their leave. Do not let it stack up at the end of the year and discourage people from carrying over leave from one year into the next unless they have planned something special, like extended travel, honeymoon, study leave, etc.
- Keeping a holiday diary for staff to enter their leave dates in so that everyone can see when people are away.
- Encouraging staff to book their leave as far in advance as possible.
- If your company is very small, don't allow more than one person to be away at once.

Work with Meaning

In a recent survey by Roffey Park (*Management Today*, 2004), it was found that 70 per cent of managers are looking for more meaning in their working lives. The history of mankind has always been about the search of some answer to the meaning to life – *Hitchhikers Guide to the Galaxy* enthusiasts know the answer is 42 – but today we are looking for 'meaning' in the workplace. The Roffey Park annual 'Management Agenda' survey has been running since 1996, but recent results show that there has been a trend of growing disillusionment at work and a desire to be doing something more meaningful.

While over two-thirds are looking for more meaning, a startling 42 per cent of respondents said that they would be looking to change jobs in the following 12 months. Eighty per cent said that it was personally important to them that their companies are environmentally and socially responsible, yet more than half (52 per cent) are sceptical about their company's value statements. Not surprisingly, 39 per cent say that they experience tension between the 'spiritual' aspect of their values and their daily work.

So, what does it mean – 'meaning' in work? Different people have different definitions: for some it is about personal values and ideals, for others it is spiritual beliefs or personal fulfilment.

When MI5 advertised for new recruits in 2004 – on a starting salary of just £20 000 – thousands of higher paid people applied. Perhaps they wanted to do something for the UK rather than just work for a fat pay-cheque. The Joseph Rowntree Foundation research backs this up; they described 'Generation X' as depressed. Other research identified 'TIREDs' – Thirty-something, Independent, Radical, Educated Dropouts – people with good prospects leaving their high-flying jobs to do something more meaningful with their lives. Meanwhile, Voluntary Service Overseas (VSO) regularly targets its recruitment programmes at Britain's managers – fertile ground for new helpers.

So, what prompted the introspection and feelings that a good job with prospects and a stable salary couldn't satisfy our deeper needs? Is it that we spend so much of our waking time involved with getting to and from as well as at work? Roffey Park research showed that 83 per cent of managers work longer than their contracted hours, leaving less time for other pursuits that might offer a sense of meaning, whether that is more time with home and family, doing volunteer work, travelling or learning a new skill.

A 45-year-old today is around one-half of their way through their working life – why spend the second half doing something meaningless? Given the time and duration of work, it is hardly surprising that 'work' is so central to our lives. It provides a sense of community and identity; we expect to make friends and meet partners there. Yet previous generations worked long hours, often in monotonous jobs in unpleasant conditions, and fully expected a shorter retirement. So, are we better off and just don't see it or are we more demanding?

Frank Furedi, Professor of Psychology at Kent University and author of *Therapy Culture*, concluded that higher expectations are crucial – we expect work to be more than just work. People have always tried to find meaning in work, which is understandable, but work cannot always meet all our needs. The media provides a steady diet of people actively changing their lives, whether that is building properties aboard, travelling round the world on a motorcycle, switching jobs (even wives!) or downshifting.

Couple that rising expectation of life's meaning, the time commitment people give to their work, with the sad fact that companies are generally not treating their people that much better and we have a nation of cynical 'Dilberts' counting the hours until they can go home.

There are a number of employer practices that can exacerbate a sense of meaningless in work:

- Demanding longer hours
- Increased demands leading to stress
- Lack of appreciation for individual effort
- Relentless focus on shareholders

- Managers that do not do what they say they will (walk the talk)
- A lack of adherence to stated organisational values – such as corporate social responsibility
- Mismanagement of change.

Such practices lead to employee cynicism, particularly following the Enron and WorldCom scandals and evidence of widespread fat-cattery. The Roffey Park research found that nearly one-half of managers say these events have made them more cynical, while one-quarter have lost trust in corporate leaders.

There is a strong business case for helping staff find meaning in their work. Companies can benefit by:

- Change management being more successful
- Retaining staff better
- Having greater staff engagement
- Improved employee performance
- More productive workforce
- Greater creativity
- More commitment.

So, what are the activities that companies can do to engender a sense of meaning? These include:

- A strong customer focus – as opposed to shareholders
- A clear role for individuals
- Flexible working practices
- Recognition by managers of work well done
- Giving employees room to develop and grow in the company
- Paying more than lip service to company values.

Companies that manage change effectively and have 'clarity of purpose' provide employees with a greater sense of meaning. Companies where employees feel a sense of belonging can also have a positive effect – although having Yahoo! tattooed on yourself as some proud US employees of that Internet portal have done is probably a step too far.

A few UK companies have tried to help staff find meaning through encouraging them to take sabbaticals or spend office time on charitable causes. Unilever and Deutsche Bank are two that have staff involved with 'Arts and Kids', a new venture to enable staff to work with children and the arts.

Blaming companies that do not do such things sidesteps the personal responsibility people need to take for their own destiny. People are generally pretty grown up; they do not have such a patriarchal relationship with their employers. While companies can do nice things to make their people valued, that does not make their work and lives meaningful. Many people are unhappy as they feel trapped in the wrong job and get stressed as they cannot see an exit route – many cannot even see when their next holiday will be. As we saw in the section on confidence building, self-esteem and achievement, people need to make a coherent plan and set about doing it – once they start, say, exercising more, they begin to feel a change to spur them on further.

Clearly individual needs and circumstances affect what can be planned. While people cannot change their lives completely overnight, there may be small gains that one can achieve – even if it is cutting down on 'down time' wasted at work and getting out to explore other interests. While employers should do what they can, it is up to each individual to make their own decisions about life and work out what is best for them. Those who are not happy are doing something that is not right for them.

So, find your own *motivation*, develop your *ability* to do it, and have the *confidence* to see it through and build your own future – and, if you are a manager, help your people do it too.

Good luck!

Summary

In this chapter you have:

- Explored some factors that will have an impact on organisations in the future
- Reviewed information technology and its influence in the workplace activity, particularly e-collaborating
- Seen that e-learning is making inroads and have considered how to help it find its place
- Reviewed the importance of flexible working and recognised some of the pitfalls of working from home and how to manage a virtual team
- Reviewed interim working and discovered its attractions for many people
- Considered future trends in work regarding children, pensions, incapacity benefit and older workers
- Looked further at women in work in the future
- Seen the importance of a work/life balance and approaches to achieving it
- Reviewed the term 'work with meaning'.

Questions

1. Consider events over the last five years that have affected your organisation, or one with which you are familiar. How many were 'predictable' and how well did your chosen organisation deal with them? Then, what do you feel is likely to be the range of 'issues' that need to be managed over the next five years?

2. Imagine that you or one of your colleagues wishes to work more flexible hours. Make a written case to management for that change.
3. Imagine that you or one of your colleagues wishes to work more remotely/from home more often. Make a written case to management for that change.
4. Consider how you might help your people discover more meaning to the work that your organisation is engaged in. What would you do to help them feel more committed?

References

Bolchover, D. (2005) *The Daily Telegraph*, 29 September, p. B7.

The Daily Telegraph (2005) 5 October, p. 10.

The Daily Telegraph (2006) 23 January, p. B2.

Evening Standard (2005) 6 October 2005, p. 25.

Hayward, M. (2004) *Management Today*, September, p. 69.

Mackay, A. R. (2007) *Recruiting, Retaining and Releasing People*, Butterworth-Heinemann.

Management Today (2003) June, p. 33.

Management Today (2004) May, p. 46.

Management Today (2005) July, p. 70.

Orr, D. (2006) *The Independent*, 25 January, p. 27.

Professional Manager (2003) March, p. 20.

Professional Manager (2004) Chiumento report 'Coming of Age', September, p. 29.

Professional Manager (2006), January, p. 23.

Reeves, R. (2005) *Management Today*, April, p. 29.

Further Reading

Covey, S. (1999) *Seven Habits of Highly Effective People*, Simon & Schuster.

Drucker, P. (2001) *Management Challenges for the 21st Century*, Harper Business.

Duarte, D. L. and Snyder, T. (2001) *Mastering Virtual Teams: Strategies, Tools and Techniques That Succeed*, Jossey-Bass Wiley.

Fisher, K. and Fisher, M. (2000) *The Distance Manager: A Hands-on Guide to Managing Off-site Employees and Virtual Teams*, McGraw-Hill Education.

Houston, D. (ed.) (2005) *Work–Life Balance in the 21st Century*, Palgrave Macmillan.

Mackay, A. R. (2007) *Recruiting, Retaining and Releasing People*, Butterworth-Heinemann.

Index

ABCs of behaviour, 175
Ability Development, 211, 227
Ability Development Model, 227
Accepting people, 298
Achievement, 106, 280
    Social-cognitive approach, 292
Action-Centred Leadership Model, 52
Adair, John, 7, 51
Adult Education, 182
Advancement, 106
Affective domain, 205
Aggressive behaviour, 269
Alderfer, Clayton P, 64
Appraisal, 33
Appreciating people, 299
Argyris, Chris 11, 58, 160, 165
Assertive behaviour, 270
Assertiveness, 266
Assertiveness and Rights at Work, 275
Atkinson, John, 286
Attributes of leadership, 214
Attribution theory, 173, 290
Auditory learning style, 204
Authority, 107
    vs Freedom, 217
Autocracy, 44

Balanced scorecard, 129
Behavioural analysis, 177
Belbin, Meredith, 89
Benefits packages, 120
Bennis, Warren, 213
Benyon, Huw, 110
Blake and Mouton, 7
Blake and Mouton Grid Theory, 216
Blake, Robert, 49
Blanchard, Kenneth, 65, 218
Blanchard–Hersey, 137
Bloom's Taxonomy of Learning Domains, 205
Bodily-kinaesthetic intelligence, 199
Branden, Nathaniel, 249
Bullying in the Workplace, 252

Burns, James McGregor, 222
Business Process Re-engineering, 338

Centre for Leadership Studies (CLS-Europe),
    126, 165
Change, 44
    defined, 334
    managing organisational change, 342
    motivation checklist, 349
    planning, 345
    resistance, 337
        dealing with it, 340
Children, 379
Classical conditioning, 175, 176
Cognitive domain, 205
Cognitive maps, 177
Competence, 191
Conditioned reflex, 175
Conditioned stimulus, 176
Confidence, 29, 202, 297
Confidence Development Model, 310
Conscious Competence, 191
Constructive Feedback, 297, 303
Continuing Professional Development (CPD), 185
Conversation, 86
Covey, Stephen, 260
Criticism, 303
Culture, 59, 129

Democracy, 44
Denning, W. Edwards, 8, 11, 24, 53
Difficult people, 276
Disgruntled employees, 74
Double-loop learning, 162
Drucker, Peter, 3, 50, 112, 285

E-collaborating, 365
E-learning, 367
E-mail protocols, 70
Effectiveness, 112
    Orientation, 220
Efficiency, 112

Effort and performance, 105
Effort, performance and reward, 102
Effort–performance, 103
EFQM Excellence Model, 168
Ego, 254
Emotional intelligence, 23, 201, 260
Employee surveys, 33
Empowerment , 24
Encouraging people, 300
Energy at Work, 69
Envy, 22
ERG Theory, 64
Espoused theory, 138, 160
European Foundation for Quality
    Management, 168
Expectancy Theory, 62, 109
Expectations, 288
Experiential learning circle, 195
Extrinsic rewards, 104

Families, 379
Fat cats, 120
Fayol, Henri, 38, 51
Feedback, 105
    giving and receiving, 302
Fiedler, Fred E., 215
Flexible working, 369
Follett, Mary Parker, 6, 40, 49
Ford, Henry, 24, 106, 307
Freedom, 30
Freud, Sigmund, 41
Fry, Roger, 195
Future Trends, 356

Gannt, Henry, 5, 39
Gardiner, Howard, 199
Gardner, John, 214
Gilbreth, Frank and Lillian, 39
Goleman, Daniel, 23, 260
Grid Theory, 49

Hackman, Richard, 82
Hackman, Richard and Greg Oldham, 55
Handy, Charles, 8, 13, 59, 248, 334
Hawthorne Experiments, 6, 9, 111
Hersey, Paul, 218
Herzberg, Frederick, 7, 45, 51,
    81, 105
Honey and Mumford, 349
House, Robert, 54
Human Capital Accounting, 24

Human Capital Management, 23
Human Relations Management, 9

Image orientated workers, 293
Incapacity benefit, 379
Incentives, 289
Information Technology and Working
    Practices, 361
Ingham, Harry, 193
Intelligence Quotient, 203
Interim Working, 378
Interpersonal intelligence, 199
Intrapersonal intelligence, 199
Intrinsic rewards, 104
Investors in People, 167
IT project management, 83

Jarvis Experiential Learning Model, 198
Job Characteristics Theory, 55
Job competence assessment, 302
Job enrichment, 29, 106
Johari Window, 193, 201
Juran, Joseph M., 11, 54
Just-In-Time (JIT), 56, 88, 289

Kilmann, Ralph H., 268
Kinaesthetic learning style, 204
Kirkpatrick, Donald L., 207
Kirkpatrick's Training Evaluation Model, 207
Knowledge economy, 159
Kolb, David A., 195
Kolb Learning Styles, 195

Law of Effect, 175
Leadership, 10
    behavioural theories, 214
    contingency theories, 215
    style theories, 215
    trait theories, 213
Learndirect, 184
Learning domains, 205
Learning from failure, 157
Learning Management Systems, 168
Learning orientated workers, 292
Learning Styles, 188, 195
Legislation Growth, 359
Lewin, Kurt, 43, 195
Lifelong Learning, 172, 183
Likert, Blake and Mouton, 137
Likert, Rensis, 7, 48

Lindeman, Eduard C., 182
Linguistic intelligence, 199
Lippitt, Ronald, 43
Logical-mathematical intelligence, 199
Luft, Joseph, 193

Mach One, 285
Mackay's Ability Development Model, 227
Mackay's Confidence Development Model, 310
Mackay's Motivation Development Model, 136
Management by Objectives (MBO), 50, 56, 107,
    112, 223
Management by vision, 223
Management Standards Centre (MSC), 184
Management style, 211
Managerial Achievement, 285
Managing virtual teams, 374
Martin, Peter, 13
Maslow, Abraham, 7, 42, 51, 81, 137, 224
Maslow's Hierarchy of Needs, 64, 201
Maternity leave, 377
Mayer, John, 262
Mayo, Elton, 6, 41
McClelland, David, 286
McGregor, Douglas, 7, 23, 41
McKinsey, 60
McKinsey 7S Model, 12, 345
McNamara, Robert, 59
Measures, 128
Meetings management, 92
Mentoring, 33
Mobile communications, 364
Mobile technology, 361
Moss Kanter, Rosabeth, 8, 13, 36, 57
Motivating People Through Change, 348
Motivation:
    national economic model, 21
    self-actualising model, 22
    social model, 22
Motivation Development Model, 136
Motivation to Study, 293
Motives, 287
Mouton, Dr Jane, 49, 216
MP3 theft, 361
Multiple intelligences, 199
Musical intelligence, 199

National Occupational Standards
    (NOS), 184
Naturalist intelligence, 199
Needs theory, 286

Network economy, 367
Nicholls, John, 13

Observational learning, 179
OK Corral, 254
Older workers, 378
Oldham, Greg, 82
One Minute Manager, 65
Operant conditioning, 177
Optimism, 284
Organisational learning, 164
Outcomes, 105
Overconfidence, 298

Parental Rights Bill, 379
Part-time Working, 377
Passion, 126, 133
Paternity leave, 379
Path-Goal Theory, 54
Pay, 117
Pensions, 378
Performance, 111
Performance appraisal, 115
Performance outcomes, 104
Pessimism, 284
PEST, 333
Peters and Waterman, 8, 190
Peters, Tom, 12, 60
Porter, Michael, 19
Praising people, 299
Psychological contract, 123, 132
Psychomotor domain, 205

Qualifications, 184

Rational–Economic models, 6
Reassuring people, 301
Recognition, 106
Reddin, Bill, 220
Relationship Orientation, 142, 232, 317
Responsibility, 106
Rewards, 117
    non-cash, 119
Role Effectiveness Model, 113

Schein, Edgar H., 12
Schmidt, Warren, 47, 217
Schön, Donald, 159, 165
Self-concept, 248
Self-development, 41

Self-discipline, 41
Self-esteem, 7, 29, 77, 247
Self-motivation, 258
Senge, Peter, 159
Single-loop learning, 162
Situational Leadership, 65, 218
Skinner Box, 177
SMART, 77, 107, 307
Social learning, 179
Spatial-visual intelligence, 199
Submissive behaviour, 269

Tactile learning style, 204
Tannenbaum and Schmidt, 7, 137
Tannenbaum, Robert, 47, 217
Task Ability Control, 229
Task Confidence Control, 313
Task Motivation Control, 138
Taylor, Frederick W., 5, 37
Team Leadership, 85
Teleconferencing, 93
Telephones, 360
T-Group movement, 44, 195
The Learning Organisation, 155, 159
Theory X–Theory Y, 7, 41, 48, 76
Theory-in-action, 138
Theory-in-use, 160
Thomas, Kenneth W., 268
Thomas–Kilmann Conflict Mode Instrument, 268
Thorndike, Edward Lee, 177, 260
Total Quality Management, 8, 11, 25, 56, 88, 338

Training effectiveness, 207
Transactional Analysis, 254
Transformational Leadership Style Inventory, 222
Transition cycle, 189
Trist, Eric, 11, 81
Trust, 72, 130, 149

Unconditioned stimulus, 176
Underachievers, 291
University of the Third Age, 185

Videoconferencing, 93
Virtual teams, 374
Vision, 58, 126
Visual learning style, 204
Visual-Auditory-Kinaesthetic Learning Styles Model (VAK), 204
Vroom, Victor, 11, 62, 81

Waterman, Robert H., 12, 60
Weblogs, 75
Wickens, Peter, 13
Women in Work, 391
Work ethic, 32
Work with Meaning, 133, 385
Work/life balance, 32, 69, 77, 364, 366, 370, 373, 377, 378, 383
Working from home, 372
Working remotely, 362
Workspace, 71